THE HISTORY OF THE EUROPEAN FAMILY

THE HISTORY OF THE EUROPEAN FAMILY

EDITED BY DAVID I. KERTZER AND MARZIO BARBAGLI

Volume One

Family Life in Early Modern Times

1500–1789

YALE UNIVERSITY PRESS
NEW HAVEN AND LONDON

For information about this and other Yale University Press publications, please contact:
U.S. Office: sales.press@yale.edu   www.yale.edu/yup
Europe Office: sales@yaleup.co.uk   www.yaleup.co.uk

Set in Sabon and Meta-Caps by Best-set Typesetter Ltd, Hong Kong
Printed in Great Britain by St Edmundsbury Press, Suffolk

A catalogue record for this book is available from the Library of Congress and the British Library.

10 9 8 7 6 5 4 3 2 1

Published with assistance from the Annie Burr Lewis Fund.

CONTENTS

PART IV
FAMILY RELATIONS

ILLUSTRATIONS

Introduction

Marzio Barbagli and David I. Kertzer

Over the past 35 years hundreds of scholars from many countries, in many languages, and from a variety of disciplines—historians, demographers, anthropologists, sociologists—have published studies focusing on family life in the past. In doing so they have made use of new sources of information, new approaches, and new interpretations. These works have tremendously enriched our knowledge of Western family history, demolishing many commonly accepted stereotypes of what family life was like in the past, and undermining many commonly accepted theories of social change.

By their very nature, as pioneering empirical studies these works have typically focused on very limited geographical areas—a few parishes, a town, or sometimes a small region—and their results have primarily been published in journals and books not easily accessible to non-experts. What has been lacking to date is a work of synthesis by the leading scholars in the field that makes the results of this new research available to a broad public, while focusing on both a long sweep of history and on Europe as a whole.

This work, which is being published simultaneously by Yale University Press in the United States and the United Kingdom and by Laterza in Italy, is designed to fill this need. Its 30 chapters, written by prominent scholars in the field, recount the history of the Western family over the past half-millennium in simple, straightforward style, yet reflecting the current scholarly state of the field. Our focus is on all of Europe, its 10 million square kilometers including all the land from the Atlantic Ocean on the west to the Ural Mountains on the east, from the Arctic Sea in the north to the Mediterranean in the south. It is a continent that at the beginning of our period, in 1500, had 81 million inhabitants; today it has 730 million.

There will, in all, be three volumes. The first, presented here, covers the period from 1500 to the French Revolution in 1789. The second deals with the nineteenth century, and the third covers developments in

European family life in the course of the twentieth century. Each is alike in examining many aspects of family life—economic, religious, demographic, social, legal, cultural—in a comparative perspective. Indeed, this is the key aspect of our approach here, and perhaps the feature that makes this work most distinctive, for we do not look separately at family history in each of several different countries: there is no chapter on family life in France, in Germany, in Italy, etc. Rather, we try to shed light on the larger patterns of geography, social differences, and historical changes. The books' authors analyze processes of convergence and divergence in family life in various European societies. One of the questions that we have tried to address throughout these volumes is if, when, and to what extent European societies over the five centuries examined here became more similar or grew more different insofar as family life is concerned.

THE FAMILY IN PRE-INDUSTRIAL EUROPE: THE MYTH

It had long been assumed that practically everyone in Europe in pre-industrial times married (outside of those who entered the Church) and did so at a young age. According to this classic portrait, people spent their lives in large, patriarchal households, composed of two or more related nuclear family units. Marriages (which were monogamous) were assumed to be stable and prolific. They were dissolved only by death and people had a large number of children. In these patriarchal families there was a rigid hierarchy, defined on the basis of such ascribed characteristics as age, sex, and birth order. Elders counted more than young people, men more than women, and first-born children more than other children. Ruling over such large domestic groups was an older man whose wife, children, daughters-in-law, and grandchildren were all completely subordinate to him.

This image of the family in pre-industrial Europe remains widespread today. In newspapers, on television, in daily conversations, the large and stable patriarchal family in which all people in the past spent their lives is continually contrasted with the state of families now: small, fragile, and having few if any children. Yet, the chapters of this first volume of our *History*, based on results from the best recent research, show how distant this image is from the reality of domestic life in Europe in the sixteenth and seventeenth centuries.

This is not to deny that this traditional image of the European family captures some of the large differences found between families of the past and families today. There is no question that couples in the past bore more children than they do today. It is also true that illegitimate births were relatively few in the 1500s and 1600s, while today the proportion of children born outside marriage is greater than 30 percent in several European countries.

It is, moreover, undeniable that the tensions and conflicts between husbands and wives were much less likely in the past than they are today to lead to a rupture in the marital bond. Yet even when divorce was either impossible or rare (a situation we will turn to later), there were non-legal means of ending a marriage. One was abandonment. The husband simply went off one day, never again to be seen by his wife or children. In England there was another type of extra-legal means of dissolving a marriage. A man brought his wife to the market and sold her to another man; this served simultaneously as a form of divorce and remarriage.[1] But these forms of marital breakup were infrequent and in practice the end of a marriage almost always came as the result of the death of one of the spouses.

Nevertheless, the image of the large, stable patriarchal family is, we discover, far from an accurate portrait. This is for two reasons. First of all, it overemphasizes and exaggerates certain aspects of the families of the past. Secondly, it offers a view of a European past that is undifferentiated. As we shall see, at different times and in different areas there were major differences in how families formed, transformed, and divided, and in the authority relations that existed between husbands and wives, parents and children, first born and later born, and parents-in-law and children-in-law. There were also major differences in kinship relations beyond the household, in the extent to which kin who lived in different households interacted and aided one another, and pursued common strategies aimed at building their economic holdings, their political power, and their social standing.

While couples in the past did have more children than they do now, the common view that women of the past gave birth to large numbers of children is clearly mistaken. The image of the large, stable patriarchal family typically recalls such cases (made famous by Peter Laslett) as that of Ann Sackett, a woman born in Kent, England, in 1779, who married at age 18 and gave birth 20 times to a total of 21 children. Yet a great deal of research has established the fact that, on the average, couples in pre-industrial England had only five or six children.

No less exaggerated is the idea that in the European family of the past the man who was the family head was a despot with absolute powers. Along similar lines we find the idea that children's marriage partners were chosen by their parents. It is true that parents often did exercise a strong influence on their children's marriages, sometimes to the extent of determining whom the child should marry. And it is also true that the greater the parents' wealth, the greater their likelihood of succeeding in exercising such control. But all this should not make us forget that, even at the beginning of the sixteenth century, norms could be found in much of Europe that favored the child's freedom of choice of a spouse and enabled children to stand up to their parents, at least to the extent of discussing and negotiating their preferences. In not a few cases children simply refused to go along with their parents' choices.

In the course of the Middle Ages, the so-called "consensualist" marriage doctrine came to be affirmed in the Christian Church. This held that marriage was a matter of the exchange of vows between bride and groom. This was both the necessary and sufficient condition for the formation of an indissoluble conjugal union: paternal approval was not necessary. On the basis of this doctrine, the Church considered as valid even "clandestine" marriages, concluded by individuals who had passed a certain age as specified by canon law (age 14 for boys and 12 for girls). Such marriages required neither parental consent, nor the presence of a priest to celebrate the rites, nor any witnesses. Such clandestine marriages could take place in two different ways. In one form they involved the exchange of *verba de presenti*, that is, a statement of present intention, with such words as "I take you as my husband; I take you as my wife." In a second form, they could take place through the exchange of *verba de futuro*, that is, a promise for the future, with such expressions as "I will take you as my husband; I will take you as my wife," if later followed by sexual intercourse.

THE GEOGRAPHY OF MARRIAGE AND FAMILY LIFE IN EUROPE

Had a census been conducted at the beginning of the sixteenth century, it would have revealed that the families in which the 81 million inhabitants of Europe lived varied tremendously by country and by region. In most of Europe the monogamous family prevailed and people could have only one spouse. But this was not the case in the Balkans, which had been conquered by the Turks. At the beginning of the sixteenth century the Ottoman empire included Greece, Albania, Serbia, and parts of Bosnia and Romania. Even if the Turks allowed the peoples they conquered a certain degree of autonomy in practicing their own religion, the process of Islamization began to make some headway. It is estimated that about 18 percent of the European population under Ottoman rule was Muslim.[2] The marriage model followed by the Muslim population was quite different from that found among the rest of the European population. The Muslim religion permits polygyny and a man is allowed to have up to four wives. Yet only the very rich could afford more than one wife and so only 2 or 3 percent of families in such areas were in fact polygynous. Among the elite, however, polygyny was common, and so the relations between husband and wife and between parents and children were very different in the Islamic areas than they were elsewhere in Europe.

At the beginning of the sixteenth century, there were also marked differences in Europe with respect to the dissolution of the marital bond. After a long period of discussion and uncertainty, the Christian Church in the West took a definitive stand against divorce and medieval canon law proclaimed the principle of the indissolubility of marriage. Only in exceptional cases did the Church allow for annulment (with the possibility of remarriage) or marital separation. But dissolution did remain a possibility, at least in principle, for three other groups. One was the Jews. The second consisted of the Muslims of the Balkan peninsula, for whom marriage could be dissolved by the husband simply pronouncing the words "I divorce you." The third lived in that vast area of Eastern Europe in which the Orthodox Christian Church was dominant. The Orthodox Church permitted divorce, although the grounds for divorce differed for men and women. The husband could obtain a divorce if his wife committed adultery or if she had tried to kill him. But for a wife to obtain a divorce, it was not enough for her husband to have betrayed her. It was necessary for him not only to have done so repeatedly, but also to have beaten her or forced her into prostitution.[3]

One of the most important and distinctive traits of family life in the past is, without doubt, the high level of mortality. In the words of historian Lawrence Stone, in the past "Death was at the centre of life, as the cemetery was at the centre of the village."[4] Moreover, death struck people of all ages, especially the very young. Before the nineteenth century, life expectancy in Europe was low, ranging from 25 to 35 years. Research results to date have shown, however, that mortality in general, and infant mortality in particular, varied greatly from one area to the next.[5]

The probability that an infant would die before celebrating its first birthday varied from 16 percent in England to 18 percent in Germany and 28 percent in France, and up to 33 percent in the region around Moscow. But there were also enormous differences within countries or even in the same region. In France, for example, infant mortality was much higher in the northeast than in the southwest. Similarly, in Germany, children survived at much higher rates in the northern regions than in the south. Numerous causes—not all of which have yet been identified—are responsible for these differences. One was the climate. Another involved the community's economic resources and nutritional level, which certainly influenced the mother's health. But just as important was the mother's breastfeeding and, in particular, how long this continued, as breastfeeding had a protective effect on the newborn's health.

Major differences were also found in the nature of the systems of family formation. In Shakespeare's *Romeo and Juliet*, Juliet's father says:

> My child is yet a stranger in the world
> She hath not seen the change of fourteen years.
> Let two more summers wither in their pride
> Ere we may think her ripe to be a bride.

Yet in the following scene, Juliet's mother tells her:

> Well, think of marriage now. Younger than you,
> Here in Verona, ladies of esteem,
> Are made already mothers. By my count
> I was your mother much upon these years
> That you are now a maid.[6]

On the basis of such early literary sources, it had long been thought that women used to marry at a very young age, at 12 or 13 years. Peter Laslett, however, has compiled results from many English studies that show that, at least by the seventeenth century, women in fact did not marry so early.

The demographer John Hajnal, in a 1965 publication that is now considered a classic, and to which many authors in this volume refer, drew a line down through Europe running from St Petersburg to Trieste. For many centuries, he argued, the lands to the west of the line were marked by a marriage model that was "unique or almost unique in the world." This European marriage pattern had two distinctive characteristics. In the first place, both men and women married late (men around 26–27, women at 23–24 or later). Secondly, a rather high proportion of the population (from 10 to 15 percent typically) never married at all. By contrast, in the countries of Eastern Europe marriage more closely resembled a pattern found more broadly outside of Europe, and which Hajnal accordingly labeled a "non-European marriage pattern": in this system, both men and women married early and virtually all adults married.[7] Subsequent research has revealed that there were areas of Western Europe (Ireland, the southern portion of the Iberian peninsula, and Sicily and Calabria in Italy) that did not follow the Western model, for in those areas marital age was low. But for the rest, the Hajnal line—as it has come to be called—has stood up, capturing this major difference in marriage system between two large areas of pre-industrial Europe.

Corresponding to these differences in marital age we find differences in household structure. Comparative historical research on household structure has benefited from a typology that was first developed by E. A. Hammel and Peter Laslett (1974). According to this typology, households formed by a single married couple, with or without children, or by a single parent (typically a widow or widower) and children are defined as *nuclear*. Households without a married couple, or a parent and child, are termed *non-family* households. These may contain either individuals bound by other ties of kinship, such as two unmarried brothers, or consist of individuals not related by kinship. *Extended* family households are those having a single conjugal unit plus one or more coresident kin (but not including a second conjugal unit). Such households might, for example, include a widowed parent or unmarried sibling of the husband or wife. *Multiple* family households are those that contain two or more kin-related conjugal units. Depending on the type of bond that unites the component units, these are further subdivided into those that are extended *vertically* (e.g., husband, wife, son, son's wife) and those extended horizontally (e.g., two or more brothers who all live together along with their wives and children). When only a single son remains at home with his parents after his marriage, the term *stem* family is also used. The term *frérèche* is employed for the horizontal multiple family household in which two or more married brothers live together. To complete this terminological overview, the term *complex* family households is used generically to refer to all households that are either extended or multiple.

In northwestern Europe (in Scandinavia, the British Isles, the Low Countries, and northern France) people at marriage followed the rule of neolocal residence. That is, upon marriage they formed their own new nuclear family household in which the husband became household head. But before marriage a substantial proportion of young people (in some areas up to 40 percent) spent various years living outside their parental homes, working for other families as servants.[8] This allowed them to put aside the resources that would be necessary to allow them to live by themselves when they married. This practice also enabled the agricultural families to remain nuclear, for it gave them flexibility in providing for the changing labor requirements of their farm without requiring them to take in additional relatives. By contrast, in Eastern Europe new couples generally followed a patrilocal residence rule, going to live with the groom's natal family in a multiple family household, in which there was another, more senior couple (typically the groom's parents). As we have seen, in these cases marriages took place at a younger age and were not preceded by a period of co-residence as servants in other, unrelated households.

But in both Western and Eastern Europe there were important regional differences. In Russia in the eighteenth century, in serf communities only 7 percent of families were nuclear, 10 percent were extended, and 75 percent were multiple. In southern Estonia similarly, complex family households dominated, but in the north nuclear family households were more common. In Hungary multiple family households were common among the peasant serf population, while nuclear households characterized the zones where agricultural wage laborers lived. In the Balkans, large complex households dominated (some reaching 50 persons), but in Romania nuclear households were common. Turning to Western Europe, in northern Portugal and in northwestern Spain the stem family household was common, while in the southern regions of Iberia newlyweds typically established their own households. In Sicily, Puglia, and in the other regions of southern Italy the nuclear family prevailed, while in Tuscany, Emilia, Umbria, and the Marches—in central Italy—patrilocal residence was typical and, for a period following the death of the older generation, people lived in *frérèches*.

There were also major differences among areas in the lives of the elderly. In keeping with the general popular impression today, people often assume that in pre-industrial times those over 60 or 70 years old lived surrounded by relatives, in households containing their married children, daughters-in-law and grandchildren, or with siblings who either never married or were widowed. But it turns out that the lives of older people in major portions of Europe were quite different.

In Russia, the Baltic area, and the Balkans, older people did often live in three-generation multiple family households with at least one married child. Such was the case as well among the sharecropping population of central Italy. Elsewhere in Mediterranean Europe, especially when they were in poor health, the elderly, who had previously lived in nuclear family households, would move in with a married child, in some regions on an alternating basis among their children's households (referred to as *ir por meses* in Spain). But in many parts of northwestern Europe the situation was completely different. For example, in England in the seventeenth and eighteenth centuries, almost a quarter of the widowed or never-married women over 65 lived alone and almost half of those who had a husband still alive lived without any children in their household.[9]

Throughout pre-industrial Europe, before the advent of the modern pension system, it was the family that was primarily in charge of providing assistance and care for those old people who were in need. However, although research on the subject remains scarce, what information we do have makes clear that the role of the collectivity differed greatly by zone. In Mediterranean and eastern areas, there was no source of aid for older people other than the family. By contrast, in England, from the beginning of the seventeenth century the state provided some assistance. The English Poor Law provided that old people who were in need (that is who were above a certain age and suffered from chronic disability) were assigned a permanent subsidy. Usually they were not sent to a home for the poor, but were assisted while remaining in their own home.[10]

Major differences were also found between the cities and the countryside. In urban centers age at marriage was higher, and the proportion who never married was greater. Moreover, single-person households were more common in the city, as were non-family households and those composed of a single parent (usually the mother) and children. More surprisingly, perhaps, urban women had higher fertility than rural women, possibly because women in the cities were less likely to nurse their own babies and when they did so nursed them for a shorter time than did women in rural areas.[11] Given the different degrees of urbanization found in different parts of Europe (see Table I.1), these rural–urban differences further contributed to the differences in family characteristics across the continent. In the sixteenth century, the highest level of urbanization was found in the Low Countries, but Italy too had a relatively high rate. Moderate levels of urbanization were found in England, Germany, France, and Spain. In Russia, Scandinavia, Poland, and Austria people lived overwhelmingly in rural areas.

Notable differences existed within local areas as well, often linked to social class. In the 1500s and 1600s it was much more common for those from noble families to remain unmarried throughout their lives than it was for others. In many countries, too, aristocratic and bourgeois men married on average at a more advanced age than others, but took as their wives women who were younger than the brides of men from lower classes. Yet, in the period under study in this volume, some of these class differences either disappeared or, strikingly, reversed. For example, in the Italian cities in the early 1500s, the higher the couple's social status, the more likely they were to go to live with the groom's parents after their marriage. By the late 1700s, by contrast, neolocal coresidence typified all urban Italians, regardless of class. Similarly, in the sixteenth and seventeenth centuries, the risk of dying in the first months of life was *higher* for the children of aristocrats than it was for the lower classes (because the former were more likely to be nursed by someone other than their mother), while adult life expectancy did not vary by class. By the second half of the eighteenth century, however, the positive relationship between

Table I.1   Urban percentage of total population, by territory, 1500–1800

Territory	1500	1600	1700	1800
England and Wales	3.1	5.8	13.3	20.3
Ireland	0	0	3.4	7.0
Netherlands	15.8	24.3	33.6	28.8
Belgium	21.1	18.8	23.9	18.9
Scandinavia	0.9	1.4	4.0	4.6
Germany	3.2	4.1	4.8	5.5
France	4.2	5.9	9.2	8.8
Switzerland	1.5	2.5	3.3	3.7
Italy	12	15	13	14
Spain	6.1	11.4	9.0	11.1
Portugal	3.0	14.1	11.5	8.7
Austria-Bohemia	1.7	2.1	3.9	5.2
Poland	0	0.4	0.5	2.5

Source: De Vries, 1984: 39.

social class and life expectancy emerged that still exists today. The rich began to live longer than the poor.

These differences among different geographical areas, between city and countryside, and among different social classes reflect a variety of factors. The likelihood that agricultural households were complex increased when they were units of production, for these households' composition was shaped by the labor needs of the farm. This is what happened with the peasant-proprietors of southern France, northern Spain, and north-central Italy, where the larger the farm the larger the household.

Even those social strata who owned only a part of their means of production (tools, livestock) were likely to live in large multiple family households when their contract obliged the family to live on the farm. Such was the case of the sharecroppers of north-central Italy. The farm owner required the assurance that, for the duration of the contract, the family to whom he gave the farm would include a large enough number of adult "arms" and would not be weighed down by too many *bocche inutili* (useless mouths, that is, people too young or too old to work). The contract thus specified that no member of the household could get married without the owner's permission. A similar phenomenon was found in Russia, where the lord strove to ensure that the members of the large serf households stayed together. It is to this phenomenon that Tolstoy referred in *War and Peace*, when he wrote of Count Nicholas Rostov: "He kept the peasant families together in the largest groups possible, not allowing the family groups to divide into separate households."[12] By contrast, when residence and workplace were separate, the agricultural population generally lived in nuclear family households.

Another important factor in explaining the differences in family life was the kind of inheritance system found, that is, the rules regarding the transmission of property from parents to children. The most common type of partible system found in Europe specified that all sons had the same rights to participate in the division of the paternal property, while daughters were supported as long as they lived in their parents' house and received a dowry when they married. In principle, this inheritance system was compatible with various family formation systems. However, in general it favored the rise of nuclear families, for each son had access to his own productive property.

The most common impartible system by contrast specified that all of the paternal property go to a single son. In some cases it was based on an institution known as *fideicommissum*, which mandated that the person receiving a certain inheritance keep it intact and transmit it to his descendants following the order that had been determined once and for all by the testator (for example, that the property should be passed down to the first-born son). This impartible system led to a situation where, upon marriage, the inheriting son brought his wife to live with his parents (forming a stem family), while his brothers, if they married, left and formed nuclear family households of their own.

Finally, the bilateral system of partible inheritance, identified in particular with the period following the French Revolution—whose laws mandated it—specified that all children, regardless of sex or order of birth, had the right to share in their parents' inheritance. Such a system strongly favored the formation of nuclear family households.

The differences in household formation systems were linked to different cultural norms. Aside from specifying where a newly married couple should go to live after marriage, these norms also influenced people's attitudes toward aging parents, when the parents were no longer able to work and were in need of the aid and care of others.

MAJOR CHANGES IN FAMILY LIFE

Social scientists long believed that a single, great historical division marked the history of the family, separating the "traditional" family from the "modern" family. The turning point was usually placed in the period of great social and economic transformations that occurred between the last two decades of the eighteenth century and the first decade of the nineteenth. The periodization that we have chosen for our *History* (this first volume concluding with 1789, the year of the French Revolution) should not lead the reader to think that we share this view. Certainly, no one can doubt the fact that the industrial revolution and the French Revolution each produced great changes in people's family lives, as they did in economic, social, and political life in many European countries. But it is wrong to think that any simple passage from a "traditional" to a "modern" family took place in this period, just as it is an error to look for a single sharp turning point. The chapters of this volume, based on the new research conducted over the past three decades, show that, from the beginning of the sixteenth century to the end of the eighteenth, many important changes in the domestic world took place. We mention a few of these here.

Population Growth

From the early 1500s to the end of the 1700s major changes took place in the European population. In three centuries, the number of inhabitants of Europe grew considerably, from 81 to 180 million (Table I.2). But, as in previous periods, this population growth resulted from the alternation of phases of expansion with phases of population decline. Beginning in the middle of the fifteenth century, following the terrible epidemics of the plague, a demographic rebound began that lasted until the end of the sixteenth century. In the following century population growth continued, but at a considerably slower pace.

Yet this general trend masks large differences among the various parts of Europe. For the entire seventeenth century, the population grew in the British Isles, France, Poland, and Russia, while it declined in the Iberian peninsula, Italy, Germany, and Central Europe, due especially to the large increase in mortality brought on by the Thirty Years' War and by the waves of epidemics of the plague that swept through many of these areas between 1630 and 1657. The pace of demographic growth then picked up in the first half of the eighteenth century and increased further in the second half.

Over these three centuries the pace of population growth differed considerably by area. The number of inhabitants in the British Isles and in Russia tripled, while that of Germany doubled, and France and Italy increased by 90 percent. As a result, the relative weight of the population in these various zones altered. While at the beginning of the 1500s the country with the largest population was France, with 15 million residents, at the end it was Russia, which had 36 million. One result was

Table I.2   The European population from 1500 to 1800 (in millions)

	1500	1600	1650	1700	1750	1800
Scandinavia	2.00	2.25	2.50	3.00	3.75	5.25
British Isles	5.00	6.25	7.50	9.25	10.00	16.00
Germany	9.00	12.00	11.00	13.00	15.00	18.00
France	15.00	18.50	21.00	22.00	24.00	29.00
Iberian peninsula	7.75	10.50	9.25	10.00	12.00	14.00
Italy	10.00	12.00	11.00	13.00	15.00	19.00
Central Europe*	8.25	10.25	9.50	11.00	13.25	18.50
Poland	4.00	5.00	5.50	6.00	7.00	9.00
European Russia	12.00	15.00	17.00	20.00	26.00	36.00
Balkans	4.50	6.00	6.00	6.25	8.00	10.00
Total Europe	81.00	100.00	105.00	120.00	140.00	180.00
Percent by zone						
Northwest[†]	45.0	43.8	46.7	46.9	43.9	42.5
South[‡]	27.5	28.5	25.0	24.4	25.0	23.9
East[§]	27.5	27.7	28.3	28.7	31.1	33.6

* Central Europe: Austria, Hungary, Czech Republic, Slovakia, Romania; European Russia: with Moldavia and the Baltic countries; Balkans: ex-Yugoslavia, Albania, Bulgaria, Greece, European Turkey;
[†] Northwest: Scandinavia, British Isles, France, Low Countries, Switzerland, Germany, Austria;
[‡] South: Iberian peninsula, Italy, Balkans;
[§] East: Russia, Poland, Czech Republic, Slovakia, Romania, Hungary.
Source: Bardet and Dupâquier, 1997: 251.

that the proportion of the continent's population living in Eastern Europe increased.

Population and Family

Demographic changes are tied in many ways to the transformations that took place in systems of household formation, in household composition, in relations among family members, and in kin relations more generally. If in some cases it is the demographic changes that affect these various family relations, in other cases the exact opposite is found: changes in the domestic world influence the course of population change.

The great mortality crises—due to epidemics, wars, and famines—had a dramatic impact on families. Not only did they cause the death of a large number of people, but they also reduced household size and led to changes in household composition, bringing about an increase in the proportion of people living alone (such as widows or orphans) or living with non-family members, and a corresponding decline in the proportion of people living in nuclear and complex family households.

Important changes also occurred in the periods following such crises. After falling dramatically during periods of high mortality, the number of marriages and of conceptions rose. Age at marriage and the proportion of people who remained unmarried fell, the interval between a woman's births declined, and fertility increased. All of these demographic reactions affected family life. The birth of more children tended to increase household size. The lowering of marriage age, by increasing the likelihood that the parents of the newlyweds were still alive, favored the formation of households containing two conjugal units and so led to a change in household composition.

In some cases, the changes that took place in systems of family formation (especially in decisions regarding marriage or number of children) influenced the size of the population itself. As we have seen, from the beginning of the sixteenth century to the end of the eighteenth, the increase in population size in England and Russia was more rapid than that of France. But, while England and Russia were similar in this respect, they had very different demographic regimes. Britain (whose demographic system has been labeled one of "low pressure") was characterized by low mortality, and by moderate levels of both marriage and fertility. By contrast, Russia (whose demographic system is termed "high pressure") had high mortality, and high rates of both marriage and fertility. We do not yet know whether there were changes over the course of our period in these features in Russia. But in the case of England we know quite precisely that the sharp increase in population that occurred in the 1700s was largely brought about by an increase in the rate of marriage. Over these years the mean female age at marriage declined (from 25.8 to 24.1), while the proportion of women who married increased. That is, fewer women remained unmarried.

The situation in France differed from both of these. The fact that England's population was growing faster than France's was due to the fact that in the eighteenth century France not only had a higher level of mortality than England, it also had lower fertility.[13] In contrast to England, in France female mean age at marriage rose over the course of the eighteenth century, increasing from 24.5 to 26. And in the last two decades of the century, we find the beginnings of a change in parts of France that would have tremendous importance—as we will see in the next volume—over the course of the following two centuries. For the first time people began to consciously limit the number of children they bore.

Voluntary birth control means that couples plan the total number of births that they want and the spacing of their births. This means that their reproductive behavior is affected by the number of children that the woman has already borne. Many studies have shown that the first families to employ contraceptive practices were those belonging to the higher social classes. It seems that the principal means that they used was *coitus interruptus*—that is, withdrawal before ejaculation—"assisted no doubt," as Lawrence Stone wrote, "by oral, manual and anal sex."[14] In fact, although condoms first appeared in the seventeenth century and began to spread in the eighteenth, they were used less for contraception than as protection against venereal disease. Their use was popularly identified with prostitution and sexual relations outside of marriage.

Yet while the exact methods used may still not be precisely known, what is certain is that, among upper-class couples, fertility began to decline sharply. To take a couple of examples, among the aristocracy of Milan, the number of children per woman (born to her between age 25 and 50) declined from 6.7 in the first half of the seventeenth century to 3.3 in the second half of the eighteenth. Among the bourgeoisie of Geneva, in the same period, the number of births per woman declined from 6.8 to 2.9.[15] This decline in fertility was not due to any increase in age at first marriage, but to changes that took place in couples' decision-making, as they started to plan the number and spacing of their births. They began waiting longer after their wedding to have their first birth, and then spent more time between each subsequent birth. Most dramatically, women began to stop their childbearing earlier. From the first half of the seventeenth century to the second half of the eighteenth, women's mean age at last birth declined from 38.4 to 35.2 among the Milanese aristocracy, and, amazingly, from 38.2 to 31.9 among the bourgeoisie of Geneva.

Initially limited to couples from the highest social strata, birth control slowly began to spread, over a long period, into other portions of the population throughout Europe. It was in some of the departments of France in the last twenty years of the eighteenth century that this process of diffusion started. It was here that birth control first became a mass phenomenon, adopted and followed by both middle classes and the lower classes and it was in France that the general decline in fertility first became irreversible. The other provinces and regions of Europe (even the most industrialized and urbanized portions of England) would only begin to follow this model much later, at least half a century and in some cases more than a century after France pioneered the fertility decline.

Religion

A new and highly important line of division in marriage and family norms arose in Europe following October 31, 1517, the date that officially marks the beginning of the Protestant Reformation. In matters regarding marriage and family relations, as in other spheres, the Protestant reformers began to put forth and enforce a doctrine that, in certain key respects, differed from that of the Catholic Church.

In the first place, they affirmed that marriage had a positive religious value. Criticizing the Catholic idea that the conjugal state was only one of regrettable necessity for those who could not follow the ideal model of sexual abstinence (a thesis nicely expressed in Cardinal Bellarmino's phrase: "marriage is human, virginity heavenly"), the reformers argued that the marital state was not inferior to celibacy and therefore should be encouraged. This new position had two important implications. The first was that marriage should be made easier, and so at least some of the many impediments that canon law had, up to that time, placed in its way should be abolished. The second was the abolition of the requirement of clerical celibacy; priests thereby gained the right to marry.

The Protestant reformers also rejected the Catholic idea that marriage was a sacrament and argued, instead, that it was a civil contract. This thesis had various consequences, some of which favored the process of institutional secularization, that is, the passage of some social functions from the Church to the state. Luther had argued that, because marriage was a worldly matter, it was the task of the government to regulate it through its laws. His teaching was followed in the Protestant countries. Parliaments and monarchs increasingly came to involve themselves in the legislation and regulation of marriage and the family, formerly a church monopoly. And the ecclesiastical courts that had been responsible for dealing with the dissolution of marriages gradually lost their importance.

Moreover, the Protestant reformers introduced an innovation with regard to the problem of the relations between parents and children in the choice of spouse and in the celebration of marriage. They severely criticized the "consensualist" doctrine of marriage that had been affirmed in the twelfth century with Alexander II's decretals. These specified that the conjugal bond was formed through the free choice of the man and woman who were being wed, and did not require paternal consent. The reformers believed that this doctrine was the major cause of the large number of clandestine marriages that were celebrated each year in Europe. Such marriages were viewed as a result of the "egoism" and the "individualism" of those who, in choosing their spouses, disobeyed their parents' wishes in order to follow their own whims. Reacting to this unacceptable state of affairs, the reformers sought to re-establish the authority of the paterfamilias. To reaffirm the public nature of marriage, they specified that its celebration had to be preceded by a public announcement made in church during a religious service. They also specified that parental consent was required for marriage. While there was some disagreement among them—the Calvinists were more committed to these views than were the Lutherans—the reformers argued that in the absence of such consent a marriage could be annulled.

In response, the Catholics, sensitive to the criticism of clandestine marriages and concerned about the innumerable legal cases that came before the ecclesiastical courts as a result of them, partially modified their doctrine on marriage. During the Council of Trent (1545–1563), after years of heated debates, the bishops succeeded in finding a compromise. With the Tametsi decree (so named for its first word), they introduced three significant innovations. They established, first of all, that marriage should be preceded by the publication of the wedding notice, and that for three consecutive Sundays, the parish priest must announce the name of the future spouses at mass. Secondly, it was ordered that henceforth marriages must take place *in facie ecclesiae*, that is, they must be celebrated by a priest, in the presence of "two or three witnesses." After receiving the consent of the couple, the priest was to solemnly declare: "I unite you in marriage, in the name of the Father, the Son, and the Holy Ghost." Thirdly, on the most ticklish question, they again condemned all those who "affirm erroneously that marriages contracted by children without their parents' consent are void." But at the same time, and in apparent contradiction, they added that "nonetheless the Holy Church of God, for the most just reasons, has always detested and prohibited" such unions.[16]

Protestantism certainly encouraged patriarchy. Partly this was a product of its opposition to the consensualist doctrine of marriage and of introducing the norm that the couple must have their parents' consent. But Protestantism highlighted the role and the power of the man in other ways as well, strengthening the notion of the husband and father as family head. To the concept of the *Hausvater* (household head), Luther and other Protestant reformers added two other authority figures: the *Landesvater* (the political head) and the *Gottesvater* (the religious head), representing among them the "three orders of Christian society: *ecclesia* (church), *politica* (state), and *oeconomica* (family)."[17] Like the king and the patriarchs of ancient Israel, the *Hausvater* possessed an authority that was both mandated by God and inviolable; those who dared to challenge it provoked the anger of the *Gottesvater*. As an evangelical treatise of 1524 put it, "For it is written, the head of the wife is the husband, the head of the husband is Christ, and the head of Christ is God. . . . there is no nobler, greater authority on earth than that of parents over their children, since they have both spiritual and worldly authority over them."[18]

According to some scholars, however, Protestantism favored patriarchy in another way, provoking the transfer of some of the functions of the Church and the parish to the family, and the transfer of part of the authority and the power of the priest to the male household head. Indeed, prayers increasingly came to be said at home. Husband and wife began to confess to each other rather than going to a priest. In another innovation, the husband began to read passages from the Bible each day, aloud, to his wife and children.[19]

The most important innovation that Protestantism introduced in Western Europe in terms of norms dealing with marriage and family was the possibility of divorce followed by remarriage. This was not an easy decision for the Protestant reformers, and they abandoned the principle of the indissolubility of marriage only very slowly, after overcoming doubts and uncertainties of all kinds. The refusal to consider marriage as a sacrament—which was one of their firm positions—removed an obstacle that would have otherwise blocked this path. But what most pushed them toward this conclusion was the conviction that the separation of bed and board (*divortium a mensa et thoro*) provided for by the Catholic Church, which left the conjugal bond intact and did not permit remarriage, was profoundly unfair to the innocent spouse.

Protestant marriage doctrine, which remained substantially unchanged until the 1960s, held that divorce could be granted only in exceptional cases, when one of the two spouses had committed some grave sin (most importantly, adultery). The principle of sin was so crucial that it was only the innocent spouse who could ask for a divorce, and the dissolution of the marriage was not permitted in cases where both spouses were adulterers.[20]

The Protestant cities and states of continental Europe immediately followed Luther's and Calvin's approach, allowing for the possibility of breaking the marital bond and permitting remarriage in cases of adultery and "malicious desertion." But in the course of the sixteenth century the courts were cautious and permitted divorce to a limited proportion of the people who requested it, oscillating between 35 percent and 55 percent.[21] Meanwhile, at the Council of Trent the Catholic Church reaffirmed the indissolubility of marriage. The Anglican Church remained faithful to this principle as well. Thus, divorce only entered into the law in England in 1670 by a private Act of Parliament. But the procedure to obtain one was so complicated and so expensive that in the following 130 years only 131 divorces were granted. Almost all involved noble or wealthy husbands who wanted to remarry.

Gradually divorce legislation grew more permissive in the Protestant countries. The list of reasons for which divorce could be granted lengthened. In some areas in the course of the eighteenth century the divorce rate increased considerably. Yet, seen by today's standards, their number remained exceedingly modest.[22] In effect, pre-industrial Europe lacked the economic and social conditions that would permit divorce. The economic interdependence of the married couple (well expressed in the Scandinavian proverb "no man can be a fisherman without a wife")[23] and the presence of many children made the decision to break the marital bond very difficult. Moreover, the couple's expectations about what marriage would bring were rather low and extremely flexible, capable of adapting to behavior that would today be seen as insufferable: infidelity, violence, and lack of affection.

There is no question, however, that the Protestant Reformation introduced major lines of division in the domestic world. If, at the beginning of the sixteenth century, the Christian population of Western Europe all lived under a system of the indissolubility of marriage, by the end of the eighteenth century it was deeply divided on this question. If at the beginning of this three-century period divorce was possible only among the Jews, the Muslim population of the Balkan peninsula or in Eastern Europe where the teachings of the Christian Orthodox Church were followed, at the end of the period divorce was available in Germany, Switzerland, Scandinavia, England, and Scotland. Thus, when at the end of the nineteenth century at least some of the conditions began to develop that made it possible for couples to avail themselves of divorce, divorce rates began to increase and the differences between Catholic and Protestant countries would become even greater.

Parental and Spousal Relations

In the noble families of his time—the Milanese Pietro Verri wrote in 1777—children might have admonished their parents as follows: "I don't owe you any thanks for my life. . . . Hardly had I been born when you wrenched me from mother's breast and gave me to a mercenary wet-nurse, almost as if you felt it beneath you to practice such a duty of nature. You left me crying miserably bound up in my swaddling clothes which prevented me from using the muscles I needed to develop; you kept me filthily wrapped up in my own feces, bound so tightly it sometimes cut off the circulation of my blood and my own breathing."[24]

Verri's testimony reminds us how different child-raising was in the past. First of all, the practice of swaddling the newborn from neck to feet was common. Secondly, in the middle and upper classes parents often gave their newborns to paid wet-nurses, despite the fact that this further reduced their babies' already poor chances of survival. Thirdly, some parents abandoned their newborns, often at a foundling home.

Many historians have interpreted these practices as signs of parental "indifference" or of their "lack of love" for their little children. A variety of evidence has been adduced for this thesis. Lawrence Stone, for example, has cited the "laconic" phrase written in 1665 in Daniel Fleming's ledger at the time of the death of his son: "Paid for my loving and lovely son John's coffin: 2s. 6d."[25] But other scholars have criticized this interpretation. Alan Macfarlane, for example, has observed that the passage quoted by Stone proves nothing because ledgers in the past served only to record income and expenses and not sentiments.[26] Another English scholar, Christopher Hill, argued that it is dangerous to infer the sentiments of parents in the past with regard to their children from their behavior. Among the poor, he noted, a new birth may threaten the family's ability to feed the previous children, and in such a context infanticide may be a sign of the parents' devotion to their existing children rather than testimony to parental indifference.[27]

But even if we do not know what sentiments mothers and fathers had for their children, it is clear that relations among family members were once very different from those found today. A patriarchal model of authority was everywhere dominant, with a hierarchy of roles and positions defined on the basis of age, sex, and birth order. At the top was a male, the father and husband. A rigid separation of roles divided husband and wife. The parents trained the children from a young age to be submissive and deferential. Children were kept at a distance and shown little trust, so that they learned to see themselves as different and inferior.

This patriarchal model began to disintegrate a long time before industrialization began: in Italy in the last decades of the seventeenth century, in France and England even earlier. Even if the father and husband continued to be the most powerful figure in the household, he no longer had autocratic power. The social distance between husband and wife and between parents and children began to diminish. The frequency with which the various members of the family interacted increased, along with the time that they spent together, and the attention and care they showed one another.

CONVERGENCES AND DIVERGENCES

At the beginning of the sixteenth century different countries and areas of Europe were marked by major differences in family life. Over the following three centuries significant changes occurred in the ways families formed, transformed, and divided, and in the authority relations among family members, as well as in kin relations. Some of these may have resulted in a convergence of various countries and regions, making them more similar. But the crucial transformations moved in the opposite direction and accentuated the differences. Such was certainly the case with the Protestant Reformation. But these forces were found in other areas of domestic life as well.

Although incomplete and unsatisfactory, the data we have lead us to believe that in some parts of Europe in our period the proportion of people who lived in complex family households actually increased. In Russia multiple family households became more established and proliferated.[28] Changes that were taking place in the political-economic sphere were triggering a growing divergence in the mode of family formation between Eastern and Western Europe.

Between the thirteenth and the nineteenth centuries, Western and Eastern Europe experienced radically different social and legal structures of agricultural landholdings, systems by which agricultural properties were managed, and living conditions of their rural populations. In Western Europe, that is west of the Elbe river, feudal relations between lords and peasants, along with medieval serfdom, completely disappeared and systems of farm rental and rural wage labor became entrenched. The agricultural population gained freedom of movement, to go and live and work where they pleased, along with the freedom to sell, buy, and rent land. The large feudal holdings were at times transformed into autonomous units that were rented to wealthy farmers (who themselves employed wage laborers); sometimes they were subdivided and given out to sharecroppers, or rented to peasant families who paid in money or in kind.

By contrast, east of the Elbe a serf economy spread. The noble's holding consisted of two parts. The first was composed of farms, of different sizes, which were given to peasant families. The second, the domain economy, was managed directly by the lord. In contrast with what happened in Western Europe, in the 1500s through to the 1700s peasants in Eastern Europe did not pay the feudal lord a rent in money or in kind. Instead, they had to participate in the *corvée*, that is forced labor on the lord's *riserva*. There they were obliged to work, one or more days each week, plowing, sewing, harvesting, threshing, or transporting the crops.

The peasants' freedom of movement was progressively reduced in this period, as they came to be ever more closely tied to the land on which they lived. According to a Russian census of 1730, of more than 5 million peasants, 87 percent were serfs, most of whom were dependants of the nobility.[29] Lacking rights of their own, the serfs owed their lords blind obedience and indeed sometimes were bought and sold as if they were cattle.

The relative weight of complex family households probably also grew in Mediterranean Europe over these centuries. Available evidence certainly suggests this for the countryside of north-central Italy,[30] due above all to the process of breaking large, often only partially used holdings into smaller farms, a process that continued up until the end of the eighteenth century and led to the further growth of the family farm economy. Growing economic investments by urban families led, throughout this period, to an increase in the number of farms. On these new farms an agricultural population came to live. The needs of such farm enterprises as well as the interests of the farms' owners came to be the principal factors influencing the composition of peasant households. The proportion of stem family households may have increased in Portugal as well. After having increased from 1550 to 1650, the proportion of the population living in urban areas—that is in communities of over 10,000 residents—which had grown from 11.5 to 16.6 percent in those years, fell sharply over the next century. By 1800 it had shrunk to 8.7 percent.[31]

Within northwestern Europe, too, it appears that differences in family organization increased over these years, due in particular to the spread of proto-industrialization. This term describes the development of rural industry that preceded modern industrialization. It spread, in the second half of the seventeenth century and in the eighteenth century, in various regions of England, Ireland, Flanders, the Low Countries, and in northern France and in some regions of Germany. In this period, industrial work in the home, which had earlier been concentrated in the cities, began to spread in the countryside. In certain sectors in particular—most notably textiles—a large part of production, destined for expanding markets often located at great distances, was done by peasant families, to supplement their agricultural incomes. Such was the case especially in areas where there were many poor families, who lacked sufficient land to support themselves, and where high population pressure meant agriculural wages were low. But it was also common in areas where, for certain seasons of the year, such families had no work. Proto-industrialization was less common in southern France and central Italy, where the presence of a variety of agricultural products (grapes, olives, mulberries) meant that there was work year-round for all members of the household.

Proto-industrialization did not involve the appearance of any new kind of family. But in some areas, where conditions were favorable, it did lead to significant changes in domestic life. In England and in some parts of Switzerland, for example, the spread of rural industry favored the formation of new households and produced a decline in age at marriage. But this was not the case everywhere, as in those areas where proto-industrial production offered a lower income than did agricultural work, or where various institutional barriers discouraged the formation of new households. Similarly, proto-industrialization sometimes led to less complex households, favoring, for example, neolocal residence and the formation of nuclear family households or offering economic independence to unmarried women and widows, enabling them to live alone instead of with their relatives. In other cases, however, proto-industrialization had the opposite effect, leading kin to want to live together to take full advantage of the new economic opportunities.

Differences among different parts of Europe also increased in relation to the prevalence of infant abandonment. From the beginning of the sixteenth century special institutions began to spread in Europe dedicated to taking in and raising babies who were abandoned. They first appeared in Italy (the foundling home of Verona dates from 1426, the foundling hospital of Santa Maria degli Innocenti, in Florence, opened its doors in 1445). They spread through France, Spain, and parts of the Austrian empire, and then, at the end of the seventeenth century, came to Portugal. While operating in countries that were quite different socially and politically, the foundling homes were remarkably similar. Everywhere they took in abandoned children and gave them to peasant women to wet-nurse in their homes. The children then remained in peasant homes in the countryside while the foundling home continued to offer a salary to the women who raised them to a certain age.

In the sixteenth and seventeenth centuries the foundling homes proliferated in Catholic countries, but not in Protestant areas. In Northern Europe—in England, Germany, the Low Countries, and Scandinavia—there were few such institutions and, where they existed, they tended to be ephemeral (as, for example, was the case in London). The exceptions—most notably Ireland—confirm the importance of the religious difference. In Protestant countries there was a much more pronounced tendency to hold both parents responsible for the cost of raising their children, regardless of either their economic ability or their marital status. In Catholic countries greater weight was given to defending the family's honor, which would be besmirched by the sight of an unwed woman with a child.[32]

In the medieval period children of unmarried parents were accepted by society, although in some places they had fewer rights than others. But the situation changed dramatically following the Council of Trent, in the second half of the sixteenth century. The Church came increasingly to insist that unwed couples either marry or separate. The subsequent stigmatization of illegitimate children led a growing number of unwed mothers to abandon their newborn babies.

We have here given only a brief overview of the nature of family life in early modern times, trying to provide a sense of how it differed from family life today and attempting along the way to dispel some common, but erroneous stereotypes. We have also emphasized the need to distinguish among different regions of Europe, and to identify those aspects of the family that changed over the three centuries from 1500 to 1800. The chapters that follow, examining a series of aspects of family life in comparative perspective, offer a rich view of European family life in the past.

PART I

ECONOMY AND FAMILY ORGANIZATION

CHAPTER 1

The Material Conditions of Family Life*

Raffaella Sarti

(Translated from the Italian by Caroline Beamish)

THE HOME

Living Conditions in Rural Areas

A family huddled together in semi-darkness around a smoking fire lit in a hole in the ground, with the animals nearby for warmth. The house has one or two rooms, walls made of wood or vegetable matter mixed with mud or clay, a roof of straw or reeds, a floor of beaten earth and frequently no windows: such scenes were common during cold nights in rural parts of Europe during the late Middle Ages. In early modern times, however, some important changes took place.

First, the fire. The fireplace built into a side wall, probably invented in Venice in the twelfth or thirteenth century, became a common feature of houses. True, it wasted a lot of heat, but it guaranteed a much less smoky atmosphere. Even better in this respect was the closed stove, which also utilized the heat in a more rational manner. These stoves—built of simple masonry or tiled—were also on the increase. They were often located between two rooms, heating both simultaneously; around the stove were benches on which people could keep warm, sometimes in crowded conditions. An Italian traveling in Poland in the sixteenth century spent his nights in houses where the whole family slept around the stove on benches covered in furs. He took advantage of the lack of privacy to make advances to some of the women. Stoves of this kind were popular in Central and Eastern Europe. From the seventeenth century onward, there were also stoves of cast iron. Fireplaces predominated in Italy, France, Portugal, Norway, and England. In the southern Slavonic areas open fires continued to be the norm. In Spain braziers were preferred, but in the Tierra de Campos and the Tierra del Pan straw was burned in underground ducts.[1]

Transformations such as the removal of the hearth from the center of the room to one wall, the addition of extra fireplaces or the concealment of the fire inside the stove imply a radical alteration of the way people lived, and of the way living was perceived.[2] The symbolic balance of the house was thus transformed, as were (more prosaically) the materials from which it was constructed. It was no coincidence that changes in the way a house was heated should combine with other changes. In the early modern period dwellings like the ones described above were with increasing frequency abandoned, demolished, replaced, rebuilt, or used for other purposes. New houses were more spacious and higher and the interior space was divided more clearly. Especially since the eighteenth century houses were usually built of stone or brick, with roofs of tiles or slates. They were much less flammable, more solid and more durable. They offered less shelter to mice and insects. On the other hand they were liable to cost 15 times as much as a house made of wood or other plant material.[3] The quality and cost of a house did not depend solely on the materials used. Even the humblest dwellings were made of stone where this was in plentiful supply (in the Mediterranean area, in Brittany, Cornwall, Burgundy, the Ile-de-France, etc.). The *Fachwerkhäuser* of Central and Northern Europe, although consisting of a wooden structure filled in with wattles and daub, clay and straw, or some similar mixture, could evidently be both elegant and comfortable.[4]

Well-known architects were hired by Italian landowners keen to make the most of their estates also by rebuilding their country houses.[5] In sixteenth-century France a new architectural genre appeared, albeit one with familiar antecedents. This new type of house was called the *maison rustique* by the humanist Charles Estienne, whose precepts were to influence house-building for more than two centuries.[6] From the late sixteenth century onward, intense building activity in England, particularly in the Midlands and the south, made cottages consisting of one or two rooms much scarcer.[7]

These transformations generally first affected the prosperous echelons of rural society in wealthy areas, then the lower social strata and the poorer areas.[8] In the Polish countryside, for example, the commonest type of house in the nineteenth century was made of wood on stone foundations, with a clay floor and a roof of thatch or wooden shingles. It usually had no more than two rooms, only one of which was heated.[9] The *Heuerlinge* of north-western Germany, on the other hand, lived in miserable hovels near the houses of the *Altbauern*, who gave them land in exchange for labor.[10] The miners of the Auvergne lived in wretched one-roomed hovels (*barriades*), and agricultural day laborers in Sicily suffered a similar fate.[11]

In fact, houses differed according to where they were situated, and also according to the social status of their inhabitants and the functions they had to fulfil.[12] For day laborers they were often no more than a refuge; for richer folk they were a status symbol and an investment. For farming families, they were a tool of their trade. Farmhouses in central Italy had storage space for grain, olives, grapes, etc., and places where these crops could be processed, according to what was cultivated.[13] Big houses, with various wings, were built as they were because they had to fulfil a variety of functions, not necessarily because they housed a large and complex family. These multifunctional homes, however, be they the palaces of the nobility or large farmhouses in central Italy, were frequently inhabited by large, often complex, families, sufficient in number to perform all the various tasks.[14]

Let us now pay a visit to a house inhabited by prosperous peasants, for example the large *Fachwerkhaus* belonging to Jacob Grösser and Agatha Deuggerin in about 1625, in the German village of Jungingen (Zollernalbkreis).[15] The front door opens on to a space which leads to another door. Propped against the wall, or hanging from it, there are various agricultural tools. On the left hand side are store-rooms and perhaps a laundry room; on the right is the stable. Under the staircase a glimpse might be caught of a hen coop, a cage with some piglets in it and a stake for slaughtering animals. On the first floor the *Stube* is large and bright. It has two rows of windows, almost certainly glazed. From the late Middle Ages glass began to spread from churches and the grandest palaces to ordinary homes.[16] The *Stube* is heated by a tiled stove, surrounded by benches. In the opposite corner near the window stands a table. There are benches fixed to the wall and a large chest for sitting on. There are shelves bearing dishes, jugs, and the Bible. Clothes and utensils hang on the wall. Somewhere there is probably a candlestick or a lamp holder. A spinning wheel dominates one corner of the room and we can imagine Agatha sitting there spinning. The *Stube* is not only used as a place to eat, or for social life but also for work: here textiles are spun, clothes are sewn, tools are mended.

Let us have a look at the kitchen: there is probably a cupboard, there are iron and copper pans, dishes of terracotta and wood, baskets, a container for water, a churn, a bottle of cider, a knife and wooden block for the preparation of meat, a pile of wood. There is also the opening through which the stove in the *Stube* is stoked and this is probably where the cooking is done—there is no chimney.[17] There are a few openings in the ceiling to allow the smoke to rise through the loft and out of the thatched roof. The smoke dries the grain and fruit stored in the loft, and also protects the beams from infestation. Beneath the loft, on the first floor, are some more (unheated) rooms, probably three. They are bedrooms. Agatha and Jacob possess three beds at most. But the family consists of five people and two servants. Seven people in three beds? Sharing a bed was perfectly normal: a bed with a mattress, sheet, and blankets was more or less as valuable as a cow.

On the whole, Jacob and Agatha's house was comfortable. At that time, small animals often lived in the main room.[18] The stables were frequently located right next to the living room so that none of the heat from the animals was wasted, and they could be minded without anyone having to venture outside.[19] In Brittany, for example, until quite recently, people and animals lived under the same roof in longhouses, the people separated from the animals by just a few pieces of furniture. Sometimes the intimacy was even greater. According to a late eighteenth-century source, crofters in the Outer Hebrides shared their home with chickens, sheep, goats, and cows, whose combined excrement was removed only once a year.[20] Moreover between 1650 and 1700 in the Vale of Berkeley, in Gloucestershire, and in East Kent (one of the richest parts of Britain, with bountiful agriculture and well-developed commercial and craft activities in small towns and villages)[21] 50 percent of the poorest households[22] possessed no chairs, although the majority had a table, and about 80–90 percent a bedstead. Every household, however, owned at least a mattress to lay on the floor as was the custom in the sixteenth century.[23]

A few decades later, seats became the norm in almost all English houses. In the early modern period the availability of consumer goods went through a period of extended growth, although the pace of the growth quickened or slackened from time to time. It is not easy to give an exact date for the beginning of this expansion. Some scholars maintained that "there was a consumer revolution in eighteenth-century England." In their eyes modern consumerism was born there. Others noted that Renaissance Italy experienced a spectacular growth both of material culture and consumption: "Modern consumer society, with its insatiable consumption setting the pace for the production of more objects and changes in style, had its first stirrings, if not its birth, in the habits of spending that possessed the Italians in the Renaissance." Thus more recent research concludes that "the emergence of a consumer society was by no means sudden—certainly not confined to the late eighteenth and early nineteenth century—nor was it limited geographically to Britain." Sometimes growth continued in spite of general economic decline. In any case, different parts of Europe developed at different rates.[24] In the valley of the Duero, in Spain, in the poorest households chairs were a rarity even as late as 1750.[25] In the Plain of Caen at the beginning of the eighteenth century there were chairs in three-quarters of the houses; by the end of the century every household owned chairs. (In the early part of the century every family owned a bed. Tables became universal 50 years later.) This expansion was not uniformly spread through society, nor were the wealthiest people necessarily the most innovative.[26]

Smaller possessions multiplied, as well as furniture: the acquisition of consumer goods stimulated and satisfied new needs and habits. In the Tuscan countryside, the number of sheets owned by every family doubled between the sixteenth and the eighteenth century.[27] In Normandy during the periods 1700–1715 and 1770–1789, inventories listing at least one tablecloth, glasses, and forks increased respectively from 61 to 76 percent; from 28 to 50 percent, and from 4 to 60 percent.[28]

Living Conditions in Urban Areas

The conditions of life described so far existed predominantly in rural or semi-rural areas. The material life of someone living in the country, however, is different from that of someone living in a town, even though in the countryside large houses and mansions belonging to wealthy people existed alongside the homesteads of peasants and artisans.[29] What were conditions like in the city at this time? In the three centuries we are looking at, houses grew taller and more densely crowded together because of population growth. In Naples, Genoa, Venice, and Rome buildings divided into apartments became more common during the sixteenth century; in seventeenth-century Amsterdam the number of four-storey houses increased. In Paris an edict of 1667 forbade the erection of buildings more than 15.6 meters high, and in 1783 the requirement to respect the ratio between the width of the street and the height of buildings was introduced. During the eighteenth century, however, buildings were rising to six storeys in height and sometimes (according to one witness) as high as nine.[30] In some areas of the city the density of population was about 500 people per hectare. In some parts of London it was 800.[31] Urban growth was due predominantly to immigration, as the mortality rate in the city was higher than it was in the country.[32] Such density of population encouraged the spread of illness and it also made the disposal of waste difficult, even though much of it was recycled. The dung of animals kept in interior courtyards, or of animals used for transport,[33] the contents of chamber pots emptied into the street and other refuse made the urban habitat unhealthy.

Liquid from this refuse percolated down into the aquifers, which were also threatened by the increasing number of septic tanks. By the end of the eighteenth century there was at least one lavatory in nearly all buildings, usually in the courtyard or in the common areas.[34] Wells, frequently polluted,[35] at which women and children often waited in line for hours at a time,[36] were one of the main sources of water. In London, where in the sixteenth and seventeenth centuries pumps and piped water were introduced, to have water brought directly to your house remained the privilege of the few. In Paris, even after the brothers Perrier had inaugurated their domestic water deliveries in 1782, there were around 20,000 water carriers and vendors in the town; the water came from the polluted Seine river. Not surprisingly, the average daily consumption of water at the beginning of the eighteenth century in Paris was less than 5 liters per head; by the end of the century it had risen to 10 liters. (In 1976, in cities with more than 10,000 inhabitants, the daily consumption was estimated at more than 400 liters per head.)[37] In Bologna, Italy, where a system of sluices delivered water to many cellars in town, in summer the water used for laundry was dark and muddy.[38]

In the second half of the eighteenth century, however, perceptions of health and hygiene began to change. For doctors, hygienists, and administrators, washing the streets to clear the air, and opening cities to wind and light became urgent necessities.[39] In addition to being dirty, cities were dark: although as early as the sixteenth century streets were widened to allow carriages to use them, and to provide an appropriate setting for new architecture, in general the urban landscape was characterized by narrow streets running between houses piled one on top of another.[40]

The problem of nocturnal darkness was also being tackled: in Paris there were 2,736 lamps in public places in 1697, and at least 7,000 in 1766.[41] Lighting began to lose its reputation as a luxury reserved for the few.[42] The means of illumination, mainly candlesticks, increased in private houses, particularly after 1750–1760. In eighteenth-century Paris there were on average five per apartment. They were in widespread use among the lower classes too.[43] The lights of the city were in sharp contrast to the darkness of the countryside.[44] In the Plain of Caen, for example, between 1700 and 1715 only 57 percent of all families possessed a candlestick (by 1770–1789 this had risen to 88 percent).[45]

The lighting of the interior of the house was improved by an increase in the number of windows, in Paris particularly notable from the 1720s and 1730s onward. Relatively large panes of translucent glass replaced paper and oiled canvas or small panes of glass. Only the richest, however, were able to flood their rooms with light through really generous windows.[46]

The desire for sunlight conflicted with the need for warmth, even in the wealthiest households. In 1695 in Versailles water and wine froze on the king's dining table.[47] Humbler dwellings, which were small and crowded, were sometimes less cold. In Bologna in the eighteenth century, the *camino* (i.e. "hearth", a room with a fireplace) represented the minimum space that was normally rented.[48] In eighteenth-century Paris there was an average of one fireplace for every two rooms. One-roomed dwellings nearly always had one, but a house with more than 20 rooms might only have four. In the houses of the rich the servants' rooms seldom had a fireplace: being warm was a prerogative which employers tended to keep for themselves. After 1720, however, technical developments improved the output of heat. New houses were more likely to have one fireplace per room. In the second half of the century, in Paris as in Turin, stoves began to become more widespread. Even as late as the French Revolution the poorest were still warming themselves at dangerous braziers, and this was in Paris where, in spite of the problems of procuring and storing fuel, people were generally better heated than they were in the countryside and in other French cities.[49]

The need to survive the cold makes the importance of the bed comprehensible. A bed was often brought to a marriage by the bride, along with the chest containing her trousseau, and was another focal point (with the hearth) of family life.[50] This is why in many wealthy Dutch houses in the seventeenth century it took pride of place in the middle of the room.[51] In Parisian probate inventories of the period it is usually the first item of furniture to be listed, and also the one described in most detail. On average its value represented about 15 percent of the estate of a poor man or woman. Among wage earners a bed represented 25 percent of the cost of furnishing a dwelling, or 39 percent among domestic servants. Every household possessed at least one, but they could vary from a simple mattress to a four-poster bed with hangings.[52] The differentiation between beds developed especially in the fifteenth century when the custom of sleeping on straw or on a palliasse laid on the ground, or on planks, began to decline.[53] In the period between 1690 and 1789, a sample of more than 3,000 beds in Paris reveals that 72.5 percent had curtains round them which created a sort of "house within a house." Sometimes the bed was placed in a niche with a curtain or a door.[54]

In the country it was common for people to share a bed. What about the town? In Norwich, at the end of the seventeenth century, it seems that almost everyone, apart from couples and children, had a bed to him or herself.[55] There were differences between the social groups all the same. In Paris between 1695 and 1715 among domestic servants each bed housed an average of 1.9 people, 2.3 among wage earners. By 1780 the figures were, respectively, 1.8 and 1.9. Poor families often snuggled up in a single bed.[56] In wealthy families in the eighteenth century, on the other hand, even the children often had their own beds. Couples frequently shared a bed with their youngest children in spite of the risk of suffocation.[57] Upper-class husbands and wives often had separate beds, even separate bedrooms. The nobility would sometimes receive visitors and friends in bed,[58] particularly in France, where the king received ministers, and—so to say—governed the country from his bed.[59] The opulent beds from which such social activities took place were not the beds in which their occupants slept: they were "ceremonial beds," in use especially in the second half of the seventeenth century.[60]

Besides the bed, in urban interiors there were other items of furniture. Houses in towns were generally better furnished than peasant houses in the country, where in the eighteenth century many dwellings were still without tables and chairs. In Paris such things abounded: while stools and benches were declining, armchairs and sofas were becoming more common. A certain abundance characterized lower strata homes as well: often there were more seats to sit on than there were inhabitants. In addition to three or four tables, often collapsible, there was an average of a dozen seats per dwelling. One-roomed dwellings, which accounted for 31 percent of homes, were generally lived in by two to three people; dwellings with two or three rooms (42 percent) by three or four people and the same number for dwellings with four to seven rooms (20 percent). Only larger houses (7 percent) housed a greater number of people, most of them domestic servants. The large number of chairs probably indicates a busy social life: we can imagine lower-class homes full of friends or relations sitting on rush-seated chairs chatting, playing games, or listening to one member of the company reading. Or drawing rooms belonging to highly educated society hostesses where guests, seated on elegant chairs, made conversation while sipping the fashionable beverage of the day from decorated cups.[61]

Pots, pans, and cutlery were on the increase and were changing. Stoneware, glass, pottery, earthenware were coming into use, replacing wood and, to some extent, metal. Many items cost less than they had in the past, and were more numerous. New consumer goods were emerging too, linked to new habits (such as tea, coffee, and chocolate services, with their sugar bowls).[62] The taste for comfort and elegance was increasing: comfortable, handsome easy chairs, small tables, knick-knacks, porcelain, clocks, mirrors, paintings, hangings, and tapestries for decorative purposes and to insulate rooms against the cold. Moreover, new items of furniture were invented in which the growing volume of domestic objects could be neatly put away: the old chests in which everything used to be piled were replaced by cupboards, chests-of-drawers, bookshelves, and wardrobes.[63] In the kitchen the crockery and cooking pots were no longer scattered around the fireplace, thanks to the presence of kitchen cupboards; there were tripods with space for burning embers over which caldrons could be placed; stoves built into the wall and, from about 1750, heavy metal kitchen ranges. It became possible to cook without squatting on the floor.[64]

The increase in the number and specialized function of furnishings was accompanied by specialization in the use of rooms. Even in the Middle Ages the elite used particular rooms for particular purposes. Kitchens are one example.[65] For a long time, nevertheless, activities generally carried out today in separate rooms were all pursued in the same room.[66] In seventeenth-century London, where the process of reserving rooms for particular uses was fairly well advanced, to the extent that upstairs rooms were mainly bedrooms while food was usually prepared in the kitchen, there were beds in shops, kitchens, and halls.[67] They could also be found in the most unexpected places in eighteenth-century Paris.[68] Rooms were often partially multifunctional even in the spacious palaces of the nobility. This explains why Madame de Maintenon undressed, with the assistance of her chambermaids, and went to bed in the very room where Louis XIV was deep in discussion with his ministers separated from his mistress only by the bed curtains.[69] It was during his reign, in fact, that the upper classes began to have "dining rooms"; *salons* spread from the 1720s to 1730s onward, while rooms defined as "bedrooms" became more common during the second half of the eighteenth century.[70]

For a long time there was no special place to eat. During the Middle Ages, tables would be set upon trestles, generally in the main room, and these would be dismantled after the meal.[71] In the palaces of the Renaissance, however, rooms began to appear, called *salette* or *salotti*, where the master of the house's family could be accommodated for the meals, even if they could eat elsewhere as well: in the main hall, antechambers, private apartments. . . .[72] In the English country house in the seventeenth century the hall ceased to be the place where the whole family ate and lived, and where some of the servants slept, because the master's family began to take their meals in a room set aside for the purpose. The hall degenerated into a refectory for the servants. Then, when a room where servants could eat became the norm, it became simply the entrance to the house.[73]

Obviously the development of specialized rooms did not involve the whole of society at an equal pace. In late eighteenth-century France, the middle classes had no dining room or drawing room. In Paris only one tenth of the population had a real bedroom, and only the same proportion a kitchen used solely for preparing food. Many families adapted the space under the stairs, or storerooms and closets outside the apartment itself, to make small rooms within which a bit of intimacy could be enjoyed.[74] This helped to demarcate the boundaries between inside and outside more clearly. Until about 1750, the rooms inhabited by a family were spread over various floors. Therefore even the growing popularity of the "horizontally" arranged apartment in the second half of the century contributed to this developing demarcation.[75]

The disposition of available space was subject to increasing attempts to use it more rationally from the fifteenth century onward, but in the early modern period it changed in a number of different ways.[76] In the Renaissance palaces of Italy (which were imitated all over Europe) service areas, reception areas, and private areas began to be differentiated. For the master of the house, then for other members of his family, apartments consisting of a series of connecting rooms were developed: one or more antechambers, a bedroom, a few small rooms (a study, a wardrobe, a lavatory). Proceeding through these rooms one entered spaces of an increasingly personal and private nature. At the end there was generally a door or a concealed staircase by means of which the master of the house could come and go without passing through the public rooms.[77]

In order to facilitate movement around the house, the number of doors increased—a rational measure in dwellings with connecting rooms where, in order to move from one room to another, all the rooms in between had to be crossed. In dwellings like this—and they were extremely prevalent in the period we are describing—any activity might be interrupted by someone passing through. Members of the family ran into one another as they moved about. The corridor changed this state of affairs. The first modern corridor probably appeared in a residence in Chelsea designed by John Thorpe in 1597. The (gradual) introduction of the room with a single door opening on to a corridor transformed each room into an isolated space, decreased casual encounters, and facilitated communication that had a particular aim.[78] This transformation embodied and reinforced the growing preference for choosing the people with whom one had relations, a new sense of modesty, and an increasing need for solitude.[79]

In the seventeenth century the architect Roger Pratt justified the introduction of the corridor as the answer to the householder's need not to have to pass through the service areas. It also prevented the servants from having to pass through the parts of the house where the owners spent their time. Some categories of domestic servant had lived in very close contact with their masters for centuries, although in the larger palaces of the Renaissance they had their own quarters. Louis XIV had a manservant who slept in the same room as he did.[80] In 1751, when the first wife of the nobleman Francesco Albergati requested the annulment of her marriage on grounds of her husband's impotence, the *marchese*'s manservant was able to testify to his master's virility because, while helping him to dress in the morning, he had sometimes seen him with an erection.[81] As time passed, however, the need for privacy prevailed over the need to have domestics close at hand, ready to serve. The spatial segregation of servants and masters consequently grew ever greater.[82] The servants may also have come to appreciate their own private space. From the later years of the seventeenth century, fewer male servants seem to have lived with their masters (on the other hand, the female servants continued to live in the master's house for a long time).[83]

In conclusion, new boundaries appeared in domestic space, which over the years became more clearly divided from external space; interior space was organized into specialized areas dedicated to private activities (such as sleeping) or more public activities (such as receiving guests). Of course, a proportion of the population, larger or smaller according to location and period, was completely uninvolved in such changes, or at least only very minimally. Where they did take place, however, the change in function of the various rooms and in their spatial arrangement was the physical embodiment of changes taking place in interpersonal relations, and these in their turn were affected by the domestic changes.[84] Having discussed the spread of tables and chairs, the increase in the use of saucepans and cutlery, and the identification of a room for use as a dining room, and bearing in mind that "the most important social relations are expressed at table,"[85] let us now focus our attention on food and eating.

EATING

In a description of a dinner taken in the second half of the seventeenth century with a family of Tyrolean cow-herds, the French nobleman Jouvin de Rochefort recalls that "they gave me the best of their seats, in other words an upturned basin," and laid a table "on which there were no cloth, napkins, knives, forks, nor spoons." A wooden bowl containing some turnips, and another with six eggs, half a cheese, and some pieces of bread was put on the table. The family sat on the ground. First the father passed the dish with the eggs in it to the visitor and, when he had helped himself, passed the rest around. Then he passed the turnips and, once the guest had helped himself, everyone put his hand into the dish. The cow-herds drank only milk but honored the visitor by giving him a small amount of rather stale wine in a wooden cup. Then they brought him a little cheese and a dish "of small fruit, somewhat similar to grapes . . . which grow in the woods," probably bilberries.[86]

Jouvin de Rochefort looked benevolently upon the poverty of his hosts. In the eyes of many members of the middle and upper strata, however, the scarcity of crockery and cutlery (as well as of food) of many rustic households was taken as evidence of the alleged crude nature of the peasantry. Knowing how to behave "correctly" at table was a strong social identifier.[87] Nevertheless in France as late as 1730 the use of the fork was uncommon even at court.[88] The fork appears to have been invented in Byzantium and to have appeared in Italy in the tenth or eleventh century, but its use became widespread in the thirteenth or fourteenth century. From the Italian peninsula it spread gradually to other European countries. On the other hand, the plate quite rapidly replaced the medieval wooden platter. From the sixteenth century onward, every guest (in decent society) was given a plate, a glass, a spoon and knife and, possibly, a fork of his own.[89] The old "convivial promiscuity" was on its way out: now everyone could eat from his own plate and drink from his own glass.[90]

What did eating together signify? One author has said that "commensality is a sign of trust and fraternity, or of proximity of status."[91] Nearly all marriages were celebrated with a banquet. "Eating together" could be one of the characteristic features of a genuine family: to live *a uno pane e uno vino* (i.e. "with the same bread and wine,") as the Tuscan saying goes.[92] Conversely the breakup of a family unit could be reflected in eating separately: Roman Catholicism does not permit divorce, but the separation of "bed, *table* and dwelling" is possible.[93] "We have one hearth between us, but each does his own cooking," a woman from a village on Lake Lugano explained in 1769; she was in conflict with her daughter-in-law.[94] Social hierarchies were manifest at table, as were hierarchies of gender and generation. The Tyrolean mountain folk reserved their wine and their solitary seat for their important visitor. Basque tradition forbade women from sitting at the table of the paterfamilias.[95] Similarly, in other parts of Europe men ate sitting down while the women and/or children stood, and often were not served until after the men had finished.[96] In northern Germany several methods of eating meals have been described: in the first, probably the oldest, women and children stood; in another, all the members of the family, including servants, sat at the table. The head of the family sat at the top and the highest-ranking servants and older children were placed closest to him, with women and men on opposite sides; in the last, the master and family ate separately, the servants being relegated to another table in another room.[97] In aristocratic households in the modern period it was the custom to have separate tables. In 1782, in the summer residence of the nobleman Francesco Albergati, there were at least four: one for the *marchese*, his wife, their two children, the children's tutor, and the resident violinist; one for the female domestics at which the valet also ate once he had served at the master's table; one for the steward and his wife, in their private apartment and one (or more) in the kitchen where the remaining servants ate.[98]

There were no women in the Albergati kitchen. In elite families all those entrusted with important jobs such as the preparation and cooking of food were men, often men of relatively high class, especially those serving at table in princely houses at the beginning of the early modern period.[99] Poisoning was greatly feared. It is interesting to note that, in Italian, the word for both the piece of furniture on which cold food and dishes were placed, and for the method of proffering food without touching it with the hands, was *credenza*, derived from the Latin *credo*, I trust.[100] The success of a banquet, an important opportunity for members of the upper classes to display their wealth and power,[101] depended on the skill of the domestic staff. A "normal" meal for the Czar of Russia consisted of 150 different dishes, 50 types of strong drink, 10 varieties of beer, and kvass.[102]

Although customs differed in different parts of Europe, in general it was not until the eighteenth or nineteenth century that elite kitchens were populated by female cooks.[103] In France the first cookery book for women appeared in 1746. In just over fifty years, about 93,000 copies were printed. Appropriately enough it was called *La Cuisinière bourgeoise*.[104] In the eighteenth century, *haute cuisine* in France (admired all over Europe) developed a certain simplicity: "bourgeois" food prepared at home by housewives or household servants came into fashion. Because cookery was an important factor in family wellbeing, the preparation of food in middle- and lower-strata families was delegated less frequently to servants than were the cleaning and washing. However this probably varied according to where you were: in England it appears that women of relatively high class were expected to know how to cook, whereas in Italy and France cooking was regarded as the work of the maidservants and ladies took no part in it. Moreover only a minority of women of gentle birth in Europe nursed their own babies: it was not until the late seventeenth or mid-eighteenth century, according to circumstances, that the practice of wet-nursing began to be abandoned. Only certain categories of working women used wet-nurses anyway, so even this practice connected with food and feeding differed according to social group.[105]

Food itself was a tremendous clue to social class and hierarchy. It was held that all should eat according to their "quality," i.e. according to their social condition (as well as according to their constitution, state of health, age, and sex). The Italian writer Giulio Cesare Croce tells the story of a peasant, Bertoldo, who was obliged to eat dainty foodstuffs when he unexpectedly embarked on a career at court: "He died in severe pain because he could not eat turnips and beans."[106] Along these lines, at the beginning of the early modern era it was considered that birds and fowl were suitable fare for the upper classes and turnips for peasants, since up was considered positive and down negative. Poultry was thought to enhance sexual excitement: widows, who were supposed to be chaste,

were discouraged from eating chicken.[107] Servants and masters living
under the same roof (and even domestics of different rank) usually ate
different food. Today "family pack" indicates inexpensive food in large
quantities, not always of the best quality; this derives from "family
wine," the wine given to the servants.[108] Similarly a "family loaf" was a
loaf of low quality.[109] In the early modern period people seated at the
same table might be offered different food: the best bits went to the most
important people.[110]

Food was different in town and country too. In town even the middle
and lower strata ate bread made of wheat, although the bread grew
whiter as it rose through the social scale. The bread eaten by peasants
was generally dark in color and made of inferior cereals, chestnut or
lupin flour, or flour made of a mixture of whatever was locally available.[111] In addition, city dwellers, particularly the middle and upper
classes, ate fresh bread every day, made in a bakery or at home (in the
latter case, it might be taken to the bakery to be baked).[112] To save time
and fuel, and in order to eat less, peasants baked rarely. In some Alpine
areas, bread was baked only twice a year. Cereals that were too unsuited
to bread-making were made into pap, farinaceous foods, and polenta.[113]

Modern attitudes to nutrition in Europe derived from a combination
of the Roman diet, centering around bread, wine, and oil (enriched by
milk, cheese, vegetables, and meat), and the "barbarian" diet of meat,
dairy products, beer, and cider combined with oat porridge and flat
barley bread. The success of the Germanic tribes in battle had persuaded
everyone of the value of eating meat, while the "success" of bread was
linked to the spread of Christianity: bread, with wine and oil, occupied
a central role in Christian worship. Interestingly, the Reformation also
affected diet. The Protestants rejected the dietary practices of the Roman
Catholic Church, with its fast days. Ancient differences between Northern and Southern Europe re-emerged: in fact they had never completely disappeared. The north was more carnivorous, the south more
vegetarian; the eating of meat and animals in the Catholic south was
prohibited on about 140–160 days in the year.[114] Fast days were even more
numerous in Orthodox Europe: there were about 200 in the Russian
calendar. Jews, scattered throughout various European countries, also
had their own dietary laws.[115]

While religious beliefs and customs dictated what could or could not
be eaten, the opportunity to satisfy one's hunger depended on the availability of food. After the catastrophic plague of 1347–1351, until about
the middle of the sixteenth century, the European diet was, in general,
rather adequate and balanced. After that, however, it became impossible
to adapt resources to the requirements of a growing population. It was

not until the eighteenth century that innovations designed to increase agricultural productivity caught on and trade in foodstuffs intensified.[116] Most people were then forced to eat less meat and more bread.[117] The quality of bread deteriorated, however. Even in the cities, where white bread had been eaten since the thirteenth century, wheat was mixed with inferior cereals or pulses—or even sometimes replaced by them. Apart from Norway and Iceland, where the diet was predominantly fish,[118] for many people in Europe cereals provided more than 80 percent of their caloric intake.[119] A poor harvest was enough to cause famine.[120] To confront a famine situation, people began growing plants which previously had been little cultivated in Europe, such as rice and buckwheat,[121] or new plants recently arrived from America (peppers, capsicums, tomatoes, beans, maize, and potatoes).

Maize was imported into Europe by Columbus in 1493 and spread rapidly in many regions of Spain, Portugal, south-western France, the Veneto, the Balkan peninsula, and Hungary. For a long time it was used only as fodder, or was cultivated only in kitchen gardens.[122] The transition to the cultivation of maize in fields took place mainly at moments of crisis, particularly in the eighteenth century.[123] In the Balkans, for example, this happened after the famine of 1740–1741. In various parts of northern Italy maize polenta became the staple food of the peasantry, to the extent that deficiency of niacin in a monotonous diet dominated by maize provoked the spread of pellagra.[124]

The potato was known in Peru in 1539, but for a long time Europeans viewed it with profound suspicion. Only hunger, particularly during the famine of 1770–1772, encouraged its wider cultivation. In fact, the potato has almost twice the yield of grain.[125] In addition, because potatoes grow underground, the harvest of a field of potatoes is assured, even if an army camps on it for months on end. War encouraged the spread of the potato,[126] particularly in the northern part of Central Europe.

By the end of the eighteenth century, therefore, the geography of vegetable foodstuffs looked different from the way it had looked two or three centuries earlier: north Central Europe was predominantly potato eating, whereas in Southern and Southeastern Europe there were large areas where polenta was very common.[127] In the mountainous areas of the Mediterranean, chestnuts were the main food (dried, boiled, or ground into flour to make bread, *ciacci* or polenta). In spite of its appearance, the chestnut is a nourishing food.[128] In southern Italy pasta became an important element in the diet of the poor from the seventeenth century onward.[129]

Although potatoes and maize helped increase the availability of food,[130] they also contributed to the deterioration in nourishment suffered by the majority of Europeans between the sixteenth and eighteenth centuries, causing the decrease in average height revealed by recent research.[131] In the eighteenth century, peasants in the Veneto, who ate only polenta, suffered a fate similar to that of the first English industrial workers who lived on bread and sweet tea.[132]

Sugar originated in India and was used in Europe from the Middle Ages onwards. In the sixteenth century it became a luxury seasoning for all types of meal (the passion for sweet-sour food died away in the seventeenth/eighteenth century). As production increased, sugar became more widely available. Tea, Chinese in origin, arrived at the beginning of the seventeenth century. It became popular in England, winning favor first with the elite, then with the populace at large. In the second half of the seventeenth century the first coffee shops appeared. Here the beverage introduced from the Middle East and familiar to the Venetians as early as the 1570s could be sampled, and here too a new form of social life was born. Coffee was a stimulating drink, the symbol of bourgeois rationalism and efficiency—in contrast to chocolate, which was popular particularly among the aristocracy or as a drink to be enjoyed while fasting (it came from America).[133]

Like tea, cocoa, and coffee, spirits were first used pharmaceutically.[134] From the seventeenth century on, however, they were drunk along with more traditional drinks, i.e. wine and beer.[135] Wine was predominant in Mediterranean Europe, but the elite enjoyed wine everywhere. Beer was the favorite in Central Europe and was also drunk widely in the Iberian peninsula. Although the poorest of the poor often drank plain water, the consumption of alcoholic drinks was presumably very high. It seems that anyone who drank wine would drink at least a liter a day, although the alcoholic content was often low. In English families in the seventeenth century adults and children daily drank probably about 3 liters of beer per head. Alcoholic drinks were drunk because drinking-water was difficult to come by. Liquid was needed to supplement the diet, to assist with the mastication of stale bread, and to quench the thirst caused by very salty food (salt was used to preserve meat and fish and to add flavor to cereals and pulses). People also drank in order to forget the rigor of their harsh lives, or to dispel the memory of hunger pains (they took hallucinogenic plants for the same reason). Throughout the early modern period hunger, whether experienced or feared, was central to the lives of a large proportion of the population. The excess that was part of the feasting on high days and holidays helped to exorcize the specter of hunger.[136]

Nevertheless, the peasant diet was not necessarily one of total deprivation. Women used aromatic plants in the kitchen to prepare tasty food even if they could not perform miracles.[137] Kitchen gardens provided vegetables and fruit: soups were prepared from onions, pulses, cabbage, potatoes, turnips, often mixed with cereals or stale bread, dressed with butter, lard, dripping, or oil and if possible enriched with a little meat. Turnips and cabbage were ubiquitous. In Central Europe, where there were no fresh vegetables in winter, sauerkraut was an essential part of the diet; in Southern Europe salads were vital, and in fact were often all there was to eat.[138] According to one witness, Tuscan peasants in the late eighteenth century had three meals a day: one consisted of polenta and salad, one of bread and boiled beans and other vegetables dressed with a little oil, and the third of soup. A little meat was eaten on Sundays.[139] In Mediterranean countries olives, dried figs, and fruit were very common; some of the peasants of southern Italy survived in winter on nothing but bread and figs.[140] Apples, pears, and cherries were widely eaten in Central and Eastern Europe: dried, they were sometimes used as a substitute for bread. Nourishment was also derived from nuts: almonds, pine nuts, hazelnuts, walnuts. It was also obtained from hunting (or poaching) and fishing, from stable and farmyard, although eggs, poultry, and rabbits were mainly reserved for the landowners or for sale.[141]

It was usually the women who looked after the kitchen garden and farmyard. In many areas, including England, women were also responsible for making butter and cheese.[142] In other countries this was man's work, work that was sometimes central in defining gender: among the Basques of Saint-Eugrâce only sexually mature males were allowed to make cheese. Those too old to beget children were not allowed into the mountain huts where the milk was processed for cheese; they stayed at home with the women and children and were assimilated back into their midst.[143]

The division of labor according to sex varied from place to place. It was usually quite rigidly observed, but not immutable. Women's tasks were many: it has been calculated that, in Britain, on average, the preparation of food took three to four hours a day, fetching water and wood about one hour, one hour was spent keeping the fire going and suckling or feeding children. Women then worked in the kitchen garden (one hour), saw to the animals and milked them (two or three hours), made bread and beer (three hours per week for each activity) and sometimes preserves. Not counting any work done outside the home, women expended their energy on doing the washing (four hours per week), cleaning the house (two hours a day), spinning for clothing (two hours), looking after children (three hours).[144] A male cook is preferable to a female, wrote Vincenzo Tanara in the mid-seventeenth century, because "the female puts the pot on the fire . . . and while the food is cooking

... she spins."[145] It is not difficult to believe that for many women this is the way things were. As the English folk-song says: "A woman's work is never done."[146]

CLOTHING

During the period in question, spinning was an everyday activity for women. In many areas the distaff and spindle featured in the wedding ceremony as traditional symbols of the virtuous, diligent wife. Girls spun to prepare their trousseau, women spun for the family. Spinning was also carried out as a money-making activity. Although silk spinning, increasingly mechanized, was done not only by women but also by men,[147] domestic spinning was almost exclusively done by women. On the other hand, weaving organized by merchants who supplied the materials to home workers, also involved men.[148]

As well as spinning and weaving, women cut and stitched to produce or alter linen and clothing. Old clothes were regularly recycled: they were passed from one member of the family to the other, sold, bought, received as gifts, inherited, or even stolen.[149] Dressmakers were employed as well, and fabrics could be bought.[150] Home production remained considerable, nevertheless, in spite of increased competition from the textile industry, professional tailors, and shops. Thanks to the development of industry and commerce, consumption grew.[151] Clothes and linen were becoming more widely available. The Tuscan peasant began to have much greater access to both.[152] In the eighteenth century the quantity of clothing and linen possessed by the "populace of Paris" tripled.[153]

This was due partly to the concept of bodily hygiene which developed in the sixteenth century. The battle against syphilis and plague, and the attitudes against sex promulgated by the Reformation and the Counter-Reformation led, in Western Europe (not in the east), to the closure of the Roman-style public baths—they were places of entertainment as well as of public hygiene.[154] It was believed that water, especially hot water, dilated the pores and encouraged pathogens to enter the body via the skin. Even newborn babies were not washed, and until the eighteenth century they were swaddled in bands of cloth which were usually changed twice a day at the most.[155] This "dry" interpretation of bodily hygiene lasted until about 1760: underclothes were now thought to absorb dirt and changing the underwear often was considered to prevent impurities from "breeding" fleas and lice. One of the duties of a diligent mother was to de-louse her children.[156] After 1760, however, baths and bathrooms began to spread: in the mid-eighteenth century only 6 percent of grand private residences in Paris had a bathroom, whereas in those built between 1770 and 1800 one third had one. The spread of bathtubs and washtubs was greater, but practical difficulties and deep-rooted prejudices made the pace of change very slow.[157]

When the changing of underwear constituted the main measure of hygiene, there was obviously a lot of underclothing about. In court circles as early as the sixteenth century people apparently changed their shirt almost every day.[158] In 1700–1715, in the wardrobes of Parisian domestic servants (who were influenced by the lifestyle of their employers), many shirts were to be found. Maidservants often owned a dozen, menservants an average of ten (25 between 1775 and 1790). Even in Paris, however, probably the European city with the largest supply of linen, not everyone was so well supplied, wage earners in particular. At the end of the eighteenth century, it seems, anyone owning a single shirt would wash it fortnightly or weekly, at least in summertime.[159] In Sardinia a sign of mourning was that the shirt would not be changed for a whole year.[160] In England children would be smeared with grease and sewn into their vests when winter began; this made sure that they were always clothed.[161]

Clearly, clothes were important as protection from cold, even if this was not their only function. In badly heated, early modern Europe, clothes often were worn in layers and were heavy, sometimes being lined with fur. In the eighteenth century they grew lighter and more colorful. In Paris women's wardrobes began to include cottons and silks. The populace turned blue, yellow, green, pink. . . .[162] Dark, faded colors continued to predominate in the country, but blue began to spread there in the eighteenth century.[163]

Throughout the centuries, certain colors had been the privilege of the few: in Württemberg, for example, green was a court color and was also worn by the Duke's huntsmen. In Bologna only the nobility were allowed to clothe their servants in multicolored livery, or livery trimmed with silver.[164] The sumptuary laws imposed in many countries regulated the shape and fabric, and the decoration permitted on clothing.[165] In Württemberg in 1712 peasants were not permitted to wear imported fabric, and the lower orders in the city could not wear Indian cottons. Only the upper ranks were allowed to wear clothing in the French style.[166] During the sixteenth century, European elites followed the Italian fashion, with its crimson velvets decorated with gold; later the darker, austere Spanish styles were more sought after. The seventeenth century saw the rise of French fashion, which was more colorful. By the end of the century such fashion was changing more rapidly than it had in the past.[167] Sumptuary laws were first passed in Italy to counteract aristocratic privilege. By the early modern period the legislation had become a means of protecting the privileged classes from "attempts at imitation" by the less fortunate. Although it was only partially effective, it illustrates the idea of dress as an indicator of social class.[168]

Clothing conveys very precise information even without being codified by law. In the German village of Laichingen, for example, in about 1750, blue began its "triumphal march" as the color of respectability and distinction.[169] Black was associated with death, although in Italy this could also be indicated by mixed shades of red and black. In many parts of Italy red was the traditional color for weddings: except in Venice, white did not become fashionable for bridal wear until the nineteenth century.[170] Clothes could therefore be used to mark key events in family life, such as mourning or marriage. Certain garments also assumed an important ritual significance. In Florence during the Renaissance the husband made his bride his wife by clothing her—providing her with clothing and jewelry.[171] In the Asturias, after a wedding a boy took a special belt off the bride: and the groom, in order to win his wife, was forced to redeem the belt by giving the boy a present.[172]

In particular since the fourteenth and fifteenth centuries, clothing emphasized the sex of the wearer above all: men stopped wearing the long gown—which metamorphosed into a cape worn only by women (apart from priests, old men, and children). Especially among the upper classes, clothing began to emphasize male and female attributes: the breeches of the Renaissance sometimes had inserts that were obviously phallic. In our period, bodices, whalebone, farthingales, and padding imprisoned the female body in order to impart a narrow waist and wide hips.[173] Clothes, accessories, and hairstyles and the manner of wearing them distinguished the men from the women, and also girls of marriageable age from girls betrothed, married women from widows, bachelors from married men. . . . In France, for example, the angle at which a man wore his cap demonstrated whether he was a bachelor or a married man.[174]

There were also clothes which demonstrated the social position of the family. During the entire early modern period, the livery of the domestic servant was a guide to the house in which he was employed. The elegance of the livery provided evidence of the wealth and power of the master. It could also give information about specific events in the family: baptisms, weddings, funerals. When marriages took place, the domestic staff often wore new uniforms to celebrate the union of bride and groom. After the marriage, the livery could even be a guide to how relations between the couple were faring: in the seventeenth century a gentlewoman who had been betrayed by her husband decided to "open her house . . . and adopt a livery quite different from that of her husband."[175]

Changes dating at least from the seventeenth century (with the growth of the urban economy, the spread of fashions that did not betray social distinctions, etc.) made the idea of an *ancien régime* of dress, characterized by the correspondence (regulated by law) between clothing and social rank, only partially applicable.[176] In France, on the eve of the French Revolution, everyone dressed as he or she wished, or as his or her purse permitted. The domestic livery still represented an *ancien régime* of dress and was extremely widespread, however. The revolutionaries, who wanted to demolish the *ancien régime* in its entirety, were well aware of the areas in which its influence persisted: on June 19, 1790 they abolished with one fell swoop the hereditary nobility, titles, coats of arms, and livery.[177] On October 29, 1793, in even more radical fashion, they declared that freedom of dress was one of the fundamental rights of man.[178] The desire to create free, independent citizens led to the elimination of one of the methods by which social rank was rendered identifiable (or, in the case of livery, the means by which one was marked out as belonging to the master's household). In spite of this, the position of the family remained for years central to the socially accepted way of defining the identity of domestic servants (or, even more, of the women and underage children).[179] However, these reforms, associated with the French revolution, surely indicate a profound change in the way material possessions were used and therefore a profound change in material culture, which is not simply a kind of pre-condition or neutral container of our life.

In fact, things and goods can embody family values, as was the case, for example, with ancient palaces or family portraits. Dowries were important when a new family was created. The transmission of family wealth was an important part of family reproduction and different inheritance systems could contribute in shaping different family relations and family forms. Emotions as well as kinship relations could be expressed through material goods, while at the same time being influenced by them. Material possessions could (and can) be used to create bridges or to erect barriers between people, as I have tried to show, however sketchily, in this chapter.[180]

CHAPTER 2

Serfdom in Eastern Europe

Karl Kaser

INTRODUCTION

Over the past decades an increasing number of studies has been devoted to European family history research. The results are quite encouraging. However, scientific research has concentrated mainly on Western, Central and Mediterranean Europe whereas Eastern and southeastern Europe have been relatively neglected. This has had a noticeable impact on our knowledge of family history in the European east. It may be too early to make generalizations regarding historical family forms in this part of Europe, since we are now limited to but a few reliable studies, which, strictly speaking, are only of regional significance. This is especially true for the vast areas to the east of the Alps and Carpathian mountains. Current research for Hungary and the Balkan countries is encouraging. But studies of family life in early modern Russia, for example, are still few. Therefore we should be careful not to draw quick conclusions.

The fact that this chapter is embedded in the context of economy and family organization suggests a correlation between family organization and the continuation and intensification of serfdom in Eastern Europe since the sixteenth century. However, there are at least two reasons not to assume a conclusive connection: first, serfdom was not the only form of economic and legal relations under which peasant families in Eastern Europe lived; secondly, in this chapter I want to question whether a system of serfdom, which undoubtedly shaped the peasant's everyday life, actually had a decisive impact on family organization or whether it provided only a general framework for the development of family forms.

Clearly, a relationship between economic conditions and family organization in Eastern Europe in early modern times exists: nonetheless for the sake of clarity we should differentiate between family organization and family functions. It was mostly family functions that were subjected to the economic demands of East European feudal lords, not the traditional forms of family organization.

Family organization and structure in Eastern Europe leaned strongly towards complexity (unlike in Central and Western Europe, where there was a strong tendency towards a nuclear family organization). By this we mean family households were typically formed by several *conjugal* units (with or without children), living in *multiple family households*. In the older literature these collective family constellations were related to a misconceived notion of Slavic collectivist mentality. We now know that this perspective is not valid: the spreading of certain family forms in historic times generally knows no ethnic or state boundaries; it is determined by a complex network of economic, cultural, fiscal, administrative, legal, and demographic factors.[1] So it is only natural that various East European ethnic groups shared the same forms of family organization and household formation: various Slavic peoples (Russians, Poles, Serbs, Croats, Slovaks, Bulgarians—to name only a few), Baltic peoples (mostly Estonians and Latvians), Balkan-Romanic *Vlachs* and Romanians, Finno-Ugristic Hungarians as well as Albanians, Greeks, Turks, and Tartars. This list is by no means complete.

What is the geographic concept embodied by the term "Eastern Europe"? A generally accepted definition of geographic Eastern Europe has never been agreed upon over the past centuries. As this chapter primarily deals with historic family forms, we need a definition that takes these forms into account. In this context we simply cannot overlook the so-called Hajnal line,[2] dividing east from west. This line, which marks a transitional zone reaching from Trieste to St Petersburg, is particularly interesting for us in relation to varying marriage patterns, customs of inheritance and household formation patterns. We will deal with this in detail later in the chapter. This Hajnal line, which did not lose its significance until the twentieth century, stretches approximately along today's border between Slovenia and Croatia as well as between the Czech Republic and Slovakia and runs through Poland and the Baltic States, defining our geographic frame of observation in a sufficiently precise way. We will not take into account the Mediterranean regions of today's Greece because they greatly differ from East European forms with regard to family structures. To draw an eastern border is not useful since our knowledge of historic family forms thins out progressively the further east we go.

Since the sixteenth century over large areas of Eastern Europe we can see an intensification of feudal relations, i.e. an increasing economic and legal dependency by peasant families on their feudal lord. Many peasant families reverted to the status of serfdom or they were confronted, as in

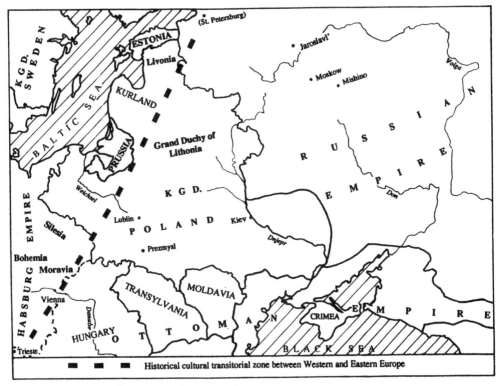

Map 1. Eastern Europe in the Sixteenth Century.

the case of the expanding Ottoman empire, with a new, Muslim class of lords. In any case, various paths led to increasing exploitation of the peasantry. Since there was no real system of legally or economically autonomous cities, which could have grown into centers of trade and exchange, the few urban centers that did exist ended up being dominated by the landowning nobility who were socially as well as economically dominant. These urban centers were restricted in their development, in contrast to the expanding cities in Western and Central Europe. East European cities and their evolving lifestyles and family forms were of lesser importance to their respective societies. In early modern times the countryside dominated urban life. This is why we will concentrate solely on family forms that developed in villages.

THE NOBLEMAN AND THE PEASANT FAMILY

Unlike Western Europe which, since the sixteenth century, gradually moved from a subsistence to a more market-oriented agricultural economy—thus weakening feudal ties—Eastern Europe took a quite different turn. Feudalism became stronger. In this context we often speak of "refeudalization" or of "second serfdom," terms that assume that there was an earlier serfdom or feudal system. This generalization is incorrect: it was during the fifteenth and sixteenth centuries that large numbers of free East European peasants first became subjected to serfdom.

Western Europe witnessed a swift transformation of the feudal economy which led to the early development of capitalist structures. Eastern Europe underwent this process much later. Terms such as "development" and "underdevelopment" should be used cautiously, but measured in terms of economic development the East has clearly lagged behind the West.[3]

When we speak of "serfdom" in this context, we have to understand that this term does not adequately describe the various relations that existed between feudal lord and dependent peasant. We must take a closer look at these differing systems if we are to judge to what extent they conditioned the emergence of different family forms. Was there a direct link between economic systems and family forms? Did developments in Eastern Europe result in an altogether different family structure? Nor must we forget that Eastern Europe in this period was politically dominated by four powers: the Habsburg, the Russian and the Ottoman empires, and the Kingdom of Poland.

The Domain in the Open Plains and Lowlands

The system of the domain economy existed throughout the vast plains and lowlands of the eastern Habsburg empire, including the Hungarian plains, Poland, the Baltic States, and Russia. There are various forms of the domain system; here we use the term "domain" to refer to a large estate in which the feudal lord's personal share was a substantial one. Only a relatively small part of the domain—also due to low density of population—was given to the dependent peasants in exchange for varying labor contributions. Consequently, the feudal lord's income from the domain came primarily from labor services and not from duties. Furthermore, since the sixteenth century feudal lords had become largely independent of the centralized state authority. This made it possible in certain areas for domains to grow into states within a state, which naturally had a destabilizing effect on the political system. Lords were able to wield legal as well as economic power over peasant families.

In comparison to these domains, on the estates of Western Europe the estate owner had a relatively small share of property; the larger share was given to the peasants for their use. They, too, had to contribute labor services; however, this was typically not the estate owner's main source of income. The main income came from the peasants' contributions. These differences had a determining effect on the differing developments in Western and Eastern Europe.

The domain systems of the East did not appear at the same time; nonetheless we can observe similar forms everywhere during the fifteenth and sixteenth centuries. In Hungary, for instance, there were various means by which owners increased their share of cultivated property: former castle fields were cultivated, clearings of the Hungarian plains took place, communal land was taken away from the village communities, communally shared pastures and forests were declared personal property of the lord, and vacant holdings were no longer filled by peasants. To put this into perspective, in this early phase the personal share of the lord never amounted to more than a quarter or a third of the property and was thus always considerably smaller than in neighboring Poland. Nonetheless, labor service increased noticeably in the second half of the sixteenth century (from one day to two or three days per week). Soon labor services were to make up 60 to 70 percent of a domain's income. Towards the end of the eighteenth century around 150 noble families ruled over three-quarters of Hungary's land and peasant population.[4]

In the Great Principality of Lithuania, which was fully integrated into the Polish kingdom in 1569, the nobility had been freed from all duties towards the Grand Prince since 1529; this paved the way for larger and more independent domains. The majority of peasants were considered dependent as early as the beginning of the sixteenth century: they were tied to the land and had to contribute duties paid in crops, as well as labor services.[5]

In the Kingdom of Poland huge domains evolved during our period. Around the mid-fifteenth century domains with more than 500 farmsteads accounted for about 13 percent of all domains; towards the end of the eighteenth century 42 percent of all domains were of that size. On certain domains the income was higher than the whole state income; these domains even had their own armies. This proved to be a serious threat to state power, and in the second half of the eighteenth century led to the collapse of the Polish state. Among the consequences of this development were the disappearance of the lower nobility and, since the sixteenth century, the decline of the largely free peasantry to the status of land-tied, hereditary subjects without rights. Livonia, which was conquered in 1561, was to undergo development along the same lines.[6]

A similar process can be witnessed to the south in neighboring Romanian Walachia. Here, too, during the sixteenth century a class of greater nobility appeared and started to expand their power on behalf of

Map 2.   The Baltic States in the Sixteenth Century.

the state by bringing free villages under their control. Only the villages in the Carpathian mountains avoided the expansion of the domain economy. In Walachia domains of considerable size were formed and formerly free peasant families became hereditary servants of the feudal lord.[7]

Matters were a little different in the swiftly expanding Russian empire. Although the peasant community was significant as it was in Walachia, in Russia the peasant village community usually functioned as an authority mediating between the feudal noblility and the peasants, and they were generally able to defend their freedom up to the seventeenth century. The independent peasantry then stopped expanding and the nobility's share of property rose sharply. Up to the eighteenth century there existed three different laws of land ownership; those pertaining to: (1) the estates of the Czar; (2) state estates, which were given to courtiers as a form of payment for their services (in the eighteenth century they numbered a half million); and (3) inheritable and non-inheritable church-related properties and their secular estates. Since the seventeenth century a new aristocratic class also emerged thanks to the Czar's donations in the newly conquered regions.

Simultaneously the number of serfs, who until then had been free peasants, increased dramatically. By 1678, 90 percent of the total population of peasant families were subject either to the secular nobility, the Church or the state, i.e. the Czar. They were still a heterogeneous group: they had to contribute varying forms of duties and were also subjected to varying legal conditions laid out individually by their respective lords. Then at the beginning of the eighteenth century a uniform tax for all peasant families was introduced and all hereditary and land-tied serfs were given the same legal status.[8] So since the eighteenth century the Russian empire had a domain system analogous to that of its neighboring states.

Timar- and Çiflik-Economy in the Ottoman Empire

From the fourteenth through to the sixteenth century the Islamic Ottoman empire conquered the major part of southeastern Europe. By the end of the seventeenth century the border with the Habsburg empire ran right through Croatia and Hungary.

Up to the sixteenth century the *timar* system characterized most agriculture: this meant that the Ottoman state had sole authority over "holy" Islamic soil and allocated benefits (*timars*) as rewards to members of its cavalry for waging war. These benefits were territories producing a certain amount of income derived from the mostly Christian peasants who lived on them and who had to pay dues. The dues amounted to 10–20 percent of the harvest and several days of labor service per year. In this phase we cannot yet speak of serfdom, since the *timars* were not hereditary and were also tied to military service. The peasant families legally remained free from their lord and the law was enforced by state judges. This freedom was relative, however, since peasants who did not convert to Islam were treated as second-class citizens. In 1630 there were approximately 8,000 such *timar* owners in the European part of the empire.

Towards the end of the sixteenth century there was a profound change in the relations between owners and peasant families. New military technology had made heavily armed cavalry obsolete and increasingly required a well trained, professionally paid infantry. At the same time the *timar* system lost much of its importance following a change in the administration of the empire. The benefits were increasingly turned into hereditary domains and, due to a weakened central power, were often illegally enlarged. The more powerful these owners became, the more likely it was that demands on the peasant families would increase. This, in turn, made it easier for the owners to refuse to pay state taxes and to take on legal authority over their subjects. The peasants' status changed from relative freedom to the servitude of the *beys* and *agas*. Larger numbers of villages and their peasant families came under a new system, which can be termed the *çiflik* economy. A *çiflik* was a large territory, similar to an East European domain, and based on the deteriorating legal status of peasant families. These families were even worse off than their non-Ottoman-empire counterparts since they were mostly Christians in a Muslim state: up to the nineteenth century this put them at a serious disadvantage.[9]

The Colonat System along the Adriatic Coast

The Republic of Venice controlled much of the Adriatic coast (with the exception of Ragusa/Dubrovnik) and parts of the eastern Mediterranean during this period, falling only in 1797 to Napoleon's army. Under Venetian rule a distinctive agricultural system adjoined the Ottoman empire. This system differed from both the empire's as well as the East European domain systems. It was known as the *colonat*, and its roots stretched back to the Roman empire.

In the second half of the sixteenth century we can observe an economic innovation in the Venetian aristocracy. Up to then the aristocracy was traditionally urban in its orientation and although it was common to own lands in the surrounding countryside there was little interest in an agricultural economy, the main concern still being trading. This changed during the second half of the sixteenth century, when land ownership increasingly became the basis of economic power.

The peasant families and their village economies were strongly linked to urban economic activities. Like the urban population, the rural *coloni* enjoyed personal freedom, meaning that the landowner generally had no legal power over peasant families. Serfdom—being tied to the land and oppressive labor services—was unknown to these peasants. Nonetheless there existed economic dependencies in the form and the amount of the contributions due to the property owner. These depended on what kind of agreement had been negotiated. Basically there were two types of contract: a *laborer* cultivated small vineyards or olive orchards and contributed a quarter of the harvest in kind and a fixed monetary sum to the owner. A laborer's contract had no limits. As *peasant* the head of the family received a holding to cultivate. Mandatory labor services on the remaining land of the nobility hardly existed; apparently it played a minor role in the owner's income and in the lives of the peasant families. Originally these contracts, at the request of the owner, were short-term. Later, during the second half of the sixteenth century, the limits were adjusted in favor of the peasant families for the rest of Venetian rule.[10]

Border Societies: Free Peasants and Soldiers

Since the sixteenth century special conditions had developed along the Ottoman borders with Russia, the Habsburgs, and Venice. Starting in the Don region in southern Russia and running all the way to the Adriatic coast, border societies evolved from purposively organized settlements. Despite varying legal and economic conditions these distinct border societies all had one thing in common: their people were, in relative terms, free. They were obliged only to defend the borderlands. In the south Russian steppe these were Don Cossacks, who had to defend the long border against the Ottomans. Along the Habsburg–Ottoman border that ran through the middle of Croatia, it was Serbs who had originally fled Ottoman rule who were the soldiers.

Let us take a closer look at this particular setting. The long wars in the sixteenth century in the border region of these two empires left the country devastated and its population depleted. On the one hand, the domains of the nobility had lost their value and, on the other, an uninhabited border region was impossible to defend for long. This paved the way for thousands of Serbian refugee families to be settled on these completely ravaged domains. They were given certain privileges, received a degree of autonomy and were freed from all taxes. The only obligation was that in case of Ottoman attack the men had to serve in the military.

This set a basic structure for the border societies: personal freedom and ownership of land and soil without feudal ties, in exchange for military service. This socially privileged status of border families was intricately linked to their ownership: military service was tied to land ownership, and vice versa. The interplay of freedom, ownership, and military service made any other form of activity besides cultivating the property impossible. Unlike in Eastern Europe or in the regions ruled by the Ottomans or by the Venetians, where the estate owner played a

Map 3.   The Balkans in the Sixteenth Century.

decisive role, in this border cordon reaching from south Russia to the
Adriatic Sea the army commander had a determining role in the everyday lives of families.

Freedom in the Mountains

In the interaction of land ownership and power over the people inhabit-
ing the land, the basis of European feudalism, there is an ecological component. It was no coincidence that the vast domains extended through
the plowed open plains of Eastern Europe. It was here that the economic
basis was optimal for the owner and here that the exploitation of the
peasant family was the most severe.

The mountain regions of the Balkan peninsula, however, created a different setting. Feudalism and state administrations had very little influence on the almost inaccessible world of the Dinaric and the Pindos mountains on mainland Greece, which extends to the Peloponnese. The same holds true for the mountain ranges in Bulgaria and to a certain extent for the Carpathians. These areas were not sparsely populated—quite the contrary. When the Ottomans conquered the Balkan peninsula, thousands of families escaped to these mountains and adapted to a living based mostly on sheep- and goat-keeping. They arranged their lives as nomads and semi-nomads according to the annual rotation of pastures known as transhumance. The summer was spent in the high regions (at altitudes of about 2,000 meters); in the wintertime they moved to the plains and coastal areas. Thus in the winter they were more likely to come into contact with representatives of Ottoman rule[11] and with the Orthodox merchants who were involved in intensive trade in mountain areas. It is no accident that men from the mountains were so prominent (as contrasted with people from the plains) in the early migrations to North America.

There are many indications that these mountains were more populated from the sixteenth century onward. Far away from feudal lords and state representatives people were able to live in isolation and freedom. It was a freedom that came at a high price: life was tedious and perilous. People had no choice but to develop protection mechanisms through tribal and pastoral organization based on patrilineal principles. Of all the systems described so far, in the mountains family and kinship had the highest importance and had to fulfill many functions. These very distinct economic and ecological conditions were probably mainly responsible for the strong patriarchal structures that were to evolve here. Honor, hospitality, and the feud became central values.[12]

Similar Family Structures despite Varying Political and Economic Systems

Despite the different agricultural and legal systems under which people lived in Eastern Europe in early modern times, the family structures—but not family ideologies and forms—barely differed from one another: they strongly leaned towards a complex structure (this does not mean that a nuclear form did not develop in certain phases of the household cycle) with the tendency for the household group to function as the labor group as well. At the same time in one of these systems, that of the domain, certain family structures stood out: in Romanian regions (in the Principalities of Moldavia and Walachia) the nuclear or stem family system dominated due to the distinct nature of feudal structures.

Should these findings be confirmed, this would mean that the economic relations that evolved from the sixteenth century onwards were not the main influence on existing family patterns. Furthermore it would mean that feudal lords may not have intervened in family structures at all, or only to a minor extent. Otherwise how could we explain the fact that the free people in the mountain regions had similar or the same family structures as the peasants living in the Russian lowlands under feudal rule? We need to find out whether feudal lords intervened in the composition of households and if so, to what extent they were able to structure households to conform to their economic interests.

In the case of the people living in the mountains on the Balkan peninsula the answer is clear, but for the societies along the Ottoman border in southeastern Europe and in Russia we cannot give a general answer. To my knowledge there is no specific research on the family structures of the Don Cossacks, for example, whereas we know a fair amount about the people in Croatia on the Ottoman–Habsburg border. In this region there is clear evidence that the local officials intervened in the composition of households up to a certain point. The border population had various origins and there was great ethnic diversity. Research shows that the Serbians, who made up a major portion of the total populace, were more prone to complex households and larger families than were other ethnic groups, especially the Croatians who also formed a large part of the population. Up to the mid-eighteenth century the military organization in this area had as its sole purpose defense against attacks from the Ottomans. This generally did not require the men to be absent from their families for too long a period. Military needs thus did not require the authorities to intervene in household formation. Around the middle of the eighteenth century a reorientation of the organization along the border took place. This enabled the integration of these local troops into the regular army of the Habsburg empire and led to longer absences from their families. To make this new system as efficient as possible military authorities decided to enforce the Serbian household model on all households. Obviously it was easier to recruit one or two men out of a larger household than from a small one with a single eligible male member. In 1754 a law proscribed household division. The consequence was that the number of large and complex families rose sharply in the second half of the eighteenth century.[13]

Such measures were easy to put into practice in military areas. Was it as easy for Ottoman and other East European feudal lords to control household division? In the Ottoman area the existence of differing family forms was mostly linked to different religious beliefs. For instance, because of the prevalent Islamic law Muslim families could structure themselves quite differently than Christian families. Islamic law permitted polygyny, the marriage of parallel cousins, and the marriage of two brothers to two sisters. The *spahis* (a kind of feudal lord) were not interested in changing the traditional household organization of the peasants in the period of early Ottoman agricultural development, since they (discussed above in connection with the *timar* system) were simply beneficiaries of certain taxes and not true landlords. They had no legal rights over their peasant families. The big question is whether the transition from this early *spahi* system to the *çiftlik* system that was much closer to a feudal system had any influence on family forms. It is impossible to give a definite answer, since this question has not yet been systematically investigated. Hints from a later period lead us to believe that Ottoman lords intervened little in traditional family patterns.

In this context we can see differences between eastern and western regions within the East European domain system. In eighteenth-century Poland we know of strong interventions in family structures by feudal lords in western but not in eastern sections (see p. 40 below). For example, sons who after marriage wanted to stay on the parental holding were forced to leave and take on a holding of their own. Attempts by peasant families to distribute their land evenly among all sons were prevented. Widows and widowers were forced to remarry promptly. Unmarried sons, on succeeding to their father's inheritance, had to marry within a year. These are all examples of the Polish lords' interventionist methods; their aim was to have as many efficient and profitable households of peasant serfs as possible.[14] In the Baltic States in the sixteenth and seventeenth centuries we likewise see the strong influence of feudal lords on the formation of households. Studies on Kurland prove this point. Feudal lords intervened if they feared that a less capable son would inherit the holding. They also pressed for prompt remarriage and insisted on the principle of indivisibility of an inheritance, going against the habits of the peasant population. Their consent was required for any partitioning of land.[15] It is worth mentioning that the feudal lords kept copious records of their serfs, in direct contrast with the Ottomans who were interested only in the head taxes on their non-Muslim population. This also results in a direct contrast in methods of imperial administration with important ideological implications, i.e., greater local autonomy under the Ottomans.

In areas where strong village communities acted as an intermediary between feudal lord and peasant family and thus averted direct intervention in household formation by the lord, the feudal lord's influence was weakest. Individual peasant families were not forced to make contributions but the village as a whole was allocated a fixed amount to be delivered. How this amount was shared among the holdings was a village matter; thus the village community also functioned as an agricultural unit, i.e. the village decided on its own how the land was to be distributed. The individual's share was determined by the number of people who were fit to work. We can deduce that in this system the village community could be flexible in reacting to ever-changing household sizes. Village communities intervened in family formation to the extent that early marriages were encouraged and young women persuaded not to marry into other communities in order to prevent a reduction of property lost through dowries. This was particularly the case in the Romanian principalities and in Russia, where the feudal lord was not primarily interested in administering village properties but thought in the larger terms of his own domain. We have no detailed account of the historical roots of these village communities; however, we can assume that they stem from tribal confederations which were territorialized some time before the thirteenth century. Although the village communities in Russian and Romanian regions apparently developed independently of each other, they have similar organizational structures.[16]

In conclusion, we cannot observe any immediate connection between the varying agricultural systems that existed in Eastern Europe and the kinds of household structure. Only the military borderlands in Croatia could serve to argue the contrary. In this region larger households functioned as military and economic units. This was not due to the agricultural organization as such but because land ownership was strictly tied to military service. Larger households were created by the administrative measures of a military bureaucracy. This general statement is underlined by the fact that feudal lords had less impact on household structures than customary laws the further east we go. Overall we can assert that the owner's intervention in household composition is largely a West European phenomenon, a fact we may want to keep in mind in the following section where we deal with household formation systems in Eastern Europe.

HOUSEHOLD FORMATION SYSTEMS IN EASTERN EUROPE: VARIANTS WITHIN THE SYSTEM

Western and Eastern Europe are characterized by two differing sets of marriage patterns and varying systems of household formation. The West European marriage pattern before World War II, unique world-wide in its characteristics, has people marrying late and a high percentage of men and women never marrying. The East European marriage model is much less distinctive in comparison to the rest of the world. People marry at a relatively young age and practically everyone marries.[17] The importance of the transition zone between Western and Eastern Europe has not been refuted to date and arguments in the next section will support it. In historic Europe we have two distinct marriage patterns, but can we therefore conclude that they corresponded to two different family systems?

We can also distinguish two differing household systems in pre-industrial Europe: the simple one covers the area of the European marriage model, which encompasses northwestern Europe (Scandinavia, the British Isles, the Netherlands, and the German-speaking areas as well as northern France). The other, which is termed the region of the "joint household system," covers the rest of Europe, as well as India and China. Scholars define three rules of formation for the simple household system: (1) late marriage (men on average at age 26, women at age 23); (2) the married couple is in charge of the household, the man being the head of the family; and (3) young people circulate among various households as servants. The three rules for the joint household system are: (1) early marriage (men on average below age 26, women below 21); (2) the newlyweds do not start their own household but live together with an older couple; (3) households with several couples can break up into two or more households.[18] The existence of male and female servants and their delayed marriage are truly exceptional features of the northwestern European household. Although male and female servants existed in other household systems, they generally played (with the exception of large parts of northern and central Italy) a negligible role, accounting for less than 2 percent of the populace and generally not living in the house of their employer. Women married very early and in any case in these eastern systems people not related to the head of the household rarely lived in the household (they made up less than 2 percent).[19]

Thus in pre-industrial Europe we have a dividing line according to marriage behavior: in regard to household formation rules the simple household system can be linked to the West European household pattern, while the complex system tends more towards the Eastern European pattern. We have to emphasize that these patterns show only general tendencies, leaving much room for exceptions. Western Europe offers an unusual pattern that demands explanation: the prevalence of nuclear families; the late marriage of men and women, leading to relatively long spans between generations; the relatively minor age difference between the partners (which increases the tendency to partnership); and the fact that servants not related to the couple also belong to the family (so-called "life-cycle servants," whose time of service is a transitional period in their lives). Extended or multiple family forms barely exist in much of this area. The fact that complex family forms did exist within the area of the East European marriage pattern is not surprising, because it is clearly a common or even universal pattern, which took on different cultural forms.[20] We can learn much about East Europe when investigating the reasons for the West European exception.

Reasons for the West European Exception

In this context there has been much talk about a connection between family organization and the process of industrialization. However, this has not been convincing. We have to assume that the Western European exception goes back to the early Middle Ages.

Due to the so-called Eastern Colonization new borders were drawn: the border that developed during the Middle Ages approximately matches the division in marriage and household formation patterns. A migratory development from West and Central to Eastern Europe started in the eleventh century and caused an increase in the amount of cultivated land. This development pushed colonization further east and paved the way for important agricultural innovations such as the three-field rotation system. The *Hufenverfassung* (the legal provision of fixed plots of land per holder) with its impartible inheritance and the introduction of the wheel plough were important legal and technological innovations. Organized village structures (*Angerdörfer, Straßendörfer, Waldhufendörfer*—villages arranged around the village green, along the street, or along woods) as well as the *Gewannflur* (a large field which due to its size needed to be cultivated by several peasants) were further features of this development. The eastern border of this migratory development reached far into the Baltic and included east Prussia, Pomerania, Brandenburg, Silesia, Bohemia-Moravia, upper Hungary, parts of west Hungary, lower Austria, Styria, and Slovenia. The above village structure was less prevalent along the borders. The significance lies in the fact that this relatively homogeneous structure from Central and Western Europe was transferred to the colonized area. Beyond the border the traditional structures continued to exist.[21]

The key to the forming of the nuclear family system and the European marriage pattern lies in the so-called *Hufenverfassung*. The *Hufe* was a fixed plot of land which was given to the peasant for cultivation. The plot varied in size according to regional circumstances. The size was sufficient for the peasant's family to provide for itself and also pay a certain amount in contributions to the estate owner. The *Hufe*, which was originally impartible, was the basis for various contributions and services given to the owner. The nuclear family group must have been the family form of choice from very early on, given the size and stability through inheritance of the various plots. Thus the regulation of inheritance favored nuclear family forms and the owner was not interested in having a large family inhabit a plot.[22]

It was in the interest of the owner that the plot be cultivated continuously, and within the medieval feudal law it was possible to pass on a *Hufe* to a person not related to the former inhabitant. This meant that household formation at this time must also have involved neolocality, and patrilocality was not the only alternative. In most West European regions it was common for a widow to remarry, so the *Hufe* would be passed on to the second husband and the lost labor was thereby replaced—a solution very much in the interest of the owner.[23] An extended household system would have provided less flexibility with its emphasis on the kin group rather than on the holding.

In this system it must have been difficult for a couple to pass on their plot during their lifetime. To alleviate this problem a system evolved that to this day is known as the *Ausgedinge* (the senior part or quarter). Its uniqueness lies in the fact that it does not follow the principle of seniority which pervaded those areas that held on to indivisibility of the plot, particularly in eastern Central Europe. Wherever, due to a lesser influence of the feudal lord, divisibility was prevalent, this principle was not in use. Passing on the plot relied on the principle of unigeniture, which means that an undivided property was passed on from one generation to the next. Marriage was then not possible until the *Hufe* or the plot had been taken over, which largely explains the late marriages in this region.[24]

Another consequence of the *Hufenverfassung* was the servant system: for the siblings of the inheriting son a temporary phase of service was unavoidable until they were able to afford to marry and found their own household. The servant moving from one plot to the next thus became the prototype of an unrelated household member and because they were not allowed to marry with this status, servants also contributed to the relatively high age at marriage.[25]

Partible Inheritance

The border area of the Eastern Colonization also marks the border between the various systems of inheritance. In the region where the *Hufenverfassung* dominated, impartible inheritance (*Anerbenrecht*) became prevalent—befitting the logic of individual property—and replaced the historically older collective concept of partible inheritance. There are regions to the west of the transitional zone between Western and Eastern Europe that practiced partible inheritance well into the twentieth century; however, they are not relics dating back to the historic

Gesamthanderbe (community inheritance) but developed much later from a unitary or impartible inheritance system. Furthermore the principle of partible inheritance in the western regions was a privilege reserved for independent peasant families. Dependent peasants did not have this option. To the east of the line the earlier systems of inheritance, supported by concepts of the collective, endured. In this system property could remain undivided over generations or it could be distributed equally among all lawful heirs. These were patterns that also existed in the West before the introduction of the system of impartible inheritance. Originally in Roman law property was considered to be tied as a whole to the family or to blood relations and was not subject to the will of the person leaving the inheritance. It was the whole household community which inherited and only people without family could appoint heirs at will. This meant that legally several heirs were joined to one inheritance group. All inherited the property as a group and all were considered the successors with the inheritable property. The individual heir did not have free disposal of his "share" in accordance with the principles of the partible inheritance; however, he could demand that the property be divided. This right of dividing mostly existed in theory because its execution had serious economic drawbacks and was therefore avoided by peasants. In Franconian times (sixth to ninth centuries AD) this changed and it became more common for one to have the right to decide what was to happen to one's property.[26]

The principle of equal inheritance for male heirs was not difficult to carry out at a time when mortality rates were high. We can assume that in earlier times it was possible to live on an undivided property for several generations without ever running into the problem of an overcrowded household.

A brief look at the customs of inheritance around the transitional zone between Western and Eastern Europe can document this theory. Let us first turn to Slovenia, to the west of this border area. Here the original partible inheritance system was apparently overlaid by intensive Germanic colonization activities since the ninth century. In the process the country was divided into *kmetija* or *zemlja* (holdings) and the nuclear family system as well as primo- or ultimo-geniture was promoted.[27]

In the Hungarian part of the Habsburg empire it appears that there were different systems of inheritance. The equal right to inheritance by male heirs and the right to mobile belongings for daughters seem to have dominated. Among the German population the tradition of impartible inheritance predominated. In the plains there existed divisibility, which also applied to daughters who married a man from the same village.[28]

In Bohemia (west of the transitional zone) the Middle European custom of the holding's indivisibility ruled. The widow had to become head of the household after the death of her husband; if she refused the holding was passed on to the next in the inheritance line.[29]

In west Polish areas there was strict indivisibility. Generally the youngest son was the heir and even if there were other married brothers on the holding there was still only one legal heir. Sharing the property among the sons was possible only with the permission of the feudal lord. Repeatedly Polish peasants tried to side-step this regulation and resorted to secret divisions, which would be annulled by the feudal lords. In Lithuania, likewise, it seems that the principle of impartible inheritance was practiced as early as in the thirteenth and fourteenth centuries. Here even before the link-up with the Kingdom of Poland in 1569 a major agricultural reform around the middle of the sixteenth century divided the entire cultivated land into *voloks* (holdings). Depending on the quality of the land a *volok* was some 21 to 23 hectares and tied to a fixed amount of contributions and taxes. The formerly irregular settlement and land distribution structures were replaced by systematic ones.[30]

In Bulgarian areas in accordance with the oldest Slavic written law from the second half of the ninth century there also existed the equal right of inheritance among males. The Ottoman conquest had no real impact on this regulation and although Ottoman law generally favored impartible inheritance and primogeniture, the common-law practices of the area prevailed. Their administration did not interfere with the civil and criminal matters of "heathen" villagers and most regulation was left to village elders. This practice can be generalized to all regions in the Balkans under Ottoman rule. This was the case in Romanian principalities where the partible and equal system of inheritance persisted.[31]

In Russia this too was the case. Here, however, the village community (*mir*) intervened with measures to even out potential extremes in the distribution of land, in accordance with local common law. Every son on coming of age had the right to found a holding the size of his share in the common and partible property. Generally, however, house and land remained in the undivided ownership of all male household members.[32]

As described above, the *Anerbenrecht* (impartible inheritance) allowed only one of the sons or daughters to inherit the holding, whereas the systems that existed outside the *Hufenverfassung* provided for collective inheritance with the option to divide the property, usually among the sons of a family, after the death of the father. Demographic changes and the availability of land were thus determining factors in the lives of peasant families. As long as there was low population growth, division by inheritance could be kept under control. As soon as the population increased, however, problems arose. Either a division was performed after each generation—with the consequence that the economic base would shrink and disappear altogether due to the small size of the holdings—or this detrimental effect was avoided by keeping all sons and their families under one roof, resulting in large, complex household systems.

In many regions it appears that the estate owners intervened and enforced an undivided household. They did this not because they wanted larger households but rather because they wanted to avoid the shrinkage of their subjects' economic base with a resultant lack of tithes (feudal duties). So in areas where there was a concept of collective inheritance we can expect to find complex household and family structures following a persistent rise in population. Monocausal explanations cannot separate the concept of impartible inheritance from the law of fixed plots per holder. We cannot cite a collective inheritance system as the sole reason for multiple household forms. It has to be seen as part of a larger and more common system of values and norms, which has historical origins.[33] For the same reason it would be wrong to cite a certain marriage pattern as the universal explanation for a particular system of household formation. Nonetheless the differing systems of inheritance play an important role in household formation—an observation that has received surprisingly little attention in historical anthropological family research.

However, we cannot expect uniform household formation patterns either in Western and Eastern Europe. Research in France and Italy, for example, has revealed regional phenomena of complex family constellations. Similarly in central and north Italy (Umbria, Tuscany, Emilia Romagna) we have well documented research on complex household and family systems since the fifteenth century, which is closely linked to the sharecropping system.[34]

Household Formation Systems in Southeastern Europe

At this point we know only the general rules of East European household formation systems. Detailed research will bring out regional variations. There is as yet too little research material on the area of the East European plains and lowlands to determine regional trends; for southeast Europe research is more encouraging. Here we can attempt to draw a map of the systems of household formation. With the exception of the Greek islands in the Aegean Sea, whose household forms cannot be seen as a variation of the general East European family formation system, we can speak of three basic types of system: the neolocal system based on nuclear families; the patrilocal system, based on life-cycle complexity; and the patrilocal system based on household-cycle complexity. Once again our sources are mostly from the nineteenth and twentieth centuries and we are forced to project our observations back into earlier times.

The *neolocal nuclear formation system* was dominant in Romanian-colonized areas (which reached into eastern Serbia), but we must not think that this was a national characteristic. The system worked like a stem family, though with partible inheritance: when sons were of marital age they were given equal parts of the property. They would then leave the parental home and set up their own holding before marriage. The youngest (rarely the eldest) son would remain with his parents. This neolocal form prevailed although sometimes an uxorilocal solution was chosen and sons-in-law were brought in to compensate for the lack of sons. Thus the Romanian household went through different phases: first a couple without children, then with unmarried children, then two couples of different generations. With the death of the older couple and the birth of children the household cycle starts again.[35]

Generally there was a sincere effort to allocate the family's land equally among all sons. Each household was to have the same access to all land categories. There was strong pressure to divide the property while the father was still alive. This system of transfer of property was embedded in a rural communal system: village territory would be divided among the households and each family branch in the village had a right to equal shares of the various land categories. The early transfer of property and neolocality were obviously dependent on this communal system, because it was the village community and not the individual owner that took charge of distributing the land.[36]

The *patrilocal life-cycle formation system* was very common in southeastern Europe. It seems to have been the prevalent system in Hungary proper, Bulgaria and continental Greece. The paradigm was the following: after marriage sons would remain in the parental home with their wives. The division and transfer of property in equal parts would either take place after the last son was married or after the father had died. In cross-sectional household statistics we therefore observe a dominance of nuclear families, along with a smaller share of complex households. Ideally individuals experienced household complexity at two points in their lives: in the marrying phase until the division of the household took place and in older age when the sons married and remained at home with their wives for some time.[37]

Studies show that this system was mainly practiced in regions with a low population density and an excess of land; in regions where conditions were reversed there was a tendency toward household-cycle complexity. The many German settlers in this region in the eighteenth century, who brought with them the system of impartible inheritance, formed exceptions to this system of household formation. The shepherd societies in Bulgaria and northern Greece as well as the Hungarian group of shepherds called "Palocians" also formed an exception to this model—they leaned more toward a third variation of household formation, the patrilocal household-cycle system.[38]

The *patrilocal household-cycle formation system* was also widespread in southeastern Europe; it appeared in several areas of Hungary proper, in Croatia and Slovakia, in most Serbian regions, in western Bulgaria, Macedonia, Bosnia-Hercegovina, Albania, northern Greece as well as in smaller areas such as the southern Greek Mani region. In the typical case a couple had children, the daughters would marry and leave, while the sons remained at the parental home even after they married and the same held true for grandsons. The transfer of property generally did not take place until a household separated into new units. At this point the property would be shared evenly by all in the lineage. Division of households and the transfer of property could become part of both an individual's life cycle and most certainly of a household cycle that could affect several generations simultaneously.

This system developed under different ecological and economic conditions. On the northern fringes of the Hungarian plain it was probably the scarcity of land that led to such generation-spanning solutions. In the Dinaric mountain regions there was probably a connection with the pastoral economy which emphasized inheritance of animals and rights to pastures; cross-cultural comparisons have shown that this form of economy tends towards this kind of solution. Furthermore here the household formation system was accompanied by marked patriarchal elements such as strong agnatic ties, ancestor worship, marriages by purchase, patrilineality, patrilineal kinship structures, and blood revenge.[39]

By way of summarizing, we can say that in Eastern Europe there was a strong tendency to form complex household structures, with few regional exceptions. This tendency is apparently strongly linked to agnatic male communal property and related processes of inheritance. These complex structures were not rigid but showed variations in strategies.

THE LARGE AND COMPLEX FAMILY AS AN IDEAL?

The formation of large and complex families is both a demographic and a cultural phenomenon. It is cultural in that people in historic times considered this family form desirable. Demographic circumstances in this period entailed both high birth and high mortality rates with a low life expectancy (on average 40 years). It is worth questioning whether under these conditions the formation of large and complex families was at all possible. Census records from the sixteenth and seventeenth centuries offer little information on this subject; however, census records from the eighteenth century show that complex family formation was feasible and indeed quite common.

The other question that can be posed is one of cultural desirability. At no point in time and in no region on this earth can we speak of a "natural" constellation of family; rather, we have to regard family forms in their overall social and economic context. In general, family relations in pre-modern societies played a more significant role than they do today and the family included relatives beyond the household. Even today in Greece the term "family" denotes a much larger circle of relatives than simply the conjugal couple and their children: one does not necessarily have to live in the same household in order to be considered family. Neither was the West European nuclear family ever prevented from having forms of relations such as the neighborhood, the village community, or the parish, which took the place of the kin relations found in large and complex families.

With a few exceptions, the nobleman did not exert a strong influence on the household formation system in Eastern Europe. Lords did not generally enforce a system that differed from the commonly practiced form. The system of partible inheritance requiring the males of a household to have collective ownership offers many possibilities for the transfer of property. This is what made large and complex families possible, because the transfer of property could occur when the eldest son got married and created a nuclear family. But household fission and property transfer might not occur within an individual's life span. Feudal lords certainly tended to influence this system to some extent, but people reacted to these pressures with their own social and economic strategies for survival. They were not easily persuaded to give them up, as can be seen in parts of Poland and the Baltic, where attempts by the feudal lords to enforce the principle of unigeniture were successfully opposed.

Questions pertaining to the structure and size of a household are often answered with the help of statistics and quantitative means. The following brief overview of the spread of complex household forms in Eastern Europe shows that such forms were apparently possible, even if we have little evidence, particularly for the early modern period. Thus, we do not have enough statistical material from the areas under Ottoman rule to allow reliable reconstruction of households. Ottoman administration, well organized as it was, modeled its census according to the needs of financial affairs and not according to the needs of family historians of the twenty-first century.

One of the first census records in Eastern Europe after 1500 that allows a reconstruction of the household formation of a particular region dates to 1712 and comprises just over 2,000 households and approximately 25,000 inhabitants. It comes from the regions of Lika and Krbava on the western outskirts of the Habsburg military border in Croatia. The census was carried out four decades before the family partition laws of 1754 were passed. It is remarkable that over 50 percent of the households were structured in a complex manner and that there was a sizeable number of households with around 20 members. The largest household consisted of 54 persons.[40] This shows that even in the early eighteenth century (possibly this also holds true for the previous two centuries) unfavorable demographic circumstances did not prevent the population in this region from living in complex households.

Hungarian demographers estimate that around 12 to 15 percent of households in the Hungarian part of the empire in the eighteenth and nineteenth centuries were structured in a complex manner, not including families which lived apart from each other but formed a joint household nonetheless. In general, it can be said that this form starts to appear in the seventeenth century in the Hungarian regions that were not under Ottoman rule. During the course of the eighteenth century, this form seems to have become even more prevalent. Towards the end of the eighteenth century, the number of complex households rose noticeably—at least in certain regions. Due to a sharp increase in population, sons would remain within the parental household in order to avoid splitting their property into small parts. Census records from the years between 1784 and 1787 indicate that Croatia-Slavonia and the northern (primarily Slovak) regions were the main areas where this phenomenon could be witnessed. In the northern regions complex households made up 40 to 50 percent; in Baranya which borders Croatia-Slavonia they accounted for around 20 percent of households. Population density in these areas was relatively high or, rather, land was scarce, which may be a further reason for the formation of complex family forms. The frequency of complex households differed by social category: among dependent peasants, families were larger and also more complex, unlike those of landless cottagers, where a contrasting trend can be observed. In the second half of the eighteenth century, there was clear predominance of two-generation households (between 60 and 80 percent). In the six communities under examination, three-generation households accounted almost everywhere for less than 30 percent; four-generation households were rare.[41]

Seen overall, Hungary is part of the transitional zone. Furthermore, we have to take into account the significant migratory processes that took place in the eighteenth century, which brought to the region mostly German settlers, who came from a completely different background, namely that of the Central European family tradition. The Baltic regions for which we have quantitative data on household formation from the second half of the eighteenth century lie in a cultural transition zone, which also marks the eastern margin of the *Ostkolonisation* (eastward colonization movement) in the Middle Ages. The interesting aspect here is that different traditions overlapped and thus lost their typical characteristics.

One of these characteristics is that the complex household is also the labor group (east of the transitional zone). Another characteristic is that male and female servants were not allowed to marry as long as they were in service (west of the transitional zone). In Estonia in the seventeenth and eighteenth centuries we find that quite a few households were structured in a complex manner but that married servants were also employed. Another interesting phenomenon is that in the south of the country (starting in the first half of the sixteenth century), we encounter *Hälftner* (equal halves or partners), which can be regarded as a counterpart to the Hungarian households where families lived separately. This means that more than one household shares the same holding and they pay their dues as a group. Nonetheless, it seems that they did not form a common household. In most but not all cases, they lived in separate houses. Only a few were relatives (father, son, or brothers). In Vändra, a village in southern Estonia, 30 of the total 132 households were part of such holdings. In the census year of 1782, in Vändra 65 percent of families were structured in a nuclear family form and 24 percent were structured in a complex form. In the northern village of Karuse, the ratio was 48 to 39 percent—showing that the share of complex families could be substantial.[42]

Let us take a look at Kurland, which is separated from Estonia by Livland. As in Estonia, strict serfdom prevailed since the fifteenth century. Towards the end of the eighteenth century (1797) there were almost no independent peasants left—merely 1 percent of the peasant population in the domain Dandzewas in the parish of Nerft. Here, too, we can observe the same phenomenon as in Estonia: married servants as well as *Hälftner*. On average, households consisted of 14 members—a considerable size—the smallest household having 7 members and the largest 23 members. The household formation processes are remarkable and a further indication of the fact that Kurland lay in a transitional zone between two systems. The households consisted of peasants, who ran the holding, their nuclear families, and related or unrelated persons. Individual owners and unrelated persons (lodgers, male and female servants) in one household represent the West European system, whereas the integration of kin-related persons aside from the owner's nuclear family is a characteristic of the East European system. In the domain of Kalizsa in the year of 1797, on average 12 percent of the household members were nephews and 6 percent were nieces of the household head. A few households consisted of kin-related people only; most included a considerable number of unrelated household members.[43]

Only peasant families with land formed complex structures, which implies that there were economic reasons for the existing complexity. In the domain of Dandzewas in the year 1797, 64 percent of these peasant families had a complex structure and only 24 percent were nuclear. This complexity was associated with a certain phase in a life cycle. The married brothers of the inheriting son remained on the holding even after their parents' death and founded their own holding only at a later point in time or waited until they were given a holding by the feudal lord. This phenomenon is reflected in the fact that in the census of 1797 in the Kurland village of Spharen (in the district of Tuckum) on average 37 percent of household members consisted of the brothers (and their families) of the head of the household.[44]

The neighboring Great Principality of Lithuania was not touched by the Germanic *Ostkolonisation* of the Middle Ages. Nonetheless, the *Hufenverfassung* was introduced by the middle of the sixteenth century. There is little reason to doubt that the nuclear family had been the family form of choice since the thirteenth to fourteenth centuries. We extract this information from the most important legal sources of the time, the so called "Christburg-Contract" (1249) and the "Prussian Book of Law" (1340), where there is mention of a law of inheritance that can only have been applied in a nuclear family context. However, it seems that the prototype of the undivided holding, which was worked on by only a single family, had not yet arisen. Particularly in the Belorussian regions of the principality it is probable that complex family forms were widespread; here too, *Hälftner* (as in Estonia and Latvia) substituted for family-related labor. They did not live within the household but built their own houses and thus lived with or without family in close proximity to the existing holding. They gave half of the harvest to the peasant and were exempt from any other dues. In some cases such partners were integrated into the existing peasant household. In 1557, with a major agricultural reform, the process of *Hufenverfassung* was introduced. This marks an important turning point in family history. Only the eastern border regions of the Principality remained untouched by the new system and here the share of complex families continued to be significant.[45]

In all other Lithuanian regions since the sixteenth century the nuclear family clearly prevailed. It is proof of the interventionist methods of Lithuania's feudal lords that at times they forced families to keep their property undivided in order not to lessen its economic potential. Initially, Ukrainian and Belorussian peasants in particular attempted to side-step the *Hufenverfassung* by dividing their property or by joining together to form complex households according to the traditional pattern. To prevent this, a year after the introduction of the *Hufenverfassung*, the law was amended: it was intended that "where peasants had divided among themselves and [too] many of them lived in a village on too small a plot, they were to be given waste land and only one or two brothers or the father with only one son were to remain on the original holding."[46] This was a clear incentive to separate and divide and thereby the Western type of the nuclear family household on an undivided and complete holding was legally established. Thus a fundamental shift in inheritance patterns occurred, from the principle of partible inheritance to that of impartible inheritance.

Our knowledge of family structures in Russia in early modern times is incomplete. We have to rely on censuses in the form of "soul counting" conducted in two Russian regions: Mishino (175 kilometers southeast of Moscow) and Jaroslavl' (250 kilometers northwest of Moscow). Generalizations thus have to be viewed with the utmost skepticism. With only a few census recordings to rely on, we can learn that household members were listed according to their status as a relative and not their status in the holding (e.g. as male or female servant). Only related persons lived within a household and the labor group was also the household group. A study on Mishino makes a further generalizing assumption when it speaks of the *dvor* (holding) as a complex household. It contends that this patriarchal form of organization was the prevailing household type of ordinary peasants in pre-revolutionary Russia. Duties existed in the form of taxes and in other forms, and were paid to the lord as well as to the state. If in the west of Europe it was common for the family to align its structure with the existing conditions, it was quite the opposite here: the above-mentioned structure of the village community made it possible via periodic redistribution of village land for change in family size to be accommodated rather than the other way around. Moreover, the basis of taxation was not the household but the conjugal couple. This meant that the greater the number of conjugal couples within a household the more land this household received from the village community and the more duties it had to pay.[47] If this system was actually practiced in most areas in Russia then indeed it supported the formation of large family households. However, we should compare this to the Romanian example which shows a completely different development: here the village community did not result in a complex family system but led to a nuclear family system!

The reason for diametrically opposing results can probably never be given conclusively, for the state and the feudal lord taxed couples regardless of whether they were alone or part of a complex household. The same was true for the village community which was responsible for turning in the duties. It may have been due to the peasant family's cultural conventions or to economic considerations: more workers permitted a larger division of labor and production. This must have been true for the Romanian peasants also. Why otherwise should they want to diminish their performance potential?

When taking a closer look at these two Russian regions we are reminded that we have to be cautious about making generalizations. In the region of Mishino, which in 1782 was inhabited by 1,162 people, we have two types of worker: *krest'jane* (dependent peasants) and *dvorovye ljudi* (servants of the feudal lord, who were paid directly by him); the first group constituted 90 percent of the population. In Jaroslavl', on the other hand, we have a much more differentiated social structure, with servants as well as dependent peasants, but with a distinctive feature: villages under the guiding hand of the feudal lord specialized in certain services and products. Additionally there was a third large group of inhabitants: laborers in the three factories of that region.[48]

The consequence of this was variation in household structure, which is indicated by the very size of a household. In Mishino in 1782, a household consisted on average of 10 members, whereas in Jaroslavl' in 1762–1763 there were 5 persons to a household. Obviously in the second case, we cannot expect a high percentage of complex families. In Jaroslavl' 31 percent of peasants and servants (21 percent of factory servants) lived in complex families, whereas in Mishino 69 percent did.

In conclusion, despite many regional variations, household structures in Russia were characterized by holdings that were controlled by households whose members were related; furthermore the village community was also in control of the land. Property was divided among male household members at the appropriate time for division. Women could not acquire property. The similarities in the functioning of patriarchal family patterns and patrilineal kinship groups suggest that both originate from a mutual source, namely a tribal structure which dates far back into history.[49]

A Few Comparisons

In order to make apparent the differences between the complex household structure in Eastern Europe and the structure that existed in the border area or transitional zone (which was permeated with "Western" elements), it is useful to compare examples of the composition of households in Russia (Mishino in 1814)[50] and in Kurland (Dandzewas in 1797).[51]

In the example in Kurland, household composition reveals obvious West European features. The most striking difference is that in Mishino only persons related to the head of the household are actually household members whereas in Dandzewas the share of non-related persons is considerable, with servants, lodgers, and foster children making up the most important categories. Before dealing with the specific aspects of servants, let us take a look at lodgers and foster children. Lodgers (a kind of tenant on the peasant holding) are a typically West European phenomenon. Foster children (i.e., children who were taken in for a certain length of time) are practically unthinkable in an East European household. At times unrelated children would be taken in permanently; however, these were then adopted and thus became relatives.[52]

Sons-in-law, who were not blood-related, can be regarded as the only non-patrilaterally related household members in Eastern Europe, this occurring only in the case of a family without a son. In the census of Mishino, there is not a single son-in-law and in Dandzewas only a few existed (which would point to an East European influence). Sons-in-law had low social status; they generally came from a poor background and often had to take on their wife's family name and thereby undergo a certain kind of adoption. In Russian, the word for son-in-law is *primak*, meaning the adopted. Through the act of adoption, he received all the rights of a family member concerning property and inheritance. Whether this held true for persons who were not related to the family in a matrilineal fashion is not possible to ascertain. Generally speaking, acceptance into a household by means of adoption occurred when a lasting addition to the family labor force became necessary.[53]

Two further important elements of the East European household system are patrilineality and the principle of seniority. Earlier we discussed the principle of patrilineal inheritance, which excluded wives and daughters. This principle was practiced quite rigidly in Mishino, whereas in Kurland it was less prevalent. Consequently daughters had to marry and leave while the sons remained in the paternal home, a fact which is underlined by the findings in the Mishino census where 16 percent of all those in households were related to the household head as sons and only

10 percent as daughters of all ages. For the same reason there is not a "sister of the head of the household" category in Mishino, whereas in Dandzewas this category accounts for 9 percent. The category "brother of head" (4 percent in Mishino, 17 percent in Dandzewas) hints at lateral household expansion, meaning that several married brothers with their families remained in the household. This is a feature which is particularly evident in Kurland. On the other hand, in Mishino brothers were equal co-holders and thus got equal shares of the inheritable property, a custom which did not exist in Kurland, where the feudal lords permitted only one of the sons to inherit the paternal property; the other brothers were only servants. One of the married and cohabiting sons took a favored position over the others. The other brothers had a choice of remaining on the holding, of leaving and serving on another holding (which explains the unusual phenomenon of married male and female servants), or of taking over another holding, which did not happen very often.[54] Thus, in Kurland the phase of cohabiting brothers could be a limited one, whereas in Mishino it was generally permanent. The odd difference of percentages in the category "brother of head" between Dandzewas and Mishino derives from the fact that in Mishino the brothers were equal co-holders who separated into nuclear families from time to time; this was not the case in Dandzewas, where the division of the household was not permitted.

One may conclude that in Russia the patriarchal principle was more pervasive, as was that of seniority. In Mishino, the principle of seniority was firmly established and senior quarters did not exist. In East European households, the question of caring for the elderly never arose, because they were in charge and kept their status until they died. This principle of seniority created a strict sense of authority, which is quite logical because it is almost impossible to imagine how a household with more than 20 to 30 members could otherwise stay organized and functioning. In the Central European nuclear or stem family systems, the head of the household generally belonged to the second generation. There the change of authority from one member to the other was implemented by the feudal lord, whose interest was in having as head of a holding a man who was in his prime. In Russia seniority might well have been a tradition established before serfdom fully existed.[55] In our comparison, the complete respect for the principle of seniority becomes apparent for Mishino, where there is no category for "father" or "mother" in relation to the head of household, which means that the head of the household was always the oldest man on the holding. In Kurland this principle was much less dominant; after all, 5 percent of household members were fathers and 10 percent mothers. As in parts of Central and Western

Europe, the transmission of property from father to son took place before the elder's death.

What cannot be deduced from our census records are the differences in remarriage. In Central Europe a peasant had to be married. If his wife died, a man had to remarry promptly; if he was too old, he passed on the holding to his successor. Matters were similar for the widow, so the household was usually headed by a couple. In the East European form of the complex household the need to remarry was much less pressing, since filling the gap was easier; thus it was possible for household heads to remain widowers. It was unthinkable that a widow should remarry and stay in the household. This would have meant a shocking break with the principle of patrilineality.

Labor Organization and Household Structure

In several places in this chapter I have pointed out the correlation between labor organization and household structure. At this point, I would like to summarize these thoughts and make a few additional remarks. To the west of the transitional zone between Western and Eastern Europe elements of the *Hufenverfassung* existed. These included the nuclear family system combined with the system of the stem family in the phases of property transfer to the succeeding generation. Other elements are individual property and the law of unigeniture. In the ideal case, the noninheriting siblings would leave to become servants at some other holding. This period of service could also be spent at the family holding. With the help of these male and female servants, the regional "labor force" could be regulated within the peasant community. In the areas where the *Hufenverfassung* was common practice, the household's property could seldom be expanded, therefore a delicate balance had to be maintained between the number of people in the household and the size of the holding.

Male and female servants were the key to flexibility in this struggle for a balance of forces. This is why they were forbidden to marry while still serving, leading to the relatively high number of late marriages in Western Europe and the rather high percentage of people remaining unmarried. There were also other groups who played a major role in this balance of forces: hired laborers, who were called on when extra labor was needed, and lodgers, who lived on the holding and were required to fulfill a specific task. Often members of these two groups were non-relatives. Male and female servants were the most important of these and for the time of their stay they were regarded as members of the household.

The East European household and labor organization were completely different. It was not the amount of labor that determined the composition of a household but rather the reverse. It was the number of household members capable of working that determined the work that could be carried out. Here the *Hufenverfassung* did not exist so it was easier to expand or reduce the amount of cultivated land. In the areas where village communities played a major role, as in the Romanian and Russian regions, this was especially evident. Periodically land would be redistributed, with the size of each household being taken into account. Moreover vast parts of Eastern and southeastern Europe were sparsely populated at the time. By clearing, new arable lands could be created, making it easier to match the size of the holding with the needs and the size of the various families. Numerous sources report how households would simply annex land and soil.

We have to keep this in mind when looking at the complex family forms in Eastern Europe. Flexible elements in the system of labor organization such as male or female servants did not exist; nor would they have fitted into the overall system where men were the collective and equal owners of the property which was passed on patrilineally. They were attached to the land; giving up their share of the property would not have made sense. Daughters had to marry and thereby strengthen their husbands' households with their labor potential. The fact that men remained on the property that had been passed down by their ancestors for generations reinforced patrilineal thinking. This can be seen as one of the decisive factors encouraging early marriage. In view of high death rates and an extremely high rate of infant mortality, it was socially useful to start reproduction at a young age—which explains the phenomena of universal marriage and the low age at marriage in East European households. Thus in the East European case we can observe a logical system where labor organization and family structure interrelated.

This interrelation of household size and adjustments to the size of a holding is found not only in the agricultural societies of the East European plains but also among the sheep and goat herders in the mountainous regions in the Balkans.

Cross-cultural comparisons have shown that in pastoral economies men have the responsibility for extra-domestic economic matters. As a consequence of their ecological adaptation, pastoral societies are at risk, found in remote regions where the authority of the state is weaker and there is little protection for shepherds and herds. Here there is a strong agnatic nucleus manifested in lineage structures linked to clan organizations.

The household was the primary unit for production and consumption for the mobile shepherd. The size of the herd was closely linked to the number of household members. The household needed an adequate number of animals to secure its basis for survival and required a certain number of shepherds for its herd as well as people for the processing of the milk and wool products. These elements resulted in a number of regional variations. In stressful times a division would occur because the members of the household would be expected to split the risk. However, the opposite strategy could be just as successful. Pasture is a collective property in most nomadic societies and usually the property was passed on collectively to the males of the next generation. Pastoral societies did not usually give their brides a dowry; instead the grooms paid a certain sum of money to the family of the bride (bride price). The success of their political organization depended on the availability of water and pasture resources. Lack of resources resulted in acephalic and segmentary political structures as well as a lack of resolution of individual rights to access pastures on a household basis.

Apparently in this form of pastoral economy, it was not the correlation between the size of the herd and the need for subsistence which was most important but the interconnection between the size of herd and the size of household. The larger a household, the larger the potential labor force, which permitted a larger herd. There is no difference between sheep and goats as far as the labor required is concerned. Pastoral labor organization puts the emphasis on male labor. Therefore when a male child is born the herd can grow at a much larger rate. A pastoral society can afford sizeable households because by growing in number they can keep a larger herd and thereby increase their material base. However, this did not automatically lead to large households since due to demographic factors a large family was an ideal that could not necessarily be achieved.[56]

In closing, let us take a look at the source material in order to find out whether our assumptions are correct with regard to the connection between nuclear family and servant system to the west of the transitional zone between Western and Eastern Europe. In Bohemia and Moravia, which are west of the line, servants have existed since the sixteenth century. Indeed, there were even uniform regulations for servants. In western Poland both male and female servants were found. In Hungarian areas in the eighteenth century, by contrast, census data list few servants of either sex. The average number per community was less than one. For Estonia, part of our transitional zone, we have data showing male and female servants since the seventeenth and eighteenth centuries as well as for the Baltic provinces of Russia toward the end of the eighteenth century.[57]

Despite the fact that we need to be very cautious in our assumptions, our analysis has shown that the West European household model was carried far into the east by the *Ostkolonisation* of the eleventh to thirteenth centuries. Transitional zones, which included Hungary, Poland, and the Baltic, exhibit elements of both the West and East European household models.

FAMILY AND KINSHIP WITHIN
THE PATRIARCHAL CONTEXT

Kinship can be seen under various aspects. Rarely does this concept refer only to the household group. At times (as is the case in Eastern Europe), ancestors may be viewed as active members of a group of relatives, turning the group into a community including both the dead and the living. We would like to deal with the kinship group under two aspects: (1) the significance of the group for the component families; and (2) the way it influences the structure of individual families.

On the question of significance, we have to look at the context in which kinship could develop. Once again we must turn our attention to the historic cultural border between Western and Eastern Europe. In the context of household and family organization, we have observed that in the West patrilineality was not strictly followed and could be interrupted quite easily by the widow remarrying after her husband's death. The Eastern household and family model was by contrast characterized by strict patrilineality. Each holding had been passed on patrilineally for generations and was practically always under collective male ownership. This led to a special kind of feeling of belonging within a patrilineal descent group, i.e., all those who descended from one particular ancestor through the male line. In Western Europe kinship referred to the household and to bilateral kin, in Eastern Europe only to one line, the patriline.

Another factor was the Church: all in all, Christianity, both in its Western and its Eastern forms, had no interest in supporting ancestor worship—quite the contrary. In the Catholic as well as the Orthodox Church the male and female descendants were considered equal and in both Churches a set of rules was established which determined at what point along the line of descent this relationship ended. The only difference between Catholicism and Eastern Orthodox Christianity was in the enforcement of these principles. In general, in Catholic areas, the religious principle matched the secular principle as far as the transfer of property and the neglect of patrilineality were concerned and secular authorities actually helped the Christian principle succeed. In Orthodox areas, these secular powers were not nearly as supportive. In addition Orthodoxy incorporated family lineage festivals such as the *Slava*.

Although the Orthodox Church did not originate them, it was glad to offer its support.

This is why Orthodox populations tended much more to ancestor worship than Catholic ones. The concept of ancestral community and the patriline competed with a horizontal and bilineal concept of kinship ideology. It must have depended on regional circumstances whether one or the other system was more prominent. In the mountainous Balkan regions, which were hard to administer, for example, Christian principles were less important even among Catholics.

In mountainous isolation the significance of the kinship group was the strongest for the individual, for the household and for community life. The Balkan regions are a good example of this and since we know much about these regions we will go into more detail in this case because the principles developed here are—in a modified way—valid for the rest of Eastern Europe. In the mountainous regions where a pastoral economy was practiced, there existed a kinship system that was characterized by a patrilineal descent group or patrilineage. We can assume that this form of kinship had dominated Europe up until the beginning of Christianity. Under the influence of Christianity this form was replaced—at first in the upper class, then slowly expanding to wider circles. Particular agricultural systems could support or impede this process. The Balkan regions were (despite missionary activities) not influenced by this; we can therefore assume that their system has considerable historic depth. During early modern times, the Christian system mostly affected the inhabitants of the Dinaric mountains and the northern Pindos mountains and only later as a result of large migrations did it reach the plains. These migrations started in the second half of the eighteenth century and peaked during the nineteenth century.[58]

We can differentiate between two primary forms of patrilineal descent groups: the tribe, which holds a defined territory and inhabits it, and descent groups with no fixed territory, whose households were scattered among various villages or who formed their own village quarters.[59] The first type we find mostly in northern Albania and the bordering Montenegrin areas; the second type existed prior to the above-mentioned migrations in Hercegovina, Kosovo, and southern Albania.

Patrilineal descent groups in the Balkans shared certain characteristics. They were of different sizes (depending on the generational depth and links to the original forebear). In our time frame (1500–1789) they were not large in size and may have reached back six or seven generations. They could be organized in subgroups, which had degrees of corporate responsibility. They formed exogamous units, i.e. one's wife had to be found outside the group. They owned common property (in the form of pastures, forests and water rights); they shared a common ancestor name and lived mostly in villages named patronymically.

The concept of the descent group in the Muslim part of Bosnia-Hercegovina was less dominant than in the Christian part. Although the basis for the organization of relationship was also the patrilineal descent group, its actual significance was comparatively moderate. Albanian Muslims in Kosovo, who were organized in clear and pronounced patrilineal descent groups, prove that it is not religion but ecology that is the decisive factor in this difference.[60]

For the group it is important to define who is a member and who is not. Members legally share corporate identity and represent the whole group, which has collective responsibility. This becomes apparent in the case of blood revenge. Such cases cannot be dealt with by individual families arbitrarily but have to gain the approval of group public opinion, as represented by the descent group. Thus corporate units and clearly defined descent groups become one and the same. Bilineal relationship systems cannot rely on such a principle.[61] They cannot be feuding or vengeance groups or control property such as pastures.

Although the line between the patrilineal descent group in the Balkans and the bilineal system outside the central Balkan regions is a relatively clear one, we cannot draw such a line for the East European regions. Nonetheless, we can assume that both principles existed alongside each other. Overall we can assume that the basic elements of these systems also existed in the other East European regions. In the remote Balkan regions they developed fully, whereas in other areas they intermingled with other ways and systems.

In general one might say that the significance of relationships could be modified by the Church, the village community (if not based on kinship), or the domain (for this period we cannot really speak of the state as a determining factor).

In Croatia and in parts of Hungary and Poland it was probably the Catholic Church that played a decisive role in minimizing the effect of the patrilineal descent system. In Romanian regions it seems that the village community took on this role; however, in Russia, where the village community was also strong, this was not the case. Everywhere the domain system had a minimizing effect on the functions of the patrilineal descent group; however, as has been repeatedly stated, the domain system was never overly involved in household affairs. But it provided the administration, guaranteed a form of judiciary, and saw to it that church rules were respected. Therefore, we can conclude that kinship was one of several possible factors in determining the life of families and households and that in Eastern Europe kinship was more significant than in the West.

The other question is whether the character of the kinship organization affected family life. Quite obviously its patriarchal character shaped family ideology. Again Church, domain, and village community would have a modifying impact. From materials on Russian history we know that since the ninth century a pronounced patriarchal society existed. During the time of the Kiev Rus (ninth to thirteenth centuries) there is talk of polygyny, abduction of women, and of bridal rewards—elements which were also common in the central Balkan areas in early modern times. The oldest Russian Code of Law from the eleventh century also depicts a strictly patriarchal society and although towards the end of the tenth century Christianity was adopted, little changed in the patriarchal tradition: women and daughters continued to have no right to inherit. Starting at the end of the fifteenth century (after Mongolian rule ended) the situation for women improved considerably, but this was confined to the upper classes. The broad mass of the populace continued to live under the common law, with a patriarchal order that still prevailed in the second half of the nineteenth century.[62] What we know of this common law allows us to assume that it shared several basic similarities with the so-called "Balkan patriarchy."

The Balkan patriarchy can be described as follows: first, men were assigned not only a dominant but even a repressive role; this was characterized by the principles of patrilineality, patrilocality, and a legal system that strongly favored males. Secondly, there existed the principle of seniority, which ensured that the elders ruled over the younger (fathers over sons, the older generation over the younger generation, older brothers over younger brothers). Unlike the cognatic, bilineal relationship system, which accepts male and female heirs alike, the agnatic, patrilineal system only recognizes males as rightful heirs. The female line is accepted in principle but in practice is never used. Patrilineal systems are characterized by the practice of ancestor worship and by the exclusion of females from owning property and inheriting. Patrilineality and patrilocality go together. In the agnatic system (and only there), where a group can have a collective property of fixed and mobile goods, women become interchangeable and disadvantaged in marriages. The wife marries into her husband's family. Neolocality (i.e., founding a new household upon marrying) cannot be part of this system because the husband's share of property is not divisible as long as the household is not being divided. The legal system which so strongly favors males assumes that only men will represent the family to the outside world (only in exceptional cases might the widow take on this responsibility). Men deal with the various authorities, they are responsible for the other family members, only they can sign contracts and do business. Although this obviously male-dominated society put women in a disadvantaged position, it did not mean that it was impossible for women to develop a life of their own. Due to the polarization of the genders women could play a significant role in certain areas of society.

Thus when comparing patriarchal structures in the Balkans and in Russia we can observe not only similarities but also certain differences. There were differences in regard to the strong system of patrilineality in the Balkans (ignoring the female line completely in family lineage) and in regard to ancestor worship, which was crucial to maintaining the patriarchal ideology. Also important here is the nature of the different historical experiences, e.g. of the Balkan peoples under the Ottomans and the population under Russian statehood and the system of serfdom. Here the nature of hierarchy, the life beyond the village, and the type of state become important.

CONCLUSIONS

Our survey has offered support for a geographical division of Europe into two systems of family organization. It has become apparent that, in addition to two different marriage patterns and differing household formation systems, there existed two very dissimilar agricultural systems, which naturally also resulted in different forms of domestic labor organization.

For Eastern Europe from the sixteenth through to the eighteenth century, serfdom did not lose any of its dominance nor was there any major capitalization of agriculture or pronounced expansion of urban centers. In these three centuries feudal relations intensified, resulting in an increase in serfdom in the vast plains of Eastern Europe. In the Balkan regions, which were under Ottoman rule (after a complete restructuring of agricultural relations), forms similar to serfdom also prevailed.

It was also in the interest of the East European feudal lords to intervene in existing household and family structures. Clearly the West European agricultural system under the influence of the estate owner was more efficiently organized; however, although East European feudal lords intervened in different ways in the lives of their formerly independent peasants, like their West European counterparts they did so to maximize their profit within the context of existing family conditions.

It seems that in these three centuries the relations between lord and peasant, and between countryside and town, became more rigid and stable. Family history shows us that family and household organization reacted quite swiftly to changing conditions. Apparently, there were no major changes in Eastern Europe except in the enormous role of colonization movements. Since the eleventh century the *Ostkolonisation* had brought the West European family and household formation pattern far into Eastern Europe. In the eighteenth and nineteenth centuries parts of the Balkans, e.g. the Serbian Šumadija region, were resettled and colonized; in Russia the colonization of the steppe and Siberia had a significant impact on agrarian and family structures. Aside from this there was little change in the family, kinship, or patriarchal structures. Such changes would occur only with the onset of the nineteenth century and its agricultural reforms and modernization processes.

CHAPTER 3

Proto-industrialization

Ulrich Pfister

The term "proto-industrialization" refers to the mass production of manufactured goods before the onset of mechanization, that is, before *ca.* 1800. It was characterized by three features which distinguished it from other types of handicraft production: first, producers were located not only in towns but also in the countryside; manufacture became largely a regional phenomenon during the early modern era. Secondly, proto-industrial manufactures were supplied to inter-regional and international markets rather than to a local clientele. Thirdly, complex arrangements developed for the integration of different steps of production and for linking producers and merchant-manufacturers. Beyond the simple *Kaufsystem* (merchants interacting with producers through markets), there existed various forms of advance contracts involving raw materials and semi-finished goods (*Verlagssystem* or putting-out system) and of centralized production in manufactories.[1]

Why is the family important in considering early modern manufacture production? On the one hand, given the absence of major technological advances capable of raising factor productivity, production growth presupposed the expansion of labor and capital inputs.[2] Patterns of the household economy and of family formation in agrarian Europe, insofar as they were conducive to a rising supply of labor for manufacture production, are key to the understanding of proto-industrial growth. On the other hand, considerable efforts have gone into showing that proto-industry broke traditional patterns of family formation and contributed to the emergence of new modes of family life that opened the way to population growth and proletarianization.[3]

This chapter examines these issues by exploring, first, the relationship between proto-industry and short-term demographic rhythms. The second section is devoted to the family economy in proto-industrial settings, and the third looks at implications of manufacture for the life course and for the family cycle. While it is now widely recognized that proto-industry involved both town and countryside, the present chapter focuses primarily on the household and family structures in rural areas.

PROTO-INDUSTRIALIZATION AND FAMILY TIME: SHORT-TERM RHYTHMS AND DEMOGRAPHIC PATTERNS

The development of a proto-industrial sector provided rural families with a new source of household income besides agriculture. On the one hand, this income derived simply from supplying labor to the manufacturing sector. On the other hand, proto-industrial income could also derive from a rent on household capital invested in proto-industry, such as instruments (a weaving loom or a forge, for instance), housing space to place and use these instruments, as well as from circulating capital used to acquire raw materials and semi-finished goods (such as bar iron, raw cotton, or thread). The availability of household income from the proto-industrial sector could alter the pattern of family formation in the sense that it contributed to the dissolution of the traditional "European marriage pattern" characterized by a high age at first marriage and a high proportion never married. In the parish of Shepshed, England, for instance, age at first marriage declined from 28.1 and 29.4 for women and men, respectively, during the seventeenth century to roughly 24 years for both sexes during the second half of the eighteenth century. An analysis of 26 English parishes suggests a similar downward trend for the national level as a whole, this tendency being particularly strong in proto-industrial parishes.[4] At least in some continental regions, proto-industry has been likewise associated with a low age at first marriage. In the Canton of Zurich (Switzerland), for example, a writer of the early nineteenth century commented on the new material basis of family formation by saying that "early marriage between two persons, who bring two spinning wheels but no bed with them, occurs fairly frequently among these people."[5]

However, a declining or low marriage age was by no means universal among populations earning their livelihood from proto-industry. Rather, it seems to be confined to certain circumstances. Both cases referred to above concern situations where high labor incomes could be earned with little capital outlay; in Shepshed for instance, hosiery looms were provided by entrepreneurs, and in the Canton of Zurich piece rates in cotton spinning rose above the wages of agricultural laborers during the boom period of *ca.* 1740–1785. Further preconditions for an increase in the marriage rate in parallel to an expansion of the proto-industrial sector are the absence of institutional barriers to the formation of new households and of industrial regulations that limited access to handicraft production. Where these conditions did not hold, other patterns prevailed, and the available evidence renders it possible to discern two major patterns.[6]

On the one hand, there were many branches in which capital requirements, such as the possession of a loom in the textile or a forge in the metal trades, constituted a formidable obstacle to early family formation. In such cases, age at first marriage remained constant over much of the proto-industrial period and was sometimes even higher than in agricultural regions or higher than among farmers within the same region. Examples include the silk-ribbon weavers around Lyon, ironware producers in eastern Belgium, linen weavers in eastern Westphalia and worsted weavers in the Black Forest.[7] An interesting case is provided by a parish in the eastern Comasco (Lombardy) whose population combined ironware production with ancillary work for silk milling by the early nineteenth century. While the majority of forgers usually had to wait to marry until their father's death and the inheritance of a forge, the marriages between forgers and silk spoolers (an activity exclusively performed by women) occurred at a particularly young age. Apparently, the employment of the wife, which was not constrained by capital requirements or energy resources (the number of forges was dependent on locally available water power), vastly increased the possibilities for young couples to make a living entirely in the proto-industrial sector.[8]

On the other hand, many types of proto-industrial commodity production were poorly remunerated and, therefore, were performed by only a fraction of the family labor force, that is, by women and/or children, or as a seasonal side-activity. Since proto-industry generated only a subsidiary income in this situation, family formation had to conform to the traditional pattern among rural lower classes, which was one of late marriage. Typical examples include cotton spinning in the Pays de Caux (Lower Normandy), which expanded only slowly and was practiced exclusively by women, and work in rural silk milling in the central Comasco. While spouses were frequently both engaged in this sector, it was characterized by low wages, so family formation required a long period of saving.[9]

Changes in the patterns of family formation rested on shifts and fluctuations in short-term work rhythms. A comparison of seasonal fluctuations of textile production in different German regions demonstrates that in places where trade with raw materials and semi-finished goods was absent and where agrarian institutions precluded the formation of households engaged entirely in the proto-industrial sector, textile production remained imbedded in the seasonal cycle of agricultural production: within most households hemp was harvested in early autumn, spun during winter, woven and sold during late spring and summer. In regions where trade and labor division had developed, by contrast, linen production became detached from seasonal rhythms in agriculture and tended to be spread evenly over the year.[10]

An analogous pattern holds for demographic behavior: in agricultural regions, marriages (and to some extent, births) were concentrated in seasons with a low labor intensity and a low exposure to economic and (in the case of births) health risks. The continuous flow of work and income in proto-industrial households meant a flattening out of seasonal fluctuations in marriages and, at least in part, births. A low seasonality of marriages in regions with a strong manufacturing sector has been demonstrated for England, and there are at least some continental parishes which display a similar tendency affecting both marriages and births.[11]

The low seasonality of marriages in proto-industrial contexts seems to be partly related to the operation of the land market, on which young couples must heavily rely where neolocal residence is the norm. A comparison of contrasting communities in the Canton of Zurich suggests that land transactions were more evenly spread over the year in a proto-industrial than in an agrarian context. This was certainly due to the relatively continuous income flow of proto-industrial workers. In addition, the prospect of future cash income increased the debt servicing capacity of proto-industrial households and enabled them to pay for a larger share of their land purchases by incurring debts than could households engaged in subsistence or even commercial agriculture.[12]

In sum, if the preconditions mentioned earlier were at least partially met, family time in proto-industrial households became less determined by the agricultural cycle and corresponding rhythms of acquiring cash, of spending and feasting. Likewise, time tended to become an abstract concept, with work rhythms determined less by specific tasks varying in time than by regular transactions with the market or with entrepreneurs.[13]

Beyond seasonal fluctuations, the changing level of real proto-industrial income could influence the propensity to marry. In some regions, year-to-year fluctuations in marriages were correlated with the ratio between prices for manufactured goods (or the aggregate value of proto-industrial production) and grain prices as an index for real income, the marriage rate being high in years of high real income and low in years characterized by a slack in the manufacturing sector and/or high prices for agricultural goods.[14] This relationship partly detached household formation from agricultural price cycles and allowed for population growth beyond regional agrarian resources. At the same time, labor supply in the mid-term could be brought in line with the demand for proto-industrial labor. Thus proto-industrialization provided for a type of economic growth in which the expansion of output depended mainly on increases in the inputs of the relevant factors of production.

However, it should again be stressed that this pattern emerged only where institutional restrictions and requirements of household capital were largely absent and where proto-industrial incomes were so high as to render it attractive not only for women but also for adult men to work in manufacturing rather than in the agricultural sector. Such a constellation appears to have been relatively rare and may have been confined to the short boom phases of the linen and cotton sectors, and here in particular to spinning, during the eighteenth century.

Nevertheless, even if family formation continued to occur late and was not responsive to fluctuations in proto-industrial income some population growth could still occur by way of other processes.[15] The extra income provided by cottage industry to households otherwise entrenched in an agrarian economy could contribute to an improvement of nutritional standards, either directly by increasing purchasing power for food or indirectly through providing funds that could be invested in the improvement of agricultural techniques such as the construction of fences to convert pastures to meadows, the building of stables, the increase of flocks, etc. A good illustration of this variant is eastern Westphalia where proto-industry went hand in hand with an increase in agricultural productivity. At the same time, at least part of the area was characterized by a system of low demographic pressure, i.e. a high age at first marriage and low mortality, particularly of infants. Due to low mortality, population grew rapidly between the late seventeenth and the early nineteenth centuries. Similarly, the combination of ironware production and silk processing in the eastern Comasco seems to have contributed to favorable and stable income conditions and, consequently, to a demographic system characterized by low infant and adult mortality.[16]

In conclusion, the variability of the demographic concomitants of cottage industry suggests that, in the majority of cases, the supply of proto-industrial labor was responsive to variations in demand to a limited extent. The marriage rate (as a major means to increase labor within a given population) was correlated with real income in only a few instances. This fact may account for the frequent complaints about labor shortage during the boom periods of the eighteenth century and, therefore, may have provided a major incentive for the mechanization of labor-intensive stages of production such as cotton spinning.

THE PROTO-INDUSTRIAL HOUSEHOLD ECONOMY

The foregoing suggests that dimensions of family organization, such as in terms of work rhythms, market interaction, and demographic events, varied considerably according to institutional and economic circumstances. The present section provides a more detailed analysis of the variables that governed the proto-industrial household economy. It does so by examining the extent to which different strata of the rural population engaged in cottage industry, then by looking at household size and composition and finally by considering the household as a working and earning unit.

Proto-industry and Social Structure

According to a widely held view, proto-industrial activities were primarily engaged in by a rural proletariat that was unable to gain its whole livelihood from subsistence agriculture. Since recent research draws a much more nuanced picture, it is preferable to review in a systematic fashion the existing relationships between the amount of land a household owns and the share of its labor it allocates to proto-industrial work. A survey of the available evidence suggests three general patterns of the household labor allocation process.[17]

First, there exists a more or less linear negative relationship between farm size and the share of household labor engaged in the proto-industrial sector: the smaller the acreage a household owns or uses, the higher is the share of its labor devoted to work in the domestic production of manufactured goods. Table 3.1 provides a concrete example of this relationship for an eighteenth-century Swiss village. Among the landless, 34.0% of all household members are reported as being proto-industrial workers other than weavers, which means in most cases that they are cotton spinners. With rising size of arable land (other types of land, such as meadows, are not considered in the analysis), this share declines continuously until it reaches 3.6 percent among those living on the largest farms. The interpretation of this result is simple: the less household income provided by subsistence farming, the higher the share of labor that needs to be employed outside the family farm.

Of course, work in the manufacturing sector obviously constitutes only one alternative among others; temporary emigration and employment as a day laborer on neighboring farms are other options, particularly for males. A systematic comparison of several parishes for which listings of the type as used in Table 3.1 are available suggests, therefore, that the strength of the relationship between holding size and the share of household labor employed in cottage industry is subject to a trade-off between labor productivity and income opportunities in the manufacturing sector and of its opportunity cost in terms of forgone income opportunities in agriculture.[18]

The second pattern refers to cases characterized by a curvilinear relationship between holding size and the share of household labor devoted to manufacture production. In these situations, proto-industrial activities were most frequent among the middle class of small proprietors and less frequent both among the land-poor and landless households as well as among well-to-do farmers. In Table 3.1, for instance, the share of household members engaged as weavers *rises* continuously, albeit slowly, from 24.5 percent among the landless to 31.9 percent among the households possessing between five and ten *Jucharten* in field land. Only among the largest ownership category is this trend reversed (8.9 percent), yielding a relationship with a curvilinear shape. Similar results have been obtained for other populations where weaving was widespread. The most notable cases include linen weaving near Bielefeld (eastern Westphalia, Germany), French Flanders and, possibly, upper Württemberg, silk weaving in the Stephanois (west of Lyon, France) and wool or worsted weaving in the Haut-Givaudan (Massif Central, France) and western Württemberg.[19] The concentration of proto-industrial activities among middle-class households is all the more pronounced where typical lower-class economic activities are not carried out in independent households. This holds true, for instance, in the case of silk thread around Lyon which

Table 3.1 Farm size and share of household labor devoted to domestic manufacture production in Mönchaldorf (Canton of Zurich, Switzerland) in 1773 (all values refer to arithmetic means).

Arable land in *Jucharten**	MHS[†]	Number of weavers	Number of other pi[‡]	Percent weavers	Percent other pi	(n)
0	4.11	1.06	1.56	24.5	34.0	(18)
Less than 1	4.94	1.36	1.27	27.5	25.7	(33)
1 to 5	5.42	1.17	1.33	28.7	24.1	(12)
5 to 10	5.38	1.50	0.62	31.9	9.3	(8)
10 and more	7.43	0.76	0.33	8.9	3.6	(21)
Total	5.45	1.15	1.06	23.2	20.6	(92)

* One *Juchart* equals some 30 acres.
† MHS: Mean Household Size.
‡ pi = proto-industrial employment. The overwhelming majority of persons classified as "other pi" are cotton spinners.
Source: Pfister (1992a: 281).

is either imported or produced in centralized mills. Likewise, wool spinning in the Black Forest seems to have been performed largely within the
households of weavers and by solitary women who were often denied an
independent household.[20]

In order to account for the existence of a curvilinear pattern one needs
to look not only at the productivity of labor (as in the first constellation
reported above), but also at the availability and productivity of household capital. The fact that a curvilinear relationship seems to be closely
linked with weaving suggests that lower-class households did not have
enough capital to acquire instruments, nor enough living space to allow
for a loom or a forge, nor enough cash to fund the regular purchase
of raw materials or semi-finished goods (such as yarn) and were thus
barred from entry into relatively capital-intensive activities. Among linen
weavers near Bielefeld, for instance, land constituted an important basis
for obtaining the credit necessary to generate the required circulating
capital. Landless weavers worked fewer looms and were more frequently
dependent on a middleman than weavers owning land.[21] However, the
income-generating potential of investment in the proto-industrial sector
was limited: as soon as all family members of working age disposed of
a machine to work on, profitable outlets for investment in the manufacturing sector within the household economy were exhausted. Investment
in the expansion or the improvement of an agricultural holding, by contrast, was much less subject to diminishing returns, particularly among
small farms. This explains why, above a certain level of wealth, the share
of household labor engaged in the manufacturing sector declined again.

Not all activities requiring household capital displayed a curvilinear
distribution over the social spectrum of rural society, however. A comparative analysis of about a dozen parishes in the Canton of Zurich suggests that this pattern was mainly confined to regions characterized by a
labor-extensive agrarian system where investment of household capital
in agriculture generated less employment than investment in the proto-
industrial sector in most households apart from the big farms. In areas
where proto-industry went together with labor-intensive agriculture, a
linear relationship between holding size and the share of household labor
engaged in the manufacturing sector obtained for weaving, too.[22]

The third pattern that can be observed is a positive linear relationship
between holding size and at least the absolute amount of household
labor devoted to manufacture production, that is, the direct opposite of
the first pattern. The prime example of this constellation comes from
northeastern Westphalia where, as mentioned before, trade with raw
materials and semi-finished goods was largely absent and barriers to
entry for land-poor households were high. In general, this implies that

where proto-industrial activities depended entirely on household resources (i.e. not only capital but also all other inputs for production), the capability of households to devote labor to the production of manufactures became directly dependent on holding size.[23]

In sum, the existence of these three patterns suggests that the share of household labor that rural households devoted to the production of manufactures depended on the productivity of both labor and capital in the proto-industrial as well as in the agricultural sectors. This complex relationship goes a long way to explain the differences in the demographic corollaries of proto-industrialization reported above. In addition, the dispersion of handicraft activities over a wide spectrum of rural society makes it difficult to speak of proto-industrial households as such. Even if this complicates the picture, the following discussion will have to distinguish carefully between proto-industrial activities with varying capital requirements and productivity characteristics.

HOUSEHOLD SIZE AND COMPOSITION

As in early modern Europe as a whole, family systems in proto-industrial regions varied widely, and this renders generalized statements about the impact of cottage industry on household size and composition difficult. In situations in which handicraft activities were concentrated among the lower classes, households making their livelihood mainly from non-agricultural activities were usually smaller and contained fewer servants and kin than the households of farmers.[24] In other words, they broadly conformed to a pattern that was widespread among rural lower classes, smallholders, and day laborers in particular. The size of a farm, which determined how many persons could make a living in a household economy, thus remained of paramount importance in proto-industrial contexts too. In the worsted region of the Black Forest, for instance, variation in the yield of arable land constitutes the principal factor explaining variations in mean household size between communities.[25] However, if we put aside questions of farm size, manufacturing production meant that a household could provide a livelihood for more persons than on the basis of work in the agricultural sector alone. Compared to other lower-class groups, the households of weavers and, to a lesser extent, spinners were thus frequently larger and more complex.

Households mainly engaged in manufacturing production contained more children of working age than households of some other non-peasant groups. In western Württemberg in 1736 the households of worsted weavers contained on average about 2.25 children, whereas households of laborers recorded only about 1.75 children.[26] In Shepshed, offspring of both hosiery weavers and laborers could find employment in the hosiery trade, and the households of these groups therefore contained more children than those of laborers in purely agrarian contexts where children had to leave the parental household at an early age in order to become farmhands. At least in the textile trades, however, this tendency was largely restricted to girls. Since many activities in textiles were mainly performed by women, young adult males continued to seek employment in the agricultural sector and left the parental home relatively early.[27]

Households depending mostly on handicraft industry were more likely to contain servants and/or other non-kin residents than other subpeasant groups, particularly laborers, although full farmers clearly employed many more servants.[28] Actually, however, what the sources designate as servants may in fact approach the status of apprentices, journeymen, and boarders. Lodgers, too, seem to have been attached to the household mainly as boarders. The presence of apprentices and journeymen was confined to regions where corporate structures had developed, mainly in the weaving and metal trades. In branches where it was possible to produce individually for the market, such as in spinning, servants and lodgers approached the status of boarders. As they made their livelihood independently, these persons, the majority of them women, stood at the margin of the family economy and the authority of the household head. A report on Mönchaltorf (near Zurich) and two adjacent parishes stated in 1774 that many persons who were reported as servants in the list used in Table 3.1 actually paid an "ordinary board allowance . . . , worked for their own profit and were their own Lord."[29] A high incidence of boarding has been found in other proto-industrial contexts, notably in England.[30] Still, we do not know how general the pattern of great autonomy for proto-industrial boarders actually was; in Württemberg, for instance, local and state authorities took repeated measures to discipline and control solitary women.[31] In any case, for middle- and lower-class families depending largely on the manufacturing sector, boarders provided a means to fully exploit the capacity of existing living and working space while at the same time contributing to family earnings, as they would later in many nineteenth-century working-class families.

Proto-industry could also have an impact on the role of servants in the households of farmers. The report just quoted also states that farmers employed their servants as spinners over much of the year and used them in the fields only during harvesting time. Similar evidence exists on the Austrian Waldviertel.[32] Combining an agrarian with a proto-industrial livelihood was thus not confined to the core of consanguine family members but extended to the household as a whole. In this case, the employment of farmhands in cottage industry may have provided a means to make better use of labor than was afforded by agricultural work alone and therefore served to retain laborers in the household or the region who otherwise would have had to emigrate.

The final variable to be considered is the kin complexity of households in proto-industrial regions. Of course, patterns of family and household organization that prevailed in a particular region greatly influenced the kinship structure under proto-industrial conditions, too. Where the formation of complex households was a strategy employed by a generally poor population, such as in the hilly areas of central France, to pool resources and to benefit from the economies of scale related to the expansion of a single household unit, manufacturing production constituted an additional source of employment that allowed an increase in household size and complexity. In the western neighborhood of Lyon, for instance, households with silk-ribbon weavers were more frequently extended than the rest of the population during the cottage industry period; and the same appears to have been true of Irish linen weavers, of cotton weavers in the Austrian Waldviertel and, possibly, of ironware producers in central Sweden.[33]

By contrast, where proto-industry fostered a neolocal pattern of family formation, manufacturing production went hand in hand with a reduction of the generational depth of the co-residing kin group. In the Canton of Zurich, for instance, households of spinners and weavers in different branches of the textile trade usually displayed a degree of kin complexity that was clearly lower than among farmers. A stem family phase, which occurred quite frequently toward the end of the family cycle among well-to-do peasants, was rare among households who made their living predominantly from proto-industry. At the same time, spinning allowed widows and unmarried women to maintain independent households rather than live with married kin (sons or brothers).[34] These findings reflect the growing economic independence of both children and solitary women, and they suggest that the employment opportunities offered by the manufacturing sector reduced the necessity for kin to co-reside for long phases of their life cycle. We do not know, however, to what extent this pattern went hand in hand with a rise in poverty during old age.

A low degree of kin complexity was not universally connected to low family cohesion, however. Particularly where marriage went together with the inheritance of the means of production necessary for proto-industrial trades, there was little opportunity for the formation of complex families. In the Comasco, for instance, the predominance of a nuclear family pattern among forgers and silk mill workers (in contrast to farmers who displayed complex family forms) has been explained by the fact that young people frequently had to link marriage with the inheritance of a forge or a fraction of a house, respectively.[35]

Even if proto-industry went together with a reduced generational depth of the co-resident kin group, this does not imply that kin beyond the nuclear group were absent altogether. For instance, although the weaver households in the western Black Forest largely lacked kin during the early and late stages of the family cycle, they frequently included kin during the middle stages, when the male heads were in their forties. It may be that during this phase, when proto-industrial earning capacity reached its peak, the capacity of these households to provide a livelihood for other members of the kin group and to capitalize on size by recruiting additional adult workers among the kin group may have been greater than during other stages of the family cycle.[36]

The Household as Work Group and Earning Unit

How did the various economic activities of household members combine with one another? Were proto-industrial households distinguished by a high complementarity of the work roles of family members and by an intensified exploitation of the household labor potential for the manufacture of a specific good?[37] Or, by contrast, did the proto-industrial household presage the proletarian family wage economy of the nineteenth century in which the household was largely devoid of an independent production function?[38] Or was the proto-industrial household economy simply a variant of the adaptive family in which households, in order to maximize aggregate welfare, employed each member in the sector where his or her labor would bring the highest possible return?[39]

All these questions can be answered in the affirmative in specific circumstances. The major factors that account for the wide variety of actual patterns appear to be the structure of the manufacturing sector itself, the extent to which a household was engaged in both agriculture and proto-industry, and the degree to which a particular activity was gendered. The examples in Figure 3.1, taken from my own work based on some uniquely detailed household listings for seventeenth- and eighteenth-century Zurich, serve as illustrations of this point.

The existence of an intensive division of labor and close cooperation of all or most family members in the manufacture of a specific good presupposes the production of a relatively complex good that requires some labor division. Weaving and possibly ironware manufacture, but not spin-

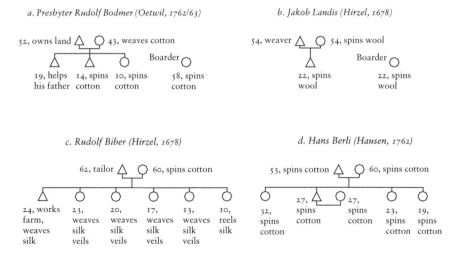

Figure 3.1 Examples of domestic work groups (Canton of Zurich, seventeenth and eighteenth centuries)

Sources: State Archive of Zurich E II 700.27, Oetwil 1762/3, Nr. 71; E II 700.50, Hirzel 1678, Nr. 38 and 70; E II 700.44, Hausen 1762, Nr. 20.

ning, offer examples. Before mechanization, between four and ten spinners were usually required to produce the yarn processed by one weaver. By employing family members, in particular adult women and children of both sexes, as spinners, weavers were able to produce at least some of the yarn they needed within the household economy. This may have provided some protection against discontinuities in work rhythms due to the periodicity of contacts with yarn markets as well as to fluctuations in these markets. Weavers in pre-famine Ulster, for instance, seem to have recruited inmates who worked as winders and spinners and could thereby substitute for children in order to reach an optimal production unit.[40] A similar logic may hold for Figures 3.1a and 3.1b: these households both contain an adult weaver (a husband and a wife, respectively) and three other family members—a wife, sons, a daughter, and inmates—who engage in spinning. It may well be that weavers and spinners formed a team in each case, and inmates may have been accepted in order to minimize the amount of yarn that had to be procured outside the household economy. A similar argument can be put forward with respect to ancillary tasks. In particular, yarn was traded in reels and had to be warped before weaving. Employing children for this task, as illustrated by Figure 1c, could save the weavers' time and, through a deepening of labor division, increase household income. The household list from which this

example is taken reports many young children, with older siblings, performing the reeling of silk.

Cooperation between household members was not exclusively dependent on the manufacture of a good that required labor division. The
contact with markets or entrepreneurs often presupposed long trips, and
so the marketing of household goods could be beset with considerable
transaction costs. In order to reduce per unit costs, the number of household members who worked on a particular type of good had to be maximized and their work rhythms synchronized. A concrete example comes
from one parish in seventeenth-century Zurich where young couples frequently formed a team for silk-gauze weaving, whereas in a later stage
of the life course married women abandoned this lucrative trade as soon
as their husbands turned to another activity which made regular trips to
the town less of a necessity, at least for the men. The long distance
between this parish and the town made it profitable to weave silk gauze
in a team of at least two, but not as an individual worker. A similar tendency is present in a rural center of silk milling in the Comasco around
1800: although most wives of mill workers were reported as being
domestic silk spoolers, wives of artisans were more likely to be designated as sewers rather than silk spoolers. It may well be that silk mill
workers were able to provide their wives with labor contracts at low negotiation costs.[41] Clearly, then, transaction costs related to the marketing
of household goods or the negotiation of labor contracts constituted an
additional factor which shaped work roles, although—as the latter
example demonstrates—not always in the direction of intensified cooperation within the family unit.

The second pattern, in which each family member worked individually in a particular sector and derived a sort of wage that would contribute to a family fund, typified lower-class households which were
largely devoid of land and engaged in a sector that required both little
labor division and little household capital. Spinning, where it was sufficiently remunerated to be performed by whole households rather than
individual members such as children and young women, could be associated with this type of family economy. In configurations such as Figure
3.1d we find that all household members performed the same activity,
that is, cotton spinning; labor division was minimal, and gender- as well
as age-specific work roles seem to have been little differentiated. At the
same time, there is evidence, both for English and Swiss contexts, that
at least female labor was exploited to the utmost among these proto-
industrial lower-class households. Female labor-force participation was
high and did not respond to variations in the opportunity cost of labor;
young girls in spinner families had very low school enrollment rates, and

adult female spinners were criticized by contemporaries for neglecting their household duties.[42]

The reduction of role differentiation in these early proletarian families should not be overestimated, however. Males often worked less in spinner families or simply tried to withdraw from the family economy. Boys had considerably higher school enrollment rates than girls, and sons left the parental home earlier than daughters. An extreme situation is found in central France: there, women worked at home as lacemakers, a highly gendered activity, whereas men hung around in *cabarets* or contributed to the family fund through temporary emigration.[43]

As the previous discussion of proto-industry and social structure suggested, manufacture production was not confined to the rural proletariat but was imbedded in a labor allocation process that operated in the majority of households in a given region. This implies that families combined subsistence agriculture and the commodity production for different markets (agrarian, local handicraft, proto-industrial) with great flexibility in order to maximize the return on the given structure of both household labor and capital. An example of this kind of pluri-activity is provided by Figure 3.1c: whereas the five daughters aged between 10 and 23 formed a partly integrated work team in that the youngest reeled silk for her elder sisters who wove silk veils, the son attended to the family farm, the father acted as a tailor and the mother spun cotton—an activity well suited to part-time labor market participation. Similarly, in Colyton (Devonshire, England) in 1851 there was a limited congruence of the activities of different family members. In particular, the mothers of young lacemakers frequently pursued a different occupation or were not active in the labor market at all.[44]

An important aspect of an adaptive strategy to maximize return on labor and capital in the various sectors of household production is the flexibility of labor allocation. One Yorkshire weaver who wrote a diary in 1782–1783 describes in detail how he divided his time between weaving, gardening, harvesting, threshing, house repairs, and so on without ever remaining idle. On a broader basis, a great flexibility of labor allocation in the short run is attested by a contemporary investigation of the ways in which men and women in late nineteenth-century Oberlausitz divided their time between agriculture and ribbon weaving.[45] This flexibility made possible a highly efficient use of time by individuals and was one of the major comparative advantages of (decentralized) forms of production such as were found in proto-industry. This is evident in the fact that work in centralized workshops or in the first mechanized workshops had to be remunerated far better than work performed in rural households.[46] While concrete information is lacking, it may also be that the comparative advantage stemming from the flexibility of labor allocation in rural households also lay behind the spread of manufacturing production into the countryside during the late Middle Ages and the early modern period.

The degree of cohesion of the family as work group and earning unit also has implications for the relationships between parents and children as well as between the sexes. Discussion of these two topics will conclude the present section.

A low degree of work group cohesion could imply a weakening of the economic bonds between parents and their adult children. If households subsisted largely on manufacture production, and agrarian property was minimal, parents had little ability to control the labor power of their children. The children could threaten to leave the parents and to become boarders in other households if they could not keep a major part of their earnings. Contemporaries deplored this phenomenon since it lessened paternal control over youths who indulged in conspicuous consumption and engaged in illicit sexual relations. The phenomenon of children living as boarders with their own parents was also thought to deprive the latter of a portion of the family income they often badly needed to amortize the heavy costs they had incurred with household formation and, therefore, to aggravate poverty in their old age. The final section of this chapter will show that this allegation may well have contained a grain of truth.[47]

The options that young adults had for leaving the household, at least in situations where proto-industrial work assumed a wage-like character, had implications that went beyond the redistribution of funds between parents and children. The threat of departure by family members with valuable labor power constituted an important pressure toward the removal of "slack," i.e. towards an efficient allocation of labor and scarce household capital. This, together with the great flexibility in allocation of time and labor to different activities, may explain why contemporary writers considered households and regions engaged in proto-industry to be particularly industrious and thrifty, and compared them favorably to the households of farmers or agricultural regions in general, where people managed their lives in a more comfortable manner.[48]

Now let us turn to the labor division, power relations, and emotional bonds between the two sexes in proto-industrial regions. Many types of poorly remunerated textile work, particularly spinning, were performed mainly by women and by children of both sexes. Other activities, such as weaving, which was frequently subjected to corporate regulations, were by contrast frequently performed by men. In the Pays de Caux (Normandy) this resulted in a constellation where men were weavers (mostly part-time) and women spinners. This meant that traditional male economic and labor power changed little; women had little scope for accumulating an independent fund or to indulge in conspicuous consumption, which remained a male prerogative.[49] This pattern was by no means universal, however. Figures 3.1a–c show that in the Canton of Zurich both weaving and spinning could be practiced by either women or men. Activities were not randomly distributed over the two sexes. Wherever possible, males preferred to work in agriculture which was often more rewarding than proto-industry. The division of labor nevertheless depended on the relative labor productivity in the proto-industrial and the agricultural sectors: if a local agrarian system was highly labor-intensive males largely engaged in agriculture and women in proto-industry, including, for instance, silk weaving, so that the sexual division of labor was strongly accentuated. By contrast, where a labor-extensive agrarian system with poor employment opportunities prevailed and labor demand in the proto-industrial sector was high, such as in the cotton boom during the second half of the eighteenth century, men engaged in proto-industry, too, and were even found in tasks such as spinning, so that sexual differences in work roles were reduced.[50]

In the few situations where such a reduction in sex role differences occurred, it seems to have been accompanied by an increase in the economic and social power of women, young unmarried women in particular. With the rising independence of children from their parents, young adult women disposed of their cash fund by using it for conspicuous consumption, especially fancy dresses and pastry. Contemporary moralists even noted disapprovingly that young women, supported by their independent labor and consumption power, began to play an active role in the marriage market in that they approached young men, rather than being courted by the lads. Since households tended to be neolocal and less dependent on the inheritance of land among this rural proletariat, the arranging of marriages seems to have been primarily an affair of the couple alone, rather than of a wider kinship group. But while marriage became less often linked to property, it still remained tied to tangible material aspects such as work capacity. This can be concluded, for instance, from the high degree of endogamy among certain professions, in particular weavers.[51] As was later to become common among the working-class population of the nineteenth century, conspicuous consumption by young adults of both sexes, being related to individual earnings, served as an indicator of labor power and thereby constituted a new element of communication between the two sexes on the marriage market.

Such an individualization of marriage seems, however, to have been confined to populations where commodity production required little household capital. Particularly where capital requirements were high and where a strong attachment to land prevailed, the kin group and adults continued to play an important role in arranging marriages. One example of this sort comes from West Yorkshire, England, where woolen cloth was produced by independent clothiers who possessed substantial tracts of land. A low age at first marriage prevailed during the eighteenth century, but courtship was organized and supervised especially by adult women, and young couples remained dependent on their kin for access to land and support some time after marriage.[52]

PROTO-INDUSTRY AND THE LIFE COURSE

Early studies have suggested that life-course strategies of cottage workers provided a major explanation for the demographic behavior of proto-industrial populations and for proletarianization. Proto-industrial households tried to overcome the difficulties associated with the early phases of the family cycle during which the presence of young children increased consumption needs and reduced working capacity, particularly of women. Couples did so by marrying early, even during slack periods, in order to get through the difficult initial period at an age when their physical labor capacity was still high. In addition, they maximized marital fertility regardless of economic conditions since children of working age constituted an asset for the household economy. However, because children left their parents early, proto-industrial families were especially prone to poverty in later life. On an aggregate level, this family strategy with its demographic implications contributed to a situation where labor supply outran demand and, therefore, contributed to proletarianization.[53]

This representation of the proto-industrial family cycle refers at least implicitly to a situation where markets, particularly for farmland and financial capital in the form of credit, were largely non-existent. Such a situation may well have prevailed in most continental regions at the beginning of the early modern period and in some parts of Central Europe even later on. Nevertheless, in the early modern period, most West European regions experienced the emergence of land and rural credit markets to which peasants had access. This had a profound impact on the ways that cottage industry could be integrated into the life course. In order to explicate this point it may be useful to draw on both the permanent-income hypothesis and on the life-cycle-saving hypothesis.[54]

Peasants, like other people, hope to have a constant consumption level over their life course. This means that during life phases in which their income (or labor capacity in an economy still partly oriented to sub-sistence production) is high, they accumulate savings, and when their income is low, they run down savings and/or contract debts. In addition, peasants make use of household capital and land property, as well as the labor of family members. Part of their permanent income strategy may consist in securing an income during old age by attaching children and/or kin to the household. This in turn presupposes that these relatives find ways to make a livelihood in the household economy. Therefore, peas-ants will use their savings and possibly their debt-servicing capacity to accumulate property which will later serve as a means to attach to the household children or kin who can, in turn, support their elderly rela-tives. The operation of such a permanent income strategy, however, assumes the existence of efficient markets for financial capital (mortgage credit, for instance) and land that allow the incremental accumulation and divestment of funds; in other words, peasants must be able to invest and divest small amounts in these markets. If this is not possible, con-sumption has to follow income, and the life course is characterized by shifts between periods of affluence and conspicuous consumption and times of poverty and destitution.

Evidence for such an incremental accumulation strategy is provided, first, by data on age-specific occupations of men. For some parishes in both the Canton of Zurich and Twente (Netherlands) it has been shown that weavers were concentrated among younger age cohorts whereas farmers tended to be more frequent among older age groups. This sug-gests a pattern of intra-generational occupational mobility whereby households saved income from earnings in cottage industry and invested it in the family farm. Interviews (not conducted until late in the nine-teenth century) suggest that the farm was explicitly considered as a kind of savings bank by textile workers, although it appears that forestalling risk was a more powerful motive for this strategy than old-age security.[55]

Secondly, there is scattered evidence that weavers in particular were richer at the end of their life cycle than at marriage. During the last third of the eighteenth century, in the Württemberg parish of Laichingen, the post-mortem inventories of linen weavers displayed greater wealth on average than the inventory established at their marriage. Linen weavers in the Ribemont region in French Flanders, apart from the serious crisis that struck both agriculture and the manufacturing sector in the 1770s, usually bought more land than they sold during the three decades before the French Revolution. This sets them clearly apart from the day laborers who continually had to sell land, mostly to rich farmers, over

the same period. The importance of the land market for the family strategies of weavers is also visible in the fact that market activity was higher
in proto-industrial parishes than in purely agrarian ones. Finally, in a
proto-industrial parish of the Canton of Zurich households containing
weavers constituted the only social group that bought more land than it
sold over much of the family cycle. Solely during old age, when work
capacity declined and land correspondingly partly lost its value for the
household economy, there seems to have occurred a limited transformation of real estate into cash income from mortgage credit extended to
the buyers of the land that was gradually relinquished through the land
market.[56]

The accumulation of real estate and the growing importance of agriculture changed men's work role and upgraded their status, but it could
also affect the roles of women in the household economy. In a Swiss parish
characterized by a highly diversified proto-industrial sector by the late
seventeenth century, the activities performed by women underwent a shift
over the life course in close parallel to the occupational career of their
husbands. One such activity was cotton spinning which was organized
locally as a *Kaufsystem* (that is, there were no labor contracts specifying
the time period during which a certain amount of labor had to be completed). Some farmers' wives combined cotton spinning with agricultural
work. Thus, as the size of a household economy grew over the family cycle
and the agricultural component became more important, the work roles
of married women diversified and proto-industrial work became less systematic. While the outward status and material wellbeing of women
probably increased in parallel to their husbands', there occurred nevertheless a clear loss of labor status in the sense that women progressively
ceased to contribute to the household economy by way of independent
contact with outside markets over the course of the family cycle.[57]

All that has been said so far relates to weaving, that is, to a proto-
industrial activity connected with a certain amount of household capital
and considerable labor productivity. This was certainly an activity on
which it was easy to base life cycles of saving and spending, of indebtedness and accumulation. Families starting their careers under less
favorable conditions were much less able to pursue such a strategy. In a
comparison of several parishes of the Canton of Zurich, it is impossible
to demonstrate a life-cycle shift from proto-industry to farming among
males in regions where spinning was dominant, and where the high initial
outlays for buildings, instruments, draught-cattle, and so on, posed a
high barrier to entry against an incremental strategy of accumulating
agricultural property. And in the industrial parish for which the land
market was analyzed, the lower-class households of spinners, combers,

and non-proto-industrial artisans, after initial outlays connected with a neolocal pattern of household formation, sold more land than they bought over the rest of their family cycle. As suggested above, if savings opportunities are lacking and if debt-servicing capacity is low, consumption cannot follow a permanent income strategy but must be adjusted to current income. The only way to make profitable use of an income that exceeds the subsistence level for a time is to spend it on conspicuous consumption. In fact, when contemporary writers in Zurich talked about new consumption habits among proto-industrial workers, such as tobacco, coffee, and bread consumption or extravagant dressing, they usually seem to have had in mind these groups that were barred from a permanent income strategy.[58]

A crucial phase that seriously handicapped the potential for accumulation in the later stages of the family cycle of many households engaged in poorly remunerated manufacturing work was the time shortly after family formation, when the presence of small children reduced the labor power of married women and led to a deterioration in the balance between producers and consumers. For one parish in early eighteenth-century Zurich, the opportunity cost of one child aged less than five years in terms of forgone earnings from spinning has been estimated at roughly one-fifth of the weekly earnings of the mother. It is no wonder if one finds that indebtedness reaches a peak during this stage of the family cycle.[59] To liquidate this debt solely on the basis of a small income and later on under the constant threat that household members with a particularly high labor power might leave was obviously too hard a task for most households of the proto-industrial lower class. Lifelong proletarianization was clearly a dire reality for the majority of these families.

CONCLUSION

Proto-industrialization did not bring about an entirely new family system in the regions where it developed. Nevertheless, it added two important new parameters to the rural household economy: the productivity of labor and capital in domestic manufacture production. In addition, some proto-industrial branches were connected with a low level of cohesion among the family work group so that there developed a market for boarding which allowed solitary residents to subsist independently thanks to their wage-like labor in the manufacturing sector. The drastic increase in the potential for pluri-activity fostered the emergence of an economy of choice within the peasant household. The allocation of labor to different sectors of activity, household size, household formation, and life-course strategies all took account of these new parameters along with the agricultural part of the household economy. The potential threat of departure of young family members to take up the opportunities offered by a rising market for individual proto-industrial laborers may have provided an additional incentive for households to exploit the opportunities offered by a household economy of choice. In that sense, the proto-industrial family constitutes a distinctive element in the history of the European family.

PART II

STATE, RELIGION, LAW, AND THE FAMILY

CHAPTER 4

Developments in European Family Law
Lloyd Bonfield

THE PLACE OF LAW IN STUDIES OF FAMILY HISTORY

Contemporary sociological studies of the modern family frequently assess the impact of the law on family structure and family relations. Indeed, investigation can be quite detailed. Take, for example, current academic inquiry into the variables considered by a couple pondering the choice of whether to marry or to cohabit: scholarly consideration of the implications of the law on the resolution of such a fundamental aspect of family structure and relations has extended so far as to determine whether current tax laws under which the tax liability of a married couple exceeds that of a cohabiting couple with the same income, may contribute to the decision to remain unmarried.[1] Likewise, consider the politically charged debate on the consequences of public assistance; analysis has been undertaken to determine whether gearing the level of payment to the number of dependent children in a household encourages childbearing by welfare recipients.[2]

In contrast, historical studies of the development of family structure and relations appear less concerned with the law and its impact, at least those that investigate pre-modern times.[3] An example can be selected to illustrate the point: Michael Mitterauer and Reinhard Seider's masterly survey of the development of the European family from the latter Middle Ages to the present. The authors characterize the underlying trend in family relations as a journey "from patriarchy to partnership." As evidence they note that research in the area of family history falls into two discrete domains: the "biological" and the "socio-cultural."[4] According to this dichotomy, the former sphere consists largely of demographic studies of fertility, nuptiality, and mortality; while the latter focuses on family structure and family relationships. One "socio-cultural" feature that contributes to the structure of the family is largely absent (or perhaps more accurately, submerged) in the Mitterauer/Seider discussion: the law.

The absence of law in their study (and in those of other scholars) is peculiar, because law in European society has always defined the extent of the family for a variety of purposes, from inheritance to marriage. Indeed the Latin origins of the word "family" (*familia*) are derived largely from legal terminology. For "patriarchy" to have been sustained, the law must have either promoted it or at the very least acquiesced in its enforcement; the control of the patriarch in medieval and early modern Europe ultimately had to have a foundation and confirmation (let alone enforcement) at least in part in law, as it did ostensibly in Rome through provisions of Roman law.[5] Finally, when attitudes toward the family altered in the nineteenth century, the law must either have changed or its tenets have been partially ignored to usher in the new order.

Where law does appear in the work of historians of the family is when rights to property are directly addressed, but discussion is confined largely to rules and practices. Law as a "socio-cultural" process is not considered, and how family law was fashioned is not addressed. Law governing family relations seems to be regarded as a product of family history, and not a participant in shaping either its biological or cultural elements. In short, family law surfaces in historical studies of the family only occasionally, indirectly, and tangentially, as a collection of rules to be obeyed or circumvented as the case may be; its origins and nature, and its role as an integral part of the family and its structure, are not discussed in any great detail.[6]

While historians of the family do not focus upon law as a major force in the development of the family and its structure, legal historians with an interest in family law frequently fail to appreciate that legal rules and practice cannot be viewed in isolation from family structure and the nature of family relationship.[7] Among academic disciplines, legal history and social history are indeed strange bedfellows. The purpose of this chapter is to broach the divide and to summarize trends in a few areas of the law—inheritance, marriage and divorce, adoption, and the legal position of women—which will place in juridical context the developments in family structure and relationships discussed in this and other contributions to this volume.

From the onset, however, the modest scope of this chapter needs to be revealed. First it must be appreciated that Europe is a large geographic area which consisted of numerous jurisdictions, many of which overlapped, in which law was created and enforced. No single scholar is competent in all the relevant law; the linguistic obstacle alone is nearly insurmountable. In addressing the variety of law which obtained in the various areas of Europe during our period, I do not refer only to the obvious distinction between the common law of England and the reborn

Roman law that obtained on the continent. Rather I mean the variety of jurisdictions that operated within each of the two systems of law: the remnants of feudal law, ecclesiastical law, the law merchant,[8] and the myriad local customs that might modify a common law or civil law "rule" of positive law. Thus, in applying law to the descent of land—to take the most obvious example—it often appears that the applicable succession rule consisted of a local exception to the "national" inheritance law.

The historian of family law is therefore hampered by the complexity and the overlap of substantive rules of law; in addition, there is also the problem of the interplay of jurisdictions that actually heard and decided cases between individuals. With respect to courts to which resort could be had, there was no shortage of forums to which the litigious might turn. Various "national" courts, municipal courts, seigneurial courts, and church courts were constituted and had competence in defined (though somewhat hazily demarcated) subject matters. Moreover, any attempt to systematize the jurisdictional system in detail runs into the problem of local variation. What is perhaps uniform throughout Europe was the central role which church courts played in determining matters of marriage and legitimacy and the jurisdiction of the secular courts over succession to land, yet even in these areas one can find a court commandeering jurisdiction in an area that was at least theoretically beyond its competence.[9]

A more fundamental and interrelated concern which the legal historian interested in the influence of family law upon family structure and relations must address is how "law" functioned in the past. Even if the various rules of law which applied to the family in early modern Europe could be organized and the jurisdictions which enforced them systematically charted, consideration must be given to how law was implemented in past societies. We must consider what it meant to an individual in our period that there was "law" governing a particular aspect of family relations. Lawyers must acknowledge that the mere fact that a statute governing civil relations was "on the books" (in force) or a custom asserted or acknowledged in a particular jurisdiction does not prove that its dictates were followed strictly or that a breach of a criminal statute engendered sanction. To offer a modern example outside the area of family law, the present law of England and Wales in effect today provides sanctions for those who commit blasphemy.[10] There have been no recent successful prosecutions for blasphemy although presumably the law is infringed on a daily basis. A future historian would mislead students if he or she concluded that because the statute was in force and prosecutions were absent, blasphemy was uncommon, or indeed even that the

existence of the law meant that blasphemy was regarded as either criminal or even anti-social. Because formal law and actual behavior may
differ, and because law is not always a reliable barometer of a culture's
values, the legal historian must consider the extent to which there was
latitude to circumvent or ignore the law (for example, if bigamy was not
permitted, how often were cases of multiple marriage ferreted out; if
divorce was not permitted how easy was it to leave one's spouse and contract marriage with or live peacefully with another?). The ability to avoid
the law is particularly important in the area of familial property arrangements: to what extent was the law governing the distribution of family
property on death of a holder an indicator of how land devolved (for
example, were property holders able to create arrangements that might
deprive a wife of dower or a child of a legitimate share prescribed by
law)?

Laws which have fallen into disuse or can be circumvented aside, other
pitfalls await the historian of family law. Consider the extent to which
conduct in our own society is governed by behavioral norms that do not
have the force of law. The historian of law interested in the effects of
family law must attempt to determine whether the law or the non-legal
norms that we can exhume actually governed society. If it was conduct
independent of law that governed society in the past and sustained patriarchy, and then allowed it to dissolve, we may suggest that law intervened
less in domestic relations in the past than it does in the present.

Having pondered the limitations of our study, let us begin our social
history by investigating the characterizations of family law that have
been offered by legal historians, and then turn to a discussion of specific
areas.

LEGAL HISTORIANS' CATEGORIZATION OF FAMILY LAW

According to legal historians who write in the area, family law in Western
Europe at the close of the Middle Ages consisted of an intermingling of
various principles derived primarily from Roman law and from Germanic
customary law.[11] A third source of law governing family relations was the
law of the Christian Church, the canon law.[12]

We shall begin our survey with the civil rather than the ecclesiastical
law. In large measure, by the later Middle Ages both Roman law and
Germanic customary law were remnants of a past order, geared to
promote a family system revolving around the *domus* or house that had
largely disappeared in most of Western Europe. Before trying to draw
substantive distinctions among the various principles which informed the

systems, and explaining how the legal concepts were related to family structure, we may first draw rough geographical boundaries for the two systems of law.

Although few areas of Europe existed in which either Roman law or Germanic customary law existed in pristine form, that is to say without interacting with and therefore being influenced by each other or with other law, Germanic customary law obtained in the northern and central parts of France as well as in Central Europe, and was arguably also the basis for the common law of England. Although Germanic custom had invaded northern Italy, principles of Roman law remained stronger there than elsewhere in Europe and also obtained in southern France.

Certain aspects of both systems were similar, particularly with respect to the law governing the family and its property. Historians generally agree that both systems of law were patriarchal, although their emphasis may have differed. The patriarchy of Germanic law developed in large measure as a result of the absence of authority of central government, while in many respects Roman law was the manifestation of the authority of the Roman state. Thus while both systems were based upon extensive sanctioned paternal control, the ideological underpinnings and the origins of patriarchy differed.

The German patriarch was at least in theory the protector of his family's person and its property: he was the executive officer or general manager of a corporate entity, the house, with the power to manage both persons and property; but he was not the outright owner of the property of his house. Customs regarding the rights of family members which were crucial in determining inheritance on the death of the father, and rights of daughters in family property upon marriage were at least in theory fixed. But to the lawyer, the relevant question is whether the customs acknowledging these rights were mandatory and enforceable should their directives be breached. Answering this question, however, requires records of litigation (or other types of dispute resolution) that either were not kept or do not survive.

One of the most extensive recent studies of early medieval customary law concerns Normandy. The fragmentary evidence that remains suggests that even the venerable *Tres Ancien Coutumier*, produced over the course of the tenth and eleventh centuries and believed to have been fixed by the reign of William the Conqueror, were not mandatory. Exceptions to its dictates were permitted by feudal courts for local custom, and even individual family practice was permitted to stray from established rules of both Norman and local custom. Transfers of property and deviation from inheritance custom can be discerned but seem to have required the consent of those relatives whose interests might have been affected by the

legal act: children whose shares might be diminished by sale or by allowing another child property in excess of the customary share. The variety
of types of disposition discerned (from *inter vivos* and *post obit* gifts,
through sales, exchanges, and rentals, to conditional gifts and mortgages) suggests that conveyancers or notaries (those who draw up documents embodying the terms of these property arrangements) had very
early on devised the means by which individualized family strategies
could be developed and implemented, even where those designs deviated
from the dictates of the customal.[13]

What can the legal historian make of one example: should Normandy
be regarded as "typical" of the vast area of Europe in which Germanic
customary law obtained? While there is no reason to believe that
Normandy should be deemed either inherently typical or atypical,
custom as written or otherwise understood was not rigidly implemented
in the duchy. Evidence suggests that there was some ability to mold
it to individual familial requirements. What evidence we have suggests
that Germanic customary law should not be regarded as immutable;
there was latitude to make arrangements that might be inconsistent with
its formal, written dictates. Moreover, patriarchal control does not
appear to be without fetters; consent of those whose interests were
affected was required, although we dare not assume that it had to have
been freely given. Germanic law might be seen as allowing a bargaining
process (admittedly not necessarily between equals) among those with
interests in familial property.

If the logic of patriarchal control in Germanic customary law may
have rested upon the need for mutual protection and assistance due to
the absence of centralized power, the near absolute power of the paterfamilias over person and property was engrained in Roman law for
different reasons; it took its cue from the authority of the Roman state.
While the legal concept is legendary, the more extreme manifestations of
patriarchal control, like the power to put children to death or sell them
into slavery, were abandoned by the time of the Christianization of
Rome, if not before.[14] What may have remained in the hands of fathers
was the ability to control the choice of marriage partner, and the ancillary right to compel divorce if a child married without paternal consent.

With respect to the devolution of property, Roman law developed an
inheritance system which allowed the patriarch considerable control over
the descent of property while endeavoring to ensure the promotion of
family members. Roman law permitted a father to select his heir by will
and under inheritance law the chosen heir succeeded to the decedent's
estate. While the individual named in the will as heir need not have been
a family member, it was necessary to disinherit expressly if the testator

excluded an individual who would have taken property under the law of intestacy. Initially it was not essential to state the cause for disinheritance in the will, but by the later Republic, it was prudent, because wills could be overturned by heirs on the grounds that the testator's act in excluding or inadequately providing for him was "undutious." By the time of Justinian, specific grounds for disinheritance were recognized, as was the legitimate share, the *legitim*, the fixed proportion of property which the testator must leave to his heirs to exclude the possibility of having the will overturned as "undutious." The *legitim* ranged from one-quarter to one-half of the estate depending upon the number of heirs produced.[15]

Thus rather like the implementation of Germanic inheritance practice observed in Normandy, the Roman law as it evolved strove to strike a balance between both rights and expectations on the part of family members in receiving property and the ability of patriarchs to control the devolution of family property. In reality, neither system bestowed upon the patriarch the power to act unfettered. Both systems recognized inchoate "rights" to family property in descendants, while conceding to the patriarch some flexibility in determining those to whom property should pass, and at what point in time in the family life cycle devolution should occur. Freedom of disposition and rights to inherit are themes which we shall return to in trying to understand the nature of inheritance law in our period. Having explored the sources of civil law that had a bearing upon the family, we may now turn to the third source of law that governed family relationships, and in particular, the means by which families were formed through marriage: the law of the Christian Church.

THE CHRISTIAN CHURCH AS LAW GIVER

While various church courts continue to exist in modern Christendom, their current control over the lives of even the most devout Christian must be regarded as modest. Indeed, few present-day Christians may even be aware of the existence of church courts.[16] That Christianity had by the time our period begins an established body of substantive law, the canon law, a set of courts to enforce that law, the array of ecclesiastical courts, and had developed a procedure to bring causes before the courts (in short created a legal system of its own) might have surprised the early Christians who seem to have had some ambivalence towards religious law.[17] After the conversion of Constantine in the fourth century, however, Christianity no longer held a disparaging view of law. From this point onwards, the Church began to develop an organizational structure to pronounce law, the councils and synods, and in the centuries thereafter, tribunals were established to deal with disputes over discrete subject matter.[18]

In ecclesiastical matters, the most important law-giving authority in Christendom was that of the Bishops of Rome. By the fifth century, if not earlier, the papacy came to hear cases on appeal from the courts of bishops and archbishops throughout much of the converted areas of Europe and to pronounce more general rules governing church doctrine, morals, and most significantly for our purposes, marriage and family relations. In retrospect, ecclesiastical competence in the law of domestic relations may seem curious, because in modern times family law is central to civil law. However, marriage, the tie that created the family unit, had interested Christians from St. Paul onwards, and the regulation of entrance into marriage amongst the faithful must have appeared crucial to the Church's mission. Indeed, the family came to be regarded as a central component of Christian life; marriage and family relations came within the competence of the Church and ultimately its system of courts. We may briefly trace how this anomaly emerged.

The fall of Rome in the fifth century resulted in the fragmentation of the Church. The authority of the popes came to be questioned, and the unity of Christendom and of canon law dissolved. Yet the development of both Christian theology and church law continued. Periods of centralized secular authority, for example relative stability brought about by the Carolingian empire, re-established (at least from time to time) the unity of church doctrine and central authority. But it was not until the reformers of the eleventh century, and in particular the canonists inspired by the papacy of Pope Gregory VII, that existing tenets of canon law were revitalized, and new law was added.[19]

Likewise, ecclesiastical jurisdiction was strengthened. The revitalized courts brought two interrelated consequences for canon law: more law was promulgated by synods; and an increased number of cases heard in church courts resulted in more judge-made law. The resultant expansion of ecclesiastical law required synthesis, and the stage was set for the great texts of the twelfth through to the fourteenth century, the most notable of which was the *Decretum* of Gratian. Secular law also made its contribution to church law. During that same period, Roman law became the basis for the development of the *ius commune*, a civil law for continental Europe. The two bodies of law, civil and ecclesiastical, complemented and supplemented each other.[20]

A substantial component of both canon law doctrine and church court business in the Middle Ages concerned the regulation of the family: law governing marriage formation, legitimacy, and sexual conduct. It is not clear why secular authority ceded control over these issues (indeed, in areas of Europe under the sway of the Eastern Orthodox Church, national courts had a more significant role to play in enforcing church law, and were frequently unprepared to follow ecclesiastical directives)[21]—areas which were of considerable importance to the laity—to the church courts, but the impact of the legal doctrine established therein still influences modern law. The requirements that had to be satisfied in order to form a valid marriage and the refusal of the church courts to sanction divorce once a valid marriage had been contracted were perhaps the most important aspects of church doctrine on family law, a topic to which we shall return.

The Church's success in securing jurisdiction over the determination of whether individuals were married had an important consequence in the area of inheritance. Church court decisions adjudicating whether a couple had contracted a valid marriage were crucial in establishing rights in property, and, in particular, the descent of land. Secular law allowed individuals to inherit property only if they were legitimate issue. Whether a child was legitimate depended of course upon whether his or her parents were married. Thus while church courts did not determine rights in property, jurisdiction to determine legitimacy vested in the Church the authority to determine whether a person might be able to assert inheritance rights.[22]

Marriage and legitimacy aside, a further important area of church concern was sexual continence. For various reasons, the Church endeavored to confine sexual relations within marriage. Church courts, primarily those at the local level, that of the archdeacon, attempted to ferret out adulterers and fornicators, as well as to uncover and to punish those who committed sodomy or incest.[23]

Thus the medieval Christian Church was an active participant in establishing the law that regulated family relations at the time our period commenced. As we shall see, the theological formulation of marriage formation came under attack, as did the question of whether marriage once contracted ought to remain indissoluble, as our era progressed. But while reform occurred in the sixteenth century in most of Christendom, medieval marriage law remained largely intact in England until nearly the close of our period.[24] Let us begin our investigation of family law with a discussion of the development of medieval marriage law and illustrate how it was transformed by the Reformation.

THE MEDIEVAL LAW OF MARRIAGE

The canon law's dictate on the formation of marriage as it evolved in the Middle Ages was striking because it required neither parental consent, clerical participation, witnesses, nor consummation for the formation of a binding and indissoluble marriage. This is not to say that the Church did not prefer solemnization in church before witnesses. Indeed, canon law prescribed a complex process for entrance into marriage which included first obtaining parental consent, then community ratification through the posting of banns in the parish church, and, finally, clerical participation in the nuptial mass. Yet the Church also came to recognize marriages which were entered into "clandestinely," that is to say, contracted outside of church and without regard to the process sketched out above. Such marriages were regarded as valid and could be entered into without consent of parents in either of two ways. The first was upon the exchange between a couple of lawful age (14 for boys and 12 for girls) who were free to marry (not already married and not barred from marriage by consanguinity or affinity) of words of mutual consent to marry expressed in the present tense (I take thee as my husband; I take thee as my wife). Alternatively, the expression of words of future consent (I will have thee as my husband; I will have thee as my wife) was sufficient to create a marriage if followed by sexual intercourse.[25]

This formulation of the requisites for valid marriage, the so-called "consent theory of marriage formation," emerged from a dialogue amongst canon lawyers in which various other requirements such as parental consent and consummation were strenuously advocated.[26] One must concede that there was a certain beauty in the simplicity of expression of these "Alexandrine rules" of marriage formation (so called because they were expressed by Pope Alexander III (1159–1181) in response to actual cases brought to him). In practice, however, the recognition of a marriage entered into without recourse to church solemnization was what modern lawyers call a "litigation breeder." Even though the requirements were minimal, conflict could arise as to whether they were satisfied, and because witnesses need not be present, it might be difficult to substantiate whether an exchange of promises in the present tense had actually been made. Two types of suit might follow: one involved church law—matrimonial causes raising the issue of whether a marriage had been entered into; and another involving secular law—disputes over property relations which resulted from an alleged union.

As to the former, marriage formation cases, the requirements fixed by canon law always left the possibility of a good faith mistake on the part of the couple as to whether consent had been exchanged. Even where the parties were acting in good faith, the difference in verbiage of present and future consent was not striking; and as F. W. Maitland, the prominent late nineteenth- and early twentieth-century English legal historian noted, of all individuals, lovers might be less likely than others to be concerned with the nuance of tenses.[27]

Cases of inexact expression aside, there was also the possibility of a dispute between a couple over whether a marriage had actually been contracted because one (or indeed both) had undergone a change of heart: one party wished not to be married to the other or perhaps even desired to be free to contract marriage with another. In cases in which the existence of a marriage was challenged, the most ticklish issue was the question of proof; because there was no need for witnesses to be present, whether words were exchanged in the present tense in certain cases might be substantiated only by the testimony of the parties themselves. Thus if both parties wished to terminate the marriage (which of course ought not to be permitted by agreement since once contracted a valid marriage was regarded as indissoluble) they could merely agree to lie as to whether words of present consent had been uttered. If the parties had cohabited, they might deny words of present or future consent had been exchanged and suffer the penalties for fornication, rather than be denied the opportunity to be free from an unwanted union. But the more likely scenario was one in which one party wished to deny that a marriage existed, perhaps because a more satisfactory match had been negotiated with another person. Since divorce was not possible, the errant spouse whose attentions focused elsewhere had to deny a valid marriage had been entered into if he or she wished to join with another in matrimony. If a spouse wished to terminate a union, it had to be proved that the marriage could not have lawfully occurred because the spouse was not free to marry or did so under duress or was barred by consanguinity or affinity.

That the Alexandrine "rules" were enforced can be discerned from the records of the church courts.[28] Why the canon law prescribed one method of marriage formation, but allowed Christians to circumvent the process is a subject of debate amongst ecclesiastical and social historians. Both logic and history suggest that the Church should have opposed clandestine marriage. In the first place, the Church, to bolster its own authority, should have required clerical intervention for a valid marriage to be created. Moreover, Germanic custom had required consummation for the establishment of a valid marriage. Finally, both Roman and Germanic law presumed parental consent to the marriage of their children. But none of the above requirements heretofore included in the tripartite

European legal heritage was embodied in the canon law marriage formation "rules."

It is not clear why individual consent as the requisite for marriage formation began to be considered sacred. Some of the many explanations
that have been proffered can be here rehearsed. Perhaps theology over-
came logic or custom. Advocates of the consent theory could point to
the example of Mary and Joseph—whose marriage was based upon
agreement alone, and had never been consummated—to repudiate a contention that sexual intercourse was necessary to render a union binding.[29]
Moreover, marriage between Christians had been transformed from a
civil relationship involving promises to a sacrament; the transition might
suggest that consent had to be individual to be binding for a person to
accept a sacrament. One could contract on behalf of another, but sacrament conveys a personal connotation. Finally, it has been noted that
canon law began to focus upon the free expression of consent to create
binding relationships in other areas.[30]

Whatever the logic of the consent theory, there were serious ramifications to accepting secret promises as sufficient to create a binding union.
While the Church ceded control over the process of joining a couple,
arguably those most adversely affected by the consent theory were
parents. If couples could privately exchange promises to be married, it
rendered parental control over the process of marriage difficult. Arguably
the method in the madness can be found in the Church's desire to free
children from parental bonds: to make choice of marriage partner personal. Though perhaps not so intended, the Alexandrine marriage
formation requirements did have the effect of strengthening the Church's
control over marriage through the church courts; the loose "rules" established were frequently the subject of litigation. Parental control over
marriage was replaced by church mediation of the marriage process.[31]

The extent to which the dictates of canon law were adhered to in practice has been the subject of debate. In particular, whether children were
really free to contract unions without parental consent has been questioned. We have noted that canon law in the thirteenth century seems to
have veered from the course established by previous law. Likewise, much
was at stake; marriage affected the inheritance of property, the continu-
ance of a patriline, and patriarchal authority. Marriage formation rules
certainly challenged the last of these, because a child could choose his
or her spouse without parental consent by the mere uttering of words.
Although we can demonstrate that clandestine marriages were enforced,
we must question how frequently such unions were contracted.

Here we can only speculate, and offer the opposing view. Historians
of marriage and the family in the Middle Ages have viewed marriage as

a process rather than as a single event.[32] In the case of both the peasantry and the landed classes, historians have described a variety of steps that were undertaken by couples and their families ranging from the economic, such as in the negotiation of marriage portions, to the emotional, the successive meetings of the couple, bundling (spending the night together, typically in a barn while clothed), and betrothal, through to the religious, the formal exchange of vows in church. The point in the process at which the community regarded the couple as married is not always easy to discern from surviving sources. The legal rules discussed above are an important indicator, because the validity of marriage was determined by the Church and its courts. As we noted, the point at which marriage was in canon law validly contracted was crucial because the canon law regarded a valid marriage as indissoluble. Because divorce was not permitted, the crucial question in the minds of those in the marriage process might be: at what point did a party no longer have the option of backing out?

While church doctrine requiring individual consent diminished the ability of parents to control the selection of a child's spouse, another position adopted by the Church limited the universe of choice of marriage partner: the rules establishing the prohibited degrees of consanguinity. In the eleventh century, the Church prohibited marriage between individuals related up to and including the seventh degree.[33] While the prohibitions were reduced by the Fourth Lateran Council (1217) to bar unions between those related in the fourth degree, the prohibition continued to extend to those related by affinity as well as tied by blood.[34] By excluding such a broad array of relations with whom union was not possible, church doctrine came into conflict with secular marriage strategies, because endogamous marriages were useful in preserving property within a patriline. Marriage of cousins, for example, might bring together a patrimony that had been divided by siblings when both a son and daughter had married.[35] By the twelfth century, however, such strategies might be pursued only after purchasing a dispensation from the Church.

Thus the canon law had pronounced on matters of marriage formation; yet there were limits to its authority. Although much academic discussion has focused upon the origins, impact, and enforcement of Alexander's formulation, papal pronouncements did not apply throughout Europe. The Eastern Orthodox Church did not accept consent as sufficient to create a valid marriage: in the Greek East as distinct from the Latin West, the priest and the nuptial blessing were required, at least in theory if not always in practice.[36] Moreover, secular authority in West European Christendom was a powerful force with considerable interest

in the practical implications of the theologically inspired marriage formation rules. Accordingly, secular law might intervene and even replace
canon law, albeit in only few instances. For example, the canon law formulation was not in force in the Kingdom of the Two Sicilies, where the
civil law required a priest to be present and a nuptial blessing given for
a marriage to be valid. Although direct opposition to canon law may have
been rare, discouraging secret marriages by inflicting civil penalties on
individuals for contracting them and on clerics for participation in them
was not. And finally the Church itself, through its power to dispense with
the canon law requirements, became a source for circumventing its own
legal mandates.[37]

DEVELOPMENTS IN THE LAW OF MARRIAGE

While the canon law dictate on marriage formation discussed above was
pronounced and enforced in church courts in Western Christendom, we
noted above that prior to Pope Alexander III's resolutions there were dis-
cordant views in the thirteenth century even amongst canon lawyers as
to what acts should be required to constitute a valid marriage. The Reformation offered the opportunity for a reconsideration of various areas of
canon law, foremost among them the law of marriage and divorce. In the
first place, Protestant reformers who sought to remake the institutions
and doctrine of Christianity questioned theology, and in particular
whether marriage should be regarded as a sacrament. But they also pondered the implications of the law of marriage, which they regarded as a
misguided body of rules geared to promote the virtue of celibacy (which
they believed was outmoded) and to reinforce the undercurrent of misogyny (which they considered the result of a misreading of Christ's teaching) that permeated the Church. Although in law as in other areas of
godly concern, Protestant theologians did not adhere to a uniform view
on precisely how the canon law formulation ought to be revised, there
was general agreement amongst them that marriage should be under the
jurisdiction of the secular courts. Yet a dichotomy was drawn. While the
enforcement mechanism of marriage law should be secular, reformers
believed that its substance ought to be governed by, and be consistent
with, biblical norms. By invoking and stressing the religious nature of
the marriage vow, the reformers reserved a significant role for themselves
in determining the substance of marriage law in Reformation Europe.[38]

Like the canon lawyers, Protestant theologians believed that consent
was the integral element that rendered the marriage vow binding. But
while the canon law in their view was concerned only with the free will

of individuals in entering into marriage, Protestant theologians considered other interests. The Protestant reformers were greatly concerned
with disorder and decay within the family, and they tied marriage formation to familial authority. For them freedom of choice of marriage
partner was a prospect to be greeted with mixed sentiments, because it
undermined support for the parental authority which was an important
feature of Protestant theology. For example, Luther seemed to regard
parental consent as in opposition to individual agreement, and regarded
the latter as the binding and legitimate force in marriage formation.
But he recognized that parental intervention was justified on economic
grounds as well as being consistent with religious authority, noting the
significant financial investment that parents made in their offspring.[39]
This is not to say that parents were to bully or impose their choice; ideally
a parent–child agreement on choice of marriage partner was to emerge
by consensus rather than coercion.[40]

The secret exchange of vows tolerated with canon law was another
concern of the Protestant reformers. The consent theory of the canon
law that sanctioned unions formed in secret, permitting vows uttered in
private to create a marriage, promoted, according to some reformers, a
variety of other ills, most notably licentiousness. The reformers created
their own idealized means of marriage formation. Luther's conceptual-
ization of the marriage process began with engagement and ended with
celebration in church. The community, as well as the couple's family, was
to be involved in the course of establishing the union.[41]

Finally, Protestant reformers were opposed to the canon law's understanding of the prohibited degrees of consanguinity for both theological
and practical reasons. The reformers were concerned by the slender biblical authority offered by canonists in justification for so wide a net of
prohibited unions. In addition, Protestant reformers saw the canon law
rules as irrational, because they added a second impediment to parental
control and inhibited the construction by families of suitable marriage
strategies: in short, according to the reformers, Alexander's rules allowed
clandestine marriages to be binding, thereby depriving parents of control
over their children's choice of marriage partner; and the numerous impediments to marriage made what might be considered reasoned choice of
partner, when considering long-term patrilineal interests, subject to a
variety of obstacles.[42]

While the reformers devoted considerable attention to reconsidering
these rules, the onset of the Reformation did not alter the law or practice of marriage formation at once. Some rural areas of Protestant
Germany, for example, did not immediately alter the existing marriage
law. Indeed, in some areas secular courts were not in place to enforce the

retailored regime; those local courts which existed were not well equipped for an expanded role. Prior to the Reformation the ecclesiastical courts had developed an impressive apparatus to enforce church law which extended into the provinces. Many rural areas had no need for expansive secular courts other than the seigneurial court, so a jurisdictional vacuum was created immediately after the Reformation when church courts ceased operation.[43]

The magnitude of the interests at stake rendered attempts at revamping marriage law and enforcing the new order more difficult. To revise and to tighten the requirements for a binding union had social consequences as well as religious ones. While parents might be pleased with the change pronounced by the reformers because they could better control their children's choice of spouse, and the village elite might be able to regulate more effectively the sexual behavior of the young, marriage as means of upward social mobility was jeopardized by the more stringent process of marriage formation. It was not only in legend that a man or woman prospered by finding an impulsive and wealthy partner who hastily consented to a union. The consequences of the enforcement of Protestant thinking on marriage formation, coupled with more rigorous checks on the behavior of youths, created a clash of cultures which characterized many aspects of the Reformation.[44]

Thus while the reformers all agreed that marriage should no longer be regarded as a sacrament, that municipal law should control marriage creation, and that parental consent should be essential to create a marriage, public acceptance of their changes was neither immediate nor pervasive. Secret marriages continued to present problems even after the marriage laws were revamped; much magistrate court business in reformed cities such as Zurich was devoted to enforcing the requirement of public ceremony.[45] Likewise even in smaller towns, marriage cases abound with the same issues of consent raised as were considered before the Reformation. It was not as easy to reform manners at it was to redraft law.[46]

Indeed, strict interpretation of marriage formation law brought with it its own series of problems. If a marriage had to be celebrated in church, what should become of the seduced, pregnant woman who had been lured to her ignominious fate by the promise of marriage? While to allow secret marriages to be created by such conduct arguably encouraged promiscuity, the reverse was not the case: tightening the requirements did not eradicate out-of-wedlock pregnancies. Most towns chose to punish transgressors who had sex prior to marriage, and even when children were produced refused to regard their parents as married.[47]

Moreover, while the requirement of church marriage increased parental control over choice of marriage partner, it could not extirpate individual choice by children. In the first place, children did not require parental consent after they reached a threshold age. This age varied by jurisdiction, ranging from about 22 to 25 for men and 20 to 24 for women. Thus if a child was prepared to wait out his or her parents, it was unnecessary to obtain parental consent. But even when underage children married without consent, it was not always easy to have the marriage dissolved. In cases in which consummation had occurred, it was often regarded as more sound by theologians and courts to have parents ratify the union, rather than seek to set it aside. In some cases, however, marriages were voided for want of parental consent, particularly in situations where the children were in their teens.[48]

It was also not clear precisely what the requirement of parental consent embodied in the reformed law actually meant in practice. Could a parent refuse to allow a child to marry anyone? A modern lawyer might ask whether parental consent to a partner could be unreasonably withheld. Although parental consent was required for marriage until the child reached his or her early twenties, developing theology and social mores were conspiring to limit parental choice of marriage partner. Over the next two centuries, a tendency, more pronounced in some areas and social classes than in others, developed to allow a child to veto his or her parents' choice in the sixteenth century, and then to permit a parent to veto the child's choice towards the beginning of the eighteenth century. But even in the early sixteenth century, the reformers expressed concern about parental coercion; ideally the choice of marriage partner should be made in concert, with the parent guiding the child's choice.[49]

Catholic Europe responded to the onslaught of Protestant reform with a reassessment of its own doctrine on marriage formation. For the purpose of revitalizing church administration and doctrine, an assembly met at Trent in the Austrian Alps three times from 1545 to 1563. In 1564, a papal bull was issued promulgating the decrees and canons of the Council of Trent which set the tenor of Catholic law on marriage until the present day. The ensuing papal bull essentially codified the Catholic law of marriage, resolving the controversial issues of mode of celebration, parental consent, and prohibited degrees of consanguinity. In the first place, the Council put an end to clandestine marriages in Catholic Europe by requiring church celebration for a marriage to be valid. Thus, with one exception, that of England, Christian Europe was united in refusing to recognize secret marriages. However, the Council refused to require parental consent to unions as some Protestant reformers had urged, and staunchly adhered to the position established by Alexander's decretals, that free and voluntary consent of the parties themselves was all that was necessary to contract a valid marriage. Finally, the Council

limited the prohibition on marriage to the fourth degree of consanguinity, but included within the ban kin by affinity (though the number
of degrees was reduced to two) as well as spiritual kin (godparents).
Finally, the Council of Trent barred the faithful from entering into any
relationship, such as concubinage, that was not lawful marriage.[50]

While the Council of Trent set out the position of the Catholic Church
on the requirements for the formation of a valid marriage, its reception
by secular law was mixed. In Italy, where the Reformation made only the
most modest inroads, Tridentine requirements on marriage formation
were respected. As noted above, the priest became the sole individual who
had authority to marry Christians, and the office became the exclusive
marriage registry. It was not until the late eighteenth and early nineteenth
centuries that the state in continental Europe asserted authority over
marriage formation.[51]

Yet adherence to Tridentine dictates was limited even in some areas of
Catholic Europe. France provides an example of two problems that faced
the Catholic Church in the post-Reformation period. In the first place,
the Church had lost its authority to legislate with binding force in the
area of marriage. It was necessary for the king to bring the Tridentine
provisions into municipal law by decree. In 1579, the main features of
the Catholic marriage formation rules were received into French law by
the Ordinance of Blois, but it was not until a decree of 1639 that French
law provided that marriage would be deemed a nullity if it was not
celebrated before a priest in the parish of one of the two spouses before
at least four witnesses.[52]

The second, and perhaps more significant, problem that faced the
Catholic Church was that it no longer held a monopoly over the celebration of marriage among European Christians. Protestants in France
until the revocation of the Edict of Nantes (1685) could be married
by their ministers according to their own rite without recourse to the
requirements either of the Ordinance of Blois or Tridentine dictates. A
marriage celebrated in France by a Protestant minister had the same
binding force as one celebrated by a Catholic priest. After 1685, however,
Protestantism (and therefore its ministers) was deemed no longer to exist.
Marriage had to follow the pattern established by post-Tridentine secular
law to be valid, and in particular, marriages had to be celebrated by a
Catholic priest. Some evidence exists to demonstrate that French Protestants traveled abroad to marry. The Enlightenment brought with it some
relief for Protestants, and by edict in 1787 they were permitted once again
to marry before a minister whose authority to marry was derived from
secular law.[53]

England presents perhaps the most curious response to the Reformation and the Catholic response to Protestant attacks upon what both sides regarded as antiquated marriage formation law. Unlike in the rest of Protestant Europe, the Church of England retained exclusive control over marriage formation, record-keeping, and litigation regarding the validity of marriage.[54] However, the Church of England largely retained the pre-Tridentine canon law of marriage. In short, Protestant England continued to adhere to the Alexandrine perception of marriage: marriage required only individual consent and was indissoluble.

The result in England was a considerable rise in the number of clandestine marriages, particularly after 1600. These unions, formed by mutual consent alone, did not follow the process set out by canon law for the solemnization of vows, but were nonetheless valid. By the seventeenth century, an alternative marriage formation process emerged. Clandestine marriages came to be celebrated by those who were (or held themselves out to be) in holy orders, but who conducted the ceremony without regard to canon law: outside of the parish of the couple, without regard to the prescribed time for marriages, and without license or the calling of banns. During the course of the seventeenth and eighteenth centuries, the demand for such marriages gave rise to a brisk business in certain areas which claimed (or feigned) exemption from the requisites established by canon law: the Tower of London in the 1630s, the Minories in the 1680s, and the Fleet Prison chapel in the early eighteenth century. In the provinces, individual clerics willing to perform such irregular ceremonies had considerable local reputations.[55]

Clandestine marriage in England, then, took on an aura of seemliness by the seventeenth century. Why it became so popular is a matter of some historical debate: it allowed privacy; it was less expensive; it allowed freedom from parental intervention. Yet it was the latter which probably led to the demise of clandestine marriage in 1753 when Parliament passed "An Act for the Better Prevention of Clandestine Marriages."[56] After nearly a hundred years of unsuccessful attempts by the landed class to protect their children and their inheritances from ill-considered unions, Parliament passed a statute which mandated that parental consent for marriages of children under the age of 21 be required for a marriage to be valid. Moreover, selection of spouse could be monitored because marriages were thereafter required to be public and could be celebrated only after the calling of banns in the parish church. Thus, about two centuries after the Reformation and the Council of Trent, England rejoined the rest of Christian Europe by sweeping aside the Alexandrine "consent" theory of marriage formation.

MARRIAGE IN OTTOMAN EUROPE

So far we have focused upon that part of Europe that was under the sway of Christianity, and subject to the secular law of Christian rulers. Yet at the beginning of the sixteenth century, a large swathe of territory in southeastern Europe was controlled by the Ottoman empire, and under the sway of Islam. Some history and geography may be necessary to place the influence of Islam in perspective. We can begin with the fall of Constantinople in 1453. After their conquest, the Turks continued to move west. By the middle of the sixteenth century most of present-day Hungary, a part of southern Poland and all of the Balkans were under Turkish administration; it was not until the end of the seventeenth century that the tide turned against Turkish military might, and the Habsburgs began the steady process of reconquest. The Ottomans created a remarkable administrative structure, as well as a set of courts of law.[57] While non-Muslims were heavily taxed and indeed subject to onerous charges (for example, the enslavement of Christian Balkan children to serve in the military), Christianity was not banished from Ottoman territory, and Christians retained a considerable degree of self-government.[58] Theologically, an uneasy détente emerged: the Turks permitted Christian religious practice, and the Eastern Church regarded Islam as a form of Christian heresy no more abhorrent than the Christianity of the Latin West.[59] In the early modern period, there was (and indeed continues to be until our own time) a significant difference between Islamic and Christian Europe with respect to legal and social conceptions of marriage, and it is to that divide which we now turn.

First let us briefly sketch Islamic marriage law. Unlike Christianity which regards marriage either as a religious sacrament or an event replete with religious significance, Islam considers marriage as a civil contract. Legal commentators observing Muslim law regard the marriage as a form of "sale": marriage occasions a transfer of the guardianship of a woman from her father (or surrogate) to her husband in which a payment is made to the wife.[60] Without the payment stipulated, Islamic law considered the marriage to be incomplete, and until payment a wife might justifiably refuse sexual advances from her husband. Other commentators on Islamic law view the relationship in a less commercial light. Although they concede that the transfer of property was an essential part of the marriage bargain, the union, they note, had to be entered into voluntarily, though arguably women may have been unaware of their right not to be married without their free consent.[61]

But perhaps the most significant difference between Islamic law and the law of Christendom is that the former allowed for polygyny, and, as we shall see, permitted divorce. Much has been written regarding the social and economic basis for polygyny, and the distinctions between the two family types are fundamental both in terms of law and with respect to family relations.[62] Yet the extent to which men had (as opposed to may have been able by law to have had) more than one wife is not clear. Regardless of the extent to which poligyny was practiced, it was permitted by law, and therefore had some connection with the underlying theory of domestic relations law.

Entry into marriage probably varied with respect to class in each society in the Ottoman empire; poor women probably had a greater freedom to marry than did the wealthy. The propertied class in both Islamic and Christian societies used written agreements to set out the obligations of marriage. Islamic marriage contracts, however, seem to have been more comprehensive than their European counterparts, primarily because the marriage might be terminated before death, by divorce. While the English or continental Christian marriage contract might set out financial arrangements incident to marriage—the marriage portion or dowry of the bride which was transferred from her family to the groom or his family; an income for the wife to enjoy during marriage; and support for her life should the prospective wife survive her husband—the marriage contract in Islamic societies went further.[63] Because a man might take another wife, or the prospective marriage might be terminated, the marriage contract might also set out the woman's rights (and those of her children) under such circumstances: whether transfers of property occasioned by the marriage (which tended to pass from the husband to his wife rather than the reverse, as obtained in Christian Europe) had to be returned; and what level of child support had to be paid. While local law might govern such situations, private agreement embodied in marriage contracts prevailed.[64] These contracts were often quite detailed, setting out residential and maintenance arrangements.

There is evidence to suggest that there was a significant quantity of litigation over the terms of marriage contracts in the Ottoman empire.[65] Some cases seem to revolve around payment of obligations occasioned by divorce stipulated in the contract. Other cases of intra-spousal conflict relate to the payment of sums required to sustain the wife in a manner appropriate to her husband's status. While litigation over fiscal aspects of marriage arrangements occurred in Christian Europe, suits were very rarely commenced between the spouses. Since divorce was not an option until after the Reformation (and, as we shall see, only grudgingly permitted), controversies tended to be related to whether obligations owed by the bride or groom's family under the marriage settlements had been fulfilled.

DIVORCE IN CHRISTIAN EUROPE BEFORE
THE REFORMATION

Whether divorce, the termination of a validly contracted marriage, ought to be permitted, and if so, under what circumstances, has preoccupied and perplexed the legal order of most European societies for centuries. Max Rheinstein, one of the most prominent comparative lawyers of the twentieth century, noted that the extent to which law recognizes the ability of a married couple to divorce could be related to societal notions of the relative importance of individual autonomy versus communitarian values. If, Rheinstein hypothesized, the individual pursuit of happiness is a natural right, and one greatly valued by society, why should the state seek to prevent the termination of an unhappy union? On the other hand, if the institution of marriage exists to serve societal interests, or indeed even to further spiritual ones rather than the needs of an individual, ought these ends to be compromised merely to accommodate an unsatisfactory personal relationship?[66] While these abstract questions may be posed, one may wonder whether these juxtaposed interests are employed to justify societal choice rather than to direct it. For permitting divorce has a number of ramifications which can be readily observed in our own day: the interests of children produced by the union are at stake, as is the allocation of property accumulated by and during the marriage. Societies which do not permit divorce must deal with the implications of unhappy unions, but they are able to avoid the ramifications of broken marriages.

The refusal of Christianity to permit divorce, largely guided by a selective reading of the teaching of Christ, is an example of Christianity's divergence from its Roman and Jewish legal roots.[67] Roman law before the conversion of Constantine permitted divorce[68] as did Jewish law,[69] although the latter may have discouraged it by creating a series of procedural formalities which had to be satisfied in order to obtain divorce. Moreover, with respect to Judaism, there was considerable discussion amongst the various rabbinical schools as to the appropriate grounds that had to be demonstrated, issues that in Roman law were resolved by edict, both before and immediately after Christianization of the empire in the fourth century.[70]

Given the later antipathy toward divorce, Christianity was slow to ban it entirely. Even as late as the twelfth and thirteenth centuries, canonists recognized, albeit reluctantly, certain circumstances that would permit not only a separation of a married couple, but also divorce with the ability to remarry. In the view of the canonists, divorce should be permitted only in extreme situations, for example, those in which adultery or impotence could be proved.[71] But with the acceptance of the consent theory of marriage, the Church came to oppose outright divorce with the ability to remarry: having consented to marry freely, the spouse was required to live with his or her choice regardless of ramifications. Rather than allow divorce, and therefore permit a second marriage, the Church allowed only separations (which did not allow the couple to remarry) in the more difficult cases of serious marital discord and impotence.[72] Annulments (which would permit a further marriage to be contracted) were granted in marriages in which an impediment could be demonstrated (for example those contracted that were within the prohibited degrees of consanguinity), but were only grudgingly conceded. Historians of marriage litigation in the medieval church courts have concluded that actions to annul were a relatively small proportion of the cases brought before the church courts, and that judges required rigorous proof of an impediment before granting an annulment.[73]

Thus on the eve of the Reformation, the Church largely had prohibited divorce with the ability to remarry.[74] Decrees of annulment, however, could be granted, although they were sparingly issued. By allowing marriages which had existed, often for many years, to be subsequently declared invalid, the Church created a thorny issue for itself and its legal order; it was necessary to categorize the status of the offspring of unions which were subsequently declared by church courts never to have existed. Logically, legitimacy would be at issue where a marriage was regarded as never having been contracted. The recognition of divorce in Roman law presented no such problem, because there was no question of whether the children born during the course of a valid marriage were legitimate; in the reign of Justinian, the rights of children of divorced parents were confirmed and strengthened.[75] However, annulment forced the Church to confront the issue. A decretal of Alexander III settled the question by holding that a child born of a marriage subsequently annulled was legitimate, and should be entitled to full inheritance rights. Moreover, such children were entitled to support from their parents regardless of whether the union which produced them had been declared to be a nullity.[76] In this fashion, the Church protected the status and the inheritance rights of children of marriages its courts "put asunder."

THE IMPACT OF THE REFORMATION ON DIVORCE

The obvious connection between marriage and its dissolution placed divorce at the forefront of discussion by the reformers in their consideration of family law. Because reformed thinkers held divergent views on the question of divorce, it is difficult to set out a common position. The view that marriage was no longer a sacrament might lead one to conclude that the reformers would take a lenient attitude toward divorce. Such was not the case. Although other reformers were more tolerant, both Luther and Calvin were reluctant to allow marriages to be set aside. Both were prepared, however, to grant a general exception for sexual misconduct, and they were prepared to sanction divorce on the grounds of adultery, or if the spouse's conduct might lead to adultery (refusal of sexual intercourse or desertion). For Luther and Calvin, however, incompatibility was another matter; they considered the inability to live in harmony insufficient grounds to dissolve a marriage: one ought to bear a cruel husband or a dreadful wife (or the reverse) with Christian patience. Even divorce on the ground of adultery, in their view, was not to be granted liberally. Often the injured party (usually the husband) had to demonstrate that he was innocent. Moreover, a repentant spouse was to be forgiven. If, for example, one party repented, the aggrieved partner was required to resume marital relations. Likewise, a spouse who returned after a period of absence was to be forgiven, though perhaps not if the partner was a wife who had committed adultery.[77]

Other reformers, however, advocated enlarging the grounds for divorce. Ulrich Zwingli, for example, advocated expanding the grounds for divorce to "any greater reason," which included madness, and violent behavior. Martin Bucer was perhaps the most liberal among the reformers. He even looked to the Roman law for inspiration, and suggested that divorce be granted to a woman whose husband accused her of adultery and to a man whose wife procured an abortion. In Zurich, for example, divorce was permitted for adultery, impotence, willful desertion, grave incompatibility, sexually incapacitating illness, and deception.[78]

Civil divorce courts were established in reformed cities and towns, and the courts strictly applied the prevailing reformed view. In Zurich, divorce was more liberally granted than in Lutheran towns. But even in Zurich a scant 35% of the petitions to the matrimonial court were approved. Lutheran towns in Germany and the Swedish Church took a more strict view, and preferred reconciliation, and even monetary fines and corporal punishment to encourage marital harmony.[79]

In England, the Reformation changed neither the canon law of marriage formation nor its prohibition on divorce. Although Henry VIII set aside two wives, and remarried, each time an annulment rather than a divorce was sought and granted. With respect to both his union with Catherine of Aragon and Anne of Cleves, the king was careful to allege grounds for annulment that would satisfy (if not ultimately persuade) a canon lawyer. Henry's refusal to seek divorce probably influenced opinion in the Church of England against the acceptance of dissolutions, and to continue the practice of the canon law to grant only annulments. Still some proposals were mooted, if unsuccessfully, by churchmen to allow divorce in cases of adultery.[80] The English Reformation, then, did not provide much in the way of relief to unhappy couples. Those who wished to set aside a spouse and be free to marry another in England either had to seek annulment or avail themselves of a divorce via the tortuous route of an Act of Parliament. Separations from bed and board, on the other hand, were granted by church courts, but the parties were not free to marry another.[81]

Above we noted that the Council of Trent reconsidered the stance of the Catholic Church on marriage formation. The Council also addressed the question of divorce. The result was a canon which asserted the principle that a validly contracted union could be terminated only by the death of a spouse. Adultery was considered as grounds for termination, and was specifically rejected, even for the innocent spouse.[82]

Yet the Reformation had its effects, even in Catholic areas of Europe. The intervention of civil authority in law on marriage formation in France through the Ordinance of Blois and subsequent edicts placed a secular slant on marriage.[83] Secular involvement extended also to its consequences. By the sixteenth century, judicial separation, which had hitherto been under the cognizance of church courts, came under the jurisdiction of royal courts. Moreover, cases brought to annul marriages likewise came to be heard in civil courts through the action *appel comme d'abus*. Thus by the eighteenth century, the Church had largely lost control over the termination of marriage, although divorce remained proscribed,[84] and judicial separations were rare.[85]

Having transformed marriage into a religious act, but one governed by secular law, the foundation was laid for the attack on the Catholic prohibition on divorce. Marriage began to appear decidedly contractual: if mutual consent was to create the relationship, should not the same be sufficient to terminate it? Enlightenment thinkers such as Voltaire and Montesquieu regarded the continuation of an unsatisfactory union as a form of tyranny, setting the stage, at least philosophically, for the divorce reforms carried out during the Revolution.[86]

But it was not only philosophers who advocated divorce; lawyers also provided arguments in its support. Grotius argued that adultery could be more broadly interpreted to include any act that thwarted the purpose of marriage, and not merely illicit sexual intercourse. Likewise, Puffendorf believed that adultery could be defined as any act that was contrary to the ultimate goals of marriage. Some legal opinion actually was implemented; Samuel Cocceji, a Prussian jurist who had advocated divorce where mutual consent was manifested, managed to legislate such a change in 1751 during his tenure as Minister of Justice.[87]

In the course of the seventeenth and eighteenth centuries, in Protestant Europe, the position of Lutheran and Calvinist theologians on divorce remained strict, but secular authority was able to wrest significant control from church courts in order to make divorce more freely obtainable. An example may be offered to demonstrate how the process developed in one jurisdiction, Sweden. At first, Swedish civil courts would only grant divorces based upon the grounds recognized by church ordinance. From the middle of the seventeenth century, however, divorces began to be granted by royal proclamation, and the grounds recognized by the Crown were expanded to include those not covered by church law. In the eighteenth century, after decades in which divorce was obtainable by royal decree in cases of incompatibility, the Civil Code of 1734 adopted it as a ground for divorce.[88]

Thus the secularization of marriage came to be inextricably bound to its dissolution. The outcome was expanded availability of separation and divorce in both Protestant and Catholic Europe. No longer was it necessary to prove adultery in Protestant lands. In Catholic Europe, and in Protestant England, separation remained the only course. But even in Catholic Europe, secularization had its consequences. In France, it became easier to obtain separation through civil courts than it had been when the Church had absolute jurisdiction.

DIVORCE IN THE OTTOMAN EMPIRE

The trauma that preoccupied Christian Europe over divorce was absent in areas under Ottoman control. Both the Eastern Orthodox Church and Islam took a more lenient stance on the dissolution of marriage than did their West European brethren.

As we noted in our discussion of marriage, the Ottomans seemed content to leave their Christian subjects free to follow the dictates of the Orthodox Church. The Eastern Church had developed a more permissive attitude toward divorce than the RC Church and many Protestant Churches. Eastern Orthodox theology permitted divorce under a number of circumstances, and local customs were recognized in various parts of Eastern Europe that extended the ability to divorce. The Eastern Church recognized that a wife's adultery permitted her husband to divorce her. The canon law considered certain acts by a wife as evidence of adultery, for example leaving the marital home. Wives, however, were not permitted to divorce husbands unless the adultery was ongoing or coupled with cruel treatment. In some areas under the control of the Eastern Church, for example Russia, a woman could divorce her husband if he seriously damaged the family's economic position, or became a serf. Serious illness was also regarded as sufficient grounds.[89] Indeed, the Eastern Church's more liberal view on divorce was an area of conflict for Eastern sects that wished to effect reconciliation with Rome.[90]

The Eastern Church, however, discouraged remarriage. This was particularly the case for adulteresses, and the law frowned upon men who married their adulterous partners whose husbands had secured divorce. To some theologians of the Eastern Church remarriage was problematic even in cases in which spouses had died: God had allocated all men a single helpmate. The marriage ceremony differed for second marriages. Serial remarriage beyond a second spouse was even more troublesome. Yet because marriage was crucial to the social organization of Slavic communities, remarriage occurred with some frequency.[91]

According to Muslim law, divorce was available to a woman by judicial decree. But as in Christian Europe after the Reformation, the available grounds for divorce may have varied from place to place. Some schools of religious thought were more restrictive, with one school, the Hanifi, recognizing only impotence as sufficient cause. Studies of divorce in the Ottoman empire generally focus on areas outside of Europe. Research in Ottoman Egypt in the seventeenth century, however, demonstrates that some Muslim societies allowed marriages to be dissolved for a variety of reasons: desertion, failure to support, cruelty, and disease. Failure to abide by terms of a marriage contract, including marrying a second wife or taking a concubine when the contract forbade such acts, enabled women to terminate unions where the ability to do so had been reserved therein.[92] Court records in a Turkish province of the Ottoman empire illustrate a similar variety of circumstances in which divorce was permitted and the medley of financial issues which emerged in marriage dissolution cases. Yet, in the Kayseri, it appears that women were unable to commence a divorce proceeding without the agreement of their husbands, and at times it was necessary for them to seek the intervention of their fathers to protect property rights incident to the marriage.[93]

INHERITANCE LAW AND PRACTICE

Perhaps no aspect of the law relating to the family has received as much attention from social historians as has the law of inheritance. For a number of reasons, such fascination is warranted; the pattern of property transmission between the generations, that is to say "how much and to whom," has wide-reaching ramifications for an individual family member, as well as for the entire family unit. Whether an inheritance is received, and its value, may determine for example: whether a child will marry or remain celibate; whether the family's social status is maintained (and whether an individual family member will rise or fall in status); whether an heir (or any child) is likely to co-reside with parents; or whether a child or children will migrate or remain domiciled in the community of his or her family's residence.

In addition to these demographic and social structural variables, the distribution pattern may provide insight into affective relationships between parent and offspring, because the economic success of children is so strongly linked to inheritance patterns. To take the most straightforward example: male primogeniture may be suggestive of a society in which daughters are less highly valued than is the eldest son produced by a union; and family continuity over generations may be more highly regarded than individual economic and social success. Partible inheritance, on the other hand, may be indicative of a society which regards children more equally and places a greater value upon financial equity among children than upon patrilineal continuity. Moreover, the extent to which parents may distribute property freely among their offspring may be suggestive of a society that has a more individualistic view of property, rather than a collectivist bent, because property holders can use personal discretion in determining who should succeed to their wealth and in what amounts.[94] Likewise, at least arguably, such societies may be more patriarchal (or matriarchal), because parents may brandish the sword of disinheritance in order to exercise a level of control over the choices which their children make. Conversely, in areas where a child or children have a vested right to a share of parental property, parents do not possess this significant element of dominion over the conduct of their progeny.

In addition to the "how much and to whom" question which inheritance law addresses, we may also consider the effect of "when": at what point in the parent's life cycle does property normally devolve to children? Inheritance law generally implements the transfer of property at the death of its holder. However, in societies which permit free disposition of property and therefore allow pre-mortem transfer, the time and legal nature of the transfer may have significant consequences with respect to family structure. For example, the logic of the stem family system turns on the co-residence of parent and heir. Moreover, in societies in which individual households are created at marriage, unions can occur earlier if parents commit property to children prior to their own death, even in circumstances in which the senior generation retains some interest in the transferred property.[95]

Thus whether property law permits some freedom of disposition, be it limited or plenary, has a significant impact upon family structure, and may also provide insights into power relationships within the family. Over the course of our period, evidence suggests that European societies were permitting greater individual control over property devolution. While inheritance law might have mandated a particular pattern of distribution, notaries (and in England, which did not have a notarial system, conveyancers of land and scriveners of wills) were able to fashion inheritance strategies which were more individual and nuanced than the rough and ready divisions (or lack thereof) sanctioned by inheritance law. By our period, then, we must look to practice as well as law: how property actually passed between generations and not merely what inheritance law dictated is probably more relevant to the historian interested in the nature and dynamics of family relationships.

Inheritance law, however, is still an appropriate point to begin a study of the inter-generational transfer of property. The forms which inheritance law assumed were limited in variety. Family property might be partible or impartible. Considering first the latter, if the inheritance passed to a single child, the paramount issue to be faced was to select the child. Although much has been written about male primogeniture, other patterns, such as inheritance rights in the youngest male or the youngest child, also obtained.[96] If property was to be divided, the question of eligible heirs was raised: did property pass to all children as in Brittany, for example, or only to male children as obtained in much of Normandy?[97]

Of course, inheritance law involved far more complications than merely the delineation of heirs. In the first place, distinctions could be made between the devolution of real and personal property; land might descend according to male primogeniture, but all children might receive the *legitim*, their "legitimate" share of personalty which each child had a right in law to claim. Moreover, the origin of property might matter. While patrimonial land might descend according to fixed patterns prescribed by inheritance law, property acquired by the holder (rather than property which had descended to him or her) might be disposed of as the holder deemed desirable. In addition, maternal land might descend in a different fashion than did paternal land. Likewise, the legal quality of land, the type of tenure in which the land was held, or whether it was held by noble or peasant might determine the pattern of descent directed by inheritance law.[98]

While permutations and complications other than the ones set out above might exist regarding inheritance law, the patterns prescribed by law were during our period increasingly circumvented by settlements of land either upon marriage or at death by last will. Such arrangements, embodied in legal transfers of land, created an individualized pattern of distribution of property and, at least technically, should have been effected only for land or personalty over which the settlor had freedom of disposition. But even in areas of Europe in which inheritance law regarded land as inalienable or non-transferable, settlements have been found disposing of patrimonial land to children other than the heir prescribed by law.[99] While most research into property settlements has focused on the landed class, settlements were also fashioned by merchants and by peasant landowners.[100]

Settlements of land were implemented to further inheritance strategies: to establish succession to family land, and also to make provisions for children who were not heirs under the patterns of distribution directed by inheritance law. The Reformation may have been responsible for accelerating the tendency towards allocating family wealth in a more egalitarian fashion.[101] Partible inheritance seems to have been favored by Protestants because it was more fair to younger children. There was also a practical element to their advocacy; some Protestants feared that primogeniture might drive non-inheriting children back to Catholicism because the unendowed might find support by entering the monastic life. In reality, however, parents retained control of the disposition of wealth, and Luther cautioned children to be content with the inheritance allotted to them by their parents.[102]

Yet convenience as much as religious teaching may have been responsible for the form in which inheritance strategies were implemented. In the course of the sixteenth and seventeenth centuries in England, for example, it became common among landed families[103] to transfer rights in land from one generation to the next upon the marriage of the male heir.[104] A present interest in part of family land in possession of the groom's father would be limited (transferred) to his male heir in order to support the newly created family, and upon the death of his parents, other parts of the family's property which remained in the hands of the senior generation would pass to him. Generally, according to the settlement, if the heir himself should not survive and produce issue (to whom the patrimony would descend ultimately under the terms of the settlement), limitations were included to direct the property to the settlor's other children, usually with preference to sons over daughters. While the settlement usually followed the pattern of succession prescribed by inheritance law, primogeniture, families were able to settle land on younger children (or) even more remote relatives if they wished to disinherit their own eldest son.

Often the process of settlement went further than merely transferring the patrimony to the eldest male child. It became more common in the sixteenth and seventeenth centuries to settle land upon younger sons and even daughters upon their marriages, although it was more usual for them to receive cash portions rather than land. Portions infused some flexibility into the inheritance system of early modern England. These sums might be used to allow a younger son to purchase a smaller estate, or as became increasingly common in the course of the seventeenth century, invest in a trade or profession. Over the course of the late seventeenth and early eighteenth centuries, the process of settlement took on a legal complexity which need not concern us here, but the development of the strict family settlement (whose mechanics and purposes have been discussed and debated at great length) allowed families to establish a master plan for the succession of their estate in one document. Included therein was the inter-generational transfer of property to the heir, a line of succession to the patrimony was mandated in default of issue produced by the marriage, and cash portions to be raised by the heir for the younger sons and daughters produced by the union. Thus the settlement resolved the distribution of family wealth for the generation as yet unborn. Through the process of resettlement in each generation, generations of settlors made provisions for generations of grandchildren; their own children's economic fate had been sealed in the preceding settlement.[105]

The strict settlement was devised in the mid-seventeenth century and reached its more complex form in the early eighteenth century. By the early eighteenth century, the strict settlement became the prevailing means by which land passed between the generations in England in the gentry and the aristocracy. However, less complex settlements emerged following the pattern of settlement upon marriage employed by the landed class even amongst the yeomanry.[106] Indeed, the process of settlement of land in England can be observed in a rudimentary form even among the peasantry as early as the later Middle Ages.[107]

Settlement at marriage or by testament in forms strikingly similar to the pattern observed in England existed elsewhere in early modern Europe, and the sixteenth through to the eighteenth centuries witnessed an increasing tendency for landed families to use notarial acts to circumvent customary inheritance law.[108] In Holland, for example, landholders used pre-nuptial settlements rather similar to the English strict settlement to fashion individualized patterns of succession.[109] Likewise, in the other areas of the Low Countries, where customary inheritance law was redacted in the early seventeenth century, *les acts juridiques*, and in particular, mortgages were used to craft inheritance strategies that circumvented the prescribed customs.[110] Similarly, in parts of northern and southern Italy, the *fideicommissum* (a form of transfer in trust) was used by larger landholders to exclude children who were assured a share of patrimonial land under prevailing provisions of Roman law.[111] Transfers similar to *fideicommissum* also occurred in Castile; evidence survives of notarial acts executed in which younger children were excluded from customary inheritance rights in both land and personalty.[112]

The attempts to circumvent inheritance custom by settlement did not go unchallenged. For example, considerable controversy over inheritance rights can be observed in litigation records in Castile, even though property law underwent a series of reforms in the sixteenth century.[113] Yet in much of continental Europe, although perhaps less so in England and parts of France,[114] landed families appeared to have been using the latitude permitted to circumvent inheritance law in order to limit the quantity of property passing to younger sons and daughters rather than to equalize wealth transfer amongst siblings; notarial acts were used primarily to consolidate the economic and social position of the family at the expense of younger sons and daughters.[115]

Most of the research undertaken by historians on settlements has focused on the documents executed by the upper classes. We may now turn from landed families to those who worked the land, the peasantry of early modern Europe. Neither our sources nor space permit a comprehensive discussion of both the strategies crafted and the legal means employed by the peasantry to implement them. Yet no discussion of law and its effects upon family relations would be complete without an incursion, albeit a cursory one.

Peasant land in Europe was frequently subject to the same inheritance customs that applied to the property of the landed class. Moreover, the desire to provide some endowment for all children rather than for merely a single heir was presumably present. However, the economic circumstances of the peasantry may have inclined them toward caution; the landed class may have had more latitude in providing for children, because they probably had more "discretionary wealth." It was necessary for the peasant family, then, to ensure its reproduction by carefully balancing the interests of family members when contemplating inter-generational transfer. A variety of other decisions might also influence both the timing of transfer and the means by which it was effected. For example, whether a widower (or widow) remarried might have implications for children produced by a previous marriage. Likewise, whether a father decided to retire and pass his holding on to his heir or heirs (and on what terms) would have immediate effects upon the economic position of his children. Individual decisions by parents in societies where access to resources by means other than inheritance was limited might require children to put off marriage or, alternatively, to induce it. The ability to control the timing and form of inter-generational transfer gave the peasant landholder considerable control over the economic destiny of his or her offspring, and affected the form that peasant family assumed.[116]

Moreover, demographic forces conspired to render the balance a more difficult one to strike. The sixteenth and seventeenth centuries witnessed population growth in many parts of Western Europe. As the population began to increase, for example in England and parts of France, partible inheritance might lead to the creation of landholdings that were too small to support families. To avoid fragmentation, parents might econo-mize at the expense of some of their children to ensure viable holdings for others. Alternatively, where parents continued to divide their land equally, the process of division might force some children to seek by-employment or even to sell their share and to migrate.[117] Still, most parents probably felt obliged to leave each child some property by testa-ment or gift in order to facilitate their progeny's start in life.[118]

What does seem reasonably clear in at least a number of areas of Europe is that the peasantry was able to effect individualized inheritance strategies. Distributions mandated by inheritance law could be circum-vented by *inter vivos* act or testament. In Germany, for example, peasants were able to dispose of land without the constraint of fixed proportions dictated by customary inheritance law. But even in villages in which custom provided specific shares of family land, it was regarded as a "rough rule"; village courts which controlled peasant affairs were prepared to sanction inheritance strategies that did not adhere strictly to the custom when family structure or the family's economic circumstances warranted deviation. Moreover, custom allowed considerable flexibility in allocation; parents could decide which parcels went to whom; agree-ments executed on marriage were upheld even in cases in which heirs were deprived of customary shares.[119] Similarly, in Castile, despite a century of reform of property law by royal authority, local custom con-tinued to be relevant in matters of inheritance and family law. The ambi-guities in the law led peasants to make settlements and testaments to secure the transmission of their estates. The complex transfers bred liti-gation, and peasants took their inheritance cases to a variety of courts, although it would appear that most disputes resulted in out-of-court compromises.[120]

In short, much inherited property passed according to terms set out by property holders either by settlement or testament. The patterns of distribution created by individual volition did not always conform to the dictates of customary inheritance law. Property holders were freer to fashion individualized strategies of inheritance than strict adherence to the customs of inheritance would have allowed. Yet the considerable quantity of litigation over dispositions suggests that the designs of property holders were not always respected. Numerous suits were probably initiated and then settled, leaving the historian with some doubt as to the actual distribution of family property. Inheritance in early modern Europe was a complex and oftentimes uncertain process, with customary inheritance law, individual volition, litigation, and compromise all playing a role, and in large measure conspiring to obscure (at least from the historian) "how much went to whom."

THE LEGAL POSITION OF WOMEN

Our inquiry into European family law began with a discussion of the current characterization of the European family during our period by historians as patriarchal. Let us return to that issue by considering, in conclusion, the legal position of women in pre-modern European society. The literature on the subject is extensive, and here (as elsewhere in this chapter) we can only scratch the surface of a much deeper historical debate.

The roots of the patriarchal family are enmeshed, at least arguably, with other aspects of male dominance in past time. For example, some historians have linked male dominance in governance with male ascendancy in the family. Thus a connection between the ruler of the state, the king, and the ruler of the family, the father, has been posited, especially for France, where, unlike England or Spain, female succession to the crown was not admitted. A number of explanations were offered to justify exclusion; legal arguments derived from public law, civil law and natural law were garnered to deny female inheritance of political office and to property. Patriarchal metaphors were created to establish males' exclusive right to political power and to link it to familial governance; for example, the king rules the political community as "husband" of the kingdom.[121]

While male dominance in political affairs is easy to document, evidence for patriarchal control of families, particularly from the law, is less compelling. The element of control by fathers that arguably lent a patriarchal quality to family life in the past may have been engrained in the mentality of early modern Europeans, but patriarchy seems to have been less explicit in the law. In short, there was no overarching principle of law in European society analogous to the Roman legal concept of the paterfamilias. Little parental control was enshrined in law, and such as there was in family law tended to be gender neutral, allowing parents (as opposed to fathers) some element of control over the activities of their children. For example, we observed that the Protestant Reformation altered the law of marriage to give to parents (as opposed to fathers) some power over choice of marriage partner for their children under a specific age. While parental authority might in reality reside in the father, law did not mandate that consent be bestowed by a patriarch. Likewise, the reluctance with which divorce was recognized preserved marriages which had been contracted, and conceded parents little ability to force their children out of unwanted unions.

Parental control, on the other hand, might be manifested in intergenerational transfer. The power to apportion property amongst children by settlement and testament gave parents (again rather than fathers) some level of control over their offspring. Yet children who were prepared to forgo an inheritance (perhaps an unrealistic option in a society in which inheritance might be crucial in establishing an economic niche) could be free of parental control.

The terms "patriarchy" and "patriarchal" have also been used to characterize relations between the spouses during our period. In this relationship, the law did intervene. In England, for example, the married couple was regarded as a single entity; the wife's legal identity merged into that of her husband during marriage. Thus the personal property of a woman became the absolute property of her husband upon a marriage, and her real property became vested in the husband during the union. Because she had no rights in property, it followed that a married woman could not contract, and was without property to pay compensation for her torts.[122] In practice, however, the theoretical constraints might not always be recognized. "Unity of person" was a legal construct. Its purpose was to create a juridical personality for the married couple; while it is telling that the juridical person was the husband, the construct itself was more a convenience than a reality. As early as the Middle Ages, there is some evidence of married women engaging in economic activities without their husbands, and even appearing in court to sue or be sued in their own name.[123] In the later sixteenth and seventeenth centuries it became more common for settlements to be executed prior to marriage in England to allow married women to hold property separate from their husbands. The practical effect of such agreements was to circumvent the "unity of person" legal concept.[124]

Litigation between spouses is perhaps the most telling evidence of discord within the family. With the exception of rare cases in which a wife sued her husband for maintenance, there was little interspousal litigation in England. Most litigation involving married women's property rights was undertaken by wives in conjunction with their husbands, for example to claim a portion owed by brides' families; or by wives joined with male relatives against their husbands for intermeddling with their separate estate.[125] An absence of litigation between spouses also characterized Castile, where inheritance matters were routinely litigated by males.[126] In other parts of Europe, however, litigation between spouses can be observed. For example, in France, where political ideology suggests strong levels of patriarchal power, women were suing their husbands in courts, illustrating their separate legal identity. Legal commentators of the era may have decried such conduct, but the courts permitted suits between spouses.[127]

It is always difficult to relate explicit manifestations of patriarchy in the legal culture of a society to social and economic reality. We may repair to the edge of Europe for an example of patriarchal ambivalence, at least as it manifests itself in the historical record: the Ottoman empire. In the mid-sixteenth to seventeenth centuries, Turkish women began to be veiled in public. The movement towards modesty was more prominent in the upper and middle classes. Historians have considered the tendency to adopt the veil as part of an attempt to isolate women from public contact with men. In addition to veiling, laws were passed in the Ottoman empire to restrict the movement of women with respect to both long-distance travel and even within their communities. During the period, the education of women and men was increasingly conducted separately, and career opportunities for women became limited to traditional female work roles such as nursing, midwifery, and the convent.[128]

Yet, at the same time, Ottoman women seem actively engaged in economic life. Women, particularly in the wealthy class, were able to inherit and deal freely with their property, and provided for their heirs through the creation of wills and trusts.[129] Moreover, women were free to bequeath their property to the same extent as males. The property rights of women were easily protected due to the complex recording of property transfers which obtained under the Ottoman empire. When transfers of a patrimony occurred, often upon the death of a surviving parent, sisters joined in the settlement with their brothers.[130]

There is also some evidence that, at least in Muslim Egypt, Islamic women seemed to take an active role in managing the financial affairs of their husbands, and their children.[131] Women were active in the land and credit market. They also appeared in court to sue and be sued on their own behalf, and sometimes in actions brought by their husbands, an interesting insight into the nature of patriarchal control.[132] Such was the case in other Ottoman territories, such as the Keyseri where women were frequently involved in litigation in their own name (though at times joined with their fathers), and appear to have been treated in a similar fashion to men, with the exception that a woman's oath had only one-half the value of that of a man.[133]

Ottoman women were not unique in pre-modern Europe as economic players either in conjunction with their husbands or in their own right. Examples of West European women can be offered to illustrate the same phenomenon. Although the "unity of person" concept obtained in England as a legal construct, diaries and letters demonstrate that married women often assisted their husbands in managing estates,[134] even running businesses.[135] Moreover, men often selected their spouses as executors of their wills,[136] suggesting that they had reasonable faith in the mana-gerial skills of their widows; such confidence could only have been gained through experience during marriage.

CONCLUSION

In this chapter we have touched upon four core areas of European family law: marriage, divorce, inheritance, and the legal position of married women. A comprehensive study of the law affecting the family in pre-modern Europe would require further investigation into the sources and a consideration of other topics: illegitimacy, the legal condition of children, and the Poor Laws, to name just a few. But we have attempted to consider the essential elements of these four crucial areas of family law, their origins and sources, and the relevant changes in the law that occurred during our period. Our goal was to observe the extent to which law actually controlled family matters. Our verdict should be that while it may have guided areas of family life in the European past, the law was dynamic and its control was imperfect.

Marriage and divorce provide examples. Entrance into marriage and divorce was controlled by law, and that law had clear religious inspira-tion and overtones. But the acceptance of divorce after the Reformation in Protestant parts of Europe and then in France may illustrate how other forces reshaped the fundamental principles cast in law. Case studies have demonstrated how difficult it was for authorities, religious or secular, to enforce the law of marriage formation and divorce. Was the recognition of divorce in law an unconscious capitulation to societal demand?

Inheritance provides an example of how the law of property func-tioned in the past. Those European societies that we have observed allowed individuals a remarkable amount of control over the disposition of their property. Inheritance customs dictated a pattern of succession to property, but settlements and wills could circumvent custom to allow families to transmit property between generations in a manner fashioned to take account of a myriad of family circumstances.

Finally, we observed that law and practice may also have diverged with respect to married women's legal position. Although the European law was reasonably consistent in manifesting authority in the husband, economic reality frequently required a partnership with the wife (or widow) in control of family property either during the marriage or at its termination.

CHAPTER 5

The Impact of the Reformation and Counter-Reformation

Jeffrey R. Watt

Martin Luther, an Augustinian monk and theology professor at the University of Wittenberg, was dismayed by the sale of indulgences which he witnessed in his native Saxony. Parishioners purchased these indulgences in order to tap into the treasury of merits, a sort of reservoir filled with an infinite supply of spiritual good deeds, allegedly the excess merits of Jesus and the saints. Through the indulgence, believers supposedly could have some of these merits attributed to them and thereby avoid spending time in purgatory atoning for sins committed in this world. In theory, for an indulgence to be effective, believers had to show genuine contrition for their sins. Luther complained, however, that many of his parishioners complacently believed that the indulgence provided them with full absolution for their sins and were thus assured of going directly to heaven after death. Further irate that his parishioners, confident of their fate, ceased going to confession, Luther posted his Ninety-five Theses in Wittenberg on October 31, 1517, the date that traditionally marks the beginning of the Protestant Reformation. Although Luther initially sought only a debate to argue over the effectiveness of indulgences, he was in fact starting a revolution that brought about the definitive disintegration of religious unity in Western Christendom.

Luther's theological dispute in many ways seems far removed from the family, but the Reformation that he initiated affected the institution of the family in a variety of ways. Luther and other reformers—including John Calvin, the most important theologian of the Reformed Protestant movement—affirmed a belief in the "priesthood of all believers," insisting that all Christians could communicate directly with God; they need not go through the medium of a priest. This notion fostered an atmosphere in which some religious education and worship was transferred from the church to the home. Protestant and Catholic reformers viewed marriage and the family as the most fundamental building blocks of society and generally attributed sundry social ills to problems in the household. Their calls for the reform of the control of marriage and sexuality reflected a general paternalistic desire for order and discipline.[1]

MARRIAGE AND THE CONTROL OF MATRIMONY

Protestantism's most obvious impact on the family pertained to marriage. Luther and other Protestants believed that one was made right before God not by performing good works but through faith alone. They also believed that human nature was so irreparably tainted by original sin that humans could not possibly lead a sinless life. They concluded that a life of virginity did not improve one's standing before God, asserting as well that the sexual impulse, itself a product of original sin, was so strong that any effort to lead a chaste existence was almost certainly doomed to failure. Moreover, their belief that the Bible was the sole authority of religious truth led them to deny that marriage was a sacrament. The belief that marriage is a sacrament, that is, an ecclesiastical ritual through which God bestows grace on believers, did not become official Roman Catholic doctrine until 1438 at the Council of Florence. Be that as it may, marriage had effectively been treated as such for centuries. As early as the fourth century, Augustine and other Church Fathers had described it as holy and sacramental. Later medieval theologians and canon lawyers were more emphatic, insisting that marriage conferred grace just as the sacraments of baptism or the Eucharist did. Even before the birth of Protestantism, however, certain individuals questioned the sacramental nature of marriage. A case in point was Erasmus of Rotterdam, a humanist who enthusiastically applied the linguistic concerns of the Renaissance to the study of Scripture and the writings of Church Fathers. A contemporary of Luther, Erasmus criticized many abuses within the Roman Catholic Church even before 1517. He condemned simony, the buying and selling of church offices; pluralism, the practice of holding more than one church office at a time; and, perhaps most important, the alleged immorality and ignorance of many clergymen. Studying the Bible and other historical sources, Erasmus concluded that the answer to whether marriage was a sacrament had varied from period to period, and he believed that the doctrine ought to change to accommodate contemporary conditions.[2]

Luther, Calvin, and all prominent Protestant reformers affirmed that marriage had considerable religious value. They identified the same principal purposes of marriage as those outlined by pre-Reformation writers: procreation, avoidance of sins such as fornication, and companionship. Reformers such as Calvin, and above all Martin Bucer, however, placed more emphasis on this third purpose than did Catholic writers.[3] Bucer wrote, "Now the proper and ultimate end of marriage is not copulation or children, for then there was not true matrimony between Joseph and Mary the mother of Christ, nor between many holy persons more; but the full and proper and main end of marriage is the communicating of all duties, both human and divine, each to other with utmost benevolence and affection."[4] In one sense, reformers enhanced the married state by rejecting the Catholic belief that celibacy was superior to matrimony. Accordingly, Protestants renounced clerical celibacy, and virtually all major reformers married and viewed married life as the "normal" state. Calvin, for example, insisted that being celibate was in no way morally superior to being sexually active within marriage. Nonetheless the reformers believed that, although sacred, marriage was not a sacrament. Reformers were unanimous in proclaiming that there was scriptural basis for only two sacraments: baptism and the Eucharist. Calvin, for example, asserted that marriage was indeed instituted by God but was not a sacrament. Agriculture, architecture, and shoemaking were also established by God; marriage was no more a sacrament than these.[5]

In part because of the belief that marriage was a sacrament, the Roman Catholic Church and its courts had enjoyed jurisdiction over matters pertaining to the validity of marriages, such as contract disputes, annulments, and separations. Luther, however, insisted that marriage was of this world, just as women, houses, and courts were; like them, marriage was subject to the state, not the Church. Virtually all areas of continental Europe that converted to Protestantism experienced to varying degrees the secularization of the control of marriage. In only a few cases was it completely laicized; in Reformation Augsburg, for example, jurisdiction over marriage and the enforcement of the moral code shifted entirely from the clergy to the city council. More often, however, as church courts were abolished, matrimonial jurisdiction passed to tribunals that included both lay and clerical authorities. The first such court was Zurich's *Ehegericht*, founded by Ulrich Zwingli in 1525, which served as a model for similar courts established in St. Gall, Bern, Basel, and Schaffhausen. Comprised of two clerical and four lay judges, the *Ehegericht* oversaw issues pertaining to the validity of marriages. Similarly, with the conversion to Protestantism in Neuchâtel, a French-speaking principality, magistrates established matrimonial courts and consistories that included pastors as judges, though secular members were more numerous.[6]

Clerical influence over the control of marriage and the family was probably greater in Geneva than in any other Protestant state. In 1541 Genevan authorities established the Consistory, a type of morals court

composed of roughly equal numbers of pastors and elders and dominated by the reformer Calvin. The Consistory heard all sorts of moral
concerns including questions related to marriage, such as divorces, contract disputes, and police actions against domestic unrest and illegal
separations. The Consistory often censured delinquents and forbade
them to take communion, but it could not impose secular penalties; any
parties who deserved punishment were referred to Geneva's chief governing body, the Small Council, along with the Consistory's opinion on
how to proceed. The Small Council also had the final say in divorce cases
and marriage contract disputes.[7]

In Protestant areas, clerical influence over the control of marriage
validity thus tended to be reduced but not eliminated. It must be noted,
however, that this process had actually begun in many places before the
Reformation. Ecclesiastical jurisdiction declined throughout Germany
from the late fifteenth century; the magistrates of many imperial and
Swiss cities had encroached on bishops' traditional jurisdiction over
marital validity several decades before the Reformation. Moreover, secularization of the control of marriage did not entail a radical change in
the institution of marriage. Marital issues pertaining to property—such
as disputes over dowries—were under the purview of secular courts even
before the Reformation. As the Roman Catholic Church lost jurisdiction
over marriage in much of Western Europe in the sixteenth century, the
state in effect assumed this jurisdiction by default, adopting to a large
extent pre-existing rules on marriage from canon law even in the area of
marital validity. In most areas, it was only during the Enlightenment that
legal attitudes toward marriage made a dramatic departure from Roman
Catholic tradition.[8]

Throughout continental Europe, Protestant governments not only
created new tribunals to deal with matrimonial litigation but also passed
laws that generally modified marriage in a variety of ways. First, they
reduced the impediments to marry, the change that ultimately proved the
least significant. Protestant reformers criticized Catholic impediments to
marry with respect to consanguinity and affinity. "Consanguinity" was
defined as the tie that binds people descended from common ancestors,
and "affinity" the relationship between two people, one of whom is
married to a relative of the other. Canon law had at one time forbidden
marriages as far as the seventh degree of consanguinity or affinity,
thereby condemning marriages between sixth cousins as incestuous. Such
extreme impediments were undoubtedly almost never imposed, and
under Pope Innocent III's leadership, the Fourth Lateran Council of 1215
reduced impediments from the seventh to the fourth degree, thus
prohibiting marriages between third cousins. Medieval canon law also

forbade marriage in cases of premarital impotence, "spiritual affinity" resulting from godparentage, deception concerning one's status (e.g. a serf who falsely claimed to be free), and sexual relations between a fiancé and a third party after betrothal. Fiancés who practiced different religions were also forbidden to marry.[9]

Reformers considered some of these impediments unwarranted. Among Protestants, Luther held an extreme position with regard to consanguinity and affinity. Citing the standards set in Leviticus 18, Luther argued that only the following relationships precluded marriage: a man could not marry his mother, stepmother, sister, half-sister, granddaughter, aunt, daughter-in-law, brother's wife, wife's sister, stepdaughter, and uncle's wife. Moreover, he maintained that marriages were forbidden only to the second degree of consanguinity and to the first degree of affinity. In attacking Catholic impediments, Luther held that they were merely a ploy to bring in revenue by selling dispensations.[10] In the marriage laws he drafted for Geneva, Calvin noted that Divine law and Roman law did not forbid marriages between first cousins. Nonetheless, because impediments to marry were so ingrained in European society, Calvin for the time being continued to prohibit marriages between first cousins, although he permitted unions between people more distantly related. More typical were the reforms introduced in a number of Swiss cantons and German Protestant states where magistrates reduced impediments to the third degree for consanguinity and the second for affinity.[11] Thus second cousins could not marry, nor could widows marry the first cousins of their late spouses. Perhaps more important was the elimination of impediments pertaining to the "spiritual affinity" resulting from godparentage. At any rate, the reduction in impediments did not effect dramatic changes in marriage practices.

More important was another change pertaining to the formation of marriage: the abolition of the so-called clandestine marriage, which is discussed in Chapter 4. As we saw there, according to canon law, consent was the necessary and sufficient condition for forming a binding union.[12]

Protestant reformers railed against clandestine marriage, condemning it because it undercut parental authority and could be the source of legal complications. To ensure that consent had been freely given, Protestant magistrates throughout continental Europe required the presence of witnesses to marriage engagements; to ensure that only eligible people married, magistrates required the publication of the banns before consecration of the union. In addition, they required the consent of parents or guardians for those under the age of majority, usually placed at 20 to 25. In theory parents and guardians could not force their children into marrying somebody; any such forced match was to be invalid.

The Introduction of Divorce among Protestants

A third and, in the long run, the most significant change in marriage law was the introduction of the possibility of divorce, as opposed to annulment or separation, and subsequent remarriage. As early as the patristic period, Roman Catholic theologians argued that marriage was indissoluble, a view inspired at least in part by the belief that it was a sacrament: to many theologians, divorce appeared tantamount to undoing the grace bestowed by God through the sacrament of marriage. True, medieval Roman Catholics recognized the possibility of annulment, a declaration that a real marriage had never existed because of pre-existing impediments. In addition to the impediments to those related by blood or marriage, pre-marital impotence, deception concerning one's status, and sexual relations after betrothal between a fiancé and a third party could all be grounds for an annulment. Beyond annulments, the only "divorce" that Roman Catholic lawyers allowed was the *divortium quoad torum et mensam*, which in reality was only a legal separation which did not permit remarriage. In canon law tradition, three causes might justify such a separation: adultery, the spiritual offenses of heresy and apostasy, and cruelty.[13]

If, as Protestant reformers insisted, marriage was not a sacrament that conferred grace on participants, only a short step was needed to deny its indissolubility. All of the main Protestant reformers recognized the possibility of divorce and subsequent remarriage under certain circumstances. Many Protestant reformers echoed Erasmus's claim that the *divortium* of the Catholics was patently unfair to the innocent party. A general theme among reformers was that divorce was possible only in cases of matrimonial fault—that is, one of the spouses had to be the guilty party, the other the victim. Divorce was not considered a remedy for marital breakdown *per se* but as "a punishment for a matrimonial crime and as a relief for the victim of the crime (the innocent spouse)."[14] Protestants held that the Catholic *divortium* was a modern innovation which was not found in the early Church and that a permanent separation was a travesty of marriage. Since the married state was appropriate for most people, it was deemed immoral to subject individuals to indefinite separations which forbade remarriage. Separated couples remained married in a legal sense, yet were not married in a social sense. As Roderick Phillips notes:

> This ambiguity implied by separation *a mensa et thoro* struck the Reformers as being intolerable to the spouses concerned and as dangerous to society. . . . Recognizing that there would inevitably be sin, that some vices practiced within marriage were unredeemable, they

believed that the marriages made possible by divorce (remarriages) would contribute more to the totality of morality, just as enforced celibacy and separated men and women detracted from it.[15]

Under certain circumstances, Protestants therefore viewed divorce as an appropriate solution to marital dysfunction.

Most prominent among the grounds for which one could file for divorce was adultery, the only ground found in all divorce doctrines and legislation among continental Protestants. Protestant reformers gave far more importance to adultery as a ground for divorce than had Catholics as a reason for separation. For Catholics, adultery was simply one of a number of possible reasons. The increased significance accorded it by Protestants was a result of their emphasis on the Bible as sole authority. Adultery was the only ground for divorce clearly and unequivocally mentioned in the Bible: "I tell you, then, that any man who divorces his wife for any cause other than her unfaithfulness, commits adultery if he marries some other woman" (Matthew 19: 9). Throughout Protestant areas in continental Europe, new marriage laws recognized adultery as a valid ground for divorce.[16]

While they universally recognized adultery as a legitimate reason for divorce, many Protestant reformers and matrimonial courts recognized other grounds, most prominently desertion. The principal justification for divorce for desertion or prolonged absence was that after a certain period of time, one could assume that the absent spouse was dead. In many ways, divorce in these cases resembled a "substitute death certificate" for the absent spouse. Significantly, this manner of dissolving a marriage had not been unknown before the Protestant Reformation. Most canon lawyers of the High Middle Ages avowed that it was legitimate under certain circumstances to allow remarriage on the basis of the presumption of death of absent spouses. Pope Alexander III (1159–1181) had issued a declaration allowing the dissolution of a marriage for the prolonged absence of a spouse under circumstances in which one might reasonably presume the absent party was dead. Alexander set the waiting period at ten years; Celestine III (1191–1198) shortened it to seven years, and this remained the most commonly prescribed period.[17]

In addition to adultery, Luther considered desertion and refusal to engage in sexual relations as valid reasons for divorce. Calvin took a more restrictive view, claiming that the Bible clearly stated that the only justifiable reason for terminating a marriage was adultery. He therefore denied that marriages could be terminated for leprosy or impotence. But in spite of his claims to the contrary, Calvin in effect also accepted desertion as a valid ground for divorce. Like Luther, he maintained that abandonment was a type of "aggravated adultery"—the spouse who deserted the household probably would have sexual relations with another person and so could be presumed guilty of infidelity. Zwingli went further than either Luther or Calvin, maintaining that the passage in Matthew simply indicated the least serious offense for which a marriage could be dissolved. Elsewhere in the Bible, other offenses appear worse than adultery—surely they too must be grounds for divorce. It is a far greater sin to be an unbeliever than an adulterer, Zwingli argued; therefore someone married to an unbeliever should have the opportunity to terminate the marriage. Moreover, Zwingli held that the Apostle Paul's claim that it is better to marry than to burn with passion underscores the importance of sexuality in marriage, justifying impotence as a ground for divorce.[18]

The reformer with the most radical views on divorce was Martin Bucer, of Strasbourg. In his work *De Regno Christi* (1557), Bucer expressed libertarian views on marriage, anticipating divorce laws that would not prevail until the twentieth century. As noted above, Bucer insisted that the most fundamental purpose of the Christian marriage was not procreation and the avoidance of extra-marital sex but rather companionship, which entailed fidelity, mutual love, and cohabitation. Consequently, Bucer not only recognized adultery and desertion as grounds for divorce but even approved of divorce "by mutual consent and by repudiation" by either spouse. This is not to say that Bucer took divorce lightly. He felt that divorce should be more difficult to attain if children were involved and that a person should be penalized financially for repudiating a spouse without due cause.[19]

It was Luther and Calvin who promulgated the most influential divorce doctrine of the sixteenth century. Legislation based on their work was widespread throughout Europe, primarily in the Protestant states, but also among Protestant populations within Roman Catholic states. Protestants throughout continental Europe followed the lead of Luther and Calvin; laws in Württemberg, Augsburg, Nuremberg, Neuchâtel, Geneva, and many other Protestant cities and states allowed divorce for reasons of adultery and willful desertion.[20]

If the laws passed in Protestant areas in Reformation Europe set an important precedent in allowing divorce and subsequent remarriage, they did not lead to widespread instability in sixteenth-century households. Throughout the Protestant world, divorces remained rare in the sixteenth and seventeenth centuries, despite contemporary moralists' claims to the contrary. According to archival documentation of matrimonial litigation, no European state experienced an annual divorce rate that even reached one per 1,000 residents. (By comparison, the US rate in 1980 was 5.2 per 1,000 people.) In Zurich, for example, the *Ehegericht* awarded 28 divorces for the years 1525–1531, which represents 0.74 divorces per 1,000 people per year. In Reformation Basel (1525–1592), 374 people received divorces, equivalent to a divorce rate of 0.57 per 1,000 residents. Research on marital litigation in states such as Augsburg, Württemberg, Neuchâtel, Zweibrüken, and Geneva reveals that divorce was considerably less frequent than even these meager rates.[21]

The large majority of divorces awarded by Protestant courts in Reformation Europe were based on the grounds of adultery or desertion. Although a person who received a divorce for reason of absence resembled a widow or widower, Protestant tribunals referred to this procedure as a divorce, not a declaration of widowhood. Moreover, although Roman Catholic canon lawyers had recognized the possibility of dissolving a marriage after a spouse's extended absence on the presumption of death, Catholics had not developed a coherent policy with respect to the abandoned spouse, and ecclesiastical courts were generally reluctant to permit remarriage without proof of the absent spouse's death.[22] Nevertheless, because of precedents in canon law, some sixteenth-century Protestants who obtained divorces for abandonment might have received permission to remarry even if they had remained Catholic, a further indication that the Protestants' introduction of divorce did not cause a revolution in the institution of marriage.

People seeking divorce on the ground of desertion generally had to wait a long time before filing suit. Whether it be the malicious desertion of the household or the absence of a husband who left the country on business, tribunals ordinarily would not hear a case unless the spouse had already been absent for several years, usually seven, the term set by canon law. In the absence of evidence of the spouse's death, courts strictly observed this long waiting period before granting divorces for desertion, generally requiring the same delay both for male and for female petitioners. (The large majority who filed suit on this ground were women, since men were much more apt to travel long distances as merchants or mercenaries.) Neuchâtel's matrimonial court was even known to require spouses of banished criminals to wait seven years before awarding divorces. Such a case began in 1597 when Isabelle Gallandre asked to be divorced from Jean Bedaux, who had abandoned her and fled the country in September 1596 after having severely beaten his mother and left her for dead. Although she produced affidavits of the sentence of banishment rendered against Bedaux, Gallandre was required to wait the full seven years since his departure, the divorce being granted only in October 1603.[23]

In light of the Protestant reformers' diatribes against the celibate life—they asserted that the majority of humans were incapable of such rigorous abstinence—it seems cruel and inconsistent to force someone to live chastely for years and wait patiently to see if the absent spouse will return. This is particularly so in cases such as Gallandre's inasmuch as her husband's crime seems to the modern observer to be reason enough for a divorce. Rarely, however, did the courts make exceptions to the usual waiting period.

Those who filed for divorce because of adultery received divorces more quickly. In dealing with divorce cases based on adultery, members of Protestant tribunals almost invariably exhorted the innocent party to forgive the adulterous spouse and preserve their married life. If the evidence of adultery was beyond question and the plaintiff persisted, however, he or she was almost guaranteed success. Among those suits that were rejected were those of people who were guilty of complicity by allowing their spouses to carry on extra-marital affairs or who had unwittingly forgiven their spouse's infidelity: borrowing a notion from canon law, the courts held that if a person had sexual relations with his or her spouse despite knowing that he or she had committed adultery, the coitus was viewed as a sign of forgiveness and the innocent party no longer had grounds for divorce.[24]

For a combination of reasons, adultery was more often cited against wayward wives than unfaithful husbands in divorce cases. One factor was the nature of the proof of adultery. If the concrete products of adulterous affairs were illegitimate children, then a woman whose husband was absent for a lengthy period would have a difficult time concealing a pregnancy. If, on the other hand, an unfaithful husband did not actually get caught in the act of coitus, he ran the risk of being discovered only if his partner revealed his name. Moreover, women generally had more economic deterrents to divorce than men; women who lived without the support of their husbands encountered more financial difficulties than did men who lived without the support of their wives. Social mores also played a role. Prior to the Reformation, adultery in Germany was defined as the sexual union of a married woman with any man other than her husband; a married man who had an affair with a single woman was not subject to prosecution. By contrast, in the sixteenth century married men comprised the majority of those convicted of adultery in some German Protestant and Catholic states, but adultery nonetheless was more often used against women in divorce litigation. In Reformation Europe, men undoubtedly continued to view their spouses' adultery as a greater affront to their honor than did most women. In Zurich from 1525 to 1531 men initiated nearly 60 percent of divorce cases based on adultery, and more than twice as many men as women were plaintiffs to such suits in Augsburg during the period 1537–1547. In Reformation Neuchâtel, among plaintiffs who sought divorces for reasons of adultery, males outnumbered females by two to one. During the time of Calvin, twenty men, but only six women, received divorces in Geneva from adulterous spouses.[25]

Few divorces were awarded on grounds other than adultery or desertion. Throughout Europe only the Reformed courts of Neuchâtel and Basel regularly granted divorces on other grounds. Even in these states the absence or adultery of a spouse was the basis for over three-quarters of the divorces awarded.[26] Other complaints occasionally alleged as grounds for divorce were illness and sexual dysfunction. Terminating a marriage because of impotence was nothing new. Since canon lawyers put so much emphasis on procreation and the sexual aspect of marriage, they understandably denied the right to marry to those incapable of having sexual relations. Consequently, Pope Gregory IX (1227–1241) declared impotence an impediment to marriage, and any marriage that an impotent person contracted would be null.[27] Rarely, however, was impotence cited in divorce cases in Reformation Europe, and plaintiffs to divorce cases based on sexual dysfunction enjoyed far less chance of success than those grounded on the infidelity or prolonged absence of spouses. Divorce for sexual dysfunction generally involved marriages that had not been consummated after several years of cohabitation, unions which might have been annulled in pre-Reformation Roman Catholic courts. Significantly, sexual dysfunction ceased to be a ground for divorce once the marriage had been consummated.[28] In addition to cases of impotence, a few other divorces were initiated for medical reasons. Here again, the courts clearly hesitated before granting divorces because of illness. For example, in 1552 a man in Valangin, a semi-independent seigneury within the Principality of Neuchâtel, sought a divorce from his leprous wife. Despite the fact that she had been sick seven years and showed no hope of recovery, the judges declared that the man was "still to live for a while abstaining from marriage, judging that he must not receive a marriage separation until God calls his wife to him."[29] For this couple, marriage was to endure in sickness and in health till death did them part. Simply put, neither impotence nor illness was a significant basis for ending a marriage in Reformation Europe.

Conspicuously absent among recognized grounds for divorce was cruelty. Like Catholic authorities before them, Protestant magistrates deplored excessive domestic violence and sought to minimize it. Tribunals not infrequently convoked couples for domestic discord, urging them to mend their ways. Protestant judicial authorities, however, virtually never awarded divorces for cruelty alone. That cruelty did not constitute grounds for divorce is aptly demonstrated by a case heard by

Geneva's Consistory. In August 1542, Calvin and the other members of the Consistory convoked a lumberjack who had beaten his wife so severely that he put out one of her eyes, which by any reasonable standard would appear to denote the use of excessive force. The Consistory admonished the man to be more gentle with his wife but also ordered the woman to obey and live peacefully with her husband and not to provoke him.[30] At no point was divorce even mentioned as a possible solution. While such police actions against domestic violence were not uncommon, only rarely did courts in any state allow divorce suits based on cruelty to be heard. The marriage court in Reformation Augsburg did hear five divorce cases based on cruelty, but none of the requests was granted.[31]

Throughout Europe, both Protestant and Catholic couples who could not tolerate each other might simply separate without receiving judicial permission to do so. Although such separations were illegal both before and after the Reformation, communities and magistrates often preferred to turn a blind eye to such separations rather than force unhappy couples to live together. Moreover, although reformers had criticized judicial separations, some Protestant courts did allow couples to separate in cases of extreme cruelty. Notwithstanding his overall opposition to the *divortium quoad torum et mensam*, Luther favored separation rather than divorce in such cases. By contrast, Calvin went so far as to say that a Protestant wife must not leave her physically abusive husband unless her life was actually in danger.[32] Since putting out an eye was not reason enough, the degree of abuse that merited a separation was obviously extreme. Indeed, only once during Calvin's time did Geneva's Consistory award even a temporary separation for cruelty or abuse. In 1553 the Consistory convoked Bertin Beney and his wife Loyse Leffort because they were illegally separated. Testimony revealed that Loyse left Bertin after he had repeatedly beaten and threatened to kill her. Bertin's own father, himself a member of the Small Council, testified that he saw Bertin draw his sword and threaten to stab Loyse. For his misbehavior, the Small Council sentenced Bertin to a week in prison and allowed Loyse to live with her mother until he learned to behave. They remained legally separated until 1555, when Loyse obtained a divorce because Bertin had committed adultery.[33]

This temporary separation, however, was the exception that proved the rule. In tightly knit Reformed areas, such as Geneva and Neuchâtel, authorities had the means and the will to force married couples to live together. For Protestants, divorce was supposed to replace the judicial separation. Barring the very limited grounds for divorce—basically adultery and desertion—married couples had to live together till death did them part. In short, although Protestant reformers and magistrates deplored domestic violence, they believed that cruelty, unlike adultery, did not affect the principal ends of marriage which they still identified to a considerable extent with sexuality—that is, with procreation and the quenching of the sexual impulse through monogamous intercourse.[34] Simply put, the introduction of divorce did not cause disruption in European families as divorce remained quite rare throughout the Reformation period. Although its introduction in Protestant areas set an important precedent, centuries would pass before divorce became common anywhere in Europe.[35]

Litigation Concerning the Formation of Marriage

In both Protestant and Catholic areas, on both the continent and in England, matrimonial courts in Reformation Europe generally heard more suits pertaining to the formation rather than the dissolution of marriages. Suits to enforce marriage contracts tended to be the most common form of litigation. In handling cases of disputed contracts, Protestant judicial authorities consistently recognized as valid only those marriage promises that had been contracted in the presence of witnesses and, in the case of minors, with parental permission. Although they rejected the tenet of canon law that consent was the sufficient condition for contracting a marriage, Protestants certainly viewed freely given consent to marry as a necessary prerequisite for contracting binding promises, requiring the presence of witnesses merely to ensure that consent had been given. The majority of litigants who tried to enforce disputed marriage contracts failed in their suits, primarily because they did not provide sufficient evidence that binding promises had been made.[36]

Judicial authorities in Reformation Europe took the betrothal very seriously. If both parties were legally capable of contracting promises and had freely agreed to marry in the presence of others, they were generally expected to execute their engagements. In the diocese of Ely in the sixteenth century, breach-of-promise cases were more often initiated by the church courts than by one of the parties themselves; couples in Ely could not simply dissolve a marriage contract at their own volition.[37]

In Reformation Neuchâtel, there were cases in which neither party wanted to honor an engagement but were obliged to do so. In 1618 Daniel Quarthier and Rose Milliods were ordered to appear before the Consistory of Valangin because there was a rumor that they had promised to marry each other. At first both denied the engagement. Rose had reportedly even said that if forced to marry Daniel, she would leave the country; Daniel had promised to marry another woman and had even made the first proclamation at church. As the case proceeded, Rose admitted having accepted Daniel's proposal by symbolically touching his hand and receiving a coin from him in the name of marriage—gift-giving and other popular rituals, such as drinking in the name of marriage, were commonly part of engagement ceremonies throughout early modern Western Europe.[38] Upset by her claim that she would rather leave the country than be his wife, Daniel had lost all interest in marrying Rose, although he too acknowledged they had made marriage promises. In the end, the court concluded that Daniel and Rose had strictly followed the proper procedure for contracting a marriage, that the promises had been reciprocally made in the presence of and with the consent of the closest relatives of both parties, and that both Daniel and Rose were old enough to make such an engagement. Therefore Daniel Quarthier and Rose Mil-liods must be husband and wife.[39]

Although this case was unusual, Protestant judges were essentially fol-lowing canon law tradition by viewing marriage vows as indissoluble. Indeed, in some areas, if the contract had been properly made, the judges ordinarily granted permission not to consecrate a marriage only for the same reasons that they awarded divorces: infidelity, desertion, etc.[40] Protestants began showing greater flexibility in the seventeenth century, yet tended to follow canon law tradition, deeming marriage contracts binding from the moment of consent, not from the consecration of marriage in church.[41]

In determining the validity of disputed marriage contracts, courts showed a certain flexibility, at times deviating from the letter of the law. In a few cases, courts in Protestant and Catholic areas ruled in favor of pregnant female plaintiffs to contract disputes even though there were no witnesses to the alleged marriage promises. In these cases, the male defendants typically acknowledged having had sexual relations with their accusers but emphatically denied that they had made marriage promises.

In a legal tradition that goes back to Roman law, a couple might be judged married simply by the way they acted in public and interacted in their daily lives. If a couple spent much time together and the man treated the woman as a man behaves toward his wife, courts in exceptional cases might recognize them as married even if they had not celebrated a wedding or betrothal in the presence of witnesses. Courts made such decisions, however, only when the women in question enjoyed an impec-cable reputation and were of comparable social status to the men they accused.[42]

Although matrimonial ordinances usually said nothing about class, wealth and social status were in fact important factors in contract liti-gation. For the judges, marriage was to be a union of equals, and they rejected those suits filed by plaintiffs who sought to use marriage as a means of climbing the social ladder. Throughout Europe, courts generally ruled against plaintiffs to disputed marriage contracts if they were considerably beneath the social status of the defendants; judicial authorities consciously tried to ensure social equilibrium by avoiding egregious differences in status between fiancés, a fact that lends support to the contention that the control of marriage tends to lead toward homogamy, marriages between people of the same status. Thus in early modern Holland, women had very good chances of winning suits involving men of comparable status. By contrast, female servants who were debauched by their masters might be able to secure a dowry from their seducers but had virtually no chance of convincing the courts to order a marriage between persons of such disparate backgrounds. This effort to ensure that spouses were of comparable status was certainly not initiated by the Reformation. It was the continuation of a long tradition, the roots of which can be found in Roman law.[43]

All told, Protestant tribunals did not mark a radical break with Roman Catholic traditions with regard to the control of marriage. Evidence from matrimonial litigation reveals more continuity than change in the formation and dissolution of marriages.

Matrimonial Control in the English and Counter-Reformations

England was in a unique position with respect to marriage in Reformation Europe. Although controversy over a marriage—the king's desire to annul his marriage to Catherine of Aragon and marry Anne Boleyn—was the key to Henry VIII's break with Rome, England, unaffected by the Council of Trent, remained more closely tied to medieval canon law on marriage than any Roman Catholic country. In England marriage did not definitively lose its sacramental status until the Elizabethan period (1558–1603). Although they allowed clergy to marry, English Protestants did not attack the ideal of celibacy as aggressively or promote clerical marriage as enthusiastically as their counterparts on the continent. Moreover, although annulments were still possible, divorce and remarriage were not. Spouses could procure judicial separations for cruelty more easily than in certain Reformed areas on the continent. More common were unofficial separations in which couples lived apart without having received judicial permission. Church courts, now under the crown rather than the papacy, continued to have exclusive jurisdiction over the validity of marriages, while secular courts still had jurisdiction over the transfer of property that often accompanied marriage. Evidence suggests that the English by and large were satisfied with the existing law and courts that regulated marriage. In short, the Reformation in England had little impact on matrimony or on the control of marriage.[44]

The Counter-Reformation did bring about some changes. In response to Protestant attacks, Pope Paul III saw the need, with encouragement from the Holy Roman Emperor Charles V, to convene a general council of the Roman Catholic Church to deal with the religious crisis. The Council of Trent, which met off and on from 1545 to 1563, proved to be one of the most important councils in the history of the Church. Catholic reformers participating in this council sought to end the schism that divided Christians, combat heresy, and eliminate moral corruption among the clergy and the laity. Some of the abuses endemic in the Church at this time pertained directly to the family.

Even before the posting of Luther's Ninety-five Theses, for example, some sixteenth-century Roman Catholics acknowledged that there was a widening gap between theory and practice concerning marriage and sexuality. Numerous Catholic commentators criticized clerical celibacy, not because it was evil in itself but because it produced more sexual license than it prevented. Himself the son of a priest, Erasmus and other critics lampooned the hypocrisy of priests who kept concubines, arguing that the ideal of celibacy had negative effects on both the priesthood and the institution of marriage. Erasmus insisted that there was no scriptural basis for the requirement of a celibate clergy, noting that Jesus showed no sign of disapproving of his married apostles.[45]

Nonetheless, in clarifying doctrine, the Council of Trent reasserted the ideal of celibacy and rejected clerical marriage. Catholic reformers recognized the problem of concubinage, as large numbers of priests lived with mistresses in direct violation of canon law. This was not only a moral issue but also a mundane one—priests who kept concubines and fathered children with them might use the Church's property for the benefit of their families. The Counter-Reformation took aggressive steps to eliminate concubinage, although evidence reveals that it was still common in the late sixteenth century. A visitation in 1583 of some rural parishes in the diocese of Speyer in west central Germany revealed that at least 12 of 22 priests openly lived with concubines and children.[46]

In spite of Protestant criticism, Catholic reformers reaffirmed that marriage was a sacrament, rejected divorce, and insisted that the Church had jurisdiction over the validity of marriages. (It conceded that issues pertaining to marital property were under the purview of magistrates, a common practice well before the Reformation.) Be that as it may, many Catholic jurisdictions, like their Protestant counterparts, also saw some secularization of the control of marriage. This was especially true in large territorial states such as Bavaria, Upper Austria, and France. By the late sixteenth century, the Duke of Bavaria, for example, had obtained jurisdiction over a wide range of ecclesiastical concerns, including marriage. This process, however, had begun in the century before the Reformation. Secularization of the control of marriage should be viewed less as the product of confessional conflict and more as part of the bureaucratic development associated with early modern state-building.[47]

At Trent, the most hotly debated family issue pertained to the formation of marriage. Although they still held that freely given consent was essential, through the Tametsi decree (1563), representatives at Trent declared invalid the clandestine marriage, requiring for a valid marriage the publication of banns and the presence of a priest and two witnesses, but not parental permission. In an effort to ensure public order, Catholics, like Protestants, thus deemed publication and a church ceremony complete with the benediction of the priest or minister essential to the formation of a valid marriage. For both Catholics and Protestants, consent remained the key element, and witnesses ensured that both parties freely entered the union.

Evidence indicates that neither the Protestants' requirement of parental permission nor Trent's rejection of that requirement had a dramatic impact on the formation of marriages in practice. A stereotype persists that parents played the decisive role in the formation of their children's marriages, often arranging marriages with the primary goal of securing the most financially advantageous match. A few historians have argued that this tradition, already strong in the late Middle Ages, was enhanced in the Reformation period as more power was concentrated in the hands of the patriarch.[48] Yet, while the role that parents played in their children's courtships varied, the evidence is overwhelming that arranged marriages were the exception rather than the rule in Reformation Europe. Because of property concerns pertaining to dowries and inheritance, there was generally an inverse relationship between the degree of freedom people had in forming marriages and the amount of wealth their family possessed. The poorer a family, the less influence parents had on their sons' and daughters' choice of spouse. Parental authority was not to be exercised arbitrarily; marriages that parents imposed on their children against their will were null.[49]

For all but the wealthiest propertied classes, young people generally took the initiative in courting.[50] Cases can be found in which Protestant parents were forbidden to hinder children in their marital pursuits if they had already reached the age of majority and discussed the matter with their parents. In 1553 Parmenon Vuillie and Jean Chastenetz confessed before the Consistory of Valangin that they had made mutual promises of marriage which they both wanted to honor. The couple had broached this subject with Parmenon's father, who expressed his opposition to the match. Since Parmenon was old enough to marry without her father's permission, the Consistory declared the marriage valid and required her father to give her the customary dowry. Various relatives and friends were to attempt to arrive at a mutually acceptable sum. If they failed to reach an accord, the seigneury would undertake an investigation of Vuillie's assets and the judges of the Consistory would determine the size of the dowry.[51]

On the whole, however, by insisting on parental permission to marry, Protestants did increase patriarchal control over the formation of marriage. Protestant courts more often sided with parents when disputes arose over contracts, frequently recognizing that parents had a definitive veto on their children's proposed marriages. In rural Lutheran Germany, as part of a broader search for order, courts in the sixteenth and seventeenth centuries supported the heads of families who, in an effort to annul contracts their children made without their permission, were the most common plaintiffs to investigations concerning engagements. Paternal consent was often stressed even after the age of majority. Magistrates in Neuchâtel were known to punish young men and women who had reached the age of majority and formed marriage engagements without conferring with their fathers, although their engagements remained valid and binding. In seventeenth-century Holland, parents were apparently able to prevent marriages regardless of their children's age; they generally used this power to veto only when there was considerable discrepancy in the social status of the two parties. The daughter of a Delft regent, for example, fell in love with a pastor 24 years her senior. Her father denied her permission to marry this man, deeming him beneath them in status. At the age of 25, she petitioned a provincial court to be allowed to marry the pastor, but the court ruled in favor of her father. She persisted and finally married him at 33, after her father's death. Parental supervision of their children's marriages was not unique to Lutheran or Reformed areas. Even though church law in England did not require parental consent either before or after the break with Rome, a large proportion of disputed marriage contracts in Ely, Wiltshire, and parts of Salisbury resulted from family opposition to individuals' choice of spouse, most often because the other party was deemed "too poor or too lowly."[52] At times, interest and emotion clearly did conflict.

In spite of such cases, the unavoidable impression is that young people of Reformation Europe, Catholic and Protestant, actually welcomed the input of their parents in choosing spouses. European youth generally enjoyed considerable freedom in courtship but sought parental permission to marry—whether before or after betrothal—even when under no legal obligation to do so. Although there were examples of parents trying to push their children into marriages they did not want, time and time again we encounter promises which young people made on the condition that parents agree to the match. Perhaps sons and daughters felt that the choice of a spouse was too burdensome to be made alone and felt relieved to hear their elders' opinion on the matter. Of course it could be that they were merely afraid of the possible consequences if they did not ask their parents' permission; indeed the prospect of disinheritance might be as effective a means of control as an actual veto. Whether the motivation be fear or, more likely, respect, promises made with such a reservation far outnumbered those cases in which young people were censured for not conferring with their parents before entering into engagements to marry. Both before and during the Reformation, young men and women at least appeared quite willing to consult their elders. In giving advice on the formation of marriages, parents appeared as much interested in their children's future happiness as in securing the most financially advantageous matches.

CHILDREN AND CHILD-REARING

In Reformation Europe, both Protestant and Catholic leaders viewed patriarchy and paternalism as the most effective means of preventing familial and social disorder. Convinced that humans, tainted by original sin, were more inclined to do evil than good, Protestant theologians and magistrates saw the need for paternal discipline within the household. Moreover, they viewed their own role as that of "fathers," providing guidance and coercion to their "children" in order to establish and maintain a well-ordered society.

Interest in early childhood increased dramatically in the Reformation period. With his break with Rome, Luther became convinced that the family, not the Church, was the most fundamental "school for character." To be sure, religious education in the home was not altogether new. Evidence indicates that in pre-Reformation Europe, children memorized Latin prayers, such as the Pater Noster and the Ave Maria, largely under the tutelage of their parents, especially their mothers.[53] But Luther and other reformers sought to encourage religious education in the home still further, promoting private family devotions and exhorting parents to lead the religious education of their children. Luther viewed male household heads as "bishops in their own homes" and thus responsible for the religious education of family members.[54] In Geneva the Consistory at times convoked men and asked them how they instructed their wives and children on religion. Moreover, as Europe became bitterly divided over religion, leaders of all confessions saw the need to indoctrinate the young in order to lead them down the straight and narrow path and protect them from unacceptable beliefs. To a considerable extent, this education was religious in nature. Protestants published large numbers of catechisms, many of which were intended for home use, in which a parent or clergyman would read questions to a child, who was to memorize the appropriate answers. Although they had existed in pre-Reformation Europe, the catechisms published in Lutheran Germany showed an unprecedented secular concern, aiming not only to offer religious instruction but also to promote a strong civic conscience among the young.[55]

The Disciplining of Children

Often this increased attention to child-rearing has been assumed to be repressive. Protestants, especially Calvinists, showed a much greater concern for infant depravity than had Catholics. Catholics believed that the sacraments, such as baptism, automatically provided grace to their recipients, whereas Protestants believed that the sacraments were effective only if the recipient had received the gift of faith from God. Since Protestants believed that children's natural inclination was to sin, many have assumed that followers of this new faith were inordinately harsh toward their children, relying heavily on corporal punishment to dissuade them from sinning. This contrasts, however, with the views of some sixteenth-century Protestant moralists who bemoaned contemporary leniency, complaining that parents considered childhood "only a time for fun, joy, and amusement."[56] Evidence further suggests that Protestants were actually among the first to question the utility of corporal punishment. Protestants insisted that one is saved not by good works but by the grace of God which was received through faith. One was made right before God not by obeying his laws but through faith alone. Consequently, while Protestants did indeed employ corporal punishment to make children more obedient, obedience to God's laws—including that of honoring one's father and mother—did not ensure salvation.[57]

The Puritans of England—Calvinists who sought to "purify" the Church of England of all "popish" elements—paid special attention to childhood and have often been portrayed as treating their children very severely. In many advice books on child-rearing, Puritans urged mothers to nurse their own children rather than send them out to wet-nurses, and saw the first years of life as crucial to a person's development. Since they stressed human depravity, Puritans did indeed warn against spoiling children and thought it necessary to break the will of the child. Many cited biblical passages to avoid sparing the rod and spoiling the child: "Folly is bound in the heart of a child, but the rod of correction shall drive it far from him" (Proverbs 22: 15).

A more careful reading of advice books suggests that Puritans did not view spanking as the method of choice. The goal of disciplining was to modify children's behavior, and if a scolding sufficed to bring them in line, so much the better. In *Of Domestical Duties* (1622), William Gouge wrote 50 pages on the important aspects of loving and nurturing children and then dedicated seven pages to discipline, favoring a middle ground between severity and permissiveness: "Reprehension is a kind of middle thing betwixt admonition and correction: it is a sharpe admonition, but a milde correction. It is the rather to be used because it may be a meanes to prevent strokes and blowes, especially in ingenuous and good natured children. [Blows are] the last remedy which a parent can use: a remedy which may doe good when nothing else can."[58] Such Puritan authors asserted that if a parent deemed that corporal punishment was indeed necessary, it was to be administered calmly, never in a rage. In the area of discipline, the Puritans ultimately favored erring on the side of leniency.[59] One scholar has gone so far as to describe the Puritans as the first "modern parents." If their advice books are a reliable indicator, the Puritans, far from suppressing children, actually insisted that children owed their ultimate obedience to God. Since they were a minority in England, Puritans tried to nurture a certain independence in their children, a trait necessary for their survival in a hostile environment.[60]

Protestants on the continent and in England published unprecedented numbers of books on child-rearing. These popular books clearly found a receptive audience, suggesting that the ideas expressed were not confined to the realm of ideals.[61] Even if they were motivated by their fear of original sin and their goal was to break the will of the child, Protestants were undeniably placing more emphasis on child-rearing than ever before.

The Education of the Young

In this era of religious strife, education was viewed as the key to securing the religious allegiance of the young. Although Luther, Calvin, and other reformers saw the family, the microcosm of society, as a most important arena for religious indoctrination, they did not always trust the judgment of individual parents in providing sufficient instruction to lead their children down the straight and narrow path. They therefore viewed mandatory catechism classes and the creation of schools as a vital complement to education in the family. As early as 1524, Luther wrote a letter, "To the Mayors and Aldermen of all the Cities of Germany in

behalf of Christian Schools," in which he called for elementary education for as many children as possible, including girls.[62]

Following Luther's lead, Protestant reformers and magistrates
throughout continental Europe called for the establishment of schools
and for mandatory school attendance. In light of their emphasis on pre-
destination, one might assume that Calvinists in particular had little
interest in primary education—if God had already predetermined the
destiny of all, what good could religious education possibly do? Calvinists, however, believed that the chief end of humans is to glorify God.
People had duties toward God whether they were or were not among the
elect, and they could learn of these duties only by studying Scripture.
Since they believed that everyone—not just the clergy—should read
Scripture, Protestant reformers believed that primary education ought to
be widely available.[63]

These intentions were not fully realized, and the universal mandatory
education that reformers envisioned was slow to take hold. The sixteenth
century did, however, witness the establishment of a large number of
schools in, for example, both Protestant and Catholic German territories. In Protestant Electoral Saxony, by 1580 half the parishes had established schools for boys, while 10 percent had schools for girls; these
figures increased to 94 and 40 percent respectively by 1675. The education offered in these schools could be rather meager. While urban Latin
schools often provided a superb liberal arts education for the sons of the
elite, the schools that offered instruction only in the vernacular might
teach no more than the catechism and some rudimentary reading skills.
The educational opportunities for girls were particularly limited. Schools
for girls typically offered instruction only for an hour or two a day for
one or two years. Since their studies aimed at nurturing piety, learning
the catechism was of central importance. In some German rural areas,
Protestant boys and girls attended school together and the educational
gender gap accordingly was less pronounced in the countryside than
in cities. Although ensuring school attendance was a problem in many
rural areas, the proliferation of elementary schools was surely a key
factor behind the increasing literacy rates for both males and females in
Protestant areas in the sixteenth and seventeenth centuries.[64]

Catholics continued to recognize priests as intermediaries between God
and believers, so they did not view the family as a microcosm of the
Church to the same extent as Protestants did. But Catholics saw educating the young as a key to promoting their faith. The most important new
order of the Counter-Reformation was the Society of Jesus, founded by
Ignatius Loyola in 1534. The Jesuits were known above all as educators,
establishing some of the best schools in Europe. A new female order, the

Ursulines, founded schools that offered primary education for girls. Probably the central impact of the Counter-Reformation on child-rearing was the establishment of such schools. But while Protestant schools tended to work in tandem with the family to educate the young, the boarding schools of the Jesuits and other Catholic schools appeared more as a substitute for or a rival to the family.[65] Moreover, these educational opportunities in Catholic areas were generally available only for the well-to-do. This was especially true in regard to the education of girls—during the Catholic Reformation, religious orders established some charity day schools, but there were far more for boys than for girls. The educational level of Catholics lagged behind that of Protestants for both boys and girls.[66]

The greater attention paid to children, child-rearing, and education probably represented the most important changes to the family introduced by the Reformation. The Protestant and the Counter-Reformation both had a greater interest in childhood, seeing early childhood in particular as the crucial time for the formation of the Christian.

ILLICIT SEXUALITY AND BASTARDY

Protestant reformers denied the moral superiority of celibacy but vehemently condemned all sexual activity outside marriage. In most parts of pre-Reformation Europe, secular courts, both municipal and territorial, usually had jurisdiction over illicit sexuality (and also issues concerning marital property such as dowry disputes). With the Reformation, both Protestant and Catholic areas became more efficient in enforcing sexual standards, attacking fornication and adultery more aggressively. Certain studies seem to suggest that Lutheran and Reformed polities enjoyed greater success than Catholic tribunals in enforcing sexual morality.[67] These findings, however, in part reflect the fact that many studies of Protestant control of sexuality concentrate on cities, where judicial power was more centralized and the control of morality more effective than in territorial polities which were often Catholic. Reformed Christians in French-speaking areas were nonetheless more aggressive than others in attempting to root out immoral behavior. Consistories in Geneva, Neuchâtel, and elsewhere regularly took the initiative by convoking those suspected of adultery, fornication, and even scandalous *fréquentation*, involving a man and a woman, usually one of whom was married, who were suspected of having an unwholesome relationship because they spent too much time together.[68]

Punishment of such illicit sexuality could be harsh. A few adulterers were put to death in Geneva, usually because they were recidivists or because the paramours were of unequal status (a married woman with her male servant, for example). Perhaps in an effort to keep up with the Calvinists, sixteenth-century Catholics also became more aggressive in attacking illicit sexuality. Like Geneva's Small Council, in the sixteenth century the Parlement of Paris occasionally applied the death sentence for adultery. Although the Old Testament did mandate death for adulterers, Reformation tribunals generally preferred less severe penalties. More often, first-time adulterers and fornicators were sentenced to brief jail sentences of three to five days and then required to confess their sins publicly in church. Although canon law had condemned equally the illicit sexuality of both men and women, in practice a double standard prevailed in many parts of late medieval Europe, whereby a male's sexual indiscretions were punished less severely than a woman's. Evidence suggests that this double standard persisted among both Catholics and Protestants in Reformation Germany but was largely absent in Calvinistic strongholds such as Scotland and French-speaking Reformed areas, where men and women generally received the same penalties.[69] Even if men and women were subject to the same punishments for sexual misconduct, women—be they married or single, Protestant or Catholic—invariably suffered a greater loss of reputation than did men.

First Protestant and then Catholic magistrates tried to enforce the notion that sexuality was to be confined within the bounds of matrimony. This resulted in the effort throughout Western and Central Europe in the later sixteenth century to eliminate prostitution, previously tolerated by Catholic theologians, magistrates, and canon lawyers as an evil necessary to avoid greater sins. Many geographical areas were quite successful in eliminating brothels, which had often been officially sanctioned and operated in the late Middle Ages. If authorities were not entirely successful in removing prostitution itself, they certainly succeeded at the least in driving it underground.[70]

This stricter sexual morality contributed to a growing intolerance of illegitimacy. Throughout much of the Middle Ages, men of the elite often kept mistresses and raised the illegitimate children of these affairs alongside their legitimate offspring. Bastards did not enjoy the same inheritance rights as their legitimate half-siblings, but they were not marginalized and often occupied important positions in European society. Although forbidden to marry, priests produced many children with their concubines, often raising them in households that differed little from those of married couples. The Protestant and Counter-Reformations, however, eventually brought an end to this guarded toleration of bastardy. As both Protestant and Catholic reformers emphasized more than ever before that sexual relations were permissible only after a couple had married in church, they came to stigmatize illegitimate children as the products of sin and a threat to the sanctity of the family and social order.

The legal discrimination against bastards intensified in the sixteenth century. In 1587, an unpublished ordinance of the Protestant Elector of the Rhineland-Palatinate declared that illegitimate babies, even if baptized, would go to hell.[71] Although extreme, this view provides palpable evidence that illegitimacy was increasingly vilified during the Reformation era. In response to the campaign against illicit sexuality, illegitimacy rates declined in the seventeenth century in some parts of Europe, including many Italian cities which were strongly influenced by the Counter-Reformation.[72] By the early 1600s, few men below the rank of royalty dared to raise their illegitimate children openly.

Protestants and Catholics followed different paths in handling illegitimate births. Protestants generally placed considerable emphasis on the individual, insisting that people were responsible for their actions and had to pay the price for their misdeeds. Accordingly, they sought to force the parents of illegitimate children to support them. Women were expected to nurse and raise the bastards they bore, and Protestant magistrates tried to identify the fathers of these children and require them to contribute financially to their upbringing. In certain Protestant areas, judicial authorities were known to administer an oath to unmarried women in labor, enjoining them at the very height of the agony of childbirth to reveal the identity of the fathers. Above all, Protestants strove to avoid having illegitimate children become a burden to the state. Catholics, by contrast, believed that society and the Church must take in abandoned babies in order to save the souls of the children and to restore the honor of their mothers. By the outbreak of the Reformation, institutions specifically for abandoned (and presumably illegitimate) children had already been established in France, Spain, Portugal, and above all Italy, the country which witnessed the largest number of abandoned infants in all of Europe. These foundling homes became widespread throughout much of Catholic Europe but were much less common in Protestant areas.[73]

Although Catholic reformers exhorted both men and women to be chaste outside of marriage, women, whose honor depended almost entirely on their sexual purity, bore the brunt of this campaign. Beginning in the mid-sixteenth century, institutions for "fallen" women were established in many Italian cities. An excellent example is the Casa del Soccorso di San Paolo, established in Bologna in 1589, which was a home for women who allegedly were guilty of illicit sexuality. This home had a strong punitive character, but a stay in such an institution amounted to an act of purification, allowing women to regain their lost honor.[74] True, into the early modern period, Italian courts at times helped women who had been seduced after promises of marriage to regain their honor by requiring their seducers to provide them with dowries and to give their names to illegitimate children. But since Catholic reformers placed much greater importance on the wedding itself than on the marriage promise, they attacked, more than ever before, sexual relations between fiancés, placing the blame primarily on the women. Indeed, by the eighteenth century, Italian women were deemed exclusively responsible for their sexual activity, and Catholic magistrates were generally much less active than Protestants in trying to establish the paternity of illegitimate children.[75] In the wake of the Council of Trent, the fathers of such children in Italy increasingly were required to pay nothing more than the costs of childbirth itself, bearing no responsibility for the material support of the child thereafter. While this alone served as an incentive for women to abandon children born out of wedlock, Catholic moralists viewed unwed motherhood with such repugnance that they actually encouraged the women to give up their children to foundling homes, "lest raising the child create a sense of tolerance toward sinful behavior and encourage other women to do the same."[76] The affront to a woman's honor of having conceived outside marriage could in fact best be expunged by concealing the pregnancy and then abandoning the baby. In Italy, preserving the mother's honor by keeping the birth secret eventually displaced saving the life of the baby as the foundling homes' *raison d'être*.[77]

The increasing disgrace associated with illegitimacy in Reformation Europe unintentionally encouraged infanticide. Moralists of course deplored infanticide, although Catholics in particular were less concerned with the killing of babies *per se* than with the salvation of their souls, believing that the unbaptized had no hope of eternal salvation. In any event, abandoning a baby virtually amounted to a death sentence for the child: in an age of high infant mortality, even in the best conditions the large majority of children who were left in foundling homes did not live to see their first birthday. Not surprisingly, in Germany, Italy, and other areas, both Protestant and Catholic, the late sixteenth and early seventeenth centuries witnessed a dramatic decline in the survival rate of bastards and a large increase in prosecutions of infanticide, a crime committed almost exclusively by unwed mothers.[78]

WOMEN AND THE REFORMATION

In spite of this increase in female criminality, Protestants introduced a number of changes that seem at first glance to have been positive for women. Luther, Calvin, Zwingli, and other reformers preached the spiritual equality of men and women. Moreover, the exaltation of marriage, the rejection of celibacy as the ideal state, the introduction of divorce and remarriage, the rejection (at least in theory) of a sexual double standard, all appear on the surface as progressive for women. Furthermore Protestant leaders disapproved of the "churching" of women because they regarded it as of pagan origin: this ritual, in which women were blessed by a priest outside the church before being allowed to attend mass after giving birth, derived from the notion that women were unclean after childbirth.

In other respects, however, Protestant reformers did little to change medieval Catholic attitudes toward women. They accepted without question the view, embraced by medieval scholastic thinkers who had drawn inspiration from Aristotle, that women were by nature inferior. Citing the apostle Paul, Protestant reformers believed that women were supposed to be silent in church. On this issue, Calvin stood out from other reformers by noting that this stemmed from tradition rather than from divine commandment. Although he thought women might eventually be allowed to preach, he certainly made no effort to effect change in this area.[79]

All Protestant reformers continued to believe that women should be subject to men. Like Catholics before them, Luther, Calvin, and all other reformers required that women be humble and above all obedient to their husbands and fathers. Luther clearly believed that a woman's place was in the home and that her role as breeder was fundamental: "Women are created for no other purpose than to serve men and be their helpers. If women grow weary or even die while bearing children, that doesn't harm anything. Let them bear children to death; they are created for that."[80] He further preached that God intended wives to be subject to their husbands because of their inherent inferiority: "The female body is not strong—it cannot bear arms, etc.—and the spirit is even weaker; according to the normal course of events, it follows [that] . . . woman is half-child. Let everyone who takes a wife know that he is the guardian of a child. . . . She is thus a wild animal; you recognize her weakness of mind."[81] Calvin too stressed female inferiority and, citing Paul, insisted that a wife is to the husband as the body is to the head.[82]

In the later sixteenth century, Lutheran Germany witnessed the publication of numerous pamphlets that described the proper relationships between husbands and wives. These works were part of a new literary genre, "household literature," which included various pedagogical publications, most notably sermons, that dealt with marriage and the family. Since Protestants viewed marriage as the normal state, they presumed that women were destined for the roles of wife and mother and were less tolerant than Catholics had been of women who were not under the authority of a male. With many references to Scripture, Protestant literature displayed a strong abhorrence of such "masterless" women. Moreover, some misogynist Protestant literature offered instructions on wife-beating, ridiculed henpecked husbands, and condemned domineering wives as a violation of nature. By and large, Protestant and Catholic writers of the Reformation era agreed that wives were supposed to be obedient, pious, and silent.[83]

Protestants eliminated many avenues of religious expression that had been important to women in pre-Reformation Europe, most notably the nunnery. Although this had been an option only for the well-to-do, Protestantism provided no opportunity for women to hold any church office or to live so independently of men.[84] While some nuns welcomed the opportunity to leave convents and get married, others strongly resisted and expressed resentment that practitioners of the new faith placed no value on the religious life. In Germany, some nunneries managed to survive long after the territory in which they were situated had rejected Catholicism, a testimony to the tenacious persistence of the sisters. Protestants also disbanded lay confraternities, including those solely for women, which oversaw charitable acts, provided for members in need, and offered a useful outlet for lay piety. They did not replace these institutions with any other all-female groups. Finally, the elimination of the veneration of the Virgin Mary and the saints meant that one could no longer pray to a female figure or celebrate holidays in honor of special women. Clearly prayers to the Virgin Mary and the female saints had been a particularly important part of popular piety for women; women comprised the overwhelming majority of those convoked by Geneva's Consistory for adoration of the Virgin.[85]

Nonetheless, some scholars suggest that the Protestant and Catholic Reformations did provide some significant avenues for women who sought activist roles. Among Protestants in the Netherlands, Germany, and Switzerland, for example, women were quite active in charitable institutions, overseeing hospitals, orphanages, and old age homes. Some historians assert that the growing importance of charitable institutions in Reformation Europe legitimized activist roles for both Protestant and Catholic women. Although often modeled on familial patterns, these roles enabled women to enter the public arena.[86]

Other scholars maintain that religiously active roles related to charity were short-lived. The experiences of certain Counter-Reformation female groups suggest that women's religious expression was subject to increasing male scrutiny. In 1535 in Italy, for example, Angela Merici founded the Ursulines, a group of lay women who were single or widowed, who ministered to the poor, the ill, and orphans, supporting themselves through weaving and, as noted above, teaching. Many similar Catholic women's groups were formed in cities in Italy, Spain, and France. The Church, however, drew the line when Isabel Roser tried in 1541 to receive papal approval of a female order of Jesuits, which, like the Society of Jesus itself, would not be cut off from the world but would endeavor to educate the young, serve the poor and ill, and crucially, win back converts to Catholicism. Appalled at the prospect of having female religious in constant contact with the laity, Pope Paul III rejected this request. The Council of Trent reaffirmed that all female religious were to be cloistered. In the seventeenth century, the Church required even the Ursulines to take orders and live in cloistered communities. In the end, Catholic women with a religious vocation had to be nuns in convents that were cut off from the outside world. All told, the Protestant and Catholic Reformations reinforced the belief that women's religious activities were to take place in a household: either the family household, or the spiritual household of the cloistered Catholic convent.[87]

There is a general consensus that the sixteenth century witnessed a decline in economic opportunities for women, especially for those living in cities. Work that had previously been open was now closed, and opportunities for women to achieve economic autonomy almost disappeared. This decline was in part the result of the increasingly patriarchal character of sixteenth-century society—magistrates put more emphasis on the male head of the household, and women's opportunities significantly diminished. In general, women were able to attain high-status labor— work in which they oversaw production and the distribution of their products—only so long as the home was the site of production. They lost access to high-status labor when work was shifted to larger structures that required political involvement. Given the patriarchal society they lived in, women could not participate in politics and saw their work more and more taken over by men.[88]

Protestantism may have contributed in a small way to the decline in work opportunities for women. The new faith tended to relegate women to the roles of wives and mothers. It also introduced an altogether new role for women, the minister's wife, which may have reinforced the conviction that a woman's place was in the home. These attitudes may have undermined the acceptability of a woman working outside the family: women's work outside the home might suggest financial need and be stigmatized accordingly.[89]

It is also difficult to sustain the view that the Protestant Reformation enhanced the position of women through the control of marriage. True, some historians have seen an alliance between women and matrimonial courts, with women consistently outnumbering men as plaintiffs in matrimonial disputes.[90] This "alliance," however, clearly did not exist everywhere. Adultery was a ground for divorce cited more often against women than by them. Women were more likely to file for divorce because of desertion, but terminating a marriage on this ground had precedents in medieval Catholic Europe. And most studies of court records reveal that men actually comprised the majority of plaintiffs to enforce marriage contracts.[91]

The Protestant and Catholic Reformations affected women in ways that varied according to place and class. It is hard to argue that the status of women in general declined or was enhanced by the Protestant and Counter-Reformations. For those with a religious calling, the Protestant and, to a lesser degree, the Catholic Reformations meant a step backward. For others, the modest increases in educational opportunities in Reformation Europe, especially among Protestants, represented a step forward. The large majority of women probably saw little change in their lot. Having no political voice and limited economic opportunities, they were subject to their fathers and husbands whether they lived before or after 1517, in Lutheran, Calvinist, Anglican, or Catholic territory. All told, continuity outweighed change in the domestic life of Europeans of the Reformation era, and the similarities in the family life of Protestants and Catholics outnumbered the differences.

PART III

DEMOGRAPHIC FORCES

CHAPTER 6

Mortality, Fertility, and Family

Pier Paolo Viazzo

(Translated from the Italian by Caroline Beamish)

One of the changes that has characterized European society most
strongly over the past two centuries is the shift from high levels of mortality and fertility to a demographic system in which mortality is greatly
reduced and fertility controlled. This shift, which began in some parts of
Europe as early as the eighteenth century and ended only in the mid-
twentieth century, is generally known by demographers, economists, and
sociologists as the "demographic transition." Many scholars see this
radical shift in the population of Europe and the West as a consequence,
and also as one of the salient features, of the more general process of
modernization. The economic growth brought on by industrialization,
plus the consequent improvement in diet, coupled with progress in medicine and public health, are believed to have produced a decline in mortality to which the populations of Europe, after an initial period of rapid
demographic growth, responded by deliberately reducing the number of
births.

Although the extent and importance of the demographic transition
obviously cannot be denied, if we view it as a watershed between modern
and pre-modern Europe we run the risk of promoting an image of an
undifferentiated European past in which the population remained almost
stationary for centuries, even millennia, because high levels of childbirth
were matched by equally high levels of mortality. In reality, however,
between 1500 and 1800 the population of Europe more than doubled.
Yet the increase was neither continuous nor uniform; periods of intense
growth alternated with periods of stagnation or decline. Moreover,
changes in population followed different patterns and different routes
in the various European countries, with trends that were often very
divergent and levels of mortality and natality which presented
frequent regional variations. Such variations were greater than the (more
predictable) variations to be found between different socio-economic
groups.

MORTALITY

Famine, Illness, and War: Mortality Crises

In medieval times people prayed to God to deliver them from hunger, epidemics, and war: *A fame, peste et bello libera nos, Domine.* When Thomas Robert Malthus published his *Essay on the Principle of Population* in 1798, he had no hesitation in naming these three scourges as the main curbs to demographic growth (what he called positive checks). They invariably arrested population growth every time available resources became scarce. Until recently, modern historians did not depart significantly from Malthus; they continued to regard famine, epidemics, and war as the three prime causes of the high mortality amongst pre-industrial populations, and to view the economy as the independent variable governing demographic development in European countries. Following the same logic as Malthus, it seemed admissible to suggest that each time the economic situation grew worse—if a region or a city fell into commercial decline, if wages dropped or if crop yields diminished due to the natural tendency for population to increase at a faster rate than resources—it caused an increase in mortality rates and thus a re-establishment of equilibrium.

Although historians and demographers have recognized the close interdependence of the three positive checks to growth, they have traditionally given a clear priority to insufficient food resources, i.e. to hunger. In a famous article published shortly after the end of World War II, the French historian Jean Meuvret, having examined several years characterized by high mortality at the end of the seventeenth century and the beginning of the eighteenth, claimed to have discovered a pattern. The exceptional rises in the number of deaths in many areas of France invariably coincided with an exceptional rise in the price of wheat, the best barometer of a food crisis. "First comes famine, then comes plague": 20 years later Meuvret quoted this French peasant proverb to introduce his theory according to which the peaks in mortality which affected the whole of Europe, from the Middle Ages to the eighteenth century, even those peaks that were due to raging epidemics, could almost always be traced to subsistence crises. Illness flourished against a "background of famine."[1]

In recent years the theory of subsistence crises has not received the empirical confirmation that its supporters were expecting, and the problem of priorities and the relative weight of the three positive checks on growth have consequently re-emerged. In the first place there is reason to believe that the importance of war as a limiting factor in demographic growth has been underestimated. Meuvret himself, although deeply impressed by the enormous losses sustained during two world wars, maintained that wars in the past had very modest demographic consequences compared with the "catastrophes of the modern world."[2] Recent calculations indicate, however, that during the incessant wars of the seventeenth and early eighteenth centuries, between two and a half and three million soldiers died, and that in France alone the War of the Spanish Succession of 1701–1713 cost the lives of no fewer than 600,000 soldiers, a figure which, although very high, does not include the deaths of the civilian victims of reprisals and looting.[3]

A further demonstration of the effect that wars had on populations can be found in recent estimates of demographic changes that took place in the German states during the Thirty Years War. The size of the gaps in populations caused by this war—which was almost exclusively confined to the countries of Central Europe—was very variable, even within the German-speaking world. Whereas some regions, such as Schleswig-Holstein, Westphalia, and the Rhineland, were almost completely spared, maintaining their populations, other regions lost (by death or by exodus due to war) more than two-thirds of their inhabitants. This is what happened in Württemberg, the Palatinate, and Pomerania. It is also interesting to note that within a single area the towns that were on the main travel routes were hit the hardest, whilst places tucked away in inaccessible valleys or protected by great forests were much less affected. In spite of this the Thirty Years War was responsible for a decrease in the population of the whole German-speaking area of about 40 percent.[4]

More serious doubts have been cast on the theory of subsistence crises by a number of recent scientific discoveries on the relationship between diet and mortality and, since the 1960s, by the growing accuracy of our knowledge of the timing and extent of the great epidemics. Yet, some aspects of Meuvret's theses have received empirical confirmation. In particular it has been established that mortality responded to variations in the price of grain and other staple foods, although the intensity of the response differed widely from country to country, particularly in relation to levels of industrialization, revenue, and urbanization. Mortality was high in France between 1677 and 1734 (the classic period of "great famines" studied by Meuvret), but in the same period the relationship between mortality and food shortages appears to have been much weaker in England.[5]

On the whole, however, the correlation between peaks in the mortality rate and food crises seems to be much less close than was previously supposed. What is more, the results of numerous clinical experiments and epidemiological analyses of the effects of subsistence crises during

World War II (for example the famine that hit Holland in 1944–1945) have demonstrated that the human body possesses an unexpected ability to survive for long periods with no food at all. There are special mechanisms within the body that allow it to adapt to conditions of extreme undernourishment and to survive. Of course undernourishment may weaken resistance to pathogens and favor the onset of illness. Clinical and experimental research has revealed a few surprises in this area as well. Although malnutrition certainly favors the spread of a certain number of illnesses such as cholera or measles, its relationship with other infectious diseases appears variable, or even (in the case of plague or smallpox), almost non-existent.[6] This is obviously a complex and controversial issue, but many scholars are reluctant to view shortage of food as the primary cause of the high mortality rates in pre-industrial populations. They prefer to link mortality to epidemiological cycles which, to a large extent, exist independently of the state of nutrition of the population.[7]

Today the vast literature on the subject gives a precise picture of the chronology of the mortality crises for the majority of the countries of Europe. The crises can be divided, Europe-wide, into two distinct phases. The three centuries between 1348 and the middle of the seventeenth century could be termed "the age of the plague." It was during this period that the crises were at their most intense and were capable of wiping out a third to a half of the population of a city or a region in a few months. The best-documented of these cases was the plague that afflicted London in 1603. From the bills of mortality (weekly bulletins which, from 1532 onwards, registered the total number of deaths occurring in London) we know that, before the arrival of the plague, an average of about 4,250 people died each year in London. The great epidemic reached London in the spring of 1603 and in that year the death toll increased tenfold, rising to 42,042 deaths of which 36,269 could be directly attributed (according to the bills) to plague.[8] As the city's population had reached about 200,000, the figures inform us that in the space of a few months the plague killed about 18 percent of the population. Thanks to the survival of some parish registers which record the age of death throughout the plague year it is possible to calculate the incidence of plague at different ages. This makes it clear that increases in the mortality rate were definitely higher for children over five years old and young people up to the age of 24 than they were for adults and old people.[9]

These data from London have largely been confirmed by the less detailed information available for other cities in Europe.[10] They show that the plague did not affect children, young people, adults, and the old in the way that had previously been supposed. This does not mean, however, that very young children and adults were spared. In the plague year 1603 in London the deaths of adults between the ages of 25 and 50 reached 20 percent; this caused the immediate disintegration of an enormous number of families. The death of parents or of other family members often made children more vulnerable, not only to plague but to other causes of death as well.

Having raged for nearly half a century with a violence and frequency unprecedented since the time of the Black Death, after 1660 epidemics of plague grew suddenly fewer and farther between, and their violence abated—probably thanks to the cordon sanitaire, and other preventive measures taken by European governments. The plague returned to the Iberian peninsula, to Sweden and Denmark, and several times to the countries of Central Europe. In 1720, however, after one last great epidemic in Marseille and Provence, the "age of the plague" finally came to an end, giving way to other infectious illnesses such as typhus and smallpox.

What immediately emerges when the annals of mortality crises between the mid-seventeenth century and the late eighteenth century are inspected is not only the way the crises became progressively less frequent, but also the reduction in their intensity. In some cases typhus and smallpox caused as much devastation as plague, and some regions of Europe continued to be smitten by great mortality crises right to the end of the eighteenth century. One extreme example is Iceland. In the early years of the eighteenth century an epidemic of smallpox killed one third of the population of the island, and in 1783–1785 smallpox plus the catastrophic effects of a volcanic eruption combined to triple the death rate and to cause the death of 90 percent of infants under one year old.[11] Nor should the severity of a mortality crisis be measured only by numbers of dead. Much depended also on the age class it affected. While the long-term effects of epidemics of typhus were usually contained, since it was an illness that attacked mainly adults and the elderly, the same cannot be said of smallpox, which affected the younger age groups almost exclusively and therefore made recovery time longer and more problematic. Notwithstanding all this, there was a definite extenuation of the crises in the eighteenth century: for the first time in centuries statistics point to what has been termed the "stabilization of mortality."

During the entire "age of the plague" the swift recurrence of the illness and the capricious, unpredictable nature of the epidemics make "normal" levels of mortality difficult to define. The concept of "normal" in this context is somewhat arbitrary anyway. At this time the only "normal" feature of mortality seems to have been its instability.[12] The wills left by those who died give some of the most vivid impressions of the precariousness of life and the extreme fragility of family structure. They also show how the speed and communal nature of death in times of plague affected individual and social behavior. In wills hastily drawn up during the months when the epidemic was at its height, when the end seemed nigh, it is hard to find evidence that people sought to find ways to transfer their property intact to succeeding generations. In contravention of the regulations governing hereditary succession, many left their possessions to the parish, to a monastery or another religious institution, requesting a proper funeral in exchange. This would save them from the dreadful fate of "the common grave in which thousands of anonymous bodies were heaped together, threatened by packs of stray dogs and only occasionally surrounded by an enclosure or fence."[13] The desire for an appropriate burial is particularly noticeable in wills drawn up during plague years, but the anxieties of a society with no descendants, or of people living with the fear that they might suddenly become so, can also be felt during the brief periods of respite between epidemics. This is evident, for example, in the extreme, almost obsessional care taken by testators to nominate long lists of alternative heirs.[14]

When the "age of the plague" ended, the fear that held people in its grip seemed to abate somewhat. In a more stable demographic situation, when the chances of survival seemed to be increasing, individual and collective existences began to assume a different shape and genuine "family strategies" became, perhaps for the first time, a real possibility. The stabilization of mortality seems to herald a new era in the history of the European family. It is worth asking, in this context, whether the gradual disappearance of crises and the stabilization of mortality were the primary cause of the demographic growth which began in the middle of the seventeenth century, becoming obvious in the eighteenth.

A New Geography of Mortality

Until relatively recently, few scholars had questioned the claim that mortality crises constituted the principal, indeed almost the only bar to population growth in Europe during the four centuries following the Black Death. It seemed logical to think that the gradual extenuation of these crises caused the general decline in mortality, and that this in turn explained the rise in population in the eighteenth century. This traditional viewpoint, however, became the subject of debate when, in 1981, Tony Wrigley and Roger Schofield published the results of their reconstruction of the population history of England from the middle of the sixteenth to the middle of the nineteenth century—a monumental and methodologically innovative work which has radically altered our perception of European demography before the French Revolution.

One early, unexpected discovery was that no particular correlation exists between mortality crises, on one hand, and the general level of mortality on the other. In the very early years of the seventeenth century, when London was so badly afflicted by the destructive effects of the plague, an inhabitant of England could expect to live for an average of about 40 years—a high life expectancy for a pre-industrial society, proof that moderate levels of general mortality are compatible with demographic patterns that are severely disturbed by violent waves of epidemics. During the seventeenth century, nevertheless, and particularly between 1655 and 1680, mortality increased considerably: life expectancy sank to about 30 years and the population shrank by 8 percent. The surprising fact is that this shrinking occurred without any important mortality crisis linked to famine or epidemics. In effect, during the seventeenth century mortality in England experienced a premature stabilization. Various elements, however, indicate that serious infectious diseases which formerly had occurred in epidemic form were now established in endemic form and had therefore become commonplace. As a result, they were not mentioned in the chronicles. The rise in the death rate showed that the toll taken by these endemic illnesses, although less spectacular, was more devastating than the deaths caused by epidemics.[15]

An even more surprising and significant result was the discovery that the sudden rise in the population of England in the second half of the eighteenth century was due only in small part to the decline in mortality, and in much greater degree to a marked rise in the birth rate. As Wrigley and Schofield emphasize, this does not necessarily mean that things developed in the same way in other European countries. The English case contrasts dramatically with that of Sweden, whose demographic growth was certainly caused by a perceptible decrease in mortality. To complicate the European picture even further, there is the well-documented case of France, where a slight decline in both the death rate and the birth rate represents a kind of compromise between the two extremes offered by England and Sweden.[16]

These differing models of growth demonstrate that the demographic history of Europe was characterized by experiences of many different kinds. In the eighteenth century the growth rates of the populations of England and Sweden, two countries belonging to the same "north western" region, were very similar, yet trends in the birth and death rates contrasted totally. Not only trends, but the actual levels of mortality and fertility could vary enormously. It was assumed for many years that in the whole of pre-industrial Europe a "high pressure" demographic regime prevailed, a regime characterized by extremely high birth rates (of the order of 40 or even 50 per 1,000) balanced by death rates that were only marginally lower. The great panorama of the development of the population of England as depicted by Wrigley and Schofield shows on the contrary a "low pressure" demographic regime. The birth rate fluctuates around 30 per 1,000 and the death rate (except over three brief periods) remains constant at levels somewhere between 22 and 28 per 1,000.

This of course does not mean that there were no high-pressure demographic regimes in Europe. On the contrary, there are numerous well-documented examples, particularly in Southern, Central, and Eastern Europe. In Hungary, for example, it has been estimated that in 1777 the birth rate stood at 55 per 1,000 and the death rate at 40 per 1,000.[17] Clearly the discovery of growth patterns and demographic regimes that differ so widely makes it difficult, indeed inadvisable, to make rapid generalizations about pre-revolutionary European demography, and reveals the existence of a hitherto unsuspected geography of mortality.

Infant Mortality

Early signs of the existence of a richly varied geography of mortality were already detectable in studies made in the 1960s and 1970s. These studies brought to light levels of infant mortality that appeared significantly lower in countries such as Belgium, England, and Sweden than they were in countries such as France, Spain, and southern Germany. They also indicated noteworthy variations within individual countries, even individual regions. At first these studies were greeted with skepticism, but over the past 20 years further research into infant mortality has dissipated most of the doubts while confirming the existence of considerable differences. Table 6.1 shows clearly that, over the centuries, infant mortality was much higher in France than in Germany, and especially than in England. In England the low-pressure demographic regime was based on this relatively low rate of infant mortality, which permitted an average of three out of four children of a married couple to survive to the age of 10. By contrast in France only half the children survived to this age. The English figures also show how mistaken it is to imagine that the further back in time one goes, the higher the mortality rate must be. In England infant mortality was lower in about 1600 than it was at the end of the eighteenth century, and the real decline did not begin until a century later. Figures available in sufficient quantity for Belgium, Holland, Germany, Italy, and Spain confirm that, if there was a decline between 1500 and the end of the eighteenth century, it was not necessarily either steady or linear. In fact in some countries slight increases

Table 6.1 Rates of infant mortality and of survival to the age of 10 years in three European countries (rates per 1,000)

Country	Period	Mortality below 1 year	Mortality between ages 1 and 5 years	Mortality between ages 5 and 10 years	Survival to age 10
France	1740–49	296	253	107	469
	1780–89	278	239	90	501
Germany	1740–49	182	156	58	650
	1780–89	177	161	58	650
England	1580–89	168	88	38	730
	1620–29	153	81	33	752
	1680–89	202	130	59	654
	1780–89	163	109	33	721

Sources: France: Blayo 1975; Germany: Imhof 1990; England: Wrigley et al. 1997.

can be observed over the eighteenth century and continuing into the nineteenth.[18]

There are other fundamental aspects of infant mortality that figures relating to whole countries, such as those presented it Table 6.1, may obscure. First and most important of all is the enormous amount of regional and local variation. In eighteenth-century France, for example, variation is tremendous. In the community of Samouillan, in the Haute-Garonne, the infant mortality rate was extraordinarily low (107 per 1,000) and at least 714 children per 1,000 survived to the age of 10. At Nesle-Normandeuse, on the other hand, in the department of Seine-Maritime, only one in three (341 per 1,000) reached the age of 10.[19] Similar differences can be found in England between 1675 and 1749. At March in Cambridgeshire, only 530 children per 1,000 reached the age of 10, whereas in the village of Hartland in Devon a good 817 reached 10 years, thanks largely to an infant mortality rate of less than 100 per 1,000.[20] Similar variations have been recorded in many other European countries. Particularly striking are the contrasts revealed by detailed study of northern and southern Germany, the south being characterized by much higher infant mortality rates than the north.

At the regional level the contrast between different zones was even more extreme in Scandinavia than it was in Germany. In 1749–1773 the proportion of children dying before reaching their first birthday was almost double in the Finnish province of Ostrobothnia (326 per 1,000) what it was in the Finnish province of Karelia (173 per 1,000), and the difference was even more pronounced at the local level. Whereas in a number of parishes in Sweden and Finland the infant mortality rate was only a little over 100 per 1,000, in Koivulathi, a coastal parish of Ostrobothnia, the figure was 548 per 1,000—probably the highest "normal" level ever recorded in the literature of historical demography.[21] Differences that were almost as extreme, some of them within the same locality, have been recorded recently in the Volga provinces in Russia: infant mortality among the Russian Orthodox community was extremely high compared with infant mortality among the Muslim community of Tatars.[22]

It is no simple matter to work out why levels of infant mortality should be so diverse. Two reasons seem to emerge very clearly, however. The studies conducted in Germany, Scandinavia, and Russia have proved beyond doubt that where weaning took place early, or where breast feeding was not practiced at all, mortality was invariably higher than it was in places that were environmentally and economically similar but where babies were breast-fed for a long time. We know from various sources, both medical and ethnographic, that breastfeeding was not practiced in many regions of Europe, especially in Scandinavia and Central and Eastern Europe. The sources often suggest reasons why women in these areas did not breast-feed, or did not breast-feed for very long. In a report to the Collegium Medicum in Stockholm in 1754 the exceptional infant mortality in Ostrobothnia was attributed to the local practice of feeding babies on cow's milk rather than breast-feeding them. In 1752 the great Swedish naturalist Linnaeus published a pamphlet significantly titled *Nutrix noverca* ("harsh foster mother") in which he observed that, where infant mortality was highest in Sweden, mothers did not breast-feed their young. One century later a nineteenth-century observer, writing about a parish in Ostrobothnia, confirmed that children were "fed with cows' milk which they take through a teat. When the child reaches the age of one year it is given sour milk, which often causes it to die." Breastfeeding, he added, "is considered indelicate; and anyway the men do not allow their womenfolk to breast-feed in case it destroys their beauty."[23]

So there were also cultural reasons which prevented women from breast-feeding their children, thus depriving them of the immunity conferred by breast milk. Breastfeeding was seen as a threat to the mother's beauty and sometimes as dangerous to health; or, alternatively, as an obstacle to the resumption of sexual relations, which were held to "weaken" or to "corrupt" breast milk. These attitudes were shared by Finnish peasant families and by the European aristocracy.[24] There were economic reasons too. During the winter months, women in coastal communities of Ostrobothnia only had housework to keep them busy and had no difficulty in looking after their children. In the summer, on the other hand, when their husbands were off in the fishing grounds, they were alone in the fields and they therefore preferred to wean their children early or to transfer them to bottle-feeding. This explains why, in these Finnish villages, as in many other peasant communities of Europe where breastfeeding was rare, deaths of newborn babies and infants were mainly concentrated in the summer months, whereas in communities where breastfeeding was the norm deaths were more evenly distributed throughout the year.[25]

Summer was the high season for infant mortality for two reasons: first, children received less attention during the months when agricultural labor was at its height and, secondly, warm temperatures produced a rise in gastro-intestinal ailments, the most dangerous for newborn babies and infants recently weaned. The risk was particularly high in the Mediterranean region, the hottest part of Europe. "*El mes de agosto los enfermaba y el de septiembre se los llevaba*" goes the Spanish proverb: "The month of August made them ill and September carried them off."[26] All over Europe infant mortality tended to be perceptibly lower in mountainous areas, where not only the lower temperatures but also climatic characteristics connected to altitude and the purer water helped to protect children. Not that mortality rates were uniform in all mountainous areas. For example in the Western Alps rates were similar to those prevailing in England, between 150 and 250 per 1,000; in the Austrian Alps, on the other hand, the annual mortality rate varied between 230 and 300 per 1,000. These higher levels should come as no surprise when we consider that in the Austrian Alps, as in the whole of Austria (and unlike the Western Alps) breastfeeding was seldom practiced. But even this case, given the difference between the infant mortality rates found in the Alpine zone of Austria and the much higher rates (up to 400 per 1,000) to be found in the Austrian plains, gives further confirmation of the advantages conferred by mountain climate and cleaner water—even in the absence of breastfeeding.[27]

In addition to breastfeeding, the other principal explanation for geographical variations in levels of infant mortality was therefore the environment. The influence of environmental factors was not only evident in the contrast between the mountains and the plains. Small distances and modest differences of altitude could have considerable consequences when combined with variations in the quality of the water and the air. Some of the eighteenth-century pioneers of demography, such as Muret in Switzerland and Moheau in France, had already noticed the high mortality rates in marshy areas, but precise and incontrovertible historical and demographic proof of the devastating effects of bad air ('mal' aria') and stagnant water on infant mortality has only recently been obtained. The most striking facts come from south-east England, where there was no difference in the methods of feeding newborn babies and infants (breastfeeding was the norm everywhere) but where geographical conditions varied considerably: a few miles could separate an isolated, sparsely inhabited hilltop community from a more densely populated marshy area. The demographic differences between the two places were enormous: in the late eighteenth century the infant mortality rate in the hilltop communities ranged from 75 to 180 per 1,000, whereas in the nearby marshy zone the rate could be as high as 450 per 1,000.[28]

These figures indicate that in southeast England the most distinct epidemiological boundary was not the one separating rural from urban areas but the one separating rural areas which were more favored geographically from marshy, malarial areas. Nevertheless, cities offered environments that were extremely unfavorable to the survival of children, and their effects grew more lethal as they expanded in size.

A case in point is London, the urban center of southeast England which from 200,000 inhabitants in 1600 grew to nearly one million by the end of the eighteenth century—the most populous city in Europe. At the beginning of the seventeenth century the "normal" infant mortality rate was probably about 150 per 1,000—close to the estimated rate for the whole of England in the same period. During the second half of the seventeenth century, however, it has been calculated that it had already risen to 260 per 1,000 and that it rose further in the first half of the eighteenth century, to a figure nearing 350 per 1,000—lower than the rate in some of the marshy areas, but high enough nevertheless to ensure that only 422 children per 1,000 in London reached the age of 10.[29] Although unusual in many ways, the case of London is nonetheless broadly representative of a general condition of high infant mortality in urban areas, due principally to the high density of population. Where people were so crowded together they acted as a reservoir for infection.

The boundaries between town and country were further blurred, and the geography of European mortality made more complex and varied, by a phenomenon which has now disappeared but which used to be extremely widespread: wet-nursing. When breastfeeding and bottle-feeding are compared and contrasted, the existence of an alternative method of infant feeding is often forgotten—suckling children for money. Sending children to a wet-nurse was a common practice amongst women belonging to the European aristocracy; at least until the end of the eighteenth century they had no hesitation in delegating to women of a lower class a chore which to many appeared animal-like and disgusting. Wet-nurses were occasionally resident in the house, but more frequently the children were lodged in the nurse's house, usually in the country. The fact that children who were nursed by a wet-nurse died less frequently than those who were bottle-fed, but more frequently than those breast-fed by their mother, produced a paradoxical result: often, as happened in seventeenth-century England, the nobility lost more young children than were lost by the less well born—who breast-fed their own babies.[30] As well as among the aristocracy, this custom was also widespread among the urban middle classes and even the working class. Artisans in particular found it convenient to send their newborn babies to a wet-nurse in the country. Especially in French cities the use of wet-nurses had reached pandemic proportions. In a report published in 1780 the Lieutenant-General of the Paris police made it known that out of 21,000 children born in the city, fewer than 1,000 were breast-fed by their mother and fewer than one thousand by nurses living in the parents' house; all the other babies were sent to a wet-nurse in the country. The figures may be exaggerated, but there can be no doubt about the scale of the phenomenon in France. In the decade 1780–1789 the death of babies in the care of wet-nurses represented less than 2 percent of the annual total of dead in rural Aquitaine, but 14 percent in Provence and Languedoc, 17.5 percent in the Paris region and 21.7 percent in Normandy.[31] Massive migrations of newborn babies like this dramatically altered the demographic balance between town and country and make it difficult today to estimate levels of infant mortality at the regional level. However, wet-nursing, and alternative forms of infant feeding in general, influenced female fertility as well as infant mortality.

FERTILITY

Nuptiality and Fertility

One of the first great successes of research into historical demography was, in about 1960, the finding that in pre-industrial Europe women did not have the prodigious number of children that they had always been supposed to have had. Of course there were some examples of amazingly prolific women. In one of the books that has contributed most to popularizing historical demography, Peter Laslett quotes the case of Ann Sackett, born in Kent in 1779, who married one John Cook at the age of 18; she gave birth 20 times and had 21 children.[32] However, what strikes the reader of Laslett's book most forcibly is the discovery that cases like that of Ann Sackett were anything but typical. In pre-industrial Europe women had an average of only five or six children.

What were the reasons for this relatively modest fertility? One prime reason was high mortality: for a woman the risk of dying prematurely—often in childbirth—was great, and the risk of being widowed while still young was also high. A second, no less important reason was the delay in beginning what demographers term the woman's "reproductive career." In almost all West European countries men and women tended not to get married until some years after reaching sexual maturity—on average at about 28 for men and 26 for women.[33] The tendency to marry late was accompanied by large numbers of people remaining single. It is probably not far from the truth to say that in Western Europe, before 1790, one man and one woman in ten did not marry, and in quite a number of regions (for example the Alps and the Pyrenees) this propor-tion might rise to 20 or even 30 percent.[34]

Matters were different in Eastern Europe. Although our knowledge of those areas is somewhat fragmentary and superficial, east of an imagi-nary line drawn between Trieste and St Petersburg it was much less common for an adult to remain unmarried. Both men and women married at around the age of 20 or earlier and almost everyone married. In the countries of Eastern Europe therefore the birth rate was poten-tially much higher, even though a particularly high death rate acted as a restraint. In West European countries the birth rate was held in check both by mortality, which cut marriages short, and also by what Malthus termed the "preventive check" of late marriage which robbed women of their most fertile years and condemned a certain proportion to perma-nent spinsterhood.

Having shed some light on the reasons for a relatively low birth rate, we might now look at level and "profile" of fertility, assuming for the time being that the number of children born to a woman was not limited by late marriage or by the death of one of the partners. One answer, although it only provides a rough approximation and does not claim to be totally representative, is provided by Table 6.2, which shows the rates of legitimate fertility for a few selected countries in Western Europe: the rates are calculated "net," i.e. without the influence of the death of a marriage partner or of late marriage. By adding these rates together a total rate of legitimate fertility is arrived at—i.e. the number of children a woman who married young, at about 20, and who was still married and alive at the age of the menopause, could expect to have had. The fertility profile, as the table shows, was similar in all countries: at its highest between 20 and 24 years, fertility declines gradually until the age of 40 and more rapidly thereafter. The levels present perceptible differences, nevertheless: in Swiss, French, and Belgian communities

Table 6.2   Age-specific and total marital fertility rates in select West European countries

Country	Period	20–24	25–29	30–34	35–39	40–44	TFR*
Belgium	pre-1750	472	430	366	317	190	8.88
France	pre-1750	467	445	401	325	168	9.03
Germany	pre-1750	432	399	358	293	138	8.10
England	1600–1799	383	350	304	243	134	7.07
Italy	1620–1860	430	410	375	310	160	8.42
Scandinavia	pre-1750	447	412	344	287	166	8.28
Switzerland	pre-1750	509	463	398	321	164	9.29

* TFR = Total Fertility Rate.
Sources: Belgium, France, Germany, Scandinavia, and Switzerland: Flinn 1981, p. 31;
England: Wilson 1984, p. 228; Italy: Livi Bacci and Breschi 1990, p. 392.

fertility appears to be conspicuously higher than it is in Italian, Scandinavian, German and, in particular, English communities.

Once again, a geography of demographic behaviors characterized by strong differences emerges, and once again the decisive factor is breast-feeding. It is well known that prolactin, a hormone whose secretion is encouraged by the baby sucking at the breast, not only stimulates lactation but also inhibits ovulation, thus reducing the probability of conception. Very recent studies have shown that in pre-industrial English society very few women stopped breast-feeding before their child was a year old, and that many continued until the beginning of the baby's third year. With intervals between births of 30 months or more, it comes as no surprise to learn that a woman, even if she survived past menopause, gave birth generally to no more than six or seven children, and that cases of women with ten or more children were unusual.[35] Although obscured by average figures like those presented in Table 6.2, there were however regional contrasts which were even more pronounced than those between England and other European countries. Whereas in northern Germany, where breastfeeding was the norm, the overall fertility rate was about seven or eight, in Bavaria the number of children per female rose to nearly ten. A comparative study of two Scandinavian villages—one Swedish village in which breastfeeding was practiced with great enthusiasm, and the other a village in Ostrobothnia where babies were bottle-fed—yields an estimated total fertility rate of 6.72 for the Swedish village compared with 10.05 children per woman in the Finnish village.[36]

Levels of fertility that are, if possible, even higher than those encountered in Bavaria or Ostrobothnia can be found in many European cities.

This "urban hyperfecundity" has been confirmed by a succession of studies. It was first detected about 30 years ago in a classic study of the population of Lyon in the eighteenth century by Maurice Garden. Garden, like Laslett, cited a dramatic case of high fertility. This concerned a butcher, Jacques Gantillon, and his wife Barthélémie Hodieu who, between 1723 and 1747, produced 21 children (the same number as Ann Sackett and John Cook). However, the fertility of the husband and wife in Lyon appeared less exceptional in a city where one third of the families of artisans and small tradespeople had ten or more children. The surprising fact is that the people of Lyon did not marry very early: the average age of first marriage for women was about 27.5. How can such high levels of fertility be explained? One early indication occurs in a report written in 1789 in which the Procurator Royal remarks of the women of Lyon that "their state, their work and their condition leave these women neither the time nor the means to feed their children." In another, slightly earlier report we read that for the working families of Lyon children were "unwelcome guests." These indications are confirmed by the statistics collected by Garden which show how—just at the time when, recalling Rousseau's *Emile*, doctors and the educated classes of Lyon were championing breastfeeding by the mother as the best way— the laborers and artisans in Lyon were consigning the majority of their children to thousands of wet-nurses in hundreds of rural parishes. A consequence of this massive recourse to wet-nurses was extremely high fertility.[37]

The close relationship between wet-nursing and fertility has been demonstrated in many other European cities. The most outstanding case is possibly that of Milan in the mid-nineteenth century. Unique written evidence charts very precisely the fertility of married women of the laboring classes. They abandoned their children in droves to the big foundling hospital and the hospital sent them off to wet-nurses in the country. The fertility of these women in Milan is extraordinarily high at every age: the total fertility rate measured between the ages of 20 and 44 was 13.7 children for each woman.[38] Paradoxically, the consignment of their babies to a wet-nurse "liberated" the reproductive potential of urban women from the restraining influence of breastfeeding. By contrast, for the thousands of wet-nurses in rural areas the arrival of a child to nurse (often as a substitute for a recently deceased child) prolonged the breast-feeding period, thereby prolonging the period of temporary sterility. This caused relatively low fertility in the countryside in contrast to the hyperfertility prevailing in the cities.[39]

Fertility varied enormously among the various countries of Europe, between region and region, and between town and country. Yet the different levels of fertility did not necessarily produce a different "natural balance" between the number of births and the number of deaths. By relying on bottle-feeding the peasant families of Ostrobothnia and Bavaria produced a far greater number of children, but among these children mortality was enormously high. Similarly the working people of Lyon who sent their children to wet-nurses in the country were condemning them to a risk of dying in infancy that was more than double the threat posed to the children of peasant women who breast-fed them themselves. Of the 6,000 children born annually in Lyon, says a report published in 1780, "more than 4,000 die when out to nurse."[40] Fertility and infant mortality tended therefore to balance each other out. In the less salubrious areas of Europe—marshy areas, cities—female fertility could be very high precisely because of adverse environmental factors which caused babies to die. The effects were similar to those of bottle-feeding and wet-nursing. If instead of examining the "total offspring" of a couple, the total number of children produced by them, we examine what is sometimes termed the "useful offspring," i.e. the number of children surviving beyond five or ten years, we discover that even in areas with the most diverse levels of fertility the figures tend to be surprisingly similar.[41]

The Different Paths Followed by Fertility

For many years historical demographers clung to the conviction that between 1500 and 1789 fertility in Europe remained more or less stable, although varying in different countries and regions because of the environmental and (above all) cultural factors which influenced the frequency and duration of breastfeeding. However, closer examination has brought to light a story which is somewhat different. Although recent investigations have confirmed the general level as being low, they have revealed that in England not only did fertility vary over the years, it varied substantially. From a rate of 7.53 children per woman in 1600–1624 it went down to 6.78 children in 1650–1674 and back to about 7.5 children between 1725 and 1800.[42] The figures demonstrate that fertility climbed by 10 percent from the late seventeenth century, contributing far more strongly to demographic growth in England than had previously been thought. In addition, they appear to confirm what other studies published over the last 20 years had already suggested, i.e. that during the course of the eighteenth century fertility in various regions of Europe saw increases which can only be partly attributed to simultaneous increases in infant mortality.

Two hypotheses have been advanced to account for this rise in fertility: an improvement in feeding and in the health of mothers, and a reduction in the duration of breastfeeding. The first hypothesis could account for the increase in fertility noted in the Swiss Alps, where the introduction of the potato and other new crops in the second half of the eighteenth century produced a considerable increase in food resources.[43] In the regions of Brabant and Flanders, in Belgium, where in the eighteenth century the diet seems to have become even more impoverished than it was before, a more convincing explanation could be that the breast-feeding period was appreciably curtailed. According to recent estimates it declined from 20 to 15 months in Flanders and from 16 to 12 months in Brabant.[44] These findings are of great interest to historians and demographers, but they are also interesting to biologists and ecologists. What is certainly evident is that during the eighteenth century European fertility developed in a variety of ways. Whereas in England, the Swiss Alps, and in Belgium fertility rose, in other parts of Europe and particularly in France the first signs of the reverse tendency (the tendency which eventually prevailed) manifested themselves. Fertility began to drop, provoked by the decision of a growing number of families to limit the number of children they produced.

The use of methods of contraception leaves traces in parish registers which demographers have learned to identify with increasing sophistication. Even more than a drop in the number of children, the best indication or proof that birth control is being used is a rapid diminution in birth rate after the age of 30, or a drastic lowering of the average age of women when they have their last baby. On the basis of these indications it is certain that an early form of birth control was used all over Europe by a few particular groups—the aristocracy, the urban *haute bourgeoisie*, some religious minorities—and that in some cities the example of these pioneers was extensively followed well before the French Revolution. In Rouen and Geneva, two cities in which the more affluent classes limited births as early as the first half of the seventeenth century, the number of children per mother declined by more than a third between 1670 and 1770. In Geneva, the average age of the mother bearing her final child, which until 1675 remained stable at around 40, had already fallen to 37 at the beginning of the eighteenth century and by 1770 had fallen to only 34.5.[45]

The early use of birth control has also been detected in rural areas. Of particular interest are the examples of the Swiss Canton of Glarus and, above all, the region of Ormánság, in eastern Hungary. Even before 1780 Ormánság had attracted the attention of agents of the Empress Maria Theresa because its birth rate was much lower than the rate in the rest of the Habsburg empire. Modern demographic studies have confirmed that in this part of Hungary women, in spite of marrying very young, produced very few children. The total fertility rate in some communities could be as low as six or even five children per mother. During the second half of the eighteenth century a practice, indeed a custom, began to emerge which during the nineteenth century was to become the so-called "one-child system" (*egy gyermek rendszer*), a generalized tendency to have only one child, whether a girl or a boy, which until quite recently made this area on the eastern side of the Danube one of the least fertile places in Europe.[46]

The fact that Glarus is the most Protestant canton in the Swiss Alps and that Ormánság is a Calvinist enclave in Catholic Hungary seems to lend force to the theory that Protestant families, compared with Catholic families, had a greater ability to adapt to new circumstances and a greater propensity to control fertility in difficult economic conditions. We should not forget, however, that Calvinist Geneva was very similar to Catholic Rouen, that contraceptive behavior has been identified in aristocratic Catholic, Protestant, and Anglican families and that, above all, deliberate birth control first spread to the populace at large in France, a Catholic country. The urban groups that first practiced birth control in different parts of Europe, and the populations of Ormánság and Glarus, in the foothills of the Alps, were small enough not to influence the overall levels and trends of fertility in the wider context. In France in the last decades before the Revolution contraception began to spread with increasing vigor, contributing at least in part to the general decline in fertility which reached about 10 percent. Viewed retrospectively, this was a modest decline compared with the much more rapid decline that began during the Revolution. But these early signals were evidently sufficient to arouse alarm at the time. In 1778, Jean-Baptiste Moheau complained, in his *Recherches et considérations sur la population de la France*, that "rich women, for whom pleasure is their greatest interest and their only occupation, are not the only ones to consider the propagation of the species to be the pastime of simpletons: the grisly secrets unknown to any other animal but mankind have penetrated to the countryside, and nature is deceived in our villages too."[47]

SOCIAL DIFFERENCES IN FAMILY DEMOGRAPHY

Infanticide, Illegitimacy, and Abandonment

A convincing explanation for the early spread of contraception in France, a century or more earlier than in the rest of Europe, has yet to be given. It is interesting to note, however, that in France the age of marriage, and the number of unmarried men and women, both continued to rise throughout the eighteenth century.[48] It would seem that, before choosing contraception, and in order to bypass Malthus's "checks," the French people tried first to slow down population growth by using the "preventive check" of marriage. In this they resembled those living in the many other European countries in which there was a rise in the age of marriage during the second half of the eighteenth century. Clearly the population of Europe, which almost doubled between 1750 and 1850, would have increased even faster without the restraint placed on it by delaying the age of marriage. Some scholars are of the opinion, however, that demographic growth would also have been slowed down by another means of control, which Malthus placed in an intermediate position between repressive and preventive checks, namely infanticide. According to the best-known supporter of this theory, William Langer, infanticide, whether carried out secretly or in public, was no less important in controlling population than was delayed marriage.[49]

This theory was formulated in the early 1970s and still enjoys some popularity. In 1777, Frederick the Great informed Voltaire that in Prussia infanticide was the crime that most often led to the death penalty, and that more than 200 of the 617 death sentences imposed in Sweden between 1749 and 1778 were punishment for infanticide. This might suggest that cases of infanticide rose sharply at times of demographic pressure. Yet this impression has not been confirmed by recent studies. A detailed analysis of large numbers of trials and legal statistics indicates, for example, that in eighteenth-century England the incidence of infanticide was lower than it had been in the mid-sixteenth century.[50] Historians are agreed in interpreting the violent denunciations that writers such as Defoe or painters such as Hogarth expressed as the result of increased social conscience rather than as the reflection of an increase in crime. In a more general way, they consider it improbable that "flagrant" infanticide had any significant role to play either in controlling population or as part of family strategies.[51] Langer, however, also mentioned secret or indirect infanticide, meaning mainly the abandonment of children. And, indeed, it is undoubtedly true that there was an enormous rise in the number of children abandoned, all over Europe, in the eighteenth century.

In some European countries foundling hospitals had already existed for two or three centuries. The oldest were founded in Italy in the late Middle Ages. Between the end of the fifteenth century and the middle of the seventeenth, many more appeared in Spain, Portugal, and France. In other countries care of abandoned children continued to be the responsibility of the parish or of local communities until about the mid-eighteenth century, when new foundling hospitals were opened in nearly all the principal cities of Northern, Central, and Eastern Europe: London in 1741, Moscow and St Petersburg in 1764 and 1771 respectively, Vienna in 1784, Prague in 1789. Thanks to well-stocked, detailed archives, we know that between 1720 and the end of the eighteenth century the number of foundlings admitted to old-established foundling homes, such as those in Florence, Milan, Paris, Lyon, Seville, and Oporto, tripled and that the number admitted to homes established during the Enlightenment soon turned into a major flood. By the end of the eighteenth century the number of children abandoned annually in Europe was about 100,000, nearly all of them in early infancy.[52]

One factor that contributed to this vertiginous rise in the number of abandoned children, which was far more rapid than the rise in the population as a whole, was the growth in illegitimacy. When fertility in Europe before the French Revolution is discussed the children born outside wedlock tend to be forgotten. If we except certain regions such as northern Portugal, the Basque country, the Alpine provinces of Austria, Scotland, or Iceland, where illegitimacy was frequent, in most parts of Europe illegitimate births accounted for somewhere between 1 and 5 percent of the total. During the eighteenth century there are signs of rapid growth: in England the numbers grew from about 2,000 illegitimate births per year in 1650 (only 1 percent of the total) to about 20,000 in the final decades of the eighteenth century, equal to about 6 percent of the total number of births, and trends were similar in France, Germany, and the Scandinavian countries.[53] Some have attributed this increase to growing urbanization and the onset of industrialization, two processes of modernization which are believed to have produced drastic changes in morals; a number of scholars have termed this a "first sexual revolution."[54] Others have suggested, particularly with regard to Central Europe, a connection between the growth of illegitimacy in the eighteenth century and changes then occurring in the agrarian structure of the countryside. In many cities at this time the increase in illegitimacy was truly enormous. Paris is a case in point. Not only did illegitimate births there rise from fewer than 2,000 in about 1720 to nearly 5,000 half a century later, when one child in every four born in Paris was illegitimate, but there was also a striking simultaneous increase in the numbers of abandoned babies.[55]

Although the figures for Paris leave no doubt about the close connection between illegitimacy and abandonment, the geography of illegitimacy and abandonment is as richly varied and as nuanced as the geography of mortality and fertility. Attitudes varied across the spectrum. In some regions of Europe the civil and religious authorities obliged unmarried mothers to place their children in foundling hospitals, even when the mothers or grandparents wished to keep them. In other parts, as for example in the Basque country, illegitimate children were received into the mother's family with no difficulty. The admissions policy of the foundling hospitals varied enormously, even within the same area. In 1774 the director of the foundling hospital in Florence, the Innocenti, observed that whereas most of the other foundling homes in Tuscany "receive only illegitimate children, this is an institution for children abandoned by their parents and it accepts the illegitimate as well as the legitimate, the latter being more numerous than the former."[56]

There is now a great deal of evidence to suggest that the extraordinary increase in the number of foundlings was to a large extent due to the growing tendency of impoverished parents to abandon the care of at least some of their offspring to the foundling hospitals.[57] It was not unusual for parents to return to the institution after a year or two to reclaim their children, but the chances of finding them alive were slim. It was rare for more than half the foundlings to survive the first year of life, and they continued to die in large numbers during the second. Much depended on the ability of the foundling home to place the babies with wet-nurses in the country. If this was done quickly, mortality could attain a level of about 500 per 1,000—a high figure, but not much higher than that for children placed with wet-nurses by their own parents. Quite frequently, however, there was a genuine shortage of wet-nurses. In such circumstances, with the babies condemned to remain within the walls of the institution fed by the few wet-nurses employed there, or on cow's or goat's milk, infant mortality rose to a horrifying 800 to 900 per 1,000. In the eighteenth century foundling homes were the scene of experiments in artificial feeding conducted according to the strictest dictates of the medical science of the period, but the outcome was always either negative, as in London in 1741, or catastrophic, as in the Russian foundling homes.[58] It would be an exaggeration to view abandonment as legalized infanticide, but mortality among children sent to foundling homes was extremely high and could add considerably to the negative demographic balance even in very large populations. Apart from its demographic importance, the tragic fate of foundlings is striking for another reason. Representing as it does "one of the social extremes of the mortality of the past,"[59] it demonstrates how vast the social differences were in the face of death.

Mortality Differences: Males and Females, Rich and Poor

We know from a great many historical and ethnographic sources that in many parts of the world men and women were unequal in the face of death from the moment they were born; in India, China, and Japan, where infanticide was widespread, girls were killed much more frequently than boys. It is also common knowledge that in some countries even today girls are weaned earlier, fed less well and are in general more neglected by their parents than boys—to the extent that girls die more frequently than boys. In such cases it would not be an exaggeration to talk about "indirect infanticide." Evidence of a preference for male children is not lacking in European history either. It has been revealed, for example, that toward the end of the eighteenth century in France couples would delay the use of contraceptive techniques if they had no male children. There is no evidence to suggest, however, that in pre-industrial Europe this preference was expressed either in the form of selective infanticide or in serious neglect. Suspicions have been voiced on occasion regarding generalized female infanticide, especially during the Middle Ages, but these have been shown to be unfounded.[60] The only blatant example of preference, with immediate effect on mortality, has been provided by abandonment. In areas where abandonment was the fate almost exclusively of illegitimate children, the ratio of male to female foundlings tended to be equal. However, where legitimate children were also abandoned there was a marked preference for abandoning girls. This difference was unusually strong in the late Middle Ages and the first centuries of the modern period, when the number of girls abandoned could be double the number of boys, but this imbalance diminished perceptibly in the eighteenth century, and almost disappeared in the nineteenth.[61]

On the whole, it does not seem likely that infanticide, direct or indirect, was the cause of unusually high mortality among infant girls. On the contrary, up to the age of five mortality tended to be generally higher amongst boys. Things were different in childhood and adolescence, and particularly in adulthood. To some extent this was due to the selectivity of certain diseases which attacked girls more than boys. The spread of one such illness, tuberculosis, probably explains the higher mortality of girls between 5 and 15 demonstrated in England from the sixteenth to the eighteenth centuries; this was a death toll which rose steadily.[62] In almost all the countries of Europe excess female mortality is, however, clearly detectable, especially between the ages of 25 and 45 years. The main cause of this is maternal mortality associated with childbirth.[63]

In Western Europe today the risk of dying in childbirth is slight: for each 100,000 births the number of deaths varies from between 6–7 in Norway, Sweden, Switzerland, and Spain to 15 in France and Portugal. Puerperal mortality rates are considerably higher in some of the countries of Eastern Europe (50 per 100,000 in Ukraine, 75 in Russia, 130 in Romania), but these differences fade into insignificance when compared with mortality rates in the relatively recent past. In the period between the two world wars, the rates in Western Europe varied between 250 and 700 per 100,000 births, and levels were even higher (much higher) in Europe before the French Revolution. In the mid-eighteenth century estimated deaths in childbirth in a number of European countries (France, Flanders, Germany, England, Sweden) were between 1,000 and 1,200 per 100,000 births, but in some areas this figure was almost doubled.[64] This means that a woman approaching childbirth faced a 1–2 percent likelihood of dying. This may not seem very much, but it must be remembered that in pre-industrial Europe a woman would typically have five or six children: the cumulative probability of dying in childbirth was therefore about 5–10 percent—a thousand times as great as the risk faced by a woman in Europe today, who on average confronts the risks associated with childbirth only once or twice in her lifetime.

These figures show that the fears surrounding the actual moment of childbirth were quite justified, and there is no doubt that death in childbirth was regarded in a different way from other ways of dying. The rapid, agonizing death of a mother in giving birth to a baby instantly transformed the joy of a long-awaited birth into a tragedy which overwhelmed the whole family. The death rate of women from puerperal fever nevertheless was not as excessive as has often been thought—it only just outweighed deaths of boy babies in their early infancy. On the whole, therefore, it was males who lived less long than women, and in some regions such as Brabant or southern Italy excess male mortality has been noted in the adult age groups as well.[65] The case of southern Italy is a good example of the way the rigid division of labor between men and women caused the exposure of each sex to different diseases and thus resulted in different levels of mortality. In regions dominated by large cereal farms only the men walked the long distance between fields—often through unhealthy, swampy areas—from the villages perched on hilltops where people generally lived. Economic factors (endemic unemployment among male farm laborers) and cultural factors (the idea that work in the fields was dishonorable for women) combined to drive the female workforce into subsidiary productive roles. The women stayed in the village to look after the house and to weave, so they usually avoided contracting malaria which, as we have seen, affected those who lived and worked in swampy areas and spared those who lived at a higher altitude.[66]

Particularly during the 1970s, the growing interest in women's history led to the concentrations of research on times, places, and age groups in which female mortality was especially high. These were seen as signs of the social oppression of women. For a certain length of time there was a tendency to attribute the high mortality of women of childbearing age less to puerperal fever and more to the physical fatigue caused by multiple childbirth, to the drudgery of domestic labor and to food that was poorer in quality than the food eaten by the men.[67] Much doubt is cast nowadays upon the validity of this theory, especially as it has been discovered that, amongst women surviving to the age of 45, it was the most fertile—those who had had 10 or more children—who lived to the ripest old age.[68] The high mortality rate among men in southern Italy— an area where the social subordination of women was plain to see—represents a further invitation to caution before "deducing a more indulgent social attitude to the role of women in those areas and those periods in which male mortality was higher than female mortality."[69]

The picture that emerges if we examine the mortality of rich and poor is equally surprising and paradoxical. Particularly in the Scandinavian countries, detailed evidence exists of large numbers of places where infant mortality was considerably higher among the children of the better-off farmers than it was among the small peasant farmers and the landless agricultural laborers. The key to this unexpected difference lies in the differing role of the women. Whereas the wives of small farmers and agricultural laborers had few duties besides the household chores, the better-off farmers' wives played a very active part in the running of the farm. The care of the animals and the production of butter and cheese were considered exclusively feminine tasks, and the good reputation of the farmer's wife depended—in an interesting reversal of the Mediterranean model—on the strength and endurance she displayed in the fields and pastures. The farmers' wives therefore tended not to breast-feed their children, or weaned them abruptly as the busiest time on the farm approached, thereby exposing them to serious risk of death.[70]

The importance of breastfeeding as a cause of the lower levels of infant mortality among the poor than among the rich has been noted in other European contexts, from rural, pre-revolutionary France to seventeenth-century England, where the risk of dying in the first few days or months of life was—as has been shown—higher for the children of the aristocracy (who were often sent to a wet-nurse) than it was for poor children. Even more interesting is the fact that adult mortality was no lower among the aristocracy than it was among the lower classes. Between 1550 and 1750 the life expectancy of the English nobility was substantially the same as it was for the rest of the population, fluctuating between 32 and 38 years, and there are good reasons to think that in this respect England was not much different from the rest of Europe.[71]

Mortality seems therefore to have been influenced by factors other than differences of social position. Cultural factors, such as breastfeeding, played a part as did environmental factors. One striking example of the inverse relationship between wealth and longevity can be found in the hilly areas of southeast England, a zone of extreme poverty where mortality—thanks to the salubrious surroundings—was nevertheless extraordinarily low among adults as well as children. Of a parish in Kent it was written, at the end of the eighteenth century, that "here people usually die when they are between 80 and 100 years old, and a person of 40 is considered young." These are figures which, as recent studies have shown, are exaggerated much less than might previously have been thought, since in these areas estimated life expectancy was often above 50 and could even reach 58, a survival level which in some parts of the world today remains a distant goal.[72]

The situation in the country was certainly different from the situation in the towns. In Geneva in the seventeenth century the life expectancy of the professional classes hovered around 37 years, that of artisans around 25–26 and that of laborers hardly extended beyond 20.[73] During the eighteenth century the upper classes everywhere began to manifest a perceptible advantage. In England, after 1750, the gap between the life expectancy of the elite, which rose to nearly 50, and that of the rest of the population (stuck at about 38) began to widen. In France a woman of the bourgeoisie who survived until she was 20 could expect, during the second half of the eighteenth century, to live another 45 years, seven years more than the national average.[74] Yet the surprising discovery to be made by historical demography is that, at least in the sixteenth and seventeenth centuries, privileged groups who had no worries about food, or about almost any other aspect of their material existence, had a life expectancy that was no higher than that of the rest of the population.[75]

Demographic Regimes, Household Structures, and Individual Destinies

The investigation of the different demographic patterns and outcomes between men and women, rich and poor, city dwellers and country folk— usually called "differential demography"—represents an important step toward a more detailed understanding of the relationship between demographic forces and the family. To get a better grasp of the effects of mortality and fertility on the family we need to descend from the level of the whole population to the level of single individuals, paying special attention to the relationships between relatives, husbands and wives, parents and children, grandparents and grandchildren, aunts, uncles, and their nieces and nephews, and between cousins. In other words, we need to ask ourselves how many relatives each person had at different phases of his or her life, how many men and how many women lived to see the children of their children, how many children survived their parents and how many were orphaned at a young age. In order to find answers to these questions, historical demographers can avail themselves of techniques of microsimulation which, by applying the appropriate demographic parameters, make it possible to determine the type, number, proportions, and age of the relatives that an "average individual"—usually called *ego*, a term borrowed from anthropology—has during the course of his or her life.

Table 6.3 contains estimates of the number of relatives possessed by an individual in pre-industrial England and an individual in England today. At every age the total number of relatives today is clearly lower. Moreover, the structure of "the universe of kinship" has also changed. It has extended vertically and contracted horizontally along the axis representing relations belonging to the same genealogical level as the *ego*. Because of the reduction in mortality an individual today has more relations in the older generation (grandparents, great-grandparents,

Table 6.3 Average number of relations at various stages of life: microsimulations for England in the sixteenth, seventeenth, eighteenth and late twentieth centuries*

Age	Century	Ascendants (a)	Horizontal (b)	Descendants (c)	Total
0	XVI	9.6	10.6	—	20.2
	XVII	8.7	9.2	—	17.9
	XVIII	10.5	11.8	—	22.3
	XX	11.0	1.6	—	12.6
20	XVI	5.7	18.1	0.9	24.7
	XVII	5.0	14.3	0.5	19.8
	XVIII	6.4	20.6	1.1	28.1
	XX	6.0	2.3	0.1	8.4
40	XVI	2.4	14.5	9.8	26.7
	XVII	1.7	11.0	7.5	20.2
	XVIII	2.6	16.9	11.6	31.1
	XX	3.0	2.9	1.9	7.8
60	XVI	0.2	8.6	12.0	20.8
	XVII	0.1	6.3	9.1	15.5
	XVIII	0.2	10.6	15.1	25.9
	XX	0.5	2.7	3.1	6.3
80	XVI	0.0	2.7	15.4	18.1
	XVII	0.0	1.8	10.2	12.0
	XVIII	0.0	3.6	18.6	22.2
	XX	0.0	1.4	4.1	5.5

* Male *egos* for the 16th, 17th and 18th centuries; female *ego* for the 20th century.
(a) Parents, grandparents, great-grandparents, uncles, and aunts; (b) wives and husbands, brothers, sisters, first cousins; (c) children, nephews and nieces, grandchildren, and great-grandchildren.
Sources: Smith and Oeppen 1993 (16th, 17th and 18th centuries); Laslett et al. 1993 (20th century).

aunts, and uncles) than he would have had in the past, while because of the decline in fertility the number of brothers, sisters, and cousins has decreased enormously. When a child was born in pre-industrial England he had an average of 10–12 relations on a horizontal axis (compared with under two today). To compensate, newborn babies nowadays have much more chance of finding their grandparents alive, perhaps even their great-grandparents.

These figures show the scale of the transformation brought about by the demographic transition. There are two important points to note, however. The first is that the data provided by Table 6.3 show how, even in the pre-industrial period, fluctuations in the rates of mortality and fertility caused considerable alterations in the universe of kinship. In eighteenth-century England every individual had more relations than he or she would have had a century earlier: the number of children, nephews, and nieces had almost doubled. The second point is that these average figures conceal great individual differences. Men and women without children, without brothers or sisters, nephews or nieces, lived alongside other men and women who were the center of an extended network of relations. Although some families had difficulty choosing to which of their many heirs to leave their property, many others had no descendants at all. It is probably not far from the truth to estimate that, out of 100 European families before the French Revolution, about 20 would have no descendants and in only 60 percent would a male heir, or heirs, survive.[76]

Although the probability of a father dying without heirs was great, no less great (and certainly extreme when compared with the situation today) was the probability of a child being orphaned at a very young age. This naturally depended on current levels of mortality and their fluctuations but also on the age of the parents at their marriage. This is reflected in Table 6.4, in which figures for Spain in 1900 and in 1960, and for late twentieth-century England are compared with figures relating to three populations exemplifying the variety of demographic experience in pre-nineteenth-century Europe. These are England in the sixteenth and eighteenth centuries, where late matrimony for both men and women was counterbalanced by relatively low general mortality rates, and a simu-lated population termed "Mediterranean." To this are attributed two dis-tinctive features of Mediterranean demography in the Middle Ages and in the first centuries of the modern period, namely very high mortality and early marriage for women, much later for men.[77] The differences were considerable: whereas under "Mediterranean" demographic condi-tions by the age of 10, 44 percent of children had lost either their mother or their father, in eighteenth-century England the likelihood of being orphaned at a young age of one or both parents was decidedly less, and

Table 6.4   Percentage of orphans at 10 and 20 years in select historical and contemporary populations*

Population	Period	Orphans at 10 of:			Orphans at 20 of:		
		father	mother	both	father	mother	both
"Mediterranean"	XVI century	25	19	5	49	35	18
English	XVI century	20	15	4	38	29	11
English	XVIII century	13	12	2	30	23	7
Spanish	1900	15	11	2	33	23	7
Spanish	1960	3	2	0	13	6	1
English	1990	2	0	0	5	1	0

* Male *ego* for the "Mediterranean" population and the English population in the 16th and 18th centuries; female *ego* for the Spanish and English populations of 1990.
Sources: For the "Mediterranean" population, Saller 1994; for the English populations of the 16th and 18th centuries, Smith and Oeppen 1993; for the Spanish populations, Reher 1997; for the English population in 1990, Laslett et al. 1993.

was in fact close to the estimated probability for the population of Spain in 1900.

Table 6.4 shows, however, that, even in favorable demographic conditions, the number of orphans was very high. In eighteenth-century England one child in four had lost one of her parents by the age of 10. Although there was plenty of opportunity for remarriage, many widows and widowers chose to remain single. An English seventeenth-century diarist claims that this was "for the good of the children." It was more common, however, for widows and widowers to remarry, thus bringing a stepmother or stepfather into the family and more often than not, half-brothers and half-sisters. This abrupt restructuring of family affection and authority often caused tension and a feeling of estrangement; there is touching evidence in contemporary documents, especially in diaries and autobiographies. The author of one autobiography, who lost his mother in 1608 when he was four years old, recalls that his father "remarried another woman, who made me aware of the difference between my own mother and a step mother"; another diarist confesses at the same period that, after the second marriage of his father, he "felt like a stranger in his father's house."[78]

The fate of orphans depended to a large extent on the structural characteristics of the family groups and the network of relationships—characteristics which in Europe as a whole varied enormously. In areas where the "complex" family household was the norm—the countries of Eastern Europe in particular, but also in southern France, central and northern

Italy and most of the Alps and in other mountainous areas—if one or other parent died when a child was still young responsibility for the care of the orphan until he or she reached adulthood fell to the grandparents or to the aunts and uncles who were already part of the same household. Orphans were more immediately vulnerable—as, at the other end of life, were old people who were widowed and had no children—where the household was "simple" in structure. A study of 19 communities in England indicates that more than three-quarters of the children who had lost a parent lived in small nuclear families with widowed parents who had not remarried: 52 percent with the mother, 24 percent with the father. When the remaining parent died, if the orphan was not too young the most frequent solution was to anticipate his apprenticeship to an artisan, or as a farmhand, by a few years. Orphans of 6 or 7, or even 10 years old were considered too young to begin learning this kind of work. They would therefore go to live with a relation, creating a kind of hybrid household somewhere between nuclear and extended. Such households had fluid boundaries and were extremely unstable. Besides the mother and father and their children there might be orphans of various cate-gories—children of the first marriage of the husband or wife, nephews, cousins or sometimes younger brothers and sisters of the head of the family or his wife.[79]

In some European countries decisions about the fate of orphans were taken informally by relations and friends. In other countries, when a parent died a family council was held, sometimes with a fixed number of relations. In the Brie region of France, for example, a family council took over responsibility for orphans. In theory this council consisted of four relations from the mother's side and four from the father's. We have detailed reports of meetings held by these councils. One of the best studies of the custom reveals that, in the Alpine valleys of the French regions of Dauphiné, in the seventeenth and eighteenth centuries, there was a divergence between well-off families and families of more modest means. Wealthier families had no trouble finding tutors and trustees for their orphans, and many relatives played an active part in the family council—sometimes as many as 20. Most importantly, the relatives living locally would be joined by relatives who had emigrated elsewhere and their presence gave the orphans a wide choice of apprenticeship or employment in the plains. Fewer relatives took an interest in the poorer orphans. Family councils in such circumstances were not well attended (even less so when the orphan needed material assistance from the family) and at best only the closest relations would take care of the orphans.[80]

This crisis scenario was less frequent at times and in places where lower mortality and a pattern of early marriage reduced the likelihood of a child being orphaned at a young age. In most of Europe the problem of assistance to orphans seems to have become less pressing in the second half of the eighteenth century, when the first signs of demographic transition began to emerge. During the last few decades before the French Revolution, however, other changes can be glimpsed (again we learn of these from looking at the situation of orphans) which were to herald a profound transformation of the family's role in assisting at a crisis precipitated by the death of one of its members. Particularly in the cities of Western Europe, from the sixteenth century onwards, the most innovative forms of public charity were directed toward the assistance of orphans. As well as being in harmony with the precepts of Christian charity, the founding of orphanages was a useful way for a government to reduce the number of homeless children begging in the streets, or securing a livelihood by illicit means.[81] In rural areas of Europe, on the other hand, the care of orphans remained the responsibility of the extended family.

Arising from the French Revolution the new view of government responsibility brought fundamental changes. A bill of 1792 established institutions for orphans and poor children all over France. This marked a drastic shift away from an aid strategy which had been in force for centuries.[82] The government took over assistance to orphans and enforced their reception in orphanages. The end of the *ancien régime* witnessed the birth of a new concept of the responsibilities of the state and a different way of coping collectively to solve the problems generated within the family by demographic forces.

PART IV

FAMILY RELATIONS

CHAPTER 7

Parent–Child Relations

Linda A. Pollock

The family in early modern Europe was of fundamental importance to the wellbeing of the individual, society, and the state, and the most crucial function of the family was the bringing up of children. The prescriptive literature, Catholic and Protestant, consistently emphasized the importance of the parental role in child care, and carefully detailed the appropriate duties. According to William Gouge in *Of Domesticall Duties*, one of the most popular of seventeenth-century English conduct books, the task of parents was threefold:

1. to nourish their children—with food, clothes, and other necessities;
2. to nurture their children—with the use of good discipline;
3. to instruct their children—in academic matters, spiritual affairs, and good breeding.

Children, whether considered to be tainted with original sin, or, from the eighteenth century onwards, seen as naturally innocent, were viewed as inherently malleable. They were plants in the garden, young shoots awaiting cultivation by their parents. To bring them up correctly was a demanding task. The moralists wanted parents to train their offspring, oversee their moral development and yet refrain from abusing their power, particularly as the children matured. Parents should strike a balance between severity and indulgence, a difficult path to follow since, in the opinion of many of the writers, parents loved their children too much. Most parents agreed that their children were their responsibility and assented to Gouge's view of the three-part parental task.[1]

Historians have not always accepted that this was the case. It has been argued that the past lacked a concept of childhood and that the modern notion of children as different from adults with their own special needs has emerged only gradually. Some scholars have gone further, claiming that children in the past, especially in the early years, were often ignored by their parents, who did not even mourn a child's death. Those children who survived babyhood were harshly treated and severely disciplined. Generally, these historians have not distinguished between practices which were misguided but beneficial in intent, and actual cruelty. They have also generalized from isolated instances of abuse to conclude that severe treatment was the norm in early modern Europe. It is true that child abuse, abandonment, and infanticide did occur in the past. It is also true that parents of the past had a different notion of childhood and the parental task than parents of today. However, it stretches the evidence entirely too far to maintain that children were undifferentiated from adult society or that harshness, at best indifference, was their lot. The parent–child relationship in previous centuries is best explored by attempting to find out how children were reared, rather than by condemning past parents for their failure to possess modern concepts and to implement modern methods.[2]

For most of Europe, children arrived within a year after the marriage ceremony, and every two to three years thereafter. Since women in Western Europe generally married in their mid-twenties and had their last child around the age of 40, this meant that the typical family had about six children. In Eastern Europe and some Italian cities where women married at an earlier age, the completed family size could be larger. Unlike today when child-rearing is generally concentrated in a few years of the marriage, couples in the past spent most of their married life bringing up their offspring. It is clear that people not only married in the expectation of having children but also sought parenthood. Remedies for infertility abounded. Childbirth itself could be regarded with fear and was potentially dangerous, but the birth of a child was welcomed. Sons—especially for the landed ranks who needed male heirs for their estates or for peasant farmers who wanted both a male heir and manpower—were certainly sought after, and the birth of consecutive girls could be a source of dismay; even so children of both sexes were desired. The mortality rates between boys and girls did not vary much, indicating that boys were not given preferential treatment, or at least not significantly so. Childbirth was carefully prepared for, the newly arrived infant welcomed into the world, and his or her baptism celebrated, often lavishly among the affluent. Children were viewed as gifts from God, treasures to be valued and a potential source of comfort and support.[3]

1–4. Geertruyt Roghman, *Household Tasks*, seventeenth century, Netherlands.

5. Pieter de Hooch, *The Good Housewife*, 1663, Netherlands.

6. Pieter de Hooch, *The Bedroom*, *c.* 1660, Netherlands.

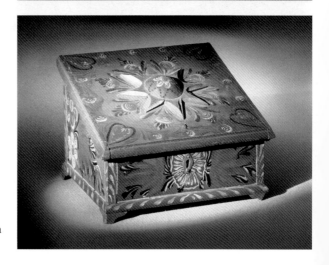

7. Pine betrothal chest, nineteenth century.

МУЖЪ ЛАПТИ ПЛЕТЕТ
ПЛЕТЕТЪ ОГНЮ НЕГОСЛ

ТЪ АЖЕНА НАМ НИТИ
ТЪ ОБОГОТЕ ТИХОТАТЪ

8. *The Husband Weaves Bast Shoes with Skill, the Wife Spins Fibres with a Will,* early eighteenth century, Russia.

9. *Many Happy Returns,* mid-eighteenth century, Russia.

ПОКОРНОПРОШУ МОИ ДРУКЪ
ВЫКУШАИ РАДОСТЬ
ПРИПОМНИ СВОЕ РОЖДЕНИЕ

ПРИИМИ ИЗАЕЦКИХЪ РУКЪ
ВПИДТНУЮ СЛАДОСТЬ
НЕОСТАВЬ ВТУНЕ НАШЕ
ПРОШЕНИЕ

10. Gortzius Geldorp, *A Portrait of a Family Saying Grace Before a Meal*, 1602, Netherlands.

11. Claes Jansz Visscher, *Family Saying Grace*, 1609, Netherlands.

12. *A Protestant Marriage*, 1768, Strasbourg.

13. John Souch, *Sir Thomas Aston at the Deathbed of his Wife*, 1635, England.

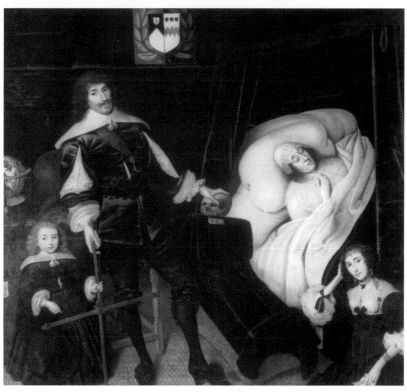

14. Nicholaes de Bruyn
after Maarten de Vos,
Children's Games, sixteenth
century, Netherlands.

15. Jan Miel, *Old Woman
Delousing a Child*,
seventeenth century,
Netherlands.

16. Abraham Bosse,
Childbirth, 1630s, France.

17. Abraham Bosse, *Marriage in the City: The Visit to the New Mother*, 1633, France.

18. Rembrandt Harmensz van Rijn, *The French Bed*, 1648, Netherlands.

19. Karl Gottlieb Löck, *The Good Mother*, c. 1770, Germany.

20. Etienne Aubry, *Farewell to the Wet Nurse*, 1776, France.

21. Jean Baptiste Greuze, *The Father's Curse*, 1778, France.

22. Jean Baptiste Greuze, *The Son Punished*, 1779, France.

23. Louis Binet, illustration for *La Paysanne Pervertie* by Rétif de la Bretonne, La Haye, 1784, France.

24. *La casalinga a il cacciatore*, sixteenth to eighteenth century, illustration for the Roxburghe Ballads.

25. *The Good Hows-holder*, 1564–1565, England, this impression 1607.

26. Rembrandt Harmensz van Rijn, *Peasant Family on the Tramp*, c. 1652, Netherlands.

27. Pieter Bruegel the Elder, *The Wedding Dance*, c. 1566, Netherlands.

28. Hieronymous Janssen, *Interior with Family Group*, seventeenth century, Netherlands.

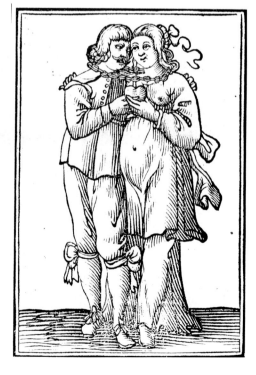

29. Jacob Jordaens, *Self Portrait with Parents, Brothers, and Sisters*, seventeenth century, Netherlands.

30. *A Good Housewife*, c. 1600, England.

31. Jan Christoffel Jegher, *Union of Houlijx*, 1644, Netherlands.

32. Rembrandt Harmensz van Rijn,
Beggars at the Door, 1648,
Netherlands.

LE CORNARD CONTANT

33. *Le Cornard Contant*, c. 1650,
France.

34. *The Happy Marriage and the Unhappy Marriage,* c. 1690, England.

35. *La Femme mise à la raison par son mari,* seventeenth to eighteenth century, France.

36. *Wedlock*, c. 1751, England.

37. *The Hen Peckt Husband*, 1768, England.

38. Cornelius de Zeeuw, *Pierre de Moucheron and his Family*, 1563, Netherlands.

39. Antoine Le Nain, *Peasant Family in an Interior*, 1649, France.

PHYSICAL WELFARE

Infancy

One of the first issues facing new parents was how to feed their infant. Many mothers breast-fed. Those who could not or those who would not relied on wet-nurses. There was no safe way of bottle-feeding in the early modern period. Some historians have portrayed the use of wet-nurses as an example of the indifference with which parents regarded infants. These scholars castigate such parents for not being prepared to tolerate the inconvenience of breastfeeding, argue that close bonds could not be forged between parent and child when a wet-nurse was used, and maintain that there was a high mortality rate for children sent out to nurse.[4] These claims require further scrutiny.

Writers, doctors, and moralists from ancient times onward condemned the use of wet-nurses. They argued that maternal breastfeeding was best for the infant and, moreover, was God's will. In spite of almost universal disapproval from the experts, parents from all ranks, except the very poorest, hired wet-nurses. They did so even though this would increase their chance of conception, and pregnancy and delivery could be as or more disruptive than breastfeeding. Convenience does not explain the reliance on wet-nurses: they were employed for a variety of other reasons. Some mothers may have been dissuaded by reading the advice literature which, although depicting breastfeeding by the mothers as natural, actually emphasized the problems. The listing of difficulties like pain, sleepless nights, or adverse consequences to the mother's health were not intended to discourage a mother from nursing, but the recitation of these matters made breastfeeding appear difficult and could undermine the confidence of women in their ability to nurse. Moreover, because children were usually not put to the breast for the first few days, they could have problems in sucking. There were also personal reasons why women would prefer to employ a wet-nurse. In theory, a nursing mother was not meant to have sex for fear she should conceive again and thereby lack sufficient milk to feed the baby. We are not sure how often married couples adhered to this taboo, although wet-nurses in Renaissance Venice were prosecuted for endangering the health of the nursling by having sex. Noble women were considered too delicate for nursing which, it was thought, would ruin the shape of their breasts. For parents lower down the social scale, maternal breastfeeding may not have been feasible. Some sent their child to nurse because of crowded or unsanitary living conditions which were not suitable for a baby. Yet others opted for a nurse because of economic difficulties: the mother's earnings were essential for the support of the family, or the constant migrations undertaken in search of work made it impossible to take care of a child. Depending on the practices of their area, children could, as was often the case in German cities such as Hamburg or in the Netherlands, be nursed at home with live-in nurses. More common, however, was the tradition of having children nursed by rural peasant women, particularly because it was thought that children needed country air.[5]

The custom did have adverse effects. In some countries, like France, the nurse's own child may have suffered or even have died as a result of the mother taking in a child to nurse. In other countries, including England, it looks as if a woman sought to nurse a child either because of a stillbirth or the death of an infant, or when her own child had reached the age of 10 months and was not so dependent on breast milk, so the practice had a less negative impact. A baby's chances of survival were better if nursed by the mother, even if she was poor. In eighteenth-century France, the mortality rate for infants was around 16–18 percent; whereas between half and two-thirds of those sent out to nurse died. There were also the notorious baby farms of the eighteenth and especially the nineteenth centuries, which took in large numbers of generally illegitimate infants, few of whom survived.[6]

Even so, the employment of a wet-nurse cannot be automatically linked with neglect. It is important to distinguish between the state-employed wet-nurses hired to feed foundlings and the private wet-nurses chosen by parents. Private wet-nurses were carefully selected, with parents combing the copious advice literature for a list of the attributes a good nurse should have. Most parents interviewed a prospective nurse and often checked the condition of her home and the welfare of any children she might have. The English gentry and the French nobility chose wet-nurses from the prosperous levels of village society who customarily had existing ties to the family: for example, they may have been former servants. During the eighteenth century, some cities like Paris or Hamburg established bureaux to help families in the search for and supervision of wet-nurses. Parents preferred wet-nurses who lived sufficiently near for them to visit the child, although if they lived in a big city this was not always possible. For London families, for instance, babies could be nursed up to 40 miles away. When frequent visits were not feasible, the parents would be kept informed of their child's progress. Private wet-nurses were paid more than the state wet-nurses. This means that parents, especially those from the poorer ranks of society, made sacrifices to pay for a nurse, believing this to be in the best interest of the infant. Furthermore, continuing payments usually depended on the child being well looked after. In some cases, mothers carefully monitored the quality of the nurse's milk and the baby's reaction to it, and the nurse would be changed if a baby was not thriving satisfactorily.[7]

The fact that the tradition of sending children out to nurse continued to be prevalent in urban continental Europe in the eighteenth and nineteenth centuries (that is, after the purported discovery of childhood), makes it difficult to sustain the argument that wet-nursing occurred because parents were indifferent to the wellbeing of their children. The poignant tale of Louise Brulé, married to a servant and unable to live with her husband, who sent her baby to nurse a mere 24 hours after his birth, underscores this point. Louise kept in touch with the nurse and a year later, seriously ill and fearing she might not have long to live, asked for her son to be brought to her so she might see him again. Alas, the child died *en route*. Although Louise was able to identify the body only by the clothes she had sent, she had been concerned about her son's welfare throughout his short life and mourned his death. It appears that wet-nursing existed so long not because of widespread indifference to the welfare of infants but because the combination of habitual practice and the structure of female employment ensured that an alternative to maternal breastfeeding was wanted and there was no other viable option. In France, for example, the great decline of wet-nursing began after the end of World War I, a time of a significant decline in female employment.[8]

Children were swaddled—wrapped tightly in long strips of cloth—for the first few months. This kept them warm and immobile as well as giving them a sense of security and keeping them out of harm's way. It was also understood to help shape the limbs into human form. A few months after birth, first the arms, then the legs would be freed from the bands. After babyhood, boys and girls were dressed alike in gowns until around the age of seven.

The physical needs of young children were attended to and satisfied as much as possible, although it has been claimed that in some cultures, such as that of Russian peasants, certain child-care practices, like the introduction of solid food shortly after birth, contributed to a high infant mortality rate. For the very poor getting enough to eat was always hard. Weaning and teething were anxious times for parents because children often became ill. Parents generally delighted in the development and exploits of their children. Those who could write recorded their children's achievement of milestones such as learning to walk or talk. In seventeenth-century England, Nathaniel Bacon reported to his wife that their 18-month-old daughter Jane "is wholly taken up with travelling by her self which she performeth very handsomely." The young child was primarily the responsibility of the mother, but fathers, even if not actively engaged in the physical care of their young children, were usually

interested in a child's welfare. Fathers have been depicted in Dutch paintings caring for small children and many letters survive documenting the
large part they took in the education of their children, especially their
sons. Parents may have employed servants to assist them in child care.
Although it has been claimed that servants in aristocratic households
neglected or were cruel to their charges, this was not a situation most
parents were prepared to accept; only trusted servants were allowed to
come into contact with their offspring.[9]

Illness

Parents and children had to contend with a great deal of disease and
many ailments in early modern Europe. In his diary from 1641 to 1683
Ralph Josselin, an English clergyman, cited 136 incidents of illness
among his ten children. They endured colds and fever, worms, measles,
rashes, vomiting, diarrhea, sores, boils, swellings and a variety of skin
eruptions. Hermann von Weinsberg, a burger of Cologne born in 1518,
recollected how often he was sick as a child: measles, smallpox, fevers,
boils, sores, worms, toothache, hernia, plague, and temporary paralysis.
About 20 percent of all infants born failed to survive the first year and
almost half did not live until the age of 10. These rates were lower
in England, Germany, and Switzerland, and higher in France, Spain,
and particularly in Russia. It has been argued that because the young
in the past were so susceptible to disease and because there was such a
high child mortality rate, parents were wary of becoming attached to
young children. The level of morbidity did affect the parent–child relationship, but not by making parents indifferent to their offspring's fate.
Parents were well aware how easily a child could die. This made them
more, not less, anxious about the wellbeing of their children and exceedingly concerned whenever a child was ill. As Elizabeth de Bouillon in
early seventeenth-century France confessed, when her children were
unwell, she suffered from "the maddening passion of a mother who is
always afraid, too weak to believe in God's promise to turn all to the
good."[10]

Far from being fatalistic in the face of illness, parents tried all the
remedies they could to alleviate suffering and effect a cure. Private and
published medicinal recipe books list many potions, ointments, and regi-
mens for children, and a repertoire of appropriate treatments was part
of a community's folklore. Home remedies may have been ineffective and
may even have aggravated the illness but their existence bears witness to
the active interest parents took in the diseases of their children. When all
hope was gone, mothers, and often fathers, stayed by the side of the child,
night and day.[11] Few parents in the past would have escaped the harrow-

ing experience of ministering to a dying child, and individuals were frequently called upon to offer comfort and support to a friend, relative, or
neighbor whose child had died. Familiarity with this situation did not
make it any easier to bear. Religion taught that it was God's will, that
the child was in a better place, and parents should accept their loss. Statements and condolences offering such sentiments are easy to find, as are
examples of parents who accepted the death of their infants without
extreme protestations of grief. This, though, was not the most common
reaction. To the majority of parents, the death of child was a cruel blow.
Many, knowing they should abide by God's will, routinely feared they
mourned too much. Magdalena Paumgartner in sixteenth-century
Germany struggled to accept the loss of her seven-year-old son Balthasar:
"I must accept God's will and let him go in peace to God, for there
is nothing left in this for me now except suffering, heartache, and
tears."[12]

CULTURAL, SOCIAL, AND MORAL WELFARE

Views on Children and the Parental Role

Good parenting was inseparable from training: parents took to heart the
scriptural dictate to "train up a child in the way he should go" (Proverbs
22: 6). The home in early modern Europe was the main instrument of
socialization. It was the duty of parents everywhere—one which they
owed not just to their children but also to society—to instruct their offspring in the ways of the world, to regulate their behavior, and to fit them
for their future role in society. Childhood was regarded as the period in
which an individual laid the foundations for a moral future and acquired
the skills he or she would need for adult life. The affluent ranks notably
considered the period of childhood as one of opportunity to construct a
model adult. The lower ranks too, at least those who were settled, took
the duty of training seriously. The actual process was influenced by a
number of factors including the rank of the family, the aims of the state,
the sex and birth order of the child, as well as cultural views on children
and youths.[13]

   By the early eighteenth century, there were three mains ways of viewing
a child. Most Christians, particularly prior to 1700, believed that
children came into the world stained with original sin. A child was
innately evil, born sinful, and needed a great deal of discipline to avoid
sliding further down the path of damnation. A second view, which
gained in currency during the eighteenth century, portrayed the child as
innately good, innocent, and pure and in need of protection from the

contaminating influences of the environment. The third position—the one held by educationalists and most eighteenth-century society—was to consider a child a blank slate awaiting experience's inscriptions. These views could coexist in any one culture, as for example, in Russia where opinion was divided over the function of education. It was either to teach good manners, civic responsibility, and a sense of propriety, or it was, through the use of harsh discipline, to inure children to their station in life. The concept of childhood was not new in the eighteenth century— the Catholic Church had long maintained the position that a child was not capable of mortal, or adult, sin before the age of seven—but it was given more emphasis. This development greatly improved state and institutional care of children but the practical consequences within the home were more muted. What mattered to most parents was that the child could be shaped. The most pervasive metaphors in early modern writings about children were those of gardening, with its intimations of growth and pruning, or of virgin wax, ready for imprinting and molding.[14]

Parental regulation would continue for as long as a child was considered to be a dependant. A youth became an adult usually only on marriage, which took place in the twenties, or with the setting up of an independent household. So long as the stage of youth lasted—which, provided it was not abruptly terminated by the death of a parent, especially a father, could be of considerable duration—young people were under a parent's authority. Despite claims that a concept of adolescence did not exist prior to the nineteenth century, the period termed youth in early modern Europe does correspond to our notion of adolescence. It was a recognized stage in the life-cycle, being understood as a period of transition in which young people were groomed for adult roles. It was also regarded as a notably difficult period, especially for young men. Although it was a time of promise, hope, enthusiasm, beauty, and vigor, it was also one of excessive passion, tempestuous behavior, and yielding to temptation. The young were either poised on the threshold of pursuing a useful life or they were about to become ensnared by worldly attractions. Even the older child required constant parental vigilance.[15]

Discipline

Familial relations in this era were conceptualized in terms of instruction and restraint. Parents undoubtedly wished for obedient children and believed that they should be "well bent when young." Submission of the young to those in authority was required. There was greater public acceptance of the necessity of corporal punishment in the past. Most parents were prepared to inflict it, usually when all else had failed, and in some families and in many schools, whippings were regularly administered. Even so, most parents did not desire repressed children; even the much-maligned Puritans wished to channel the will of a child rather than break it. The advice literature counseled moderation in parental modes of discipline, although most authors thought that parents were usually too indulgent to their children rather than too harsh with them. All advice manuals urged that children be disciplined for disobedience, but not in an arbitrary or severe manner. There was to be a good reason for the correction, the punishment should be appropriate to the offense, and the child's age, sex, temperament, and intentions should be taken into account. Parents had means other than beating to ensure correct behavior. Isabella de Moerloose of seventeenth-century Ghent was beaten on one occasion to drive out the evil spirit which her mother thought had possessed her, but more often she was told tales of spirits and devils who preyed on naughty children to make sure she conformed to house rules. Parents also attempted to shape a child's behavior by arousing feelings of guilt and shame.[16]

In practice, most parents sought a middle way: one that would induce children to follow parental counsels but that would not require the enforcement of authority with fear. Parents achieved their child-rearing aims not with brutality, but with a concept of reciprocity: parents and children had duties to one another, and children would derive great benefits from complying with their parents. Children were taught early to honor their father and mother, and they were told repeatedly that the first duty of a child was obedience. Outward marks of deference, respect, and obedience to parents such as bowing, uncovering the head, or kneeling in their presence were insisted upon. As they grew older children learned that deferential, dutiful conduct would be rewarded whereas discourteous or disobedient behavior would lead to some form of deprivation. "Tell little Balthasar," wrote his father Balthasar Paumgartner, a merchant of sixteenth-century Nuremberg, "to be good for the time being, otherwise I will bring him nothing. If he is bad, I will give the beautiful satin purse, the two pairs of shoes and the red striped stockings I have bought for him to another little boy who behaves better than he." Parents continued to exercise control over their older children, although they appreciated that it was more limited in nature and that obedience could not be demanded from older children as a right. The elite ranks composed books of advice, usually for sons, a few for daughters. These works warned youths of pitfalls in the world and also laid down rules for appropriate behavior. Advice was given on a variety of topics: business, estate management, regulating family and servants, as well as financial matters. Works such as these were intended to ease a child's transition to adulthood while reflecting the desire to continue to regulate the child's conduct. Children, for their part, expected parents to fulfill their duties, and would remind them if they defaulted in their obligations.[17]

Young people, of course, did not always accept the continued imposition of parental control. There were outbreaks of conflict as children strove for autonomy or resisted their parents' choices in such matters as career or marriage. It was a parental duty in early modern Europe to make sure their children were established in life, so a parent would take an active role in finding employment for them. Parents who owned property were also anxious to have some say in the union of their children because they did not wish to see the family resources wasted. Parents were meant to take a child's preferences into account and make sure the child approved of the choice. The amount of control a parent exercised over a child's future spouse varied according to the status of the parent and the age at which a child would marry. The younger the partners at marriage, the greater the power wielded by parents. In the elite ranks, parents may often have been the instigators of a match, whereas lower down the social scale it was more likely that the young couple would approach their parents after they had decided to wed. Parental approval was considered a necessity, since parents controlled the disposal of dowry or property. In the southern German town of Neckarhausen, children under the age of 25 who wished to marry were required to have parental consent. Parents could offer early independence to their children (young people became full adults either on marriage or at the age of 25) in return for a suitable choice of marriage partner. Although parents undoubtedly expected to have some say in marital selection, they rarely dictated the choice of spouse. What was sought was a match acceptable to all.[18]

In some families prolonged periods of discord between parents and children, usually sons, occurred. Stephan Carl Behaim and his mother in early seventeenth-century Germany, for example, were often at odds. He was frequently insolent to his mother, continually involved in fights, and drank heavily, stealing as well as borrowing money without authorization from his mother to support his habit. When an individual child's lifestyle was a source of recurring distress, parents struggled to reform the behavior. They would reproach and admonish the child and also presented disrespectful children before the church courts. Although parents could cast off an erring child, they were often reluctant to do so. Adolf Frederick of Mecklenburg in 1654 was prepared to abide by the custom of primogeniture and leave his estate to his eldest son, despite the young man having "deeply and frequently offended us."[19]

The expectation of parents that they would maintain authority over their children and the existence of episodes of intense strife were not incompatible with the forging of close bonds between parents and their children. Historians have viewed the history of childhood as the gradual emancipation from a callous and cruel regime: in the past scant attention was paid to a child's needs whereas today empathy and encouragement and understanding are accorded most children. This argument is based on several dubious assumptions. Historians have often supposed that it was necessary to recognize the individuality of a child before affection could grow. This, however, is a modern and a Western notion based on the elevation of the parent–child (especially the mother–child) bond over any other form of attachment. It has also often been claimed that the lower orders were less caring than the middle classes. Today young children have little economic value and it is easy to assume that in previous centuries a parent's need of a child's labor interfered with the expression of love. That is, it is believed that economic interest cannot coexist with emotional intimacy. The first impression of family life in the working classes of early modern Europe may be that parents had little time for their children, and did not trouble themselves much with their education or welfare because they were too preoccupied with problems of subsistence. However, a more searching examination of the life of the German lower bourgeoisie, the English coal miners, and the Parisian artisans, has refuted this idea. The poverty of the working classes and the absorption of their energy by the struggle for daily existence did not lead to a lack of concern for their children. The authoritarian aspect of child care in the past has been emphasized to the detriment of the more tender side.[20]

A great deal of affection existed between parents and children in the past. In the late seventeenth century John Churchill, an English aristocrat, wrote to his wife:

> You cannot imagine how pleased I am with the children, for they having no body at home but their maid, they are so fond of me that when I am at home they will be always with me, kissing and hugging me.

Further evidence of the warm relationship between parents and children can be discerned from the amount of contact maintained between parents and children who had left home. When they could, young people returned for visits and their parents visited them. Throughout the period of youth, the parental tie continued to have material and emotional value to young people, especially in moments of crisis or hardship. Parents, for example, mediated between master and son if the latter was unhappy in his apprenticeship, and came to collect working children who had fallen ill so they could be cared for at home. When they reached adulthood, children referred to their parents as indulgent and loving, appreciated the amount of parental investment in their upbringing, and lamented their parents' death.[21]

Spiritual Instruction

In Catholic Europe, parents played a vital role in the bringing up of pious children and in the communication of spiritual values. Theologians stressed the importance of religious conditioning from an early age and viewed the parents as playing a crucial role in forming new generations in the Catholic faith. The father was regarded as the key figure, particularly with reference to the moral instruction of sons, although the Church did recognize the extent of maternal influence and the mother's role in supplying a Christian upbringing. The Protestant reformers were equally concerned about the religious instruction of children, believing that the correct performance of this was the cornerstone of the evangelical society they hoped to build. The best gift a parent could give to a child was to bring him or her up as a God-fearing Christian. Protestant mothers had a specific responsibility to catechize children and servants in the home. The Geneva Bible at Deuteronomy 21: 18 included the marginal note: "it is the mother's dutie also to instruct her children." Notwithstanding these admonitions, it is likely that family devotions, prayers, and Bible lessons were held only in the homes of the godly, a small minority in society. Not all parents were sufficiently pious to ensure that the word of God was preached to their family; some lacked time or knowledge. The parish church largely took over the function of religious instruction for Catholics and, in the end, even the Protestant reformers were ambivalent about the role to be played by the family in the moral and religious training of children. Religious education, however, was not just the imparting of spiritual knowledge, that is of the sacraments, Bible, Lord's Prayer, and so on; it also entailed the moral shaping of everyday behavior and the implanting of Christian virtues. Here parents made a significant contribution to the upbringing of their children by passing on cultural standards of honesty, honor, fair play, social respectability, and a work ethos.[22]

Academic Education

Education in early modern Europe was not equated with schooling. As Thomas Carleton, a husbandman's son in seventeenth-century England, commented, he was "educated sometimes at school, sometimes with herding, and tending of Sheep, or Cattel, sometime with the Plow, cart or threshing Instrument, or other lawfull labor." Before the advent of compulsory education in the nineteenth century, formal education was a voluntary activity, and it was expensive. The family was an important educative agency: parents, as part of their duties, were to undertake the education of their young children, and mothers—despite the reputed weakness of the female sex—were considered the prime movers in this matter. In Sweden, which lacked a formal educational establishment, children were successfully educated by their parents at home after a campaign for improved literacy was begun by the Church in 1686. Educational provision expanded between 1500 and 1800, but access to it, and the value placed on education, varied according to the culture and was highly stratified by class and sex. In general the sons of affluent families were the chief beneficiaries.[23]

The desires of parents, religious reformers, and the state helped fuel the spread of educational establishments but their aims were not always the same. The religious reformers and secular authorities in early modern Europe wanted to promote order and obedience: social stability, not mobility, was their goal. Parents wanted to prepare the child for his or her adult life: the wealthier sections of society sent their sons and daughters to school not just for scholarly lessons, but also for social grooming and future contacts; the lower orders preferred an education grounded in practical skills. The distribution of literacy virtually mirrored the hierarchy of wealth, status, and position: only around 10 percent of agricultural laborers and small farmers were literate; whereas the nobility, clergy, and professionals were nearly all literate.[24]

The economic status of parents was the main determinant of schooling. Those living in subsistence peasant societies, especially those of Eastern Europe, probably perceived little value in literacy. Elsewhere in the poorer sectors of European society, parents struggled to make sure that their children received some education. Often, however, those in straitened circumstances lacked the funds to achieve their aims. The village of Willingham in 1593 endowed a school by public subscription. The contributions came from 102 villagers, a substantial proportion of whom could not sign their own name and yet were prepared to make a financial sacrifice for their children. In the end, though, few children of the poorer families attended the school. The offspring of laborers and small farmers needed to join the workforce as soon as they were strong enough to contribute to the family economy—around the age of six or seven. By that age a child could have been taught to read but probably not to write. Thomas Tryon, son of a village plasterer, remembered being sent to school about the age of five in late seventeenth-century England, but, he wrote, "I scarcely learned to distinguish my Letters, before I was taken away to Work for my Living" and he was put to carding and spinning. Individuals seemed to be educated only to the level that their fathers deemed essential for their future trade or social aspirations. For the middle and upper classes, education was considered to be indispensable in preparing sons for their future career. Sir Gervase Sleigh, a member of the English gentry, made certain that his two eldest sons studied the classics so that they could enter public service; whereas his two younger sons were destined for a merchant's apprenticeship and thus had to study only reading, writing, and the casting of accounts. Parents were prepared to invest in higher education, but only if a perceived advantage accrued. The prosperous farmers of the Ile de France sent their sons to university because this aided in the management of a large estate, as well as opening doors to other careers.[25]

Even basic literacy was never achieved by the vast majority of women in the early modern period. Although more girls' schools were founded from the sixteenth century on, there continued to be far fewer than there were for boys. One survey of schools in late sixteenth-century Venice uncovered 4,600 male pupils and a mere 30 girls; another for late eighteenth-century France found that two-thirds of boys received some schooling compared to one girl in fifty. Even where girls' schools existed, girls attended for a much briefer period than their brothers, meaning in effect that they often learned to read but not to write. Girls could not attend grammar school, and only rarely received a rigorous scholastic education. The evidence suggests that education at school was not demanded by parents for their daughters. There were impressive female scholars to be found throughout Europe, such as Isotta Nogarola, Marguerite of Navarre, or Margaret Roper, but many parents were against higher education or a classical training for women. This is not to say that parents were uninterested in the academic achievements of their daughters nor that they were unwilling to expend much money on their education. Girls of the middle and upper ranks would often be taught at home by a succession of tutors and governesses whose fees were expensive, at times more so than the fees for their brothers. Parents, including those of humbler backgrounds, were also gratified by their daughters' intellect and progress. But in a culture which dictated that one learned only what one would use, women, it was believed, had little need for academic embellishments. Moreover, many Catholic and Protestant parents were convinced that the moral virtue of young women might be compromised by sending them to school.[26]

Socialization

One of the priorities of parenting was what the upper ranks termed "breeding": ensuring that their sons and daughters exhibited behavior appropriate to their rank, birth order, and gender. All children learned to respect those in power at home so that they would have respect for their betters in society later. One of the most salient differences between a peasant and a noble child, though, lay in the realms of education and socialization. For the lower-class urban child whose living quarters were often cramped and overcrowded, the streets were an important venue of socialization. He or she mixed with adults in the local community, learned its shared values and customs and gradually became inured to the world of labor from an early age. The landed ranks, on the other hand, were primarily socialized in the home. As adults, elites had to demonstrate by genteel behavior that they were worthy of their high social status. Parents took great care to have their children instructed in the social graces. Children learned the correct forms of address and public conduct, indispensable for the successful negotiation of a hierarchical society. Table manners were crucial, since eating was the great public event of the day in the aristocratic household. Physical grace mattered too and so the young practiced such activities as horse riding and dancing. In regions which left the bulk of an estate to one child, the heir and the other siblings were brought up differently: one to run an estate, the others to seek employment. The heir was singled out for a particular relationship with his parents and was often used as the buffer between parents and the younger children.[27]

The two sexes were also reared differently, in all ranks of early modern Europe. Around the age of seven, boys, in an important ceremony known as breeching, would don male attire. This ritual marked not the end of childhood but the beginning of sex-role socialization: the boys received not just trousers but other accoutrements of manhood, such as a sword. After the ceremony, a boy left the world of women and prepared to enter that of men. Mothers were generally considered too indulgent to produce a masculine man so a boy's care and guidance were placed in the hands of his father and male tutors. In Russia, a strict sexual division was enforced, often involving a change of living quarters. The inculcation of the values of masculinity continued at the grammar schools and universities, with the finishing touch added by the Grand Tour, which parents hoped would enlarge the mind and cultivate understanding. Upper- and middle-class males learned to substitute courage for fear, to cultivate honor, to govern their passions, to understand the demands and obligations of service, and to take responsibility for the family. In short, they were groomed for their role as a public figures in public life.[28]

Middle- and upper-class girls were just as assiduously instructed in the mores and skills of femininity so as to be suited for their future role in society: that of wife and mistress of a household. In Dutch paintings, little girls are depicted with babies or dolls and household utensils. The daughters of French nobles received gifts of beautiful dresses, dolls, or musical instruments while their brothers were given swords or belts. Girls were schooled in the demands of running a large household, in the overseeing of an estate, and often in medical treatment. They were also trained to be modest, virtuous, and obedient from an early age. This grooming regime was not intended to make girls incapable of initiative or independent action—such talents were vital in cultures where men were often absent from home. The aim was to make certain that when a girl grew up, she would defer to and be governed by her husband.[29]

ECONOMIC WELFARE

Child Labor

In the vast majority of European families, childhood in its modern definition, as a carefree time marked by games and a freedom from work, did not last long. In families below the level of the middle class, children worked from about the age of seven. On farms, they assisted in animal husbandry and helped with agricultural tasks: herding livestock, minding sheep, scaring birds, collecting firewood, and rearing silkworms. They were also employed in rural industry, particularly in textiles. Those from proto-industrial families often had to contribute to the family budget from a young age. In Zurich, for example, more children of textile workers in the age group 5–13 were in the labor force, compared to the offspring of farmers and craftsmen. Even when not actively employed, children contributed to the family economy by taking over domestic chores and thereby freeing older members of the family to work. Girls in particular helped out with babysitting, cleaning, cooking, and fetching water.[30]

The use of child labor does not mean there was not a caring parent–child relationship; it was simply one of the realities of a harsh economic existence. For the very poor, children were an economic burden. Having a large number of small children, especially if the father had died, was one of the main reasons for claiming poor relief. Children's labor was crucial to the survival of many families: either they made it possible for other family members to work, or they supplied unpaid labor, or they earned and thereby directly supplemented the family finances. Their labor before industrialization, however, was neither as demanding nor as frequent as adult employment. Young children were given lighter tasks which did not require a great deal of strength. Moreover, they rarely worked when very young, at least outside of the home, because the costs to the employer of feeding and clothing them would outweigh their productive contribution. Parish authorities, for example, found it difficult to find masters willing to apprentice young pauper children. The small size of children was not an advantage for agricultural work, unlike for sweeping chimneys or going down mines. Before their mid-teens, when children were considered capable of adult tasks, child labor was likely to be infrequent and intermittent, prior to the nineteenth century.[31]

Child labor changed considerably with the advent of industrialization. It became more regular and more continuous, and the transition between being a child and being a member of the workforce was more abrupt. The authorities thought it better for poor children to work so there was rarely an outcry about child workers in the eighteenth century, with the exception of chimney sweeps. Although they constituted only a small number of children, the chimney sweep in England became the symbol of the poor working child. As children came to be seen as innocent, malleable, and dependent, so climbing boys were gradually viewed as the embodiment of perverted childhood, and a campaign was begun to remove children from the labor force.[32]

Service and Apprenticeship

The stage of youth was associated with moving out of the parental home. Many young children were temporarily separated from their parents: they may have been placed with other relatives or boarded out, usually for reasons of schooling or following outbreaks of plague or parental death. For older children, leaving home was more of a *rite de passage*, although there was no set age for doing so. The economic situation of the family normally determined the appropriate time. Rural cottagers and urban laborers could keep children longer and benefit from cheap labor. The most common age to depart was between 15 and 19 and most young people would leave to enter service or to take up an apprenticeship. Parental help was invaluable in securing a good place: parents supplied guidance and contact networks, assisted with making arrangements, and paid for an apprenticeship premium. Leonard Wheatcroft, a parish clerk in seventeenth-century Andover, and Jacques Louis Ménétra, a glazier in eighteenth-century Paris, took great pains to secure suitable positions for their offspring.[33]

In Western Europe about 40 percent of all children spent part of their adolescence as servants. The term covered a wide variety of workers: men and women, boys and girls, engaged in agricultural, commercial, industrial as well as domestic tasks. The institution of service was popular for

many reasons. In the cities, middle-class households offered many opportunities for domestic service. Farmers also sought servants because they
were better suited to the continuous tasks of agriculture than day laborers who were often unreliable. The supply of and demand for servants in
husbandry was greatest in those rural areas in which the nuclear family
predominated and which had a mix of small and medium farms. While
the poorer ranks needed to have their offspring in gainful employment,
those higher up the social scale wanted to widen the social and educational horizons of their children, and also to provide a stronger framework of authority and discipline. In the sixteenth century, elite children
often spent time in the service of another noble so as to build up future
patronage networks and be properly instructed in gentility. Servants
were most frequently aged from 15 to 30 and lived as members of their
employer's household, usually on yearly contracts. Young people entered
service both to save their family the cost of maintaining them and to
learn skills necessary for their future. Young women wished to accumulate a dowry.[34]

In Western and Central Europe, servants were typically young and
unmarried and hence the system has been termed life-cycle service: that
is a stage between leaving home and getting married through which
something like a tenth or more of the whole population would be passing
at any one time. Historians may have exaggerated the extent of life-cycle
service. It was certainly not universal. In Greater Russia, for example,
there were no servants in rural households. The south of Italy, despite
having nuclear families, lacked life-cycle servants. Even in areas where
service was common, there was never a time when all young people
became servants: around 25 to 50 percent in any one area was the normal
proportion. In cities, service seems to have been restricted mainly to
certain categories of youth: the poor, orphaned, or rural. In Rye, a Sussex
coastal town, over half of the servants were migrants. Local youths with
living parents were employed only when the family was too poor to
support all the children, or when the father himself could not employ all
the sons. Many sons and daughters did not leave home until marriage
and thus did not enter service. Nor did all of those who left home intend
to become servants: they might become lodgers in the city, take up an
apprenticeship, or attend school. Nor, finally, was service always limited
to a segment of the life-cycle. In Eastern Europe, excluding Poland,
a large proportion of rural servants were married, as were domestic
servants in sixteenth-century Venice. Life-time domestic service was
particularly common for women. Once in service, young people did not
necessarily remain in it till marriage. They could leave to capitalize on
other opportunities for employment and return if these did not work out.

In Renaissance Venice, service, far from representing a distinct stage of life, "was a profession that women and men entered and left as the circumstances of their lives changed." Because a large percentage of young people, around one third overall, were not servants, the onset of youth cannot be equated with the entering of service.[35]

The second major reason for leaving home was to take up an apprenticeship. The age for beginning an apprenticeship depended on the craft to be learned. Apprenticeships usually began in the mid-teens and lasted from three to seven years. Many youths, however, did not complete their terms but left as soon as they had mastered the trade. Detailed contracts were drawn up specifying the obligations of both parties. The master was to provide food, clothing, and lodging, to teach the apprentice the rules and skills of the craft, and to bring up the youth to be an honorable member of the craftsman's guild. For his part, the apprentice promised to submit to the discipline of his master's household, to refrain from gambling, drinking, and unseemly behavior, to be suitably dressed, and to go out at night only with his master's permission. Most apprentices were male. Female apprentices were few in number and usually confined to the clothing or retail trades rather than the lucrative, high-status crafts.[36]

In early modern Europe, apprentices and servants were considered to be dependants of the head of the household and hence part of the family. This was notably the case with apprentices who lived many years in their master's home and for whom the master was in loco parentis, regulating and protecting the youths like family members. We should not, however, exaggerate the familial facet of these relationships. They were also contractual relations of labor. Apprentices were not accorded the same status within the household as the master's children. For example, they ate at the lower end of the table and were sometimes given food of poorer quality. Neither did the parties involved always perform their obligations satisfactorily. Apprentices disobeyed orders, refused to abide by dress codes and curfews, and ran away. Servants, too, were often defiant, took advantage of running errands to visit friends, family, or lovers, and stole from their employers. Not all masters took care to train their apprentices: some wished only to exploit a source of cheap labor. Servants and apprentices, especially the former who were often poor and isolated from their peers, were also vulnerable to abuse from their masters or mistresses. Young female servants were sexually exploited by their masters or the sons of the household. It is difficult to discover how often abuse occurred and how serious it was. In France, between one tenth and one third of all recorded illegitimate pregnancies were a result of master–servant sex, which, on occasion, was consensual. In Renaissance

Venice approximately one case of servant abuse a year was brought before the courts. In northern England between 1600 and 1800, servants sued their masters for failure to pay wages rather than for ill-treatment. Although apprentices and servants did have recourse to the courts for abuse or non-performance of the contract, only the most egregious examples of cruelty were likely to be taken to court; when this occurred, the masters were invariably penalized. In most cases if young people did not like their situation, they left. In the cities, it was generally easy for a servant to obtain another position.[37]

Inheritance

As today, so in the past: children cost money. Starting with the provisions for childbirth and continuing until the children attained maturity, parents, to the extent that they could afford it, spent money on their children. Clothes and shoes were a constant expense, as were, for the affluent, education and entertainment. Toys for children became more readily available in the increasingly commercial society of the eighteenth century. Before then there were virtually no toyshops or toy manufacturers in Europe, and almost no books written or produced especially for children. Ensuring adequate financial provision for their children was a major concern for parents. During their lifetime they frequently distributed family resources such as domestic goods, education fees, apprenticeship premiums, marriage portions, and sometimes land, as well as making careful provision for property to be bequeathed after their death. Determining how much to give each child was a delicate and complex task. In essence, a head of household was faced with two not entirely compatible goals: to preserve the lineage, especially if land was involved, and to provide for all children. The former aim usually meant passing on the holding, farm, or estate intact to a single heir, a practice termed impartible inheritance, whereas the latter entailed the division of property among all offspring (partible inheritance).

Different cultures and geographical regions adhered to different patterns. Germany generally had partible practices in the southwest, and impartible in the north and east. The west of France tended toward partible inheritance, while an inegalitarian system predominated in the north, northeast, and south. Eastern and Central Europe were similarly varied. Russia clung to the partible system, in contrast to Austria where inheritance laws forbade the splitting of property and permitted only one heir to take over the estate. Most of the nobility—excluding the Russian and Venetian elite as well as the German princes before 1650—employed the impartible system known as primogeniture, passing the estate on to the eldest son. Primogeniture was generally used by noble families in order to avoid the subdivision of their estates and to consolidate wealth to hand on to future generations. Some noble families did divide up their estates, but had the same goals and followed alternative strategies to avoid too much fragmentation. Such families substituted a dowry for a daughter's share in the estate, or, as in Savoy, arranged for brothers to hold the estates in common, or made use of testaments to favor one son over his brothers, or, as in Venice, relied on restrictive marriage policies.[38]

In whatever system was chosen, sons customarily received more than daughters. Women in most parts of Europe received a dowry, which would normally be less than they would have received if there had been an entirely equal distribution of the estate. A daughter sometimes inherited moveable property but rarely land or the manor house. Even in areas like Franche-Comté where the law stated there was to be equal division among all siblings, brothers in most families inherited more than their sisters. Parents thus consciously gave daughters less. In parts of France and Valencia by the eighteenth century, there was a more egalitarian treatment of women. The reverse was true of England: the argument has been made that much of the legal history of the English landed elite is in essence the tale of depriving women of their common law rights. The development of the strict settlement (one made on the marriage of the heir which detailed the succession of the estate, annuities for younger sons, dowries for daughters, jointure for the widow, with the whole secured by trustees) gave the younger child a share of the estate but probably disadvantaged daughters by stripping them of their common law right to inherit in default of surviving males.[39]

Inheritance was based on laws, customs, and actual practices, and the three did not necessarily correspond. Laws required that property be divided up in certain proportions but rarely determined the exact form of the settlement, which would ultimately depend on such factors as land tenure, local traditions, parental desires, and economic conditions. The actions of landowners and of peasants often differed from legal dictates. They were prepared to defy the law if necessary, or, more commonly, to maneuver within it. The Russian aristocracy, for example, tried to avoid complying with Peter the Great's law of single inheritance, and their resistance forced the law passed in 1714 to be repealed in 1731. These nobles inserted into their wills fabricated debts to their non-inheriting children which would have to be paid out of the estate, and illicitly sold land so that the proceeds could be divided or the land resold to the non-heirs. In Valencia, where custom favored equal distribution of property, parents got around the introduction of the more inegalitarian Castilian system in 1707 by granting *inter vivos* gifts to the excluded children.

Inheritance was more a form of family strategy than a fixed practice: parents selected the best option for their circumstances.[40]

It may be that economic factors were the main influence on the parental strategy chosen. Peasants in the partible inheritance regions of southwest Germany, for instance, tended to pass estates to only one son during periods of agricultural depression. In Sweden, the custom was to have egalitarian inheritance in regions where there were substantial sources of complementary income, such as forestry and fishing. The estates of the Hesse-Kassel nobility were divided equally among surviving heirs because an estate was required if one was to become a full member of the Ritterschaft (landed and political elite), which conferred significant financial benefits. A similar reason lay behind the Russian aristocracy's opposition to impartible inheritance. A survey of the strategies employed by the nobles of the southwest German states concluded that the inheritance patterns of Catholic and Protestant nobles were similar: both religious groups implemented polices which adjusted the number of heirs to changing economic conditions in order to ensure that the estates could continue to support the family in a noble style of life. Families resorted to restrictive marriage policies, carried out divisions in only a minority of cases in which they were theoretically possible, and increasingly favored the eldest son as a means of achieving their goal, without ever formally abandoning the system of partible inheritance.[41]

The practice in most families appears to have been a compromise between extreme egalitarian and single heir systems. The nobility believed that it was their responsibility to provide for all their children. Therefore, even if the main estate was granted to one heir, the younger children received stock, grain, movables, and cash. If the family was very wealthy, a younger son might receive some land. In poorer families, if one son was made the heir, the others would be encouraged to find employment, and funds would be made available for apprenticeship or training, if at all possible. Pierre Coulet, a small farmer in Upper Provence, reminded one son in his will drawn up in 1661, that

> he should be content, without being able to demand anything else from his inheritance since, unlike the other children, he had him taught writing and reading, and given him the profession of a hatter, which has cost him much money.

Parents, for the most part, tried to give their children equality of opportunity and would take the special needs of individual children into account. They would, for example, balance the account by leaving less to those children who were to be the beneficiaries of other relatives. In the stem-family society of Haute-Provence, one son would be chosen to inherit the estate. In return, this son had to remain in the parental home, subject to parental authority until his father's death. The other siblings were given a considerably smaller share of the family property, but they received it, and their emancipation from paternal control, immediately. Most parents tried to achieve some level of parity among a multiplicity of competing interests.[42]

Property was part of a larger set of transactions and responsibilities: people exchanged resources for attention, care, and respect. In peasant societies ownership of property and tools, use rights, and labor were elements in a series of complex reciprocities which structured the relationships between parents and children. Parents in eighteenth-century Neckarhausen expected to retain control over their adult children even after the latter married and set up their own household. No child was given enough to make him or her independent: if a child was granted land, he would not be given equipment or traction animals. Traditions like this reinforced the obligations of children to parents. Generally, inheritance customs were flexible enough so that dutiful children could be rewarded—those who looked after sick parents, for instance, were given more—and unruly ones threatened with whole or partial disinheritance.[43]

Sibling Relationships

The system of inheritance affected family relationships: the manner of transmitting property influenced the interaction of spouses, parents and children, and siblings. Property conferred not just wealth and goods but status and power. The division of the family's possessions aroused acute feelings and could engender a great deal of conflict. In theory partible inheritance should have eliminated quarreling among siblings; in actuality, this was not the case. In eighteenth-century Neckarhausen immovable property was to be divided among all children. At the father's death, each child had to report what he or she had already received, and the remaining goods were then divided so as to give everyone a fair share. The custom entailed a great deal of wrangling as siblings evaluated each other's property. A similar system in Brittany also led to intense sibling rivalry, mainly because the fact that goods were not transmitted on one single occasion, such as marriage, meant that the issue of inheritance was never finally settled.[44]

In cultures that relied on impartible inheritance, children within the same family had different entitlement rights, and this could create tension among siblings. The practice in Austria and Haute-Provence where one son was chosen to take over the land resulted in a great deal of resentment: on the part of the inheriting son who resented his lack of power at home, as well as from the other siblings who knew that, without land, they would find it difficult to found their own household and were jealous of the heir's privileged status. In the case of primogeniture, no matter how generous the provision was for younger sons, there would still be a great deal of financial inequality, with the eldest son obtaining the lion's share. Inheritance was a contentious issue in brother–brother relationships in all families with property to leave, but particularly so in the elite. The system strained the friendship between the heir and his younger brothers: younger sons might envy their elder brother's fortune, and, if they found it difficult to persuade their brother to pay them their annuities, would resent their financial dependence. Primogeniture also fractured relations among the younger siblings. At times, younger children were bequeathed larger portions than the family could afford, setting the scene for rivalry as brothers and sisters vied for the favor of the oldest son. One study of an English gentry family in the seventeenth century, the Verneys, concluded that sibling relationships were "marked by a calculated reciprocity" and unlikely to be based on affection. Financial concerns also intruded in the sister–sister relationship. In 1683 Jane, the eldest Josselin daughter, was angered by the fact that her two younger sisters each received a larger dowry than she did.[45]

There is copious evidence in the archives of bitter sibling discord over property and finances. Nevertheless, younger sons did reap social and material benefits from being members of a high-ranking family and may also have derived considerable bounty from assisting the heir with business or other matters. Nor were all sibling relations conflictual; at least in some families, mutual attachment and assistance were the norm. Young people who migrated to cities in search of employment would take advantage of established siblings to locate a suitable position. Despite occasional bouts of rivalry, most families held together. And the sibling bonds could often be strong. At the deaths of Anne and Thomas Josselin within a few days of each other, their father commented that they were "loving in their lives and in their death they were not divided, lying in the same grave."[46]

STEP-PARENTS

Children in early modern Europe were likely to face the death of a parent in the course of their childhood. A relatively high percentage of marriages in this period were remarriages, perhaps as high as 30 percent in sixteenth-century England. This meant that step-parents were common. Mortality frequently disrupted families in urban areas: individuals may have undergone several remarriages and children could have lost not only both their parents, but also their first step-parents. The death of a parent was a momentous event in a young person's life, inducing an acute sense of deprivation and loss. Since the surviving spouse was likely to remarry, it also resulted in the introduction of a stranger into the family. Tales of cruel step-parents abound in fairy tales and folklore. There were certainly some apprehensions at the remarriage of a parent, particularly with reference to inheritance, for it was feared that an heir might be disinherited in favor of the children of the new marriage; or that the new couple would spend the biological parent's wealth; or that a step-parent would acquire a life interest in the estate after the spouse's death, forcing the heir to wait for his inheritance. History, though, furnishes many examples of caring, committed step-parents. Johannes Struby of Alsace, to give one instance, was a devoted step-father. His correspondence with his stepson Sebastien, aged about 13 or 14, in 1518 reveals that Struby helped the boy obtain an apprenticeship in his chosen career, as well as making sure that Sebastien acquired the appropriate clothing. Struby also took an interest in the type of training Sebastien would undergo, inquiring about the academic and religious education his stepson would receive and stressing that he wished the boy to be instructed in all necessary virtues and honor. The autobiography of Jacques Louis Ménétra describes the affection his three children felt for their stepmother and their deep grief at her death.[47]

ABANDONMENT, INFANTICIDE, AND ABUSE

Abandonment

The abandonment of children was a distinguishing feature of early modern European culture. The system developed to cope with this problem was characterized by the existence of foundling homes, the protection of the anonymity of parents, and the placement of foundlings with wet-nurses and in foster homes. Foundling homes originated in Italy in the thirteenth century and spread through much of Europe. By the eighteenth century most large towns had at least one foundling hospital, the prevalent belief being that these institutions were needed to prevent infanticide. The rate of abandonment varied through time and across cultures, increasing in the eighteenth century. Slightly more girls were abandoned than boys. The decision to relinquish a child was based on a variety of factors, including poverty, government policies, and illegitimacy, as well as rural to urban migration. It was above all a survival strategy in times of economic or personal crisis.[48]

One of the main reasons for leaving a child in a foundling home was because the mother was unmarried and the child illegitimate. In much of Europe, a woman's honor was identified with her sexuality and by surrendering her infant she could hide her dishonor. The decision to give up an illegitimate child was typically made before or shortly after its birth, and most were left within the first few months of life. In some homes, however, large numbers of legitimate children were taken in. By the mid-eighteenth century about 50 percent of the foundlings left at the Inclusa in Madrid were legitimate, as were at least 72 percent of the babies left at the Spedale degli Innocenti in Florence in the late eighteenth century. Shame alone, though a contributing factor, is not enough to explain the phenomenon of abandonment.[49]

The prime motivating factor appears to have been ability to maintain the child. The rate of abandonment increases as the economy worsens in all cultures studied. In early modern Europe, couples married when they had enough money to do so and had the means by which to earn a living. An economy in crisis postponed or prevented completely a proportion of marriages, and increased the number of illegitimate births. Employment prospects for a single woman in a depressed economy were singularly bleak. Even if she were lucky enough to find a job, her wages would probably be too low to support a child. This situation was exacerbated by the fact that in some types of work, such as domestic service—the largest area of employment for urban women—it was often impossible to keep the child and the position. The mothers of abandoned children were usually unwed servant girls or textile workers. Many were recent migrants to the city, bereft of family resources and support. It was the combination of the conditions of employment with a low income rather than poverty *per se* that interfered with a woman's ability to keep her child. Legitimate children tended to be left at an older age rather than shortly after birth, and as bread prices rose, more of them would be placed in a foundling home. Over half the infants left at the Inclusa in Madrid came from an agricultural background, and almost one third were of artisanal status. These groups were especially vulnerable to economic distress.

It looks as if the abandonment of legitimate children was intended to be a temporary expedient: parents tried to reclaim surviving children from the Inclusa, for instance, whenever possible. In places where expenses had to be paid before reclaiming a child, or where a penalty was imposed, fewer legitimate children were abandoned. That the ability to look after the child was the crucial factor in the decision to abandon can be seen from a study of the Basque country. This region had a high illegitimacy rate but virtually no children were abandoned. The area had many complex households to help with the care of children, tolerated concubinage—stable but irregular unions—and had a system whereby, if the mother so decreed, the father had to take custody of the child after the age of three. After changes in the nineteenth century which left young, unmarried mothers to look after the child alone, abandonment increased.[50]

It has been argued that the constant presence of these foundlings in early modern European society is evidence of maternal neglect, or at least indifference to the fate of children. The rate of abandonment increased, however, at the very time—the eighteenth century—when, according to some scholars, a new attitude toward children was emerging. For many women, the decision to relinquish a wanted child was heart-rending. With respect to the London foundlings, the babies were left in well frequented places so that they would be found quickly, and many had been well cared for until the time they were left. Observers commented on the grief of mothers who left their children at Coram's hospital in eighteenth-century London. Some parents left tokens so they could identify the baby, hoping to reclaim the infant later. Infants often had notes attached to their clothing explaining who they were and why they had been left. A note pinned to one baby abandoned in Rouen in 1789 read:

> I was born today, January 7, of a legal marriage. My father and mother are suffering extreme poverty and do not have it in their power to have me christened or to render me the services my tender youth requires them to give me. It is only with the most mortifying distress and acute sorrow that they abandon me.[51]

Infanticide

Child abandonment is usually portrayed as an alternative strategy to infanticide, which was regarded as unnatural in Europe. It was deemed an offense against God and the family, and included in the group of crimes considered especially heinous such as witchcraft, heresy, and incest. Horrifying sentences were imposed on those convicted, including torture, impaling, and/or burying alive. Most European states took an increasingly harsh stance in the sixteenth and seventeenth centuries, deeming it infanticide if a baby died and the mother had concealed her pregnancy. From the 1770s on, capital punishment was gradually abolished as a penalty for killing newborns. Infanticide seems to have been relatively rare: there were 42 cases in sixteenth- and seventeenth-century Nuremberg; 24 in Amsterdam for the period 1680–1811, and two to three a year in the north of England in the eighteenth century. It is possible that some women, especially those living in the city, evaded detection and prosecution. The existence of infanticide has more to do with the plight of unmarried mothers than with the concept of childhood or relations between parents and children. Those who were charged with killing their babies were invariably isolated women who lacked support networks. They were typically unmarried, often domestic servants, and frequently poor and illiterate. These woman committed infanticide to avoid the stigma of illegitimacy: the possible rejection by friends and family, the prospect of losing their livelihoods, and the incurring of church and state penalties.[52]

Abuse

As today, children in the past were at times the victims of abuse by adults. There was no specific child protection legislation in Europe before the late nineteenth century. This does not mean that children were without legal safeguards, but they were not singled out as a group in need of particular protection. Local communities differentiated between legitimate punishment and physical abuse, and ill-treatment of children, far from being condoned, was punished if discovered. Henry Machyn, citizen of sixteenth-century London, described how one woman was placed in the pillory for beating her child with rods. Most cultures dealt severely with those who sexually abused minors. State law could also be harsh on those who accidentally hurt children. In 1664, a coachman in the Hague who ran over a small boy who had run into his path, was punished with three days on bread and water in the jail and ordered to pay for the boy's apprenticeship.[53]

Children, of course, were vulnerable to secret abuse. Some of the 'accidents' that befell children, such as burnings, drownings, suffocation, or poisonings, may have been of this sort. On the other hand, there is plenty of evidence that when parents were aware that their children were in danger, they tried to rescue them, and were profoundly grateful if they managed to do so.[54]

CONCLUSION

The history of childhood has moved a long way from Philippe Ariès's early influential claim that the past lacked a concept of childhood, that childhood was an unimportant phase in the life-cycle, and that the frailty of children precluded any great parental attachment to them. Many scholars initially accepted and extended these premises, charting the emergence of a modern concept of childhood through such purported developments as the emergence of the nuclear family; the appearance of toys; the growth of sentiment; changes in education systems; the intensification of patriarchy by Protestantism; and the reduction in the severity of discipline imposed on children. The spate of works within what has been called the modernization paradigm—holding that good parental care is a modern invention—was followed by a flurry of research trying to balance the picture by stressing continuity—arguing that as far back as we can tell, most parents loved their children, grieved at their deaths, and conscientiously attended to the task of child-rearing. It is only recently that historians have begun to critique the nature of the questions asked of the historical material. Rather than search for the existence or absence of love in the past, for example, we should investigate what love meant in a given culture and era, and how it was expressed. We should also aim to present a more rounded picture of parent–child relations in the past. To date we have tended to focus on one facet of the interaction without viewing it as a whole. Parenting was—and still is— a mix of justice, severity, indulgence, anxiety, frustration, and commitment. Formality was not incompatible with intimacy; grooming children for their role in life did not preclude the growth of attachment to individuals. Groups of children for whom childhood was bleak because of acute poverty or poor parenting practices were counterbalanced by large numbers of families who aimed to do the best they could for their children.[55]

The modernization paradigm may not be the most helpful interpretative model but that does not mean that some changes did not occur. Pediatric treatises and domestic conduct books began to focus more on the child as an individual and also to include the duties of parents, rather than solely those of the child. The definition of love may have changed: from an absence of ill-feeling to doing all one could for a person. By the eighteenth century the social and economic environment in much of Europe had changed markedly. There were more commercial opportunities available to the middle- and upper-class child, meaning that a new degree of material indulgence was permitted. In some cultures, the state took a new interest in education. It is possible that there was an increased sensitivity to the needs of children by government and institutions. For the poor child, in particular, changes in the concept of childhood improved state care.[56]

The European pattern of child care places a great deal of responsibility on parents: they are charged with playing a large role in the formation of the character of each child. Changes in the concept of childhood certainly affected notions of parental accountability. In the seventeenth century, the waywardness of children could be blamed on original sin;

once it was accepted that children were innocent, their faults were laid at the feet of their parents. Parents in all periods and cultures were intent on fitting their child for society. They may have been less concerned with individual happiness in the past, but they were also unenthusiastic about imposing their will on a child. There was more negotiation in the parent–child relationship than many historians have supposed. Child-rearing was not just something done to a child; he or she participated in the process. Perhaps we should now attend to the part played by children in their own upbringing, difficult though this will be to document from the available sources.

CHAPTER 8

Marriage, Widowhood, and Divorce
Antoinette Fauve-Chamoux

From the Middle Ages onward, when marriage was socially regulated, it became the main mechanism governing population growth in West European populations, replacing mortality. Not everybody could marry, a fact reflected in high rates of celibacy. The question then is: who married, who remained single, who divorced, and who remarried?

GETTING MARRIED: MARRIAGE OBJECTIVES AND STRATEGIES IN MATING

In most early modern rural West European societies, marriage was hardly conceivable for new couples with no plans to settle down, i.e. who lacked the resources to start a separate household. Young men or women resorted to all sorts of strategies in order to get married, including migration.

Getting Married and Settling Down

In the East European steppes, abundant opportunities to start new farms and breed cattle facilitated settling down and encouraged marriage. But the case was very different in Western Europe, where rural settlements were more permanent, since practically the whole land was already appropriated. Landlords (noblemen, urban middle classes, the Church) were not prone to divide up their estates. They were much more interested in leasing them on a long-term basis to reputable farmers. As for small peasants in areas with egalitarian inheritance, each generation had to redistribute its rural patrimony, which usually provided only enough for one family to live decently. One obvious reason for this is that landholdings can only be divided so much. As a result, many brothers and sisters gave up the idea of marrying in the village. They sold off their portion to their brother(s) or sister(s), who continued cultivating the family land, and chose celibacy or migration. Survival of parents also influenced marriage. Settling down for a new couple was all the more difficult when parents lived a longer life, except if they agreed to retire and transmit or split their assets well before dying.

Stem-family societies, as found for example, in Scandinavia, in the Tyrol or the Pyrénées, were an exception to the general habit of settling down separately in a new household at marriage. Here, the married heir was bound to live with his or her parents in the family home.[1] But at times of population growth we do find the building of new houses. When possible, these were built on newly claimed land; otherwise, we observe some breaking up of estates.

In such European rural societies, sexual intercourse was practically out of the question for young people who had not received a legacy or did not earn money from employment in service or as apprentices. This was necessary if one was to establish oneself as a peasant or craftsman.

Getting Married and Social Control

Society was not capable of providing a plot of land or other opportunities for young couples until a certain age. Marriage postponement was part of the "European household formation pattern."[2] Women married at a late age and infrequent pre-marital sexual intercourse was the "contraceptive" device of European Christianity. In this, Europe contrasted with the rest of the world where females married at an early age. Controlled marriage and celibacy together were not enough to hamper European demographic growth overall, although these varied by time period. Growth was moderate during the sixteenth century, and more pronounced later. Some seventeenth-century crises concluded with quick recovery (Table 8.1), and the eighteenth century ended with a much larger population.

Table 8.1 Population increase in pre-industrial Europe (millions of inhabitants)

Date	Western Europe	Europe with Russia
1500	67	81
1600	89	100
1650	88	105
1700	95	120
1750	111	140
1800	146	180

Source: Western Europe: Biraben 1979 ; Europe with Russia: MacEverdy and Jones 1978.

In the sixteenth and seventeenth centuries, growing nuptiality and fertility counterbalanced the effects of war, epidemic, or famine. Such post-crisis recoveries were due more to higher marriage rates than to marriage at a younger age. Severe mortality crises brought a rise in the number of widows, widowers, and bachelors of all ages on the matrimonial market. In the eighteenth century, population grew at a regular pace everywhere in Europe except the Netherlands, with an acceleration after 1750, most clearly shown in Eastern Europe, Scandinavia, and Ireland. Historians, economists, and demographers still debate the main reasons for such growth in Europe during the Age of Enlightenment. Some point to the agricultural revolution that spread from England and provided abundant food to all of Europe. Others note progress in medicine and public health, which were effective in decreasing mortality rates. However, such theories remain unsatisfactory and do not account for the extent of European population growth nor for the general demographic change which seemed to occur on a worldwide scale: we now know there were similar developments in China and the Americas in the eighteenth century.

As a true representative of the Age of Enlightenment, writing at the end of the eighteenth century, Thomas Malthus referred to regulated marriage and responsible fertility as "preventive checks," much to be preferred to the "positive checks" of mortality crises, wars, and famine. Demographic historians have continued to address the links between population and subsistence, emphasizing nuptiality as the main mechanism regulating the reproduction system of European societies.[3] We will now consider just how this system worked.

Marriage

Until recently, nuptiality statistics were not thoroughly investigated, since mortality, natality, and fertility appeared to shed more light on population dynamics. When these statistics were just starting to be used for basic research, the French demographer, Louis Henry, pointed out some aspects of interest.[4] He introduced the notions of *panmixia* and *isolate* which dealt with the choice of marriage partner. *Panmixia* is a pure, theoretical situation in which random marriages occur in a given large or small population. *Isolate* relates to endogamy (i.e. a tendency to choose one's mate within the limits of one's relatively closed group). After some generations, certain groups may be called isolates. When studying nuptiality, the demographer thus creates a new concept, the *endogamic circle* which the marriage candidate is supposed to enter for a certain time. Age, social status, education, skills, religion, etc. are interacting factors that give access to specific circles of various sizes. Henry made a point of not neglecting the individual's motivations. He also paid particular attention to the consequences of accidental events, such as epidemics, wars, or emigration, which disturb the equilibrium of generations.

In the end, Henry depicts nuptiality as the result of a variety of forces. Economic and social factors (which either hasten or delay marriages) interact with demographic factors, such as the sex and age composition of the population, which affects numbers of potential mates. The subdivision of the population into more or less closed groups according to geographical proximity or social segregation also has an important effect. Permanent celibacy is viewed as often being the result of the unavailability of desired mates in the relevant population. Social factors induce one to marry someone other than a desirable partner. Let us add that, in narrow groups, such as a village or a small group of craftsmen, each man or woman has a reduced choice. Observations show that a later marriage often meant marrying someone who was considerably younger. This is unsurprising, since the older the person, the fewer the potential mates of the same age and the larger the pool of younger potential mates. The endogamic circle was thus permanently reshuffling.

Of course past societies were never totally closed. Random meeting sometimes ended up in marriage. But is it mere chance when girls and boys of neighboring villages meet on the fairground? Is it also mere chance when migrants—female and male servants—attend the same entertainment places in town, as part of their social and cultural networks which then act as another "endogamic circle"? We ought to consider more carefully these methodological caveats. Our contemporary treatment of past social networks and our finer reading of statistics give us a deeper view of certain social realities. At the same time, the possibility of individual choice ought not to be ignored.

Matrimonial markets, so it seems, should shrink during periods of demographic crisis and blossom in subsequent recovery periods. In the European context of global population growth since the sixteenth century we would expect a broadening of the matrimonial market, which would also imply earlier age at marriage. Yet, such was not the case, as far as we can tell. Let us first recall the basic features of the West European family as they can be read from a combination of various monographs (Table 8.2). They indicate late first marriage, over 25 for women and 28 for men; a two- to three-year age gap between husband and wife; faster and more frequent remarriage for widowers (see below); and a high rate of permanent celibacy.

Only half of adult women (aged 15 to 50) in Europe west of the Petersburg–Trieste line were actually living as spouses. Widows and spinsters accounted for the other half. East of this line, marriage patterns were similar to those of non-European societies: marriage was at an early age

Table 8.2   Characteristics of marriage, spinsterhood, and widowhood in pre-industrial Western Europe, seventeenth and eighteenth centuries

Variable	Mean value
1. Female age at first marriage	25.7 years
2. Male age at first marriage	28.0 years
3. Age difference between spouses	2.3 years
4. Maximum estimate of never married	13.3%
5. Minimum estimate of never married	8.6%
6. Interval from widowhood to remarriage	
Males	15.5 months
Females	39.2 months

Source: Smith 1977, p. 23 (compiled from 38 family reconstitution studies).

Table 8.3   Mean age at first marriage in early modern Europe (females)

Period of marriage	pre-1750	1740–1790
Belgian provinces	25.0	24.8
England	25.0	25.3
France	24.6	26.0
Germany	26.4	26.9
Eastern Tyrol	25.0	29.7
Scandinavia	26.7	25.2

Source: Flinn 1981; Ortmayer 1995.

and almost universal, with about 70 percent of women living as spouses, against 30 percent living as widows or nuns. Table 8.3 shows comparative data for female age at first marriage. After 1740, with the exception of the Belgian provinces and Scandinavia, female age at first marriage rose and the number of unmarried or widowed women grew.

The Never-married: Growing Celibacy

Assessing accurate numbers of the permanently celibate is somewhat difficult. Estimation of this group in a given population is usually based on the number of individuals still unmarried at age 50. For a good evaluation, given the lack of statistical data on the never-married in the demographic records of this period, one must deduct, from available data on the age group 50–59, all those who had previously been married, the widowed and separated. We must also remember that never-married individuals showed greater mobility, with a propensity to live their old age in town. Thus spinsters over age 50 often accounted for more than 15 percent of the female population in urban areas such as Lyon or Rheims against a much lower proportion in European rural areas (between 9 and 12 percent).[5] Analyzing the Floridablanca census of 1787 for Spanish Galicia, Antonio Eiras-Roel found evidence of a high rate of permanent celibacy in urban areas; more than 17 percent for men and women alike, against 8 percent for men and 14 percent for women in rural areas.[6] Male or female celibacy then appeared to be more of an urban phenomenon. We suggest that many of these single people came as migrants from rural areas, where they had not been able to marry. Towns offered more opportunities to make a living.

Louis Henry convincingly showed a global and regular growth of permanent celibacy in France from the end of the eighteenth century, as well as in most other European countries, particularly in the case of women (Table 8.4).[7]

We notice a great variability in female celibacy according to place and time. The highest rates in this sample (Table 8.4) are found in late

Table 8.4 Proportion of never-married aged 50–59, in early modern Europe (females)

	% never-married
Rural populations	
Belgium (1814)	8
Denmark (1787)	6
England (1599)	0
England (1790)	13
Norway (1801)	13
Iceland (1801)	23
Spain (Galicia 1787)	14
Urban populations	
Belgium (1814)	28
England (Lichfield, 1692)	7
Germany (Konstanz, 1774)	27
Italy (Rome, 1701)	5
Switzerland (Zurich, 1637)	4
Norway (1801)	16
Spain (Galicia 1787)	17

Source: Wall 1991, Eiras-Roel 1991.

eighteenth-century Konstanz (27%) and early nineteenth-century urban Belgium (28%). Many of the never married in town were not town-born. As for rural populations, only Iceland and Norway presented high proportions of women never marrying (23% and 13% respectively).

The Seasonality of Marriage

When in the year did one marry? Table 8.5 tries to answer this question, recording monthly indices in Europe between 1580 and 1799 in various Catholic and Protestant populations. These statistics and contemporary evidence for France point out deep drops in March/April and December and a slight dip in May and August/September, contrasting with peaks of marriage frequency in January/February, June/July, and November. February seems to have been a favorite month for weddings, with November a runner-up (and sometimes the most popular month, as in the case of Rouen or northeast of Paris). January/February apparently surpassed June/July as the prime marriage season toward the end of the seventeenth century.[8]

We might attribute this timing to the rhythm of the agricultural calendar, which in mostly rural countries must obviously have been a determinant. It may explain the figures for the harvest months August/September. The case of wine-growing areas is a revealing indicator of the role of agricultural activities. Their wedding calendar is very specific, with absolute minima in September/October, a peak in August after a dip in July.

But there is another reason for the deep drops in March/April and in December. In Roman Catholic countries, the Church prohibited marriage during Lent (March or April, according to the date for Easter) and Advent (before Christmas in December)—the so-called *temps clos*— except in some cases where a license to marry was given (or sold). From a more secular point of view, such periods would not have been convenient for marriage since one had to fast.

Was such a phenomenon a constant in places with a strong Roman Catholic tradition, as in the case of Warsaw? For the period 1750–1774, there were still fewer marriages in Warsaw than in France during Lent and Advent, apparently for reasons of stronger religious observance. But we do not observe the eighteenth-century rural French characteristic of a peak in February. The general trend in Warsaw differed more from the rural French model than did that found in urban France. Obviously, the calendar of field work or agricultural production had a lesser influence on life in this capital town than in urban France at large. Statistical data are not available for Paris, as the parish registers were burnt in 1871 during the Commune. We also note with interest that almost half of

Polish weddings occurred on Sundays (41%). Other favorite days were Mondays (16%) and Tuesdays (15%). Of course, Fridays—fast days— were avoided for such festivity, as elsewhere in Europe. Women married at a much younger age in Warsaw than in any other European pre-industrial city, be it Rheims, Rouen, Geneva, or Amsterdam.

Marital seasonality offers interesting insights into the attitudes of the first Protestant generations after the Reformation. Calvinist groups broke from the Catholics and their opposition to marriage during Lent and Advent. This change is noticeable in popular practice: March and December marriage dips disappeared quickly in Geneva.[9] From the English and Dutch Puritan marriage registers one sees that an analogous trend developed during the seventeenth century. But remnants of ancestral seasonal customs were still to be found in Scotland before 1640.[10] Wrigley and Schofield's figures for England also point to troughs in marriages during Lent and Advent in the late sixteenth and the early seventeenth centuries (Table 8.5). Old Catholic prohibitions were therefore never completely rejected. There were regional variations, even in French areas with a high ratio of Protestants, such as the Cévennes (Anduze), Montpellier, or Metz, where marriages at first were celebrated during the closed periods as a means of protest. In northern Protestant communities like Rouen or Châlons-sur-Marne, the Lenten prohibition was taken into consideration. This may have marked a desire not to offend Catholic sensibilities at a time of political insecurity. After 1662, Huguenots had to apply for a license in order to marry during a period of *temps clos*. Protestant marriage celebrations in March became less common. At any rate, after 1685 they could only be clandestine and were not officially recorded, since Protestants were no longer supposed to exist in the French kingdom.

May was generally considered an unlucky month for marriage, particularly in Switzerland. This prejudice was deeply rooted in European culture. We may trace it back to Ovidius (*Fasti*),[11] in the first century of the Roman empire and read it as a pagan prohibition. May weddings were thought unlucky for marital fidelity and prosperity. During the seventeenth century, Protestants as well as Catholics shared this aversion to marrying in May. But all these specificities began to fade with the eighteenth century, when traditions loosened. At this time we actually observe in Europe a swing from winter to spring weddings. A spirit of liberty seemed to affect the choice of month for wedding as the Age of Enlightenment neared its end.

Seasonality of marriage is thus a revealing indicator of popular traditions. But observation of marriage also gives essential insights into social life: marriage is indeed the touchstone of social differentiation.

Social Differentiation

Marriage patterns varied over time and according to country, but they also differed according to social groups. In France, for example, the age gap between spouses at first marriage was not very pronounced. But it was usually greater when a person married younger, and at a higher level on the social scale. French dukes and peers married at 25, and females at 20 in the second half of the seventeenth century. As a rule, age at marriage was higher in towns. In Lyon, between 1700 and 1750, women were on average 27.5 years old when they married, and men 29.[12] The data for Rheims show a lower marital age, but age at first marriage rose perceptibly during the eighteenth century (Table 8.6).

Few studies give extended data about social differences in ages at marriage. John Knodel's study of 14 German villages as well as Beatrice Möring's work on a Finnish community are of great value in this respect. Both studies point out differences between rich farmers and proletarians (Table 8.7). In Germany, women marrying farmers were two or three years younger than those marrying poorer grooms. The artisans' daughters were in between. In eighteenth-century Finland, proletarian girls married very late. Upper-class peasants married younger brides than lower-class villagers. There was a direct relationship in both countries between property size and the bride's age: the larger the holding, the younger the girl at the time of her first marriage.[13] This may be because lower-class rural peasants often went into domestic service in town for a number of years. They had to make money before settling down, not like their rich counterparts who could afford to marry rather young. There were many cases in Europe where daughters from upper- or middle-class families married later when the groom's status was below their own; marrying later was often related to the birth order position in the family. When they married a landless man, non-heiresses from rich families were older than their elder sister had been at marriage, the older sister having married a man of equal standing.

Social Differentiation and Transmission of Patrimony

Recent studies carried out on communities in the Pyrénées provide further evidence of social differentiation of this kind and bring to light the role of transmission of property and wealth, pointing to differences between heirs and non-heirs in age at first marriage. Where young couples lived together with the husband's or wife's parents, age at marriage was considerably lower. In the stem-family areas, children's age at marriage differed appreciably depending on their birth order. Younger brothers who would not inherit landed property married much later than the senior heir.

Table 8.5 Seasonal distribution of marriages in Europe (1580–1799), monthly indices

	Jan.	Feb.	Mar.	Apr.	May	June	July	Aug.	Sept.	Oct.	Nov.	Dec.
French Catholics												
Rural France 1580–1589	169	158	27	70	93	139	114	69	98	100	141	23
Urban France 1580–1589	177	154	19	81	116	136	107	74	101	78	139	16
Rural Paris 1671–1720	152	216	18	60	74	110	171	43	68	61	215	10
Rouen 1671–1720	130	205	25	51	95	87	113	65	59	115	242	13
Crulai 1675–1789	115	166	17	27	74	94	130	38	71	59	186	6
Rural France 1740–1792	188	318	24	54	74	96	99	45	62	71	158	11
Urban France 1740–1792	161	198	25	83	95	97	105	81	90	103	140	22
French Protestants												
Metz 1562–1568	152	128	83	94	107	106	111	108	71	72	76	92
Montpellier 1562–1568	96	115	127	130	121	96	81	114	69	80	84	89
Anduze 1562–1565	93	110	108	141	86	97	86	79	141	108	59	93
Anduze 1610–1659	120	84	108	146	51	117	82	121	93	112	79	86

	Jan.	Feb.	Mar.	Apr.	May	June	July	Aug.	Sept.	Oct.	Nov.	Dec.
Rouen												
1631–1664	125	157	20	104	127	87	112	75	118	106	104	65
1665–1684	114	126	22	85	129	94	138	76	92	116	117	91
Châlons/Marne												
1600–1642	129	78	39	120	90	110	126	103	86	106	163	52
England												
1540–1599	124	86	8	61	98	117	109	70	102	184	201	41
1600–1649	99	100	22	93	123	129	103	73	89	158	165	48
1650–1699	89	102	43	129	137	123	87	60	96	131	135	72
1700–1749	91	100	48	128	126	103	77	65	96	146	125	97
1750–1799	96	102	60	105	117	91	84	79	86	143	127	112
Switzerland												
Geneva												
1550–1574	119	123	109	104	101	113	96	84	82	81	88	100
1650–1674	105	121	110	122	33	109	82	90	103	79	114	132
1750–1774	82	105	117	140	36	125	93	94	86	107	111	102
Italy												
1570–1599	163	122	43	80	103	106	69	51	106	86	168	103
Poland												
Warsaw (Catholics)												
1700–1724	214	188	19	54	109	97	95	82	97	105	129	11
1725–1749	195	201	13	59	96	77	108	90	113	114	128	6
1750–1774	171	152	12	49	108	102	144	90	80	139	145	8
1775–1799	157	184	21	45	119	92	129	89	89	142	129	4

Sources: Dupâquier 1979, 1988; Benedict 1991; Wrigley and Schofield 1981; Perrenoud 1979; Kuklo 1990.

Table 8.6   Mean age at first marriage in early modern European towns

Date of marriage	Males	Females
Galician villages (Spain)		
before 1787	25.8	25.7
Galician towns (Spain)		
before 1787	26.1	23.2
Rheims		
1668–1699	27.7	24.3
1700–1724	27.7	26.2
1725–1749	28.3	25.7
1750–1774	27.9	26.3
1775–1791	28.2	26.7
Warsaw		
1740–1769	28.8	22.6
1770–1799	29.0	21.8

Source: Rheims: Fauve-Chamoux's data bank, parish registers; Kuklo 1990; Eiras-Roel 1991.

Table 8.7   Mean age at first marriage in early modern European towns by occupation of husband

	Farmers	Proletarians	Artisans	All
Males				
Germany (1700–1799)	27.6	28.6	27.3	27.9
Finland (1738–1749)	23.2	32.0		24.7
(1750–1789)	24.5	28.7		26.3
Females				
Germany (1700–1799)	24.1	26.4	25.3	25.6
Finland (1738–1749)	24.1	30.8		25.3
(1750–1789)	24.4	28.7		26.5

Source: Knodel 1988; Möring 1996.

In the Baronnies (central Pyrénées), between 1700 and 1789, 14 percent of women married before age 20; in the nearby Bareges valley, just after 1800, 22 percent of brides were married before 20; in the Alps (Queyras), 15 percent in the seventeenth century and 20 percent in the eighteenth century married this young, against 40 percent in the Swiss Alps (Uri) who married as soon as they reached puberty. But we know that girls married very soon in Bigorre (central Pyrénées) before 1650. Our sources mention a peak: 60 percent of girls married before age 20 in Saint-Savin

Table 8.8   Proportion of females first married before age 20, according to successoral situation in the family (1700–1789), Esparros, French Pyrénées

married	Younger sister × Heir	Heiress	Younger sister × Younger brother
14%	18%	8%	7%

Source: Fauve-Chamoux 1995a.

Table 8.9   Mean age at first marriage according to successoral situation of the couple, by period of marriage (1700–1789), French Pyrénées

	Heir × Younger sister		Younger brother × heiress		Younger brother × Younger sister	
Esparros						
1700–1789	27.5	24.7	29.6	24.6	33.1	25.1
Laborde						
1770–1789	27.6	25.5	36.4	24.0	33.4	27.6

Source: Bonnain 1986, Fauve-Chamoux 1995a.

between 1618 and 1650. Later on, in the eighteenth century, women marrying in the Baronnies before age 20 were heirs' wives. Heiresses also married relatively young, but their husbands were much older when they entered in the stem-family with the specific status of son-in-law ('*en gendre*') (Table 8.8).

It appears clearly in Esparros, as in Laborde, a nearby village, that the woman who took up residence in a stem-family household (heiress × younger brother or sister × heir) on marriage was younger on marrying than was the woman who was neither herself an heiress nor marrying an heir. In the latter case, upon marriage the couple (younger sister × younger brother) formed their own conjugal family household (Table 8.9).[14]

What counted for those women, marrying in a stem-family society, was less their status as heiress or non-heiress than the model of marriage they entered into: stem-family type or a branching-out type. Then differences of mean age at marriage make sense (Table 8.10). Younger brothers, who would not inherit the family farm, married much later than the heir. They had to amass some money before marrying an heiress or—if they did not emigrate—before establishing a branching-out family. Such eighteenth-century sons-in-law were not in the prime of their youth.

We may definitely consider nuptiality as a key to the ancient European demographic system: marriage was then a highly respected institution

Table 8.10   Mean age at first marriage according to successoral situation in the family, by period of marriage (1700–1789), Esparros, French Pyrénées

Grooms		Brides		Grooms	Brides
Heir	Younger brother	Heiress	Younger sister	all successoral situations	
27.5	31.5	24.5	24.9	29.1	24.8

Source: Fauve-Chamoux 1995a.

which shaped lives; illegitimate births remained at a low level, at least until 1750. With so many widows or unmarried women still young enough to give birth, social and religious morals were rather well observed. Less than 5 percent of all European infants born before 1750 were illegitimate.[15] This leads to the question of the nature of marriage ties at that time. What part did love—as opposed to material interest— play in the selection of a mate?

Marriage and/or Romantic Love

We may consider France an interesting experimental ground to find an answer to this question. One reason is that some French couples began to limit the size of their families by the end of the seventeenth century, much earlier than in any other country. Secondly, formation of couples seems to have been less tied to community socio-economic constraints than in other countries such as Switzerland, Germany, or Sweden.[16] The growing frequency of pre-marital relations in France toward the end of the eighteenth century, as well as the growing number of illegitimate births, may well indicate greater sexual freedom, associated with a decreasing social control of spontaneous mutual attraction between potential partners. Of course it is impossible to evaluate quantitatively the part attraction really had in the formation of couples. In well-to-do peasant circles, unions were pre-arranged and minors could not marry without their parents' consent. Young men and women probably had to choose their mate within a precisely delineated sphere of socially accept- able partners.

Possible choices would naturally increase in periods of demographic growth. Seasonal or domestic work mobilized young people, who then had more opportunities to meet. Nothing forbade a joint attraction to both the girl (or the boy) and her dowry (or his economic prospects). Fairs offered opportunities for boys and girls to become acquainted. In Savoy for instance, around 1800, according to a witness of that time, "women meet in a usually large, suitable cowshed in order to spin, sew or knit under a lamp they maintain at common expense. Old women with their tales, girls with their songs, boys with their mere presence brighten up this scene."[17] Once married, the peasant's wife, rich or not, had to face tiring daily work and repeated pregnancy, which soon robbed her of her blossoming youth. The rapid aging of both urban and rural women was a harsh reality of life in the *ancien régime*, but this did not mean that there was an absence of love between spouses, nor disharmony in family life. Among many contemporary hints, we may refer to the observation of a middle-class Norman physician in Elbeuf, who could not help wondering at the serene life of textile workers around 1770: "Closeness and a true solicitude reign in these families, which partake equally in sorrows and pleasures, in fidelity between spouses, affection from the fathers, respect from the children, to manifest such a domestic intimacy that we would think such qualities a prerogative of this happy town."[18] Marriage with love was not the only rule, but it existed. The comic theater of these times gives countless evidence of parents not having the last word when it came to the choice of their child's mate. Let us also remember that marriage then was indissoluble and lasted for life.

Intermarriage and Kinship

Marriage presumed another condition. It could not be celebrated between kin. Of course we encounter here the age-old prohibition on incest, but we cannot evaluate the effect of this prohibition without examining how exogamy rules were formulated and enforced. According to anthropologists, exogamy was a necessity for family groups in order for them to maintain mutual ties favoring peace and social or economic exchange. Christian canon law multiplied the prohibitions. It has been said that in early times the Church tried to impede patrimonial transmission within families, aiming to favor donations to the Church itself.[19] Other scholars interpret this extension of marriage restrictions in European societies as an awareness of necessary sexual difference: the mating of identical sexual "humors" had to be prevented.[20] This is the reason why prohibitions regarding affinal relations became more and more severe: marriage with a previous husband's blood relation became impossible. Moreover marriage became prohibited where there was spiritual linkage: the Church went on inventing new cases of spiritual kinship, such as the one contracted between the christened party, godparents, parents, kin, and officiant in a baptism, or the so-called "decency kinship," a by-product of illegitimate relations.

While adopting the Germanic computation of kinship grades in the tenth century, the Roman Catholic Church simply doubled the range of prohibitions: the seventh canonic grade was the equivalent of our 14th grade. This completely unenforceable legislation gave rise to countless but—for the Church—very lucrative exemption requests, and offered the reigning lords a good pretext to revoke marriages which displeased them. In the thirteenth century, the Church reduced the prohibition to the fourth grade. After the shock of Reformation, the Council convened in Trent eventually submitted the choice of spouse to the full authority of the priests, who enforced the new canons well enough: the new parish registers allowed the Church to control potential kinship or affinity ties between spouses-to-be. The Pope delegated to the bishops authority to examine exemption requests, especially for the minor cases (third or fourth grade). It was not too difficult for poor people to get the exemption they wished for: they just had to declare their condition and identity. But most importantly, they had to explain why they wanted to marry their kin despite the prohibition.

By the end of the seventeenth century, genealogical kinship diagrams began appearing in these exemption requests. In the archives of the Parisian Officialité, the church court, the requests amount to more than 6,000 for the eighteenth century. After studying 4,767 cases of declared kinship, André Burguière noted that 76 percent were cases of consanguinity, 16 percent of affinity, and 8 percent of spiritual kinship. Only seven cases referred to "decency kinship." Three out of four consanguinity cases concerned kinship relations of the lower grade, the remaining requests relating to unions of uncle and niece or between first cousins.[21] Remarriage strategies with a near relation of the first spouse were common. These maintained an already existing net of relations. There were also "continuity" strategies in the world of shopkeepers and craftsmen, which explain a widow's marrying her dead husband's assistant or companion, or the widower marrying his maid. Cohabitation in the master's house had indeed created what the Church defined as affinity ties. There may have also been some common participation of the potential partners in a past baptism.

There were many "proximity marriages," for instance in villages or within the less mobile part of the population, or for such occupations as wine growers or gardeners. All resulted in a generalized cousinhood. Reasons stated in requests for exemption were stereotypical: "too small neighborhood," i.e. not enough non-kin available to marry in the village; the claimant growing old, so that it was too late to find another would-be spouse. Previous sexual relations are mentioned only when the woman is pregnant. Nowhere is attraction or love given as a reason for exemption. It would not be recognized as a justification to lift canonic prohibitions. To allow a union that should theoretically be prohibited, the case law of the Church accepted three types of reason, all more serious than love:

1. sociological reasons: the Church must favor homogamy; marriage within the limits of village or in same socio-professional milieu must be encouraged;

2. strategic reasons: for instance, marriage for an old spinster; or remarriage if it is the only way to bring up young orphaned children, not to dissolve a household, or to maintain a family business with the help of a person already associated with it. In some cases such marriages were justified as a way to reconcile two warring families or family factions;

3. moral reasons: marriage would be a way to avert illegitimate birth or to put an end to a grave public disorder as in the case of concubinage.

Exemptions in the Rome Court

There were very few exemption requests in Rome during the half-century after the end of the Council of Trent (1563): they concerned mostly European aristocratic families and had to be paid for in gold. In the seventeenth century, one third of all papal exemptions went to French families. Later on, in the eighteenth century, requests came largely from northern France and the Austrian Netherlands (the future Belgium) where there were many requests to permit marriage at first-grade consanguinity; and southern Italy, Portugal, and particularly, southeastern Spain with its strong endogamy (one request per year to the Rome Court on grounds of consanguinity for every 25,000 inhabitants, i.e. twice as many as in France around 1750). The number of requests in Rome grew regularly over the course of the eighteenth century, reaching three cases per 1,000 French marriages in 1785, although local bishops satisfied a majority of requests locally, as we have seen. A true economic and fiscal system was at play, which many writers of the pre-revolutionary *Cahiers de Doléances* found appalling. Only a few weeks before the storming of the Bastille, Cardinal de Bernis acknowledged that flight of capital was a side-effect of these requests. He explained that it was good for the Kingdom of France, still "the eldest daughter of the Church" (June 3, 1789): "I read in some *Cahiers* of our provinces' protests against such an abuse of sending to Rome enormous sums as a payment for bulls, exemptions and unions. . . . But those who make such remarks do not know that our sugars, our coffees, our fashion yield four times more in Rome, and that money comes back to the Kingdom. . . . The whole town of Rome wears the fabrics made in the town of Lyon; if this Court in Rome gave English tradesmen, who have fawned on it for a long time, preference over us, subtracting this expense would not indemnify our commerce against such a substantial loss."[22]

By August 1789, transferring money to Rome had been decreed illegal. Marriages between next of kin multiplied. France began experimenting with divorce after 1792 and was apparently less opposed to family endogamy in the time of the Revolution. The new civil law had no objection to marriage between distant relatives, or even between cousins. The first- or second-grade endogamy rate, which was two per 1,000 marriages in 1766–1768, soared to 17 per 1,000 marriages a century later (1866–1868). Most of these unions were remarriages of parents or distant relatives which had previously been refused by the Church.

There were indeed parts of Europe where neither society nor Church perceived distant kinship links as an impediment to marriage. Such was the case in Sardinia between the sixteenth and eighteenth centuries, owing to its partially matrilineal system of family transmission. The result was a mixed situation of parallel descent where mothers transmitted their name and individual identity to daughters, and fathers to sons. Some Greek islands, with an Orthodox tradition, had a similar system, which we usually observe, like most inegalitarian transmission systems, in agro-pastoral (non-cereal-growing) communities. Here first cousins could plan to marry as they belonged to separate kin groups, the result being strong local endogamy.[23] In light of such examples, we can see that kinship systems and family transmission in different parts of Europe were so different because of local history, notwithstanding the ambition of the Church to dictate patrilineal values.[24] The fact that most requests for exemption on the ground of consanguinity presented to the Roman Catholic Church originated from rural areas was no coincidence: rural geographical endogamy very often intersected with social endogamy.

Geographical Endogamy

It has been shown that small villages during the *ancien régime* were usually less endogamous than bigger ones, where the choice within the village itself was larger. Inhabitants of small villages had to look elsewhere for marriage partners. But, although prone to endogamy, villages were never closed, isolated entities, as we observe for Alpine or Pyrenean villages as for the remotest Greek islands. Their migrants—soldiers, servants, colonists, etc.—spread throughout the world over the course of centuries. Even the remotest matrimonial areas were neither homogeneous nor completely closed: in the Swiss Valesan Alps, proportions marrying endogamously varied between 67 percent and 97 percent.[25]

Studying choice of spouse in the enlarged limits of a region allows demographic historians to analyze nuptiality models in association with bio-anthropologists. In a given population, resorting to outside spouses modifies the genotype of following generations. European marriages were usually celebrated in the bride's parish, but the new couple would not necessarily settle down there. In stem-family systems where the eldest daughter could be selected as heiress, the husband moved into her family home and became locally defined as a son-in-law—in the Central Pyrénées, one third of the cases are "uxorilocal" (female family transmission). But this was an exception. "Virilocal" residence was the general European model: the new couple usually established itself in the husband's home and parish. Thus marriage registration in a parish is evidence only of the place of the wedding ceremony—usually the bride's parish—and not of the new couple's residence. This is the reason why numerous studies based on marriage registration are so misleading. They cannot tell anything about the reality of matrimonial exchange from one locality to another. Marriage records need to be complemented by marriage contracts or census results, which are the only sources that give us accurate clues to the establishment of the new couples.

However, statistical studies of matrimonial areas are very useful when they refer to national or regional data banks, as is the case for the Pas-de-Calais studies.[26] For instance, they show growing mobility of couples at the time of the French Revolution. But even in this case we ought to evaluate the changes brought on by civil registration and secularization: maybe *ancien régime* priests were more concerned about the local origin of their parishioners than about their actual residence.

Female Condition and Marital Dependence

Besides analyzing its social, demographic, and geographical aspects, let us try to evaluate the more intimate characteristics of marriage during this period. Then, as now, a wedding was an intimate family affair, and an important moment of change in a young woman's expectations and condition. For the young woman, contracting marriage implied that she would become dependent on her husband instead of her father. In northern and eastern France, engagement was often celebrated religiously only two or three days before the wedding sacrament, so as to limit potential pre-marital cohabitation. To break off one's engagement then could result in religious sanctions of penitence or occasionally in payment of damages, but it was no breach of any juridical obligation to marry.

According to the philosopher and Oratorian priest Malebranche (*Traité de morale*, 1683), as soon as she married, the woman owed her husband "obedience in every just and licit occurrence, accommodating and yielding to her husband's manners and spirits like a faithful mirror which truthfully renders the face, without any purpose, love or thought of her own: similar to dimensions or accidents which are not endowed with any possibility of action or motion of their own, but whose acting and moving are those of the body, [women] in all circumstances are part of the husband."

For Cardin Le Bret (*De la souveraineté du Roy*, 1682), female nature justifies such dependence: political power is denied to women "in conformity with the law of nature which, by creating the woman's body and mind imperfect and weak, did submit her to the man's willpower." And it was not only a human matter. Divine order as revealed in Holy Writ confirmed the necessary submission of women: When the world began, God said to Eve, and through her to all women: "Thy desire shall be to thy husband, and he shall rule over thee" (Genesis, 3: 16). The same could be read in Paul: "The husband is the head of the wife" (Ephesians 5: 23).

Of course, reality was different: wives with a stronger personality than their husbands' were prominent stereotypes in literature of the time. There were many women with brains who would not easily be cast aside, for instance Madame de La Fayette, the well-known author of *La Princesse de Clèves*. Born Marie-Madeleine Pioche in an upper middle-class family, she married at 20. She revealed herself as a true business-woman in her private life. After just 18 months on May 6, 1656, her husband delegated her all powers, in front of a notary "to watch out and keep an eye on every and all assets and businesses of their House, to receive every and all sums of money and generally any other falling due now and in the future, be it rents from houses, farms, seigneuries, dividend warrants, promises, bonds, bills of exchange, etc., whatever the causes and occasions of such acts and whatever the amount."[27] The potential gap in a household between theory and reality was wide indeed!

The French wife could make her own will, writing her testament freely. Although law, customs, and marital conventions made her a dependant, the married woman was far from powerless, and her practice of power could be very efficient. Moreover, she was entitled to go to court at any time and require dissolution of joint estate or joint estate and common life. For a woman, ill-treatment was a valid reason for separation, but if her husband committed adultery, this was not, at least in civil courts. In this case, she could only go to ecclesiastical courts, since spouses were considered equal before the evangelical law. The civil law only recognized adultery committed by the wife, which it treated as a serious crime.

In European Catholic societies, men and women married "for life" in an indissoluble marriage. What did this mean in real terms? What was the mean duration of the married condition? Answering that question is not easy for a rural population, but it is even more difficult to trace couples in urban areas, as their mobility in and outside town was potentially greater. Stable populations allow easier observation over a longer time span. They may have been privileged by scholars for that reason. In early modern times, unions on average could not last very long due to high rates of adult mortality. Their mean duration—for stable non-migrant couples—was estimated at a little less than 20 years in rural areas around Paris in the reign of Louis XIV.[28] Thus remarriage was frequent: of 1,000 registered unions, 721 were marriages between two never-married individuals, 129 between a widower and a single woman, 75 between a bachelor and a widow, and 75 between two widowed individuals. Remarriage was an important feature of European society in the past.

WIDOWHOOD AND REMARRIAGE

Widowhood and Widows: Gendered Differences and Residential Patterns

Historical studies of West European widowhood emphasize the role of widowed women working in guilds during early industrial times. They describe the widows' role in the transmission of properties and wealth, but neglect the situation both of landless rural widows and of wage-earning urban widows in pre-industrial societies.[29]

Historians have outlined many aspects of widowhood.[30] But the household position of widows and women living alone during the early modern period is not well known. Scholars have paid great attention to widows who remarried, but not to the many women who remained widows. The specific nature of women's poverty over their life course, however, has been stressed along with discussion of the long evolution of welfare systems in European countries, which points to wide differences between systems of charity and various kinds of network support for aging women and widows.

The importance of widowhood in the urban pre-industrial population must be underlined. Great changes in Europe's population structure began to take place during the last decades of the eighteenth century. For example, life expectancy rose, even for the poorest urban class. But new economic conditions, a certain demographic upsurge, and generalized rural exodus (which drew young males and females alike to the cities) all contributed to the progressive postponement of first marriage (for example in Rheims 1775–1791, mean age at first marriage was 28.2 for men and 26.7 for women, as against 27.7 and 24.3 in the period 1668–1699: see Table 8.6). Table 8.3 shows that the age at first marriage rose in Europe after 1740, with the exceptions of Belgium and Scandinavia. Strategies of remarriage had to face the consequences of such developments, which induced changes in household size and structure. Age at widowhood changed for men and women alike.

It is obvious that age at termination of first marriage partly determined age at remarriage. In rural Europe before 1700, widowhood commonly occurred in the age group 35 to 40, and even earlier in areas where age at first marriage was low, as in Nivernais, France, a region where extended families were numerous.[31] Both widowers and widows tried to find a new partner younger than themselves. According to many monographs, 50 percent of the widowers who remarried, sometimes 75 percent, remarried during the first year of widowhood. For women who remarried, the mean length of widowhood was around two years.

Remarriage: Gender Inequalities

Was remarriage easier in urban societies, where the "marriage market" could be considered larger? In the countryside, remarriage frequency usually decreased with aging for both sexes, yet such was not the case in an urban French context at the end of the *ancien régime*. After 1760, on average, widowed men remarried at a later age, and in greater number than previously. In the same period, more men experienced widowhood at an earlier age. In pre-Revolutionary Rheims, 52 percent of widowers married again, against 20 to 30 percent before. As for women, Rhemish widows did not remarry as often as in earlier times—a feature also observed in other European towns, especially London at the end of the eighteenth century.[32] A diminishing proportion of remarrying widows is also attested to in some local studies. Louis Henry suggested that we ought to link this trend to the general trend of an older mean age at first marriage.[33] But how could we then explain that only 20 percent of all widows who remarried did so at a younger age? At the end of the century of Enlightenment, these widows neglected more and more the church recommendation for a *délai de viduité* (the time to elapse in order for a woman to be recognized as not pregnant). Of the 20 percent of females who remarried, 60 percent remarried less than 12 months after widowhood. This was indeed a severe breach of the Catholic tradition. We must note that this ecclesiastical recommendation had no canonical character, and that it was not even systematically respected in the pious seventeenth century. Clearly, a new model of remarriage was developing. For a new departure in life, a widow had to be young and remarry quickly (Tables 8.11 and 8.12). But, of course, her chances of remarriage depended upon the number of her living dependant children and her personal assets. Remarriage was much easier for men and women if they had no children alive. But having more than four children alive made remarriage a necessity if one was to be able to cope with everyday life.

Table 8.11   Proportion remarried by sex, Rheims

	1660–1699	1700–1729	1730–1759	1760–1789
Males	31.0%	22.1%	30.5%	52.6%
Females	32.2%	47.6%	49.2%	20.9%

Source: Rheims data bank. Family reconstitution.

Table 8.12   Duration between widowhood and remarriage: proportion remarried in the first year, Rheims

	1660–1699	1700–1729	1730–1759	1760–1789
Males	62.4%	61.1%	57.1%	53.2%
Females	30.0%	40.0%	41.2%	59.3%

Source: Rheims data bank. Family reconstitution.

Many questions remain to be answered if we are to explain the historical and geographical fluctuations in European remarriage patterns:

1. What was the impact of family size, that is the number of children alive at the time of widowhood, on the likelihood of remarriage of widows and widowers?
2. Are the variations in remarriage patterns correlated to changes in population mobility?
3. Did the imbalance in sex ratio play a role? In pre-industrial times, a surplus of women was a constant urban feature. This is correlated to mobility and to fluctuations in the female labor market, thus reducing chances of remarriage and creating an excess of widows.[34] With a longer life expectancy at the end of the eighteenth century, an aging female population accentuated this already unbalanced sex ratio.
4. Lastly, although female widowhood practically meant pauperization, could we not inquire more precisely into differences in levels of pauperization induced by economic crises? Could we see if remarriage was not a function of the fluctuations in the standard of living of different social groups?

Urban Widows

Many widows did not remarry. What kind of residential patterns did these confirmed widows adopt? If we consider the urban population of any large European city, only half of the female adult population (aged

Table 8.13   Marital status of household heads according to sex, Rheims, end of eighteenth century

	Male head	Female head	All heads
Married	86%	0%	65%
Widowed	5%	51%	16%
Separated and divorced	1%	7%	3%
Never married	8%	42%	16%
Total	100%	100%	100%

Source: Rheims data bank.

over 20) was currently married.[35] The other half was single or widowed. In this female population, the percentage of widows obviously grew regularly with age. After age 50, widows were more numerous than single women, even if single women still represented 20 or 30 percent of the elderly female population.[36] Consequently, widows formed the bulk of the aging women in societies where remarriage was less and less accessible, for all kinds of social, economic, and demographic reasons.[37]

In pre-industrial urban society, widows played a more important role than single women since they were more often in charge of a family household: 51 percent of female heads of household were widows, 42 percent were single women. On the whole, females headed 24 percent of all households and males headed 76 percent (Table 8.13).

The probability that a woman would head a household was directly correlated to her age and to widowhood. Beyond age 35, widows outnumbered single women among female household heads. Urban widows often headed their own households, being thus independent, even if they had grown-up children. Such was not usually the case in rural areas, where transmission of responsibilities to the next generation occurred as soon as possible. Between age 30 and 50, all urban widows were heads of household. The proportion slowed down with aging, to 50 percent for the age group 70–74, when women became more dependent, living as mothers, or mothers-in-law, in the houses of their children.

How many widows lived with dependant children? Not the majority. In Rheims, of widows under 40 years old and heading households, only 30 percent had children at home; 50 percent did when aged 40–50. After age 50, children disappeared more and more in these households: female loneliness grew with age. Consequently, co-residence with offspring was not such a common situation for widows in town: globally 40 percent of all widows lived alone against 75 percent of all single women, who were

Table 8.14   Mean household size by marital status and sex of head, Rheims, end of eighteenth century

	Married	Widowed	Separated & divorced	Single	All
Male head	3.8	2.9	4.0	1.4	3.6
Female head	—	2.4	2.0	1.2	1.9
All heads	3.8	2.5	2.3	1.3	3.2

Source: Rheims data bank.

Table 8.15   Mean household size by wealth and sex of head, Rheims, end of eighteenth century

	Rich	Middle-class	Poor	All
Male head	3.9	4.0	3.3	3.6
Female head	2.7	2.2	1.4	1.9
All heads	3.7	4.0	2.8	3.2

Source: Rheims data bank.

on average younger. Anyhow, with its many variations in early modern Europe from one region to another, the mean household size was always small in the West European urban context, due to broken families, to numerous individuals living alone, and to the number of households headed by women.

One of the main characteristics of European urban households in the past was the large proportion that were headed by women: one in four in Rheims during the *ancien régime*, and typically from 15 to 25 percent in other eighteenth-century towns.[38] Everywhere female-headed households were smaller than those headed by men, and not only because a man was missing from the house. In Rheims, 3.6 persons lived in male-headed households, and only 1.9 in female-headed households where a male companion was missing (Table 8.14). Poor people had smaller households than rich or middle-class families: 3.3 persons were living in poor households, against 3.9 in rich ones. In female-headed households, the mean size was 2.7 persons for the rich and 1.4 for the poor (Table 8.15). The age of the household head, that is her/his stage in the life course, was also closely related to the size of the household (Table 8.16).

Larger Female-headed Families in the Countryside

Things were different in the countryside, where households, whether male or female headed, were usually larger. Analysis of a 1693 census

Table 8.16   Mean household size by age and sex of head,
Rheims, end of eighteenth century

	15–29	30–49	50+	All
Male head	2.7	4.0	3.3	3.6
Female head	1.1	2.3	1.9	1.9
All heads	2.3	2.6	2.9	3.2

Source: Rheims data bank.

shows that the mean size of female households around Valenciennes—in northern France, near the current Belgian border—was larger: 3.6, against 1.9 in urban Rheims. Such a significant gap needs explanation. It partly reflects the fact that in the countryside, as opposed to in urban areas, fewer women lived alone. Moreover, the mean size of households of well-to-do farmers was much larger. The overall mean household size was 4.5 persons; the households of the poor and of daily workers were smaller (very poor: 3.7; daily workers: 4.5 persons) than the rich households, which contained around six members (5.9). Female-headed households accommodated 3.6 individuals on average, which means that most widows succeeded in keeping their children at home. These figures reflect important class differences, but they also show that the poor managed to keep their members at home with more success in the rural areas than in towns. Agricultural wage laborers certainly had fewer adult children at home than farmers did, and farmers' households were also more likely to contain elderly parents and other relatives. Craftsmen's families lived more like the poor than the well-off. Few very poor men lived alone.

In the country, female heads were able to manage a larger household than their urban counterparts: the difference between poor male and female mean household size was very slight in rural areas (3.7 for poor male heads and 3.6 for female in Picardie), compared to the urban areas (3.6 for male and 1.9 for female in Rheims, as already noted). Social differentiation was greater in the city. In town, poor people could not keep their children at home as long as rich people could. Poor women had to work, whether they had children or not. Middle-class urban babies were sent out to wet-nurses in the countryside—be it in London, Paris, Florence, or Warsaw—while lower-class children were bound to live as apprentices in another family. I would argue that the poverty of widowed families was the major explanation for the smaller size of female-headed households, both in town and country.

The Widow's Legal Capacity

With her husband's death, the widow gained full civil capacity in the eyes of the law and some prerogatives which might be considered as compensation for her inferior status while married. Besides what remained of her own dowry, she might get a life interest on a portion of her husband's assets equivalent to one third, half, or even the entire value of her dowry, according to region and to the customary law enforced in the region, by written or common law. In common law provinces, such a life interest was called a dower (*douaire*) and the amount of life interest was calculated on the size of the husband's assets (one third to one half, according to the regional custom or to the wedding contract) rather than on the settlement the widowed wife had brought in trust. In some provinces, like Normandy where the joint estate was unknown, this life interest could be taken from one third of the assets acquired during marriage. In some other regions operating under common law, the life interest could even be transformed into title deeds for part of the joint estate, provided that heirs—not the widow—would be responsible for potential debts affecting this estate. When the sole asset was a master title allowing a craftsman to practice, this title was sometimes transferred to the widow who had the right to go on practicing herself, to hire a companion, or eventually to rent her license. These complex and varied dispositions were intended to secure the widow's welfare when there were some assets available at her husband's death.

Apart from all of this, we cannot ignore the fact that for a great majority of women in early modern times, becoming a widow usually meant immediate impoverishment. Such was the case for lower- and middle-class women, and even sometimes for the upper classes.

SEPARATION AND DIVORCE IN PRE-INDUSTRIAL EUROPE

Indissolubility of marriage appeared with the diffusion of Christianity throughout Europe. According to Roman law, mutual consent was meant to justify legitimate union for life, but divorce was still possible. We recall Juvenal's famous repudiation formula, *res tuas tibi habeto* (go and take your things with you). By contrast, the nascent Christian Church was the only institution in the Roman empire to claim indissolubility of marriage, according to Christ's wording: "[man and wife] are no more twain, but one flesh. What therefore God hath joined together, let not man put asunder" (Matthew 19: 6). Since the time of St. Paul, marriage, assimilated to God's will, was a sacrament. Roman and Christian doctrines then became irreconcilable. The whole history of marriage and divorce in Europe stems from fluctuations between these two sources, according to socio-demographic conditions and to ideological interpretations.

Orthodox and Catholic Traditions

It began with a differentiation between the Roman Catholic and Orthodox Churches, the latter admitting divorce for some specific cases on two grounds. One, an interpolated clause in the Gospel of Matthew, which some theologians thought apocryphal, calls for repudiation in the case of adultery. The second is an exegesis of Origen: "even some leaders of the Church (who permitted one spouse to remarry during the lifetime of the other) tolerated this weakness to avoid greater evils, despite what has been commanded from the beginning and written in the Scriptures" (comm. in Matthew 14: 23). This third century AD commentary is very interesting as it admitted that there were cases where social and ethical considerations could contradict theological canons with some success. It explains why attitudes toward marriage, which were also a main topic for the Orthodox Church, were not as contradictory in the European Orthodox countries at in Western Europe, particularly since the Byzantine civil law, heir to the Roman one from the Justinian Code on, incorporated many conciliatory dispositions of the Roman law which faded in the Roman Catholic sphere. Analyzing the autonomous development of marriage and divorce in southeastern Europe would justify a separate study. Let us only mention that it may have influenced Reformation thinkers.

Catholics and Protestants

The emergence of the Reformation in the sixteenth century was another moment of differentiation, as Protestants denied the sacramental character of marriage. The Council of Trent (1563) confirmed the Catholic dogma: "If somebody says that marriage is not truly and really one of the seven sacraments of the evangelical law which Christ instituted, but that it is only a human invention brought into the Church and not confering Grace, be he anathemous."[39] But the Council had also to consider the realities of married life. So it differentiated legal separation (*divortium quo ad thorum*), which authorized separate residence, and divorce (*quo ad vinculum*), deemed impossible since it would have been the breach of a sacrament; *De sacramento matrimonii*, can. 17, condemned definitively the divorce by mutual consent which was allowed in the Roman empire, and still part of a custom of the Frankish kingdom (the Salic law). Another provision was taken with the Tametsi decree which confirmed the validity of so-called "clandestine" marriages: when the priest was a witness to the free and voluntary consent of both spouses, non-consenting parents could not require annulment of the marriage. Lastly, as discussed in Chapters 4 and 5 of this volume, the Council promulgated some administrative rules: publication of banns, the presence of two witnesses, and above all the institution of marriage registers, all of which are of so much interest to historians.

Of course marriage, besides being a sacrament, had also been a social contract since ancient times. When civil administration began to blossom all over Europe, more and more conflicts arose between ecclesiastical courts, which dealt with sacraments, and secular courts, which ruled on contracts. In seventeenth-century France for instance, parliaments and crown administration removed more and more cases from the *officialités* (the church courts), especially the separation cases. The division of jurisdiction was clear in 1721: "Legal separation, being a sequel to the ties of the wedding sacrament, is within the competence of ecclesiastical courts, but the secular judge usually is the only one to proceed since practically legal separation always implies separation of assets."

As a result, indissolubility of marriage was the rule in all European countries with a Catholic tradition, which admitted civil separation only on narrowly defined grounds. The Catholic Church deemed divorce "damnable and cause of all the misfortunes and corruptions of modern times"; the Protestants condemned trafficking in indulgences or marriage annulments which brought huge sums to the Court of Rome. In France, only the Alsatian Lutherans were not totally barred from divorcing between the time of annexation to France and 1692.[40] Even the Huguenots could not marry religiously: officially there were no Protestants in France after 1685 and the Revocation of the Edict of Nantes. The couples whom clandestine ministers married "in the desert" were legal concubines. The case is of some interest since it inspired the first protests of the philosophers in favor of liberty half a century later. Jewish communities also met insuperable difficulties before parliaments, when trying to legitimize remarriage according to their customs. In France, the Tolerance Edict (1787) eventually confirmed the validity of non-Catholic marriages—but indissolubility of unions was still the law until 1792. There had been a slow change in mentalities due to the influence of the eighteenth-century Philosophes.

Divorce and Enlightenment

The Enlightenment Philosophes treated divorce as one of the many legitimate consequences of their ideological principles. As liberty can only benefit reasonable beings, Montesquieu thought that liberty to divorce would bring about population growth, greater morality, and

family happiness. Nature has its own law: Diderot described with enthusiasm the marital freedom of mythic Tahitians. In the name of justice,
Voltaire condemned the persecution of Protestants. As it was politically
impossible for the Philosophes to challenge the Church directly on that
theme (with the exception of Morelly who did so in 1755, but was
ignored), they decided to try to undermine the indissolubility of marriage. The article "Divorce" in the eighteenth-century *Encyclopédie*
which Diderot and d'Alembert edited, is a good example: under cover of
a neutral history, the author Boucher d'Argis favored all the societies of
the past which had admitted divorce, observing that they had experienced
none of the disastrous consequences that the Church predicted. On the
contrary, some pamphlets wondered if indissoluble marriages were not
the real cause of many crimes of passion. Pro-divorce pamphlets began
to appear in France in 1770. The same year, Cerfvol published a new
edition of his *Mémoire sur la population* (London, 1768) under the title
Utilité civile et politique du divorce. This demographer asserted that
celibacy, adultery, prostitution, illegitimate births, and abandonment of
children were all consequences of the indissolubility of marriage and
caused depopulation. After him, for 30 years proponents of divorce systematically resorted to other natalist arguments, adding that divorce
would not only favour natality but would also improve the condition of
children: Helvetius (1770), Hennet (1789), and Condorcet (1794) added
that the possibility of divorce was a precondition of good family life and
of marital love and bliss.

When the French Revolution broke out, the Enlightenment
Philosophes had apparently already convinced public opinion that
divorce was compatible with the aims of a good citizen. How otherwise
can we explain the fact that the 1792 law instituting divorce was passed
virtually unanimously? It was a very liberal law indeed, which even
favored women. Codification in the Napoleonic *Code civil* (1804)
brought some limitations: incompatibility of temperament was no longer
a legal ground for divorce, and divorce would be less accessible to
women, who were more frequent petitioners than were men.[41] This first
legalization of divorce in France came to an end in 1816.

Separation Proceedings in the Catholic Church Courts

In the *ancien régime*, divorces, or, more accurately, annulments of marriage, were extremely rare and subjected to the jurisdiction of the
papal court. So here we will examine its lesser counterpart, separation.
Requests for separation came overwhelmingly from women (70 percent in
the diocese of Cambrai between 1710 and 1736), and only 5 percent were
the joint requests of both spouses. The number of female requests grew

during the eighteenth century, indicating a certain emancipation. More than half of all requests came from the urban middle classes. Maybe rural marriages were more carefully planned, more family oriented and, above all, more a strategy for patrimonial transmission. Separation requests often came from young childless couples, as the presence of children seems to have checked the temptation to separate. The presence in a household of the children of a previous marriage, on the other hand, apparently aggravated conjugal difficulties: almost 30 percent of the requests followed a remarriage (although remarriages numbered only 20 percent of all marriages). We know of a second husband saying that "he could not stay any longer with a wife who tried to ruin him as she wanted to make her children by her first marriage richer" (1756).[42] Material and financial rivalry often gave rise to dissension in "recomposed" families.

The grounds for separation are stereotyped: abuse, ill-treatment, and cruelty, often associated with death threats, were the most commonly mentioned. Conjugal violence was in many cases caused by an alcoholic husband. Adultery is the second most frequently mentioned ground. The mere presence of a maid in the household—servants were numerous then—could destroy conjugal peace: "this girl ate at their table with approval of her master who always took special care to serve her the dainty morsels" (1770); or the presence of old parents-in-law: "she left her spouse because she was not ready to act as a servant or still less, a slave, to his father and mother. . . . Separate residence was requested" (1752). It is easy to imagine that co-residence of two or three generations sowed discord, even though it was a provision in many marriage contracts, maybe precisely for this reason. Disagreement could vanish when it was only for a short period, for instance when the parents promised their daughter and son-in-law "to feed and nourish them for the duration of a whole year, with the proviso that they keep proper self-respect and governance as becomes to members of good families" (1665). Or it turned to conflict when parents were too inquisitive about the conjugal life of the young couple, as was the case of a shoemaker who expected that his son-in-law would take radical Malthusian precautions in his married life—contrary to the aims of marriage as defined by the Church: "He [the father] won't hear of him [the son-in-law] sleeping with his wife, there were enough children, the next to come would only be unhappy without anything to live on, so he forced his daughter to sleep in her servant's bedroom and this last one never to quit her mistress in daytime" (1763).[43] We might also mention a last ground for such requests, one never explicitly mentioned in our documents: the wife's parents might be reluctant to pay the dowry which they had agreed to give the husband when signing the marriage contract.

Ecclesiastical judges naturally sought to heal the breach between spouses, and defendants argued to minimize charges. But the fact is that in the eighteenth century, eight out of ten ecclesiastical rulings approved separation. Such a discrepancy between the severity with which divorce was treated and the ease of separation in pre-industrial Catholic Europe puts things into perspective. Of course, the principle of indissolubility implied that conjugal life could be resumed at any time, as in this 1746 ecclesiastical sentence: "We agreed to the [female] petitioner's request for legal separation and distinct residence, and that for a three year duration, but we bid both sides to behave in a Christian manner and above reproach, and exhort them to seriously consider reconciliation, so as to live conjugally and peacefully thereafter."[44] As for children, their fate was in the hands not of the *officialité* but the family notary. Cases of bigamy did not end up in separation by church courts, but in annulment of the union, the abused person being free to marry again, but damage suits and legitimization of children born to the cancelled union fell to the competence of civil courts.

The files of these church courts abound in telltale evidence, even when the legal wording covered up or disguised what the sides really said. St. Paul's texts were systematically quoted, inviting the wife to submit to her husband and not to shy away from her conjugal duty. But the husband had to treat her "with friendship and esteem" and we observe many women asserting their full right to consideration, to dignity, and laying stong claim to responsibility in household management: "instead of treating her maritally, he denies her any handling of money and takes away from her the management of their household by transferring this responsibility to the maid or servant, depriving her of any knowledge of their domestic affairs" (1637). Such a claim apparently became a valid ground for separation: "he set himself as a master in the house and maintained that he only married to get a maid" (1790).[45] The only status of the wife known to theologians was submission. But we begin to read in the jurisprudence of the eighteenth century something which is very near to legal rights for women. The household became the wife's territory. She was entitled to participate in managing money and was mainly responsible for bringing up the children. It had been a long process in the Catholic world, ever since the first centuries, until all women acquired some definite autonomy, even married women. This is a point we ought to remember as we analyze the case of Protestant countries.

Divorce and Protestantism: toward Secularization

Luther and Calvin worked out their doctrines on divorce very slowly.[46] They both agreed that marriage was not a sacrament. They both rejected marital indissolubility in principle. They admitted divorce, but considered it with palpable reluctance to be a lesser evil in extreme cases of matrimonial fault, such as adultery, the matrimonial offense *par excellence*. This was not the case in Catholic doctrine, where adultery was indeed a sin but did not in itself justify the rupture of a consecrated union. We ought to relate that difference to the fact that Protestants saw in marriage a way to ward off carnal sin, so that remarriage was a lesser evil than celibacy, whereas Catholics considered celibacy—chaste celibacy of course—the greatest perfection a person could reach. Polemics of reformers about the dubious bachelor life of some priests may be considered a sign that they were more conscious of the realities of life (and more pessimistic about it) than the Catholic doctrine was, and thus that they would later offer less resistance to socio-economic considerations, that is to secularization. They even considered cohabitation such an essential duty that they viewed desertion as a valid ground for divorce, thus allowing the deserted person to remarry. For instance, a spouse whose companion was missing for a long time could be authorized to divorce and remarry. But this second marriage was cancelled if the missing spouse returned alive and could prove that he had not deserted, and that it had been impossible for him to send news of his whereabouts.

In England, on the contrary, where the Anglican Church refused to give up the doctrine of marital indissolubility, a private Act of Parliament was the only way (but it was expensive) to dissolve marriage until the middle of the nineteenth century. For the English Puritans the family was the basic unit of social order: it then had to be preserved from evil, as can be seen from an extensive literature. But English opinion cannot be reduced to the attitudes of Church and Puritans. Divorce found a well-known advocate in John Milton, whose *Doctrine and Discipline of Divorce* (1644) not only supported divorce but admitted it in circumstances of incompatibility. According to him, marriage was not instituted primarily for procreation, but "for the apt and cheerful conversation of man with woman, to comfort and refresh him against the evils of solitary life." Of course, he did not inspire the very repressive Adultery Act which the Puritan Cromwell promulgated some years later (1650), but we can see some trace of secularization in the Marriage Act of 1653, which promoted certain aspects of civil marriage: publication of banns, ceremony before a justice of the peace, and the prevalence of secular courts.[47]

All over Protestant Europe where divorce was possible, the list of admissible grounds for the dissolution of unions was rather restrictive at first, owing to the reluctance of the various Reformed Churches to admit this necessary evil. But socio-economic pressure and changing public opinion favored a secularization process, whose ups and downs we can follow during the eighteenth century. In Sweden, for instance, a civil code was promulgated in 1734, introducing circumstances of incompatibility, besides adultery and desertion. By the middle of the eighteenth century, Prussian divorce law was also liberalized. A similar trend of secularization was evident in Catholic France, as we saw. Even in Catholic Austria, Joseph II gave civil authorities the power to hear petitions for marital separation. On the whole, the acute differences between Catholic and Protestant countries began to fade under the pressure of secularization.

There were no really permissive divorce laws and policies in early modern Europe, and divorce was still usually expensive, except in the short period of the French Revolution, when it was made accessible to ordinary people. This meant that remarriage was only open to widows or widowers, not to separated individuals. These difficulties may partly explain why the absence of one spouse in a household was so common a phenomenon, especially in towns. Rheims numbered legions of "deserted wives" at the end of the eighteenth century; in 1804, 7 percent of couples in Rouen were separated. Wife "sale" was a kind of customary divorce in England. Some family historians, like Lawrence Stone, have suggested that because people could not divorce, bigamy may have been common in some traditional European societies. This argument is far from being proved, as bigamy was regarded as a serious crime, and was severely punished. Even adultery was punished, more or less severely, according to time and jurisdictions: for women it was a capital offense in Calvin's Geneva, in Scotland and, with the 1650 Adultery Act, in England: an adulterous woman could be hanged. We then understand why adulterous couples could not flaunt their status nor act as ordinary concubines. But extramarital sexuality was tolerated in most elite societies. In eighteenth-century France, adulterous men were not prosecuted. Only some scandalous women would be deprived of their dowry or sent to nunneries. In Scotland too, even the Church was very lenient in this regard.

CONCLUSION

Are there general patterns of marriage, widowhood, and divorce in pre-industrial Europe? We saw that a high age at marriage and a high proportion of people who never married distinguished past European societies. Malthus was right in considering nuptiality, including remarriage, the main variable in population control of the time. We also noticed a slow secularization trend. So can we definitely assert the presence of a "European marriage pattern"? E. A. Wrigley, comparing England's demographic change during the eighteenth century with what occurred in France during the same period, has suggested that "the West-European marriage pattern is better described as a repertoire of adaptable systems than as a pattern."[48] We have described enough variations, adaptation processes, and conflicting traditions to show the obvious difficulty in identifying a unique European marriage pattern.

Remarriage was common in past societies. But the main changes in remarriage models occurred in urban societies after around 1750: gender differences in remarriage, as well as residential patterns were modified. Four out of five widows had to remain in widowhood and experienced poorer and poorer living conditions. In an urban context, widows were not able to keep their children at home and faced frequent solitude and poverty. These changes must be considered in the light of a general demographic transition in fertility and marriage behavior which affected remarriage strategies. Dramatic changes in remarriage rates indicate that marriage was no longer the main form of economic partnership.

Social historians have pointed to changes in marital emotions: choosing a spouse has become more and more an individual concern, sometimes based more on the personal compatibility of partners than on factors of material interest. "Romantic love" cannot be considered to have been born in eighteenth-century England. It must be understood as part of the long process of European secularization and the rise of individualism and social mobility. Moreover, romantic love had its limit: for most women, it was better to have a bad husband than none. Near Meaux in September 1694, Catherine Girardin asked and obtained separation from her husband, a brutal wine grower, but after seven months of hardship during a severe economic crisis, she came back before the ecclesiastical court, requesting annulment of the marital separation: "it would be not only praiseworthier, she said, but much more advantageous and useful, to be united in marriage again, than to remain separated."[49] Controlling emotions in order to live a decent life was a necessity: the presence of a husband in a household as a regular breadwinner was a safeguard against poverty. But more and more women—single, deserted, or widowed—were living without a spouse in early modern Europe.

Here we touch the limits of secularization in early modern times: marriage was still considered the better solution, for men and women alike, but it was often broken by demographic events. Economic conditions and the transfer of patrimony compelled one to marry, even for a short time, to guarantee the presence of offspring. But family transmission of assets and skills could also take lateral paths outside marriage: single persons wrote wills in favor of nieces, nephews, friends, servants, or illegitimate children. In early modern Europe, most family reproduction proceeded through marriage, but a large part of socio-economic transmission took place prior to, after, or outside conjugal life.

CHAPTER 9

Kinship: Thin Red Lines or Thick Blue Blood
David Gaunt

In 1476 a writer living in Salerno, not far south of Naples, published a short story. It told the tragic tale of two young lovers who had chosen death because they belonged to families that were at war with each other and had prohibited the couple from marrying. Throughout the following century this tale grew popular and was retold many times not just because it was a gripping story, but because it also gave cause to reflect on the impossible demands families could press upon their members. In the late sixteenth century William Shakespeare used this plot as the basis for *Romeo and Juliet* (1592) and that play can be seen as a general criticism of the domestic tyranny of kinship with its collective oppression of the desires of the individual. One can assume that the sympathies of Shakespeare's audience were totally on the side of Romeo and Juliet and not with the ancient heads of their clans.

In the Middle Ages the primary units of association in Europe evolved in a special way. The order of kinship was very confused, with several rival ways of reckoning blood ties and family relationships. At the same time other kinds of association, which were not based on kinship, but rather on neighborhood, religion, or trade, grew up and became alternatives to kinship. Here one can mention guilds, brotherhoods, colleges, and other sodalities one could join voluntarily. While kinship did not disappear as a principle for ordering life it was not unchallenged and often the voluntary alternatives were preferred to the mechanical bonds of kin. In the course of this rivalry it became necessary for the individual to reduce the power of kinship ties. Primarily, this meant loosening the legitimacy of customary bonds to distant relatives.[1]

By the start of the modern age, kinship in the form of a disciplinary force of the collective over the individual was often viewed as in decline. The Italian Renaissance *condottieri*, humanists, and artists, at least in Jacob Burckhardt's famous version, were individualists who had broken free from the fetters of family and community.[2] From Lisbon to L'viv and from Palermo to Bergen individuals formed brotherhoods, so-called sodalities, in order to give one another the social aid and protection that normally one might expect to have come from the kin.[3] Had the kin really functioned well these sodalities would probably not have been needed. The Reformation, on the one hand, praised the virtues of family life and in its Lutheran form supported the position of husbands over wives and fathers over children.[4] But on the other hand it made little acknowledgement of kin beyond one's closest relatives and Luther himself attacked the brotherhoods as heathen and devilish.[5]

Countries developed gradually in this respect. A contrast between the Dutch humanist Desiderius Erasmus (c.1466–1536) and the Polish scientist and administrator Nicholas Copernicus (1473–1543) can illustrate how differently kinship functioned. Almost nothing is known about Erasmus's kin and no one claimed to be his cousin. He was born outside wedlock; his father is assumed to have been a priest. Early in life he was placed in a school run by the Brothers of the Common Life and then became an Augustinian monk. These corporations formed his early career, and kinship played almost no role at all.[6] In contrast, just about everything in Copernicus's career was influenced by kin. He was a child when his father died and a brother of his mother, Lucas Watzenrode, bishop in Warmia, took the boy under his wing: he paid for his schooling in Poland, sent him away for university education in Bologna, and got him his first court positions.[7] Although Erasmus was protected by corporations he was often out of money and had to write best-selling books. Copernicus was so economically secure that his major work lay unpublished until he was on his deathbed.

Just about every major political, social, religious, or economic change between the Protestant Reformation and the French Revolution had negative consequences for the societal functions of the kindred. The Age of Reformation focused on the nuclear family, the Age of Absolutism undermined all aspects of noble corporations including the aristocratic ideology of pedigreed lineages, the Age of Revolution celebrated the individual citizen. As long as the nobility had a monopoly on political power, it tended to be broad-minded about just who could be reckoned as kin. But when the nobility began to lose this privileged status in the eighteenth century, individuals began to concentrate their attention on private estates and property. The fears of estate owners that inheritance would split the family fortune gave rise to a desire to exclude all but the closest relatives from the kin group.

Even the very language used to denote kinsmen changed. In most European tongues there had once been a very elaborate, specific, and detailed vocabulary with unique words for each relationship. Latin for instance distinguished the father's brother, *patruus*, from the mother's brother,

avunculus. By the end of the Middle Ages these specific concepts shriv-
eled in many languages, including English, French, and to a certain extent
German, down to a rudimentary vocabulary using multi-purpose terms
such as cousins, aunts, and uncles. The terms distinguishing a mother's
brother from a brother's brother or a sister's daughter from a brother's
daughter were replaced by the single simple words "uncle" (derived from
avunculus) and "niece."[8] These changes will be treated in detail further
on in the text (p. 259f.).

Linguistic changes are at best only indicative: they fail to give clear-cut
distinctions. Words can have many meanings and the history of everyday
life is filled with terms that carry multiple meanings simultaneously.
While this makes it hard for the historians to establish definite chronolo-
gies and patterns, it does reflect the fact that the forms of domestic
relationships in Europe are, and probably always have been, malleable,
adaptable, negotiable, and inventive. Because of its shifting functions,
the kin group has at all times been hard to define, and the terminology
reflects this ambiguity. The very word "family" has curious roots going
back to the Latin *famulus* meaning slave. It was thus a word which designated a relationship not of a biological nature, but one of belonging and
dependency to the superior individual who was legally termed the paterfamilias.[9] In late medieval Italy the word family had just begun to be used
in its more modern meaning of a small domestic group with a core of biologically related members. Perhaps the best expression of this new use can
be found in the Florentine humanist Leon Battista Alberti's *Four Books
on the Family*: "My children . . . let us remain happy with our little
family."[10] To denote the little family he used the diminutive form *famigli-
ola*, because normally at that time to use the Italian word *famiglia* would
also mean speaking about the entire household, including all of its servants. The ordinary North European usage of *familia* in the Middle Ages
was even more inclusive and indicated the household as well as the serfs
of major landowners. The concept covered all persons who were dependent, or under the *tuitio* (defense) of a landlord.[11]

From its original Renaissance Italian roots the concept and vocabulary
of the family (as delimiting a married couple with their children) spread
gradually throughout West and North European regions. By the late seventeenth century this linguistic transition was well underway, but in truth
nowhere completed. The transition took several steps: first the adoption
of the word family, second its reduced application only to the "entire
household," and third the evolution of the meaning "little family" or
nuclear family. An indication of the second phase comes in the Académie
Française dictionary of 1694 which defined the new term: a *famille* consists of "all the persons who lived in the same house, under the same

head." A similar use can be found in the diary of the English civil servant Samuel Pepys whose last entry for 1662 notes: "My family is myself and wife—W[illia]m. My clerk—Jane, my wife's upper-maid . . . Susan our cook-maid . . . and Waynman my boy [servant]": the household consisted of a childless married couple and their four servants.[12] Throughout most of the eighteenth century family was defined as Samuel Johnson defined it in his *Dictionary* of 1755 as "those who lived in the same household."[13]

During the transition from the medieval corporate society to modern individualism the word *family* came to be superimposed on already existing terms for a domestic unit, namely that of the dwelling house, *Haus*, *casa*, *ostel*, *masia*, *domus*, *dom* and the like. After the transition, *house* came to be reserved for the dynasties of royalty, aristocracy, industrialists and the otherwise rich, influential, and powerful. The concept *kindred* disappeared from everyday English conversation. The term *household* evolved to indicate those people dwelling together regardless of whether they were related by blood or marriage.

Today it seems amazing that Shakespeare could have written *Romeo and Juliet* without ever using the word family. As a matter of fact, in all of his writings he used the word only nine times and never in its modern sense.[14] Instead, he placed his star-struck lovers in the midst of large dynastic groups such as the House of Montague and the House of Capulet. Individual members of the houses called each other kinsman, or in sixteenth-century English slang "coz," short for cousin. The terminological avoidance of "family" is similar in many other countries. When Spanish playwrights contributed to the theme of Romeo and Juliet they too failed to use the word family. Lope de Vega in *Castelvines y Monteses* (1618) spoke mainly of the *casa* (house). Although Rojas y Zorilla in *Los bandos de Verona* (1640) did use an occasional *familia* in the meaning of kindred, he more often used the synonyms *arbol* (tree) and *rama* (branch) as well as *bandos* (bands).

Among other things this poetic use of words painted a dramatic image of a fierce tribe whose young male warriors were ready to attack and whose members bound themselves tightly together through the symbolic ropes of kinship. In all likelihood there may have been little contemporary reality behind the description of the violent urban vendettas of Italian families which at the most had flourished in the central Middle Ages when families were forced to unite in order to build defensive towers within the city walls. The tower societies had been disbanded and most towers destroyed in the thirteenth and early fourteenth centuries.[15]

BROAD AND NARROW KINSHIP

The family system of the Middle Ages had two distinctly different major principles for thinking about kinship. Simply put, one was very broad but shallow, and the other was very narrow but deep. The broad one included many living relatives whose exact blood relationship was uncertain. But it was a good way of creating the political and military strength that only large numbers can give. The narrow one isolated a single line of relationship and even excluded some blood relatives. But it was a good way to amass and transfer wealth intact within a close group. The broad kinship unit is often termed a *clan* because it was a group whose members all claimed common descent from the same ancestor; it brought together many separate branches whose exact connection to one another was not clear. The narrow kinship unit is termed a *lineage*, that is a group that recognizes only a single line of descent from an ancestor and thus does not include separate branches. It insists on clear blood relationships and often places many restrictions on marriage. A lineage usually has high self-esteem and awareness of its social importance.[16]

The broad principle is believed to be older than the narrow, but they coexisted within elites during the Middle Ages. From the fall of the Roman empire up to the twelfth century Europeans usually kept to the wide ideal of kinship and considered it to be double-sided. Each individual possessed relatives on both the father's and the mother's side (in anthropological terms it was a bilateral kinship system). The marriage of two individuals was also the alliance of two large kin groups. Women had an important role in passing property between generations and this is believed to have given them considerable social status. The Catholic Church and the medieval customary laws of many countries were based on the principle of bilateral inheritance. A person could inherit both from mother's kin and from father's kin; and both males and females could inherit. Although there were various regional regulations about the size of the daughters' portions, sometimes half of that of a son, women and their offspring were seldom totally excluded from inheritance. Sometimes families might attempt to exclude an erring son or daughter, but courts would judge in favor of the child, not the parent.[17]

In most parts of Europe, inheritance rules stipulated larger proportions for male-side heirs. The amounts inherited decreased with genealogical distance. Languages had words for each particular relationship. The broad kinship system was eased by the exact designation of kinship relationships with separate words for father's father, father's mother, mother's father, mother's mother, mother's sister, mother's brother and so on. Germans would address a mother's sister as *Muhme*, a father's sister as *Base*, a mother's brother as *Oheim* and a father's brother as *Vetter*. The Anglo-Saxons used *eam* for a mother's brother, *faedera* for a father's brother, *modrige* for mother's sister and *faðu* for father's sister. Swedes said *morbror* and *moster* to a mother's brother and sister, *farbror* and *faster* to a father's brother and sister. The Finns used *eno* for a mother's brother and *setä* for father's brother. Cousins on the mother's side were called *serkku* and on the father's side *nepaa*. For the Poles, *stryj* denoted a father's brother and *wuj* a mother's brother. In English such distinctive words fell out of use in the early Middle Ages, while in German they began losing their original meanings by the late Middle Ages. In France the terms for maternal relatives were marginalized; instead from the fourteenth century many new terms were created for lineal relatives, such as great-grandparent.[18] The Scandinavian and some other languages, however, have retained the specific kin terminology up to modern times.

In the broad kinship ideology it was not necessary to keep accurate track of dead relatives, so few languages had adequate terms for what today are called grandparents and great-grandparents. Many historians have observed that nobles in the early Middle Ages had very short pedigrees and seldom gave accurate information about their ancestors.[19]

Beginning approximately in the twelfth and thirteenth centuries a new type of kinship thinking is believed to have slowly developed and superimposed itself on the previous system. Its first appearance was among the feudal knights and may be said to reflect the world-view of the dominant warrior strata. It was the ideal of the single male lineage or patriline (in anthropological terms agnatic, male, unilateral kinship). In France the word *lignage* began to be used as a distinction from the broad kinship indicated by *parenté*.[20] Kin relationships, according to the new ideal, were passed on exclusively from fathers to sons. The lineage could take alternative forms and could either be inclusive in order to encompass many male branches, or exclusive in order to give privilege to just one solitary senior branch. Increasingly inheritance began to favor the eldest son, while younger sons and daughters would receive much less and in places even nothing. Because customary laws usually recognized both male and female inheritance, new types of property transfer had to be developed. In extreme forms, like the English form of primogeniture called the "straight settlement," all property was transferred to the firstborn male child. The assumption of permanent family surnames and heraldic arms that were passed on from the father to the children accompanied the lineage ideology.

The idea that marriage created an alliance of two separate kin collectives had little support in the narrow kinship ideology. Women lost their role of conveyor of property from their kin group. In the narrow form of kinship the various words distinguishing maternal and paternal kin became less important. One reason given for the adoption of the lineage system was the decline in opportunities and resources to support a large elite, so the lineage served to limit the size of the elite population in order to concentrate wealth in the hands of a few. The degree of self-discipline and self-sacrifice demanded of daughters and younger sons who were disadvantaged must have been almost intolerable.[21] But, of course, the military and the Church offered alternatives to marriage.

The broad and narrow kinship systems existed side by side, but the one that Shakespeare writes about in the feud between the Montagues and Capulets was that of the male lineage, which had gradually become a dominant image among the elite of France, Italy, England, and Rhineland Germany. Shakespeare makes Juliet plead, "O Romeo, Romeo! Wherefore art thou Romeo? Deny thy father, and refuse thy name. . . . 'Tis but thy name that is my enemy. Thou art thyself though, not a Montague . . . O! Be some other name." Probably this reflects an element of popular protest against the ways of the rich and powerful. Certainly Shakespeare is right in placing the words in the mouth of a young female since the lineage ideology clearly put women in an ambivalent position. In the Central and East European countries the ideology of lineage and primogeniture appeared somewhat later and aspects of the broad bilateral kinship and the higher status of the kin of the mothers survived for a longer period. It is possible that the differences in kinship between Eastern and Western Europe are connected with what sociologist Norbert Elias called the "civilizing process," which began in Western Europe and spread slowly. A key factor in the reception of civilization was the degree to which the nobility mixed with other social groups. In England, France, and Italy nobles and non-nobles were in close association. The top echelon of society was to a certain degree socially integrated. But in Germany, Poland, and Scandinavia the nobles held themselves aloof from other social strata. The exclusivity of nobility was accompanied by strong emphasis on kinship and blood.[22] This may contribute to the modern West European perception of kinship ideology and exclusiveness as belonging to an "uncivilized" view of the world.

THE THICK AND THE THIN

There has been much discussion among historians at to whether the large kin groups, which existed in some places at the end of the Middle Ages, were "natural" or "artificial." By natural they meant related by blood.

Members certainly addressed each other as kinsmen, and often had a similar symbolic name. Sometimes they even used the same heraldic signs on their shields. However, many groups were so large that it was impossible to believe that births within the family could account for them. In addition there were known cases of treaties and contracts when kin groups adopted entire families of strangers or when several kin groups united to form a single collective. Some historians, like Jacques Heers, refer to them as family clans, because, as in Scottish clans, members believed they had a common ancestor, but did not know how they were actually related to one another.[23]

In many cities of central Italy the family clans were known as *consortia*. The *consortia* were a type of very broad kinship group which joined many separate branches living far from one another. *Consortia* derived from the Latin word *sors* (inheritance), which could designate a group who shared an inheritance, and owned property in common. There were many regional dialect variants of this term. In Genoa such clans were termed *alberghi*, and in Venice *casata*. Florentines themselves occasionally used the terms *lignaggio* or *agnatio* instead. Writing in the 1430s, Matteo Palmieri in *Della vita civile* indicated the place of the *consortia* within a hierarchy of sentiments. He stated that a man should first love his sons, then "grandsons and anyone else born of our blood; among these I include first of all everybody in the household [*casa*] and then the stocks [*le schiatte*], lineages [*le consorterie*] and huge families [*copiose famiglie*] which must develop as its numbers overflow."[24] It was thus conceivable that there could exist units that were even larger than the *consortia*.

Within the Florentine Bardi *consortia* all branches had equal status, with no division into senior and cadet lines. Just as in modern family businesses, control over the Bardi family bank and leadership of the *consortia* passed from one branch to another depending not on seniority, but on individual competence. This would not be true of dynastic lineages that were strictly divided into senior and inferior branches. The *consortia* developed a strong sense of collective identity and solidarity. One manifestation of this was that nearly all great families since the late thirteenth century kept books called *ricordanze* that chronicled family history, genealogy, documents, and other events. All of the sons of the *consortia* were given their independence at a young age and received money in order to start in business. This was a deliberate strategy since the survival of the group demanded the early recognition of talented youth. Those who prospered showed their prowess. "The Tuscan commercial company, even in the thirteenth century, was not a spontaneous, natural association of heirs; it was, like Burckhardt's vision of the Renaissance state, a work of art."[25]

Among the largest clans in Europe were the *alberghi* of Genoa. There in 1479, the Spinola group encompassed 104 separate households, the Lomellini 93 households, and the Doria 59. In the early sixteenth century households calling themselves Doria occupied nearly all of the San Matteo area of the city. This geographic proximity was not unique. In 1427 in Florence of the 60 branches belonging to the Bardi *consortia*, 45 were concentrated in the quarter of Santo Spiritu and most of them in the very street now called Via dei Bardi.[26] The Genoese took their kinship system with them: since 1346 the Greek island of Chios was dominated by the Giustiniani merchant clan originally from Genoa. All newcomers to the island automatically took the Guistiniani name.[27]

In Poland large nationwide clans developed and flourished among the knights from the thirteenth to the fifteenth century. Similar systems appear to have existed in Bohemia and Croatia. In Poland they were termed *plemie*, that is "descendants," and in contemporary Latin documents this word was translated as either *stirpe, parentela, genus,* or *cognatio*. Each clan had a common symbolic name and a coat of arms that was identical for all its members. A few common surnames began to appear as early as the thirteenth century. One of the main purposes of the clans was to unite members of the elite throughout the widespread Polish–Lithuanian territory. The larger the membership and the wider its geographical spread throughout the commonwealth, the more powerful the clan became. Within the nationwide clans there were regional subgroups known as *gniazda*, that is "nests." The largest clans could have 20 family branches and these could also have a special local surname. From the fourteenth century a Polish knight would write his name in the following fashion: Piotr Lubomirski, herbu Sreniawa, that is Piotr of Lubomierz of the Sreniawa clan.[28] Large clans would be led by *seniores* who represented the wishes of the entire group at court.

Some Polish historians believe that the late medieval clans were actually built up of kinsmen sharing common descent. This was a position often held by scholars in the early twentieth century. Others believe that they were artificial political patron and client unions made up of many biologically unrelated groups, an interpretation widely held by the late twentieth century. Probably neither stance is completely adequate since, while it is true that many unrelated families were united, the original core of each clan was a single kin group to which the others attached themselves. One historian has recommended the phrase "quasi-natural" instead of artificial for this type of extended kinship.[29] The most well known incorporation of non-kin for political reasons occurred in 1413 when each of 47 Polish clans adopted Lithuanian boyar families. It was even possible for clans to make temporary confederations in order to pool resources. Twenty clans in the Kujawy, Leczyca, and Sieradz districts of Great Poland did this around 1440. The knight clans disappeared in the sixteenth century presumably because they lost their political function when individual nobles instead developed regional associations. The rank and file nobility rebelled against the clan seniors.

Other clan-like kindred organizations were the *slachte* of the peasant republic of Dithmarschen on the coast of the North Sea. Their origin went back to the tenth century when these groups built the great dikes to prevent flooding by the sea and they existed as formal associations up to the eighteenth century. The largest *slachte* were confederations of several smaller groups of kindred. Strangers could also be admitted as "cousins." The late sixteenth-century writer Neocorus states: "There are in every parish splendid old kindred of unimaginable antiquity; adorned because of their uprightness and noble deeds with magnificent blazons and coats-of-arms . . . [they] had great alliances between themselves, that no member should forsake the other, even the meanest and poorest." The kindred divided into subgroups termed cleavages, in German a *Kluft*; the members termed themselves *Vetter* (cousin). The entire corporation, according to a register from 1737, was called a *Vetterschaft*, that is a cousinhood.[30] The register belonging to the Mengermann group had 37 signatories; another journal from the Dickboleman *slachte* in 1671 listed 55 names. The cousinhoods comprised several genealogies; the register of the Hersens *slachte* in 1717 contained 58 names but only three different surnames. These groups had many functions that elsewhere were performed by the parish, for instance care of paupers; or formed voluntary associations, for example providing fire and accident insurance.

In the Balkans large male-based kin groups were prevalent among the migrating sheep-herding population and in the high mountains. In theory the members were all descended from a common founding father. The Albanian clan of Këlmendi amounted to more than 2,000 people when in 1700 they were forcibly resettled in northern Kosovo. This clan could put 400 fighting men into the field and their women would fight side by side with the males.[31] The clans (in Albanian *fis*, in Serbian *pleme*) were sometimes split into smaller groups. The Albanians and Montenegrins had clans or tribes consisting of a number of smaller male lineages called brotherhoods (in Montenego the *bratsvo*, in Albania the *vëllazëri*). According to Kaser, the more isolated and independent a pastoral society, the more it tended to be built up of separate lineages.[32] This may have been true in the Balkans but was not the case for the nomad Lapp or *saami* population of northern Scandinavia and Russia, who maintained bilateral kinship.

Although the word clan is of Gaelic origin, the large kin group in Ireland was instead known as the *cenél* and consisted of smaller segments called the *fine* led by a local chief. The size of the *fine* expanded as a result of polygyny, incorporation of weaker kin groups, and destruction of rivals. The Irish genealogist Dubhaltach MacFirBisigh wrote in 1605: "It is a usual thing in the case of great princes, when their children and families multiply, that their clients and followers are squeezed out, wither away, and are wasted. Take Ireland, and even the whole world if you desire, and there is no limit to all the instances which you will find of that." In Scotland the subgroup nicknamed "the Cumins of the hen trough" were from the beginning non-relatives who had sought protection in a powerful clan. They were accepted into the Cumin clan by baptism in a stone water-trough at the hen house just beside the castle door. In other words what has been termed a clan was often a large political and military organization based on a core of kindred.[33]

THE STRAIGHT AND THE NARROW

The problems of owning land and preserving family fortune made broad kinship untenable in the long run. Large holdings of land quickly became divided into small parcels. Property and inheritance split the clans into lineages. Aristocratic dynastic lineages differ from Polish knight clans and Dithmarschen *slachte* because of the narrow interest of the lineages in accumulating and preserving wealth and landed property within a very confined group. The large literature on the Polish clans scarcely mentions property and inheritance, the main purpose apparently being to advance the political and defensive interests of members. Usually clans were so large that they did not feel a need to prevent marriage within the group; they could even be endogamous and prefer marriage within the group. But endogamy was impossible in narrow lineages, because of the constant risk of violating incest prohibitions. In the Scandinavian countries the number of noble lineages was so small that it was almost impossible to find a husband or wife who was not closely related. Papal dispensations had to be obtained.[34]

The dynastic lineages also differ from the Italian *consortia* and *alberghi* by singling out a sole preferred line of inheritance as the chief principle of organization. Both of these organizations concerned themselves with wealth and fortune, but whereas the *consortia* were dynamic and survived through expanding business, the dynastic lineage was economically defensive and emphasized the preservation and maintenance of existing property.

Increasingly throughout the Middle Ages noble families concerned themselves with the consolidation of their landed holdings just as the feudal princes began to build up hereditary territorial kingdoms and lesser knights strove to make their personal fiefs into hereditary family real estate. Once the legal battle to make fiefs inheritable had been won, by about 1300, noble families began to apply a new strategy for transmitting property between generations. The lifestyle of aristocrats became increasingly expensive and thus there was room for fewer great dynasties. Those who desired to survive the competition began to entail their largest estates: a contract was drawn up which stated that the existing estate could never again (or for a number of generations, typically four) be divided, sold, or given away. This meant, of course, that the general rule that all children inherit at least some part of all property was sidestepped. One of the children would assume the ownership in trust. He or she also had responsibility for the wellbeing of any siblings and they would either live on the estate or receive annual support from the income of the estate.

Usually the contract specified how the property was to be transmitted intact, the most common way being primogeniture, that is the first-born (male) child would get the major share. The other children might receive some capital or some other non-entailed land or installments from the profits from the running of the estate. If the main lineage died out, that is had no male heirs, then the designated cadet branch of the kin stood next in turn. Such entailed aristocratic estates could be found throughout the continent. In Spain the system was called *mayorazgo*, in Denmark *majorat*, in France *substitution*, *droit d'ainesse* or *préciput*, in Germany, Italy, Poland, and Sweden it took its name from a Roman law institute called *fideicommissum*, which today is known as a trust. Although its roots go back to the Middle Ages, this legal institution flourished in the fifteenth and sixteenth centuries in Western and in the seventeenth and eighteenth centuries in Central Europe.

The English practice is considered one of the most extreme and exclusive. There all property would go to the oldest son and the other children would in principle receive nothing. The continental *fideicommissum* was more equitable since the favored heir was obliged to provide an income for his younger brothers and sisters through annual payments. In addition, grandparents or the property of the mother could provide for younger children or some minor property might be removed before the entailment contract was signed.[35]

In 1505 the king of Spain made *mayorazgo* obligatory for the property of the grandees. Behind this law was the wish to maintain the wealth of a few families so that they could serve the state in fitting aristocratic style. Developments in Castile show that the attempt to preserve wealth in a lineage did not always disadvantage daughters. In 1611 the Cortes decided on the general principle that in inheritance a daughter should be given priority before distantly related males. This resulted in many heiresses to large estates. Their husbands would change their names and arms to that of their wives, or alternatively add their wives' names to their own surnames.[36]

In Italy *fedecommesso* is said to have contributed to the extremely low rates of marriage among the nobility. In the last half of the eighteenth century two-thirds of all noble males in Venice never married and the proportion never married was one-third among the patriciates of Milan and Florence. Figures for women are not available for all of these cities, but in Milan during the first half of the seventeenth century three-quarters of the patrician women never married. Younger sons could enter the military or the Catholic Church and daughters could become nuns.[37] Judged an aristocratic and feudal remnant, the institute of entailment was forbidden during the Revolution in France and in several other countries during the nineteenth century.[38]

The winner-take-all strategy of a single heir was most noticeable in England, because that country had a very small nobility that could not expand in numbers. Two hundred aristocratic peers held their position through the favor of the king. The children and siblings of peers were not even considered noblemen, but were treated as commoners. On the death of a peer, the eldest male heir succeeded to his rank, property, and noble status. The other children remained commoners and needed to find occupations. There were thus no cadet branches of noble lineages.

In France things were different: all the children of aristocrats were considered nobles, so there was great need for family discipline if the property was to be kept intact. The sixteenth-century marshal Gaspard de Saulx in his memoirs recommended the following placement of children: "Wealthy gentilhommes with three children should place two in the army. . . . The rest should enter either the Church or the Law, and only the eldest should have children. Marry few daughters for that is the ruin of a noble house."[39] One can wonder what happened when his grandson Claude de Saulx married Françoise de Brulart in 1613 and they proceeded to have 11 children. Three of the four girls became nuns, two of the seven sons became abbots, two other sons died as bachelors. That left only one married daughter and three married sons. The many placements in religious orders and the two sons who never married suggest planning. In the final outcome only two marriage portions were ever paid out and separated from the Saulx-Tavane family fortune and thus eight out of the eleven children received nothing.

The entailment of estates did not mean that women were automatically disadvantaged. In a wide-ranging study Cooper shows that daughters were often provided for in the European contracts establishing the entail. They could get other land that the family owned, a large sum of money for their dowry, or yearly sums of money to be paid from the estate. Sometimes the daughters received more than the younger sons and this probably raised their chances of finding a husband. In some countries, most notably France, the sizes of the payments to dowries surged during the eighteenth century. A duchess needed a dowry of at least 200,000 livres and the huge sum of 400,000 livres was the dowry of Marie-Eléonore Eugénie de Lévis-Châteaumorand when she married the Count of Tavanes in 1759.[40]

Among the nobility of Venice unmarried adult siblings remained living in the same household in what was known as a *fraterna*. The portions that they would have inherited remained in the communal property and the large houses and estates could be kept together. Often only one of the brothers in the *fraterna* took a wife and some of the other brothers and sisters lived as bachelors and spinsters in the large house. The married brother and his wife attempted to control the number of births so as to limit the amount of tension within the coming generation. All the kin lived off the produce of landed property on the mainland. Hunecke argues that the Venetian nobility declined after the sixteenth century simply because it was all too successful in enforcing discipline to the "spirit of the family." Because of the restricted number of marriages the dynastic lineages ran the risk of dying out if the few married couples were unfortunate and had no living children. Sometimes a dynasty would even entice strangers to become adopted and move into the palace while at the same time assuming the family "arms and name" so that these symbols could survive.[41]

In Catalonia there was a single designated heir called the *hereu* if male or *pubilla* if female. Commonly the heir was the first-born male child. The Catalan parliament in 1585 established the main heir's part as about three-quarters of the total estate. The remaining quarter was divided equally among all the children. For daughters this part became their dowry; males used their portion to begin a career. In leaving home to make their fortune, the poor younger brothers, termed *fadristern* or *cabaler*, helped inspire Catalan society with a tense economic dynamism.[42] The *hereu* strove to consolidate the local landed property and one of the strategies was to marry a near kinsman. In six generations over 250 years, half of all the marriages in the Dosrius family required papal dispensations from marriage prohibitions because the intended brides and grooms were first cousins and thus normally forbidden to wed.[43]

Even among the peasantry close marriage could be a useful strategy for keeping landed property within a kinship group. Peasants' own ideology about marriage and inheritance was often endogamous. In parts of Northern and Western Europe a preferred marriage among well-off peasants was often between two cousins. This could enable ownership of farmland to continue within the same family. Although the marriage of near relatives was forbidden by Catholic and Protestant Churches, state regulations forbidding marriage of first cousins began in some places to be removed at the turn of the eighteenth to nineteenth centuries. Prior to this, cases of close marriage in Europe appear to have occurred in sixteenth- and seventeenth-century Latvia and involved first cousins. Folk-songs told that the purpose of these weddings was to make the kin "tighter." Local priests considered this a heathen custom.[44]

MILLIONS OF BROTHERS AND SISTERS

In most languages the meaning of the word for friend started out by indicating a kinsman. The Anglo-Saxon *fruint*, the German *Freund*, the Swedish *frände* as well as the French *ami* originally meant a relative. Kinship and family were major social constructs for describing the close relationships of solidarity, friendship, and loyalty. So it is not surprising that the language of kinship could be transported to situations that we today do not consider at all kin-like.

One of the major differences between modern times and the late Middle Ages is the present emphasis on the importance of biological ties, whereas previously biology was not seen as the exclusive condition for relationships. When, however, the character of the relationship was intended to be "friendly," it was a good idea in the Middle Ages to express it in just those kin-like terms. The popular metaphor of kinship created a social atmosphere of peace, trust, and solidarity among its members in a period otherwise known for insecurity, brutality, and hysteria. Later in the early modern era the ideology of blood relationships evolved. Some historians believe this can be traced to the declining fortunes of the nobility, who used the idea of blood as a defense against being forced by poverty to relinquish their noble status. A blood elite did not disappear just because its wealth declined, they argued, and the king should supply jobs just for this group. The blood relationship slowly merged with ideas of racial primacy. The idea of the primacy of blood relationships was accompanied in some countries by laws prohibiting adoption.[45] In Sweden and Norway it was common for orphans to be kept as foster-children but adoption (which gives inheritance rights) was not legal until the early twentieth century.

The language of kinship became the universal language of association in trade guilds, charities, and the fraternities of laymen. In France secret societies of workers termed *compagnonnages* called themselves "Children of Salomon" or "Children of Master Jacques." In Amiens a strike of textile workers in 1623 was led by a group known as the "big brothers." In eighteenth-century Poland the political supporters of one aristocratic group were known collectively as "the Family."

The family had become by this time a powerful political and social metaphor. A word that was rarely used during Shakespeare's age had rapidly gained new meanings and connotations. This transition, as previously mentioned, is part of a process of isolating smaller and smaller units from the wider group of all potential relatives.

Early modern kinship differed from voluntary associations because it stressed inequality. The word "kin" marked out a small group of persons who were isolated from the rest of humankind. Kinship emphasized the uniqueness and single origin of the group. In short, it had an exclusive myth of foundation and a legend of shared social obligations. Associations, however, stressed equality: "we are all brothers in God and there is no precedence before him," stated one fifteenth-century Breton.[46] Merely being a witness at a baptism was considered enough to create a spiritual bond between godparents so strong that marriage was forbidden on the premise of incest. Inside the religious orders members called themselves brothers and sisters and were guided by holy mothers and holy fathers. Other types of kinship terms can be found in the religious groups like the Bohemian Brethren, who termed themselves the "unitas fratrum," the Polish Brothers, the influential Dutch and English Anabaptist Family of Love who were also known as the Familists,[47] and in the Ukrainian associations like the L'viv Stauropegial Brotherhood which began an educational revival in the mid-1400s.[48] In Catholic countries there were confraternities of pious laymen, for instance the flagellant fraternity of the Polish *bractwa* who were famous for their ritual processions of repentance. The Holy Brotherhood of fifteenth-century Castile functioned as police to keep the peace by combating feuds. The Hutterite Brethren established a religious form of communism and called their large farms in Moravia *Brüderhofe*, "Brother farms." Within the civil service lower officials like Samuel Pepys would address the senior official as father: thus one day in August 1660 Pepys recorded that he had dinner with his former chief at the Exchequer "my father Bowyer."[49]

While it is true that there was inflation in terms of kinship when speaking of persons who were not blood relatives, this hardly means that the expressions lacked real value. Bossy calculates that between 10 and 20 percent of the European population belonged to a fraternal organization in the early modern era. The growth of brotherhoods can be seen as an alternative to reliance on blood relations.

Kinship was just as much a social necessity as a fact of life. If one lacked relatives, one had to create them in order to survive. During a journey through rural Russia in the 1840s, the German traveler August von Haxthausen observed what seemed to him to be most unusual: a large household whose members were unrelated. He commented: "The Russian cannot live without a strong family tie. If he has none, he invents one! If he has no father alive he searches for and chooses one for himself and has the same veneration and affection for him as for a natural parent! Also, if he has no children of his own he adopts some."[50]

Some persons even had trouble in interpreting the Bible since kinship was downplayed in the New Testament story of the life of Christ. The author of the widespread *Golden Legend* found it necessary to humanize Jesus by showing that he had a family and was related by blood to many of the apostles. The episodes of the New Testament made more sense this way. Therefore, he held that St. Anne had been married three times and that Jesus was only her oldest grandchild. The other grandchildren were Simon, Jude, the two Jameses as well as John the Evangelist, so each of them was a cousin. Further he assumed that John the Baptist, Elizabeth, and the Virgin Mary had been cousins. Even though the Catholic Church tried to combat this book, the presentation made good sense to readers in the fifteenth century and a new cult grew up for the veneration of St. Anne, the matriarch leader of the extended Holy Family lineage.[51]

WHAT'S IN A NAME?

One clear consequence of this creation of the "Holy Family" was the enormous popularity of baptizing children with the names of the saints. This led to a great reduction in the number of first names in use, which in turn made the adoption of surnames essential. The stock of names in Pistoia fell greatly between 1219 and 1427. There were 1,157 different names used in 1219 but only 220 in 1427, and there were 93 persons named Iacopo. The same decline occurred in Florence—by 1427 only 14 names were sufficient to account for half of the male population. Eight percent of all male household heads were named Giovanni, the most common name; other leading names were Antonio, Piero, Domenico, Bartolomeo, Iacopo, Franceso, and Matteo. The decline in the number of names is similar for women and 17 names sufficed to cover half of all the females, with Catarina the most common of all. Among the leading names were the feminine forms of masculine names, such as Antonia, Giovanna, Francesca, Piera, Bartolomea, Agnola, Mattea, Iacopa, and Niccolosa.[52]

Why did the culture of naming change? There are probably many factors at work. David Herlihy identifies several of them. One was that communal governments and the Church objected to the use of numerous unstable and fanciful names. Even when individuals had first and last names, they might change last names several times during their lives. Both religious and secular authorities needed to trace individuals in order to enforce laws or collect taxes. Herlihy believes that people were hoping for spiritual favor and protection when they chose the names of the saints. But there was also a new consciousness of ancestry that led to the exclusion of new and whimsical names. Perhaps this was also caused by a reorientation in religious psychology: the stable use of a few names made each life into a daily religious lesson. This meant that many unusual first names, which had been passed on from generation to generation as a sign of kinship, now disappeared. The kin-signifying function of the first name had to be replaced, and the surname became a suitable substitute.

The modern system with a first name and a hereditary surname is believed to have begun among the well-to-do families and *consortia* living in the towns of Italy in the twelfth and thirteenth centuries. The origin of the permanent family name is thus coterminous with the rise of the lineage principle of kinship. Even in Italy it was, however, not a universal practice. In 1427 about a third of all inhabitants of Florence had a surname, but in the surrounding villages only one person in every ten had a last name.[53] From Italy the custom spread to the nearby Midi region of France and to Rhineland Germany in the late Middle Ages.[54] The diffusion of the use of surnames was at first almost always confined to elites. In the peripheral country of Denmark the adoption of surnames came at the command of the king, who, in 1526, ordered that all noblemen take such names.[55] The Swedish–Finnish nobility also took surnames in the sixteenth century. Usually the Scandinavians turned their heraldic arms into a name, a fact that explains the many strange-sounding combinations like "Lion's Head," "Boar's Head," "Three Roses," "Laurel Wreath," "Golden Star," "Night and Day," and "Ox Forehead." This last-mentioned was the surname of the well-known Swedish Chancellor Axel Oxenstierna. The Polish–Lithuanian nobility also took surnames in the same period. Here families usually made a name out of the place or dwelling where they lived by attaching a final ending such as "ki" or "ski" if a male, and "ka" or "ska" if a female. In this way a great number of totally unrelated families came to have the same last name, such as the 30 separate groups calling themselves Dabrowski.[56]

Among the common people surnames developed out of names of their occupations like smith, carpenter, or porter, or from physical characteristics like white, red, or black hair color or from place of birth or some other distinguishing factor. In the beginning these last names were unstable and did not pass on from parent to child, but each had an individual second name. The transition to a hereditary name was gradual and probably depended upon the ambitions and needs of the families. The adoption of heritable last names was completed during the early modern period for most social groups superior to the peasantry.

In some places the need for assembling kin quickly must have been an incentive. In the Basque town of Balboa it was convenient to use a surname as a cry to summon help. A person in danger had only to scream "Gamboa, Gamboa" or "Onaz, Onaz" and all his relatives would rush to his defense.[57] Benvenuto Cellini, when writing his autobiography in 1555, saw in his name a sign that he was related to all other persons whose name was also Cellini even if they lived in Pisa or Ravenna or in France and he had never met them.[58] Casanova's characteristic Spanish surname got him into an embarrassing situation in Naples when an unexpected bearer of the same name turned up. In Scotland the surname was the premier sign of belonging to the clan.

Governments and church authorities found that it was useful if the population had a stable set of names. It was easier to collect taxes and guarantee inheritance, and it was easier to check baptisms and religious knowledge or to prohibit marriage between near kin, if persons could be identified through unique names. In the ordnance of Villers-Cotteret 1539 King François I decreed that in the lands he ruled (a smaller area than modern France) all families must adopt a permanent surname. This name could not be changed at will. He also ordered that baptismal registers should be kept in which were to be entered each individual's first and second names. From the central French regions the use of family names spread in the seventeenth century to Béarn, Artois, Flanders, Franche-Comté, and Alsace and later on in the eighteenth century to Lorraine.

Although elite surnames were known in many countries in the Middle Ages they were seldom universal until much later. In Central Europe government orders obliging all families, both urban and rural, to adopt family names were issued in Bavaria in 1677, Denmark 1771, Austria

1776, Brandenburg-Prussia 1794, and the Netherlands 1811. Jewish inhabitants were ordered to adopt family names in Austria (1787), Frankfurt (1807) and France (1808).

In many countries during the early modern era women did not automatically adopt their husbands' surnames when they married. Instead the wives kept their maiden names and in legal documents they were given their full name and then indicated as "wife of so and so." This was true for France, Germany, and Scandinavia. The first Swedish woman who took her husband's surname was married in 1691.[59] Not until the nineteenth century did most Swedish women adopt their husbands' last names. In some circumstances a woman of the lower nobility might change names, that is if her husband had an aristocratic title; otherwise she probably would not. In Castile a man marrying an heiress could be obliged to take on her family's name. In England the husband did not assume the name of the heiress, but their son would be given her maiden name as a first name, thus leading to the unusual Anglo-American custom of surnames as first names. In parts of eastern France and Switzerland both the husband's and the wife's names were combined to create a unique double surname for both.

A Parisian adoption contract from 1632 illustrates the use of separate surnames after marriage. "The honorable Marie la Rousse, wife of Gilles du Puy, a merchant and bourgeois of Paris, who has authorized her to undertake what follows . . . [has] confessed to having adopted . . . as her daughter and own child, Claire le Roy, young daughter of Pierre le Roy and of Avoye Caillet his deceased wife."[60] In Germany at the end of the seventeenth century women began to take their husband's name, but sometimes added their maiden name afterwards ("born so and so"). The Jewish writer Glikl bas Judah Leib, who was born in Hamburg about 1646, never took any of her two husbands' last names. Ashkenazi Jewish wives in Hamburg, Prague, and Vienna at that time usually signed their names with reference to their fathers and not to their husbands.[61]

The fact that wives did not always take their husbands' names is open to several interpretations. A positive interpretation could be that identification with and contacts through the mother's kindred were important and could be aided by retaining her name. A negative interpretation could be that the status of the wife's kindred was marginal and unimportant to the male lineage and therefore it would be improper for her to be symbolically taken into the lineage.

The need for a surname common to the whole kindred was strongly felt in the large towns. Among the peasantry of Northern and Central Europe family names did not exist until late in the early modern period and in Iceland as well as parts of Scandinavia some families never have had surnames. Instead peasants had a Christian name which was followed by a reference to the father's name, that is a patronymic. Per the son of Carl became Per Carlsson, his sister Anna the daughter of Carl became Anna Carlsdottir (if Icelandic) or Carlsdotter (if Swedish). This type of name was typical of a broad region starting at the mouths of the rivers Maas, Schelde, and Rhine in the Low Countries and stretching to the Baltic coast. Even in Italy about 40 percent of all surnames today are actually patronymics or matronymics (reference to the mother).[62]

The lack of peasant surnames was sometimes replaced by identification through the name of the farm, dwelling, or hamlet. This would change if the family moved to a new village. This principle held in the Pyrénées mountains and in Catalonia.[63] It also meant that if a man married the inheriting daughter and moved into the father-in-law's house, he too would carry the name of that homestead.

Among the aristocracy of France and England the use of surnames was far from simple. Some individuals might have several, depending on whether they chose to use the name of the lineage, the name of their manorial house, or the feudal title. The essayist Montaigne was exasperated by the near impossibility for an outsider to know who was related to whom within the highest social circles. It led to the "most injurious consequences in our land of France, to call each person by the name of his estate, and it is the usage that most leads to confusion between different races. The younger son of a good house, having had as his appanage a piece of land under the name of which he has been known and honored, cannot honorably abandon it; ten years after his death the land passes into the hands of a stranger, who follows the same usage: you may well guess how confused we become when we try to ascertain the origin of these men."[64]

It would seem that at least in the West European countries identity with a kin group through the use of a common name came into conflict with the strong feelings of individualism on one side and the strong identification with the personal dwelling, farm, or estate on the other.

DECLINE AND FALL?

In the sixteenth century many observers perceived that the various forms of kinship were in decline. As Shakespeare made the Prince of Wales notice as he arrived in London: "I want more uncles here to welcome me." In return he was warned, "those uncles which you want were dangerous ... God keep you from them, and from such false friends!"[65] Amity, as social anthropologist Meyer Fortes pointed out, is the best term for describing the basic idea behind kinship and this amity is expressed in "the axiom of prescriptive altruism" which holds that one must treat kinsmen with exceptional generosity and readiness.[66] A breakdown in amity and altruism could lie behind the general narrowing of the broad principles of reckoning kinship.

A large number of historians has commented on the changing role of kinship in the organization of society during the early modern period. A majority sees a decline as early as the end of the Middle Ages or in the sixteenth century. When they speak of decline they do not mean total disappearance, but rather that the size of the effective kin group shrinks and is replaced by other social institutions. Others place the decline somewhat later, often as a gradual consequence of the Reformation and Counter-Reformation. A few posit that some forms of kinship declined while other forms, for instance that of cousins and brothers-in-law, became more important. It is not easy to summarize these different standpoints, because the definitions of kinship vary greatly. However, most are agreed that in the early modern period the circle of kinship tended to be much smaller than in the Middle Ages.

Kinship in Europe can be many things: it can involve a series of ties between persons and their nearest relatives. On a basic level this is the question of who can help out in the hay harvest or who can lend a wagon. It can also involve a way of thinking about ancestors in previous generations and descendants in coming generations. This level concerns who will inherit the farm and who will have to move some-where else.

On a higher level kinship can be an administrative link between the monarchy and the individual. It can be a way of organizing primitive justice through the blood feud, or responsibility for building and main-taining sea-dikes in Frisia and Dithmarschen. One reason kings sup-ported the spread of primogeniture and entail was that it created a group of respected and wealthy local leaders who could be useful to mobilize the regional population. It is on this latter level that the greatest changes occurred. National states became organized along the principles of centralization, individualism, bureaucratization, rationalization, profes-sionalization, commercialization, higher education, merit, and literacy. During the seventeenth century, in Western Europe most all corporations, especially those of the nobility, were under attack. Many of the princi-ples of the strong central nation state were in conflict with a society based on kinship, birthrights, privilege, inherited status, and ascribed identity. In local communities the development of administration for paupers, philanthropic institutions, schools, and district courts took over func-tions which had been the sole responsibility of the family. Kinship was reduced to being just one of many intervening forces, like churches, guilds, landlords and aristocrats, which the Philosophes of the Enlightenment doomed to oblivion.

French historian Roland Mousnier gives kinship a prime position in his description of the absolute monarchy. He believes that it remained important in France right up to the Revolution, not just for the nobility but for "all the strata." However, he sees that the balance of power tilted away from the kindred and in favor of the nuclear family household. By the eighteenth century this process was completed and the conjugal family was to all intents and purposes severed from the lineage. As an example of the changing times, Mousnier names the growing paternal power over the lives of grown children. From the mid-sixteenth century parents could prohibit the marriage of sons under 30 and daughters under 25 years of age. From 1639 if children married without consent of their parents they could be disinherited. The principles of kin solidarity were, however, strongest among the aristocracy and lasted longest there. In France sons of high-ranking families could inherit not just landed estates, but high office as well. Certain families such as that of Du Plessis de Richelieu could use the elevated position of one of their kinsmen in order to gain access to money and power.[67] Individual families like the Saulx-Tavanes show how French aristocrats could combine personal interest in career and success with great concern for at least the nearest kinsmen in the lineage.[68] A study of the women of the English-Irish Lennox family in the eighteenth century reveals the same great interest in kinship as among the French aristocracy.[69] Kinship strategies remained in use, but the reach of kinship was limited and the expectations among the elite of successfully using the kinship network to place an untalented relative became increasingly uncertain.

Jean-Louis Flandrin agrees with Mousnier that kinship remained an influential social institution in the early modern period. But the extent of the kin group, he calculates, had been drastically narrowed down to only an individual's cousins, aunts, uncles, nieces, and nephews. Kin who were more distantly related had become unimportant. He attributes this to the church regulation that forbade marriage within the fourth degree of kinship: this rule existed from 1215 to 1917. The fourth degree of kinship encompassed any descendant of one's great-great-grandparents. Consequently the church prohibitions were treated as a boundary and people kept account of kin within this group, but not those more distantly related.[70] A close circle of kin does not in itself mean that ties to the acknowledged relatives were weak. On the contrary, the small group could at times function very well. Within the English middle classes the close kin group could be used for building investment capital in family businesses. In the absence of business ethics the moral obligations of kinship created solidarity.[71]

Lawrence Stone, the British historian, has proposed a transition in England from a period before 1630 when kinship was central to society to a period in which the nuclear household reigned unchallenged and the wider sense of kinship fell into disuse. The causes he singles out were "the decline of kinship and clientage as the main organizing principles of landed society" plus the rise of the nation state.[72] The Protestant religions gave strong backing to intimate family life, which led to a need to separate the mother–father–child group from the rest of the kin.

Another historian who sees a decline in patron–client relationship is the German Alfred Schröcker who studied the pattern of patronage of the Prince Bishop of Bamberg and Mainz, Lothar Franz von Schönborn, in the last part of the seventeenth century. Although Schönborn presided over vast numbers of appointments to administrative posts and was the head of a large aristocratic lineage, kinship was not the core of his patronage system. Like all families in the upper social strata, the Schönborns made calculated marriage alliances to consolidate their power; some alliances bore fruit, others did not. Even when Schönborn made an all-out effort to place a relative, he was never sure to succeed in getting him appointed. The reason for the lack of success was that every other lineage competed on the same terms and this prevented any single family from attaining too much influence. The kinship strategy was thus not guaranteed to succeed, so younger sons had to have education and experience as well as good connections.[73] In Poland the competition of rival kin groups was very destructive. Of 79 aristocratic families in the seventeenth century only 10 to 20 were politically influential at any one time.[74]

Austrian historian Otto Brunner identifies a transition from *das ganze Haus* (the whole house), which is a broadly conceived unit of production, consumption, and socialization, to the intimate little family of the late eighteenth century. Symbolic of this was the invention of words building on the French imported concept *Familie* instead of the German *Hausvater* (paterfamilias). *Das ganze Haus* was a total institution demanding discipline, subordination, and loyalty. The family however was based on sentimental feelings, primarily those between parents and children. Enlightened despots like Joseph II enacted legislation that relaxed the control of fathers and made wives, children, and servants more independent. This state of affairs made the creation of a friendlier atmosphere in the family an important binding factor.[75]

David Sabean is one of the few writers to have discovered an increasing use of kinship in the early modern period: he found that at the same time as the highest classes abandoned kinship networks, lower social strata began to utilize them. He has studied a village in southwestern Germany, an area of great migration to North America in the nineteenth century. The emigrants reported that one reason they had left was that the village was being run by cousins (*Vetterle*). They were referring to networks of local family factions. Kinship was used for exchanges, marriages, adoptions, godparents, employment, and loans of money. This was a new phenomenon: in the early eighteenth century there had been no systematic alliances between families related by blood. By contrast, by the early nineteenth century cousins created "tight overlapping repeated exchanges with each other which were replicated from generation to generation." There were many reasons behind the rising use of kinship in the village community. Population growth caused each person to inherit smaller portions of land so cooperation between cousins who had adjacent land made economic sense. Around the year 1800, artisans and other workers adopted the strategies of the well-to-do. But while landholders were marrying their first cousins, the artisans began to marry second cousins.[76]

A Swedish peasant proverb runs: "What use is a relative if he lives five kilometers away?"[77] In everyday life there were probably few occasions for peasants and workers to rely on kinship. Some exceptions are found, however, when migrating to a new place of residence and when seeking jobs. The many north Italian construction workers in Prague were recruited through kinship. In Prague the Aostallis, Bossis, Luraghos, and Spinellis came as entire clans in the seventeenth century to work in construction. Often they remained for a season and returned to their home valleys in winter. But they left a chief, a *capomaestri*, to plan the next year's projects in Prague.[78] In Vienna a dozen Italian families dominated the chimney-sweep guild.[79] Many guilds throughout Central Europe recruited on the basis of kinship and kin groups used the organization of guilds for advancement.

The American historian Natalie Zemon Davis summarizes some major causes of the compression of the kin group in sixteenth-century Europe. First, the power of feudal lords and distant kin had eroded enough to give better-off families a freer hand to plan for their own future. Secondly, the expansion of the urban economy increased movement into towns and created a large number of new occupational opportunities. Individual families had more possibilities and more chances than ever before. Davis argues that as new horizons opened for urban families, the traditional strategies for passing on property between generations had become risky. There was no longer any prescription for the best economic arrangement of marriage. These changes created a climate of opinion that called for a sharp boundary between the immediate family and more distant kin. The Protestant Churches as a rule raised the power of the father over his household—wife, children, and servants. The family of the household had become the "locus for identity, gratification and reward," and not the kindred.[80]

VENDETTAS AND BLOOD FEUDS

After the execution of Mary, Queen of Scots, English ambassadors were sent to make amends to James VI. The Scots informed them that according to the custom in Scotland a murderer must offer compensation to the kin of the victim. Because Mary was related to many of the royal houses in Europe, the English offer of recompense would also have to be directed to monarchs abroad who were her kin. This was the same for both commoners and royalty.[81]

This was one of the last remnants of the medieval custom of the blood feud in Western Europe. During the Middle Ages the court system of most countries was underdeveloped because government was weak. The pursuit of justice was therefore in the hands of the kindred. Law codes specified which of the kinsmen of a criminal were to be held jointly responsible for compensating the kin of the victim. The size of the payments (called the *wergild*) varied: the closer the relationship, the more money the kinsman paid or received. If there was no offer of reconciliation or if the offer was rejected, the kin of the victim found itself in a feud with the criminal's kin and could in the case of murder kill a member of the other family.

Blood feuds and wergilds disappeared in England and Wales during the Middle Ages, but could be found in Denmark, Scotland and along the Belgian, Dutch, and German North Sea coast in the sixteenth century.[82] In Albania and some other inaccessible parts of the Balkans, the blood feud continued into the twentieth century.[83] It would be misleading to see in this only anarchy and private justice. Although it is true that kinsmen carried out the feud, the custom belongs just as much to the history of the judiciary as to the family. Most families would probably have been more than happy to avoid being pulled into conflict by some distant cousin's rashness. The custom was well regulated by the legal codes. In Scotland the kin of the slain victim sent formal "letters of slains" to the kin of the accused slayer. Since killers often went into hiding, responsibility fell on the kinsmen to find and deliver them. In addition the joint responsibility for the crimes committed by kin ought to have helped to prevent other crimes since law-abiding persons would keep a watchful eye on the doings of hot-tempered relatives. Thus the kindred became a sort of police force.

Many medieval governments tolerated the idea of blood feud because it could be expected that when the kindred solidarity functioned well it prevented crime. When there are numerous court cases involving kindred who must pay compensation, this may indicate that the kindred was not functioning effectively. In the sixteenth and seventeenth centuries the nation states began to centralize the judiciary system, with trained judges and a hierarchy of appeals courts, and this type of justice had little use for the kindred. By 1677 the Earl of Strathmore commented that in Scotland feuds were "quite out of fashion ... the country being generally more civilized than it was of ancient times."[84]

VOLUNTARY KINSHIP

In many societies kinship was historically one of few respected ties between individuals. If two persons or two families wished to ally themselves, but were not related by blood or marriage, they had good reason to create kinship-like bonds in a socially acknowledged ritual. Anthropologists have at times deemed this "invention" of kinship to be artificial or fictive, but such a perspective misses the mark. What one culture perceives as artificial can be experienced as totally natural in another. Kinship is as much about socially recognized relationships as about biological descent. In the case of invented kinship the term "voluntary kinship" is more suitable. Because voluntary kinship involves a permanent change of personal status, it is usually surrounded by special ceremonies.

Being a godparent is in many places considered to create a tie between kindred. At an early stage the Christian Church called for outside witnesses and sponsors to the ritual of baptism. They were to be persons of both sexes and included persons who were unrelated to the infant. These sponsors were allotted a special function as godfather and godmother and regarded as having a strong relationship to the family of the child, because they were assumed to be responsible for the child if anything happened to the parents. They are called *comadre* and *compadre* in Spanish and the institution itself is known as *compadrazgo*. It appears to have been an important relationship in most of the countries on the northern shore of the Mediterranean. *Compadrazgo* was based on friendship and sociability, especially among the males, and an offshoot of this is the Latin-American *compadre* friendship between the father of the child and the godfather.[85]

The early Christian religion developed the theory that this special relationship represented a "spiritual" kinship (*pneumatikos pateras*), just as binding as a blood relationship. Hence the Church, when it constructed the list of kin who were forbidden to marry, also included the baptismal sponsors. This marriage prohibition prevailed throughout the Middle Ages but disappeared first at the Protestant Reformation and then at the Catholic Counter-Reformation in the Council of Trent of 1563. It remained, however, in force in the Greek Orthodox Church for much longer.

The *compadrazgo* is a complementary form of kinship entered into voluntarily. Since it concerns a godparent-to-child relationship it is actually based on the nuclear family, not the kindred, but it could indirectly extend to encompass the entire family of the godparent. This spiritual kinship is a question of producing amity and sociability, it plays no role in inheritance. Perhaps because it is free of the concern about inheritance the *compadre* relationship evolved more harmoniously than the tense relationships with siblings and in-laws.[86]

From the Balkan mountains to the Carelian forests in Finland the Greek Orthodox Church kept the idea of spiritual kinship alive. In modern times the ties of spiritual kinship have been best studied in Serbia and Montenegro, where the custom is known as *kumstvo,* from the Greek word *koumbari*. The godparent was called *kum* if male and *kuma* if female. In most of the world the godparent relationship is individual, but in Serbia and Albania it is collective and involves the entire kindred. Members of one kin group act as godparents for all the children of another group. The right of the child and godparents to be *kum* is a family possession and passes on through inheritance in the male line. The Balkans have throughout history witnessed much migration and political unrest. In the absence of central government, blood feuds and vendettas between kindred survived into modern times. Becoming godparents of another kin group's children made for useful alliances and the ceremony could serve to seal reconciliation between two previously feuding families. Sometimes the kin groups that stood in a *kum* relationship actually merged and would assume the same surname, celebrate the same ancestors and festivals. *Kum* could also come from the Muslim population. In such cases the ceremony involved not baptism but the ritual of the first haircut. A similar *kum* tie could be created if a Christian witnessed the circumcision or first haircutting of a Muslim boy.[87]

Another custom used by the south Slavs and Albanians in order to reconcile families in a vendetta was blood brotherhood. There was even a form of blood sisterhood. Blood feuds could be ended through a ritual. Two representatives of the kindred make a cut in their right wrist, then suck blood from each other's wrist. After the ceremony all of the kindred on both sides consider one another blood brothers.[88]

GENEALOGY AND FAMILY MYTH

The Académie Française dictionary of 1694 defined kinship as consanguinity, that is, sharing common blood. The *Encyclopédie* stated that "all kinship comes from birth and derives from the fact that persons descend from the same stock." The references to common stock and common blood are part and parcel of European kinship ideology.[89] Like all ideological statements, these definitions were only lightly reflected in the practice of kinship which in many ways attempted to exclude persons of the same blood, for instance if they were "illegitimate," or "distant" relations, or belonged to the wrong sex. At the same time these definitions hide the fact that the broad medieval form of kinship was often between persons who were not close relatives.

The Rise of Professional Genealogy and the Decline of Kinship

Starting in the Middle Ages families began to keep *ricordanze*, *livres de raison*, and *Stambücher* which included entries of births and deaths and marriages as well as narrative chronicles and biographical sketches.[90] The family book of records would begin by relating the misty origins of the ancestors. Such books were transferred from parent to children, and sometimes copies were made for separate branches. Lacking documents and based on unsure oral traditions, these works invented fanciful legends of origin and secret myths. The original book was possessed by the main heir. Sometimes the information was written into the family Bible and blank pages were included for that purpose.

In the course of the sixteenth and seventeenth centuries, European discourse on kinship shifted. Pride in mythical founding ancestors and their heroic deeds became less prominent. The idea that all persons with the same surname were related was also qualified. Part of this shift was a consequence of the growth of professional history and genealogy. Genealogy may have been invented in order to gild an insufficiently glorious origin, but when it was done with care it actually destroyed many family myths.

The French historian André Duchesne (1584–1640) is believed to have been the first professional genealogist. In principle, he never recorded as a fact any item for which there was no written proof. Thus his *Histoire généalogique de la maison du Plessis de Richelieu* (1631) printed all existing documents in their entirety. The latter take up a significant part of the volume. The first scientific handbook on how to compile an accurate family history was written by the German professor Johann Christoph Gatterer in 1788 and based on lecture notes to his course on history. About grand origins, he was a true skeptic of the Enlightenment. "No ancestor of our Christian families hid in the Trojan horse and helped to burn down Troy. King Piramus was not the ancestor of the House of Habsburg. The old Dukes of Lithuania do not have the honor of descending from a bastard son of Emperor Augustus. And the Austrians have not received their privileges from Julius Caesar and Emperor Nero."[91] Gatterer's standpoint was reasonable, but had the unfortunate result of robbing much of the magic from the lineage. The writing of professional genealogy ceased, after a while, to be in the interests of the aristocracy.

KINSHIP-IN-ACTION AND KINSHIP-IN-THINKING

Much of what has been presented here deals with kinship-in-thinking, that is as an idea, a pattern of thinking limited in time and place. Little has here been said about the practice of kinship. These two things should be kept separate. Kinship-in-action is the everyday help and support given by blood relatives and in-laws to an individual. The group of persons who can normally be activated is small and limited by availability, propinquity, and willingness. A peasant is likely to get help in his fields from his brother or brother-in-law. The peasant woman is likely to get help from a sister or sister-in-law. But if the kin live far away a good neighbor will do just as well.

Kinship-in-thinking is very different and can encompass all conceivable relatives both living and dead—provided there is some reason (however slight) to mention their names. The advantage here need not be related to material utility, but could be connected with the symbolic values of a link to an esteemed ancestor. The image of the "same blood flowing in the veins" gave honor and value to a descendant. Just as one's reach is always greater than one's grasp, the circle drawn by kinship-in-thinking will always contain many more individuals than kinship-in-action can ever mobilize.

Kinship-in-thinking employs distinctive terms for varying genealogical positions radiating outwards from any single individual. It results in groups that are basically inegalitarian and use signs like unique names in order to distinguish themselves from all others. Kinship-in-action, however, is local and can fulfill its mundane functions without elaborate terminology. In small-scale communities symbols like names may have been superfluous since all important relationships were generally known and recognized.

The decline in kinship which so many historians assign to the early modern period is to a great extent a decline in kinship-in-thinking. A decline in ideologies, symbols, signs, and discourses is in reality a decline in kinship as a legitimate social classification. Kinship-in-action, however, in face-to-face social intercourse was probably only slightly affected. It remained the basic form of social help in the local community.

NOTES

INTRODUCTION

1. Gillis 1985, pp. 211–219.
2. Veinstein 1995, p. 76.
3. Levin 1989.
4. Stone 1977, p. 66.
5. Livi Bacci 1997; Perrenoud, 1997.
6. From Act I, scenes ii and iii.
7. Late male age at marriage is not unique to the Western European experience, as societies in Africa and other parts of the world—especially where polygyny is common—have been marked by late male marriage. It is the high age at first marriage of women that marks the Western European marriage model as unique.
8. The term "servant" in this context should not be identified with "domestic servant," although some served in such a role. For most rural people, and especially for males, service meant agricultural service, doing work on a farm.
9. Laslett 1989; Kertzer and Laslett 1995; Reher 1998.
10. Smith 1984; Laslett 1989; Reher 1997.
11. Nursing tends to discourage ovulation.
12. Tolstoy 1942, p. 1271.
13. Livi Bacci 1997, pp. 131–139.
14. Stone 1977, p. 422.
15. Livi Bacci 1983.
16. Quoted in Gaudemet 1987, p. 217.
17. Harrington 1995, pp. 39–40.
18. Quoted ibid., pp. 40–41.
19. Stone 1977, p. 141.
20. Phillips 1988, pp. 40–94.
21. Ibid., p. 92.
22. Ibid., pp. 202–226.
23. Cited ibid., p. 365.
24. Quoted in Barbagli 1996 (2), p. 370.
25. Stone 1977, p. 105.
26. Macfarlane 1979.
27. Hill 1981.
28. Bérélowitch 1997.
29. De Maddalena 1974, p. 223.
30. Barbagli 1996.
31. De Vries 1984.
32. Kertzer 1993.

CHAPTER 1

* As well as thanking the editors of this volume, I should like to thank G. Angelozzi, R. Brigati, C. Calderan, M. Callari, C. Casanova, F. Cazzola, S. Cavazza, L. Gambi, H. Grassl, A. Guenzi, L. Guerci, A. Fauve-Chamoux, L. Ferrante, D. Lombardi, M. Martini, M. Montanari, O. Niccoli, M. Palazzi, G. Pomata, S. Salvatici, S. Soldani, and F. Viti. This chapter deals with the questions analyzed more fully in Sarti 1999a, chs 4–6.
1. Deffontaines 1972, pp. 96–121; Braudel 1979 (1967), Italian translation [hereafter It.tr.] 1993 (1982), pp. 272–275; Pounds 1989, pp. 196–198; Gottlieb 1993, p. 29; Yun 1994, p. 127.
2. Cuisenier 1991, p. 338.
3. Roux 1976, It.tr. 1982, p. 159; Pounds 1989, pp. 122–136.

4. Collomp 1986, It.tr. 1987, pp. 402–403; Goubert 1982.

5. Gambi 1976, pp. 496–502.

6. Cuisenier 1991, pp. 26 and 33.

7. Roux 1976, It.tr. 1982, pp. 171–172; Cosenza 1974, p. 129; Barley 1985; Horn 1994, pp. 78–79.

8. Schwarz 1989, p. 92; Pounds 1989, p. 136.

9. Pounds 1989, p. 126 and pp. 132–133.

10. Rösener 1995, p. 194.

11. Collomp 1986, It.tr. 1987, pp. 400–401.

12. Roux 1976, It.tr. 1982; Pounds 1989; Schwarz 1989.

13. Barbieri and Gambi 1970; Gambi 1976.

14. Complex families are those including other relations besides the parents and children. On the relationship between the form of the house and the form of the family, see Sarti 1999a, pp. 83–95.

15. The description of the house is adapted from Hochstrasser 1993, pp. 112–120.

16. Braudel 1979 (1967), It.tr. 1993 (1982), pp. 270–271; Pounds 1989, p. 187; Thornton 1991, It.tr. 1992, pp. 27–30; Garnot 1994, p. 22; Roche 1997, pp. 137–138; a traveler in Tuscany in 1756–1757 noted their presence in every house, but dated their introduction to 80 years previously, cf. Malanima 1990, p. 22 and 1994, p. 121.

17. The chimney appeared in the eighteenth century.

18. Dülmen 1990, pp. 56–60.

19. Pounds 1989, pp. 127–135; Cuisenier 1991.

20. Cuisenier 1991, p. 104; Davidson 1982, pp. 116–117.

21. Weatherill 1988, pp. 52–53 and p. 49, pl. 3.3.

22. Those whose property was worth between £10 and £50 when they died. Sources on the conditions of life of the poorest (i.e. those whose property was worth less than £10) are scarce (Horn 1994, p. 72).

23. Horn 1994, pp. 72–73.

24. For seats in English houses, see Green Carr 1994, p. 88. Quotations are taken respectively from McKendrick 1982, p. 1; Goldthwaite 1987, p. 16; de Vries 1993, p. 107. On this debate, see Weatherill 1988; Brewer and Porter 1993a; Goldthwaite 1993; Glennie 1995; Clunas 1999.

25. Yun 1994, p. 128.

26. Particularly Weatherill 1988. On the Plain of Caen see Dessureault et al. 1994, pp. 102, 108.

27. Malanima 1990, p. 161 and 1994, p. 121.

28. Dessureault et al. 1994, pp. 102–103, 108–109.

29. Sarti 1999a, pp. 101–104; on England see Stone and Fawtier Stone 1984 and 1986, It.tr. 1989, pp. 243–329.

30. Roux 1976, It.tr. 1982, pp. 176–211; Simoncini 1995b, pp. 10–13; Cosenza 1974, p. 124; Pardailhé-Galabrun 1988, pp. 212, 217–218, 224.

31. Roux 1976, It.tr. 1982, p. 183.

32. de Vries 1984a, pp. 175–249.

33. Braudel 1979 (1967), It.tr. 1993 (1982), p. 456; Pardailhé-Galabrun 1988, p. 244; Palazzi 1985, pp. 356–357.

34. Palazzi 1985, p. 356; Pounds 1989, pp. 247–248, 274, 277–278; Vigarello 1985, It.tr. 1988 (1987), p. 130 and passim; Montenegro 1996, p. 69. The lavatory with running water was an English invention which only spread in the nineteenth century.

35. Pounds 1989, pp. 274–280; Roche 1997, p. 156, 165; Pardailhé-Galabrun 1988, pp. 348–354.

36. Davidson 1982, pp. 12–13.

37. Braudel 1979 (1967), It.tr. 1993 (1982), p. 205; Roche 1981, It.tr. 1986 and 1997, pp. 152, 173; Davidson 1982, p. 21.

38. Guenzi 1983, p. 176.

39. Vigarello 1985, It.tr. 1988 (1987), pp. 165–179; Roche 1997, pp. 132–136.

40. Braudel 1979 (1967), It.tr. 1993 (1982), pp. 466–468; Pardailhé-Galabrun 1988, pp. 211–212; Tocci 1988; Benevolo 1996 (1993), pp. 127–160.

41. Roche 1997, p. 135.

42. Thornton 1991, It.tr. 1992, p. 275; Roche 1997, pp. 125–138.

43. Pardailhé-Galabrun 1988, pp. 342–344.

44. Roche 1997, p. 136.

45. Dessureault et al. 1994, p. 108.

46. Pardailhé-Galabrun 1988, pp. 253–255, 341–348; Garnot 1994, p. 22.

47. Braudel 1979 (1967), It.tr. 1993 (1982), p. 272.

48. Palazzi 1985, pp. 356–358.

49. Pardailhé-Galabrun 1988, pp. 332–337 and passim. My thanks to P. Cornaglia for the information about Turin.

50. Klapisch-Zuber 1988, pp. 205–206; Segalen 1981; Malanima 1990, pp. 11–12; Hauser 1994, pp. 363–373; Sarti 1999a, pp. 45–48.

51. Cosenza 1974, p. 127.

52. Roche 1981, It.tr. 1986, pp. 174–180; Pardailhé-Galabrun 1988, pp. 275–287.

53. Grassi et al. 1992 (1989), ad vocem, Thornton 1991, It.tr. 1992, pp. 111–114; Montenegro 1996, pp. 34–35.

54. Pardailhé-Galabrun 1988, pp. 275–276 (quotation from p. 275); Hayward 1965, It.tr. 1992, passim.

55. Weatherill 1988, p. 160.

56. Roche 1981, It.tr. 1986, p. 175.

57. Pardailhé-Galabrun 1988, pp. 284–286; Fildes 1986, pp. 89–90, 112.

58. Elias 1975, It.tr. 1980, pp. 43–46; Pardailhé-Galabrun 1988, p. 285; Montenegro 1996, pp. 30, 106, 110 and 156; Ranum 1986, It.tr. 1987, pp. 171–174.

59. Grassi et al. 1992 (1989), ad vocem. On the ceremonial surrounding the king of France's morning awakening, see Elias 1975, It.tr. 1980, pp. 94–100.

60. Montenegro 1996, pp. 104, 107 and 110.

61. Pardailhé-Galabrun 1988, pp. 236–

62. 242, 257, 303–305, 309–310. Amongst the wage earners we find 2.3 persons per room at the beginning of the eighteenth century, 2.7 at the end, see Roche, 1981, It.tr. 1986, p. 158.

62. Roche 1981, It.tr. 1986, pp. 192–194; Weatherill 1988, passim; de Vries 1993.

63. Hayward 1965, It.tr. 1992, passim. Braudel 1979 (1967), It.tr. 1993 (1982), pp. 275–278; Roche 1981, It.tr. 1986, pp. 190–210 and 1997, pp. 202–208; Pardailhé-Galabrun 1988, pp. 316–324; Weatherill 1988; Brewer and Porter 1993a, Schuurman and Walsh 1994.

64. Pardailhé-Galabrun 1988, pp. 291–292; Davidson 1982, pp. 47–48; Roche 1981, It.tr. 1986, p. 195.

65. Thornton 1991, It.tr. 1992, p. 315.

66. Pardailhé-Galabrun 1988, pp. 255–267; Sarti 1999a, pp. 152–157.

67. Frank E. Brown 1986, p. 580.

68. Pardailhé-Galabrun 1988, pp. 255–272, 276.

69. Vigarello 1985, It.tr. 1988 (1987), p. 128.

70. Pardailhé-Galabrun 1988, pp. 257–260.

71. Grassi et al. 1992 (1989), headword "tavolo"; Thornton 1991, It.tr. 1992, pp. 205–214; Montenegro 1996 passim.

72. Thornton 1991, It.tr. 1992, pp. 290 and 295; Montenegro 1996, pp. 66–69.

73. Stone and Fawtier Stone 1984, 1986, pp. 292–293. On servants' dining rooms in Italy, see Fragnito 1991 and infra, p. 14 para. 2.

74. Roche 1981, It.tr. 1986, pp. 158–159; Pardailhé-Galabrun 1988, pp. 255–267. For another case see Nenadic 1994, p. 149, which describes "The rise of the dining room" in Scotland.

75. Roux 1976, It.tr. 1982; Pardailhé-Galabrun 1988, pp. 248–251; Roche 1981, It.tr. 1986, pp. 149–153. On London see Frank E. Brown 1986.

76. Goldthwaite 1980; Thornton 1991,

It.tr. 1992, p. 11; Montenegro 1996, p. 30.

77. Thornton 1991, It.tr. 1992, pp. 300–314; Montenegro 1996, pp. 30 and 91.

78. Evans 1978, German trans. 1996.

79. Ibid.; Elias 1969 (1939), It.tr. 1982; Ariès and Duby 1986, It.tr. 1987; Blok 1995.

80. Evans 1978, German trans. 1996, p. 90; Vigarello 1985, It.tr. 1988 (1987), p. 84.

81. Archivio di Stato di Bologna, *Fondo Albergati, Strumenti e scritture*, b. 210, fasc. 4.

82. Meldrun 1999; Sarti 1999a, pp. 158–170, both with bibliography.

83. Sarti 1995 and forthcoming; Arru 1995.

84. See note 79.

85. Valeri 1977, p. 352.

86. A. Jouvin de Rochefort, *Le Voyageur d'Europe*, Paris 1672, partially reproduced in Montanari 1991, pp. 233–235.

87. Montanari 1991, p. viii.

88. Flandrin 1996a, p. 570.

89. Elias 1969 (1939), It.tr. 1982, pp. 167–169; Braudel 1979 (1967), It.tr. 1993 (1982), p. 181; Flandrin 1996a, p. 570; Sarti 1999a, pp. 175–176, with further references.

90. Flandrin 1996a, p. 570.

91. Valeri 1977, p. 352.

92. Klapisch-Zuber and Demonet 1972; Montanari 1994 (1993), p. 63.

93. Di Simplicio 1994.

94. Quoted in Merzario 1996, p. 232 (my cursive).

95. Corso 1948, p. 11.

96. Baumgarten 1965; Valeri 1977, p. 352; Barbagli 1996 (1984), pp. 402–408.

97. Baumgarten 1965. Some of the laws passed in the nineteenth century increased the distance between peasant farmers and their dependants.

98. Archivio di Stato di Bologna, *Tribunale criminale del Torrone, Atti processuali*, 8374/5, fasc. 100.

99. Horn 1975, p. 6; Fairchilds 1984, pp. 15–16, 51; Sarti 1994, 1999a; Fragnito 1988, 1991; Manciulli 1996; Nazarov 1997, p. 848.

100. Manciulli 1996, p. 329.

101. Faccioli 1973; Manciulli 1996; Romani 1997; Sarti 1999a, pp. 183–185, with further references.

102. Nazarov 1997, p. 847.

103. Horn 1975, p. 6; Fairchilds 1984, pp. 15–16; Sarti 1994, pp. 248–249 and 1999a, pp. 183–190; Capatti, Montanari 1999, pp. 273–284.

104. Fairchilds 1984, p. 51; Hyman and Hyman 1996, p. 653; the author was Menon.

105. Weatherill 1988, pp. 149–150; Mennell 1985, *passim*; on wetnursing, Fildes 1986.

106. *Le sottilissime astuzie di Bertoldo*, quoted in Montanari 1991, pp. 174–175.

107. Grieco 1996; Montanari 1994 (1993), pp. 104–114.

108. Battaglia 1961, vol. 5, p. 623. On "family" in the sense of servants, see Sarti 1999a, pp. 27–30.

109. Guenzi 1982, p. 26, note 26; Romani 1997, pp. 730–732.

110. Manciulli 1996.

111. Braudel 1979 (1967), It.tr. 1993 (1982), pp. 112–114; Camporesi 1980 and 1989; Guenzi 1982; Visceglia 1991; Kaplan 1996; Montanari 1994 (1993), p. 65. Flandrin and Montanari 1996.

112. Guenzi 1982, p. 25; Visceglia 1991.

113. Visceglia 1991, pp. 223–225; Flandrin 1996b, pp. 605–610.

114. Montanari 1994 (1993), pp. 24–30, 99, 141–143; Nigro 1997.

115. For Russia, see Nazarov 1997, p. 846; for Jewish diet, see Soler 1996 and Toaff 2000.

116. Braudel 1979 (1967), It.tr. 1993 (1982), pp. 98–104.

117. Ibid., pp. 168–175; Montanari 1994 (1993), pp. 91–97, 130–135; Matthaiou 1997.

118. Morineau 1996, p. 589.

119. Flandrin 1996b, p. 603.

120. Braudel 1979 (1967), It.tr. 1993 (1982), pp. 45–49; Livi Bacci 1987, pp. 70–78; Montanari 1994 (1993), p. 127; Flandrin 1996a, p. 552.

121. Braudel 1979 (1967), It.tr. 1993 (1982), pp. 111–130; Montanari 1994 (1993), pp. 125–128; Flandrin 1996a, pp. 555–556.

122. Montanari 1991 and 1994 (1993), pp. 128–130.

123. Levi 1979 and 1991; Montanari 1994 (1993), pp. 166–170.

124. Ibid.; Braudel 1979 (1967), It.tr. 1993 (1982), pp. 130–132; Levi 1979, 1991; Visceglia 1991, pp. 226–228; Flandrin 1996a, pp. 556–557; Finzi 1990 (1992).

125. Salaman 1985 (1948), It.tr. 1989; Braudel 1979 (1967), It.tr. 1993 (1982), pp. 139–143; Montanari 1994 (1993), pp. 130, 170–175.

126. Braudel 1979 (1967), It.tr. 1993 (1982), p. 141.

127. Montanari 1994 (1993), p. 171.

128. Camporesi 1989; Flandrin 1996b, p. 608.

129. Sereni 1981 (1958); Montanari 1994 (1993), pp. 175–180. For the history of pasta, see Serventi, Sabban 2000; Capatti, Montanari 1999, pp. 59–74.

130. Morineau 1996, p. 583.

131. Livi Bacci 1987, pp. 142–145; Montanari 1994 (1993), p. 181; Komlos 1998.

132. Drummond and Wilbraham 1958 (1939); Levi 1996, p. 200.

133. Mintz 1985; Huetz de Lemps 1996; Montanari 1994 (1993), pp. 154–159.

134. Ibid., pp. 153–154; Sarti 1999a, pp. 215–216.

135. Braudel 1979 (1967), It.tr. 1993 (1982), pp. 215–220.

136. On salt ibid., pp. 183–184; on wine and beer see ibid., pp. 206–214; Montanari 1994 (1993), p. 151; Sarti 1999a, pp. 216–219.

137. Thirsk 1997; Teti 1978 (1976), p. 78; Flandrin 1996b, pp. 624–625.

138. On the extent of their diffusion, see Flandrin 1996b, pp. 608–612; Sarti 1999a, p. 220.

139. S. de Sismondi, Tableau de l'agriculture toscane, Geneva, 1801 p. 99, quoted in Malanima 1994, p. 118.

140. Teti 1978 (1976), passim.

141. Flandrin 1996b, pp. 613–616.

142. Hufton 1996, It.tr. pp. 133–135.

143. Sandra Ott, "Aristotle among the Basques: the Cheese Analogy of Conception," in Man 4 (1979), quoted in Pomata 1983, p. 1439.

144. Weatherill 1988, pp. 142–145. The author draws this information from diaries and other sources. Clearly not all women did exactly the same things. Moreover, more women could collaborate doing the mentioned tasks (i.e. mother and daughters, or mistress and servants).

145. Reproduced in Montanari 1991, p. 209.

146. Davidson 1982, p. 207.

147. Poni 1994.

148. For example Laudani 1996; but see the chapter on proto-industrialization in this volume.

149. Roche 1989, pp. 313–345; Hufton 1996, It.tr., pp. 147–148; Vickery 1993, p. 282.

150. Roche 1989, pp. 247–312.

151. Malanima 1990, pp. 166–167; Shammas 1994.

152. Malanima 1990, p. 161 and 1994, p. 121.

153. Roche 1981, It.tr. 1986, p. 220 and 1997, p. 230.

154. Braudel 1979 (1967), It.tr. 1993 (1982), p. 298; Vigarello 1985, It.tr. 1988 (1987), pp. 34–46 and passim.

155. Barbagli 1996 (1984), pp. 336–363; Hufton 1996, It.tr. p. 173.

156. Vigarello 1985, It.tr. 1988 (1987), pp. 54–55; Hufton 1996, It.tr., p. 177.

157. Vigarello 1985, It.tr. 1988 (1987), pp. 114–115 and 182–183.

158. Ibid., p. 83.

159. Roche 1981, It.tr. 1986, pp. 225–233.

160. Braudel 1979 (1967), It.tr. 1993 (1982), p. 286.

161. Hufton 1996, It.tr. p. 177.
162. Roche 1997, pp. 138–139; 1981, It.tr. 1986, pp. 217–264; 1989, pp.129–141.
163. Medick 1995, pp. 764–772.
164. Ibid., p. 764; Frati 1923, p. 223; Sarti 1999b.
165. These laws did not exist in Holland. In Switzerland, Germany, and Italy they were in force until the begin-ning of the nineteenth century; see Wijsen-beek-Olthuis 1994, p. 43; Ribeiro 1984, pp. 69–75; Roche 1989, It.tr. 1991, pp. 54–56 and 1997, p. 219; Levi Pisetzky 1995 (1978), p. 34.
166. Medick 1995, pp. 761–764.
167. Braudel 1979 (1967), It.tr. 1993 (1982), pp. 288–289; Levi Pisetzky 1995 (1978); Poni 1993.
168. Hughes 1983; Visceglia 1991; Sarti 1999b.
169. Medick 1995, pp. 764–765.
170. Corso 1948, p. 55; Levi Pisetsky 1995 (1978), pp. 69, 73.
171. Klapisch-Zuber 1982, It.tr. 1988, pp. 161–162, 167 and 186.
172. Corso 1948, p. 8.
173. Levi Pisetzky 1995 (1978), pp. 172, 210–211; Giorgetti 1992; Metken 1996.
174. Roche 1997, pp. 211–212.
175. Ricci 1891, p. 153; Sarti 1999b.
176. Roche 1989, pp. 59–61 and 1997, p. 214.
177. Maza 1983, pp. 311–314; Roche 1989, p. 103.
178. Fairchilds 1993, p. 850.
179. Rosanvallon 1992, It.tr. 1994; Sarti 1999a, pp. 248–262.
180. Sarti 1999a; Douglas, Isherwood 1979, It.tr. 1984, p. 14.

CHAPTER 2

1. Mitterauer 1990c, pp. 109–122.
2. Hajnal 1965, pp. 101–143.
3. Kaser 1990, pp. 49–81.
4. Ibid., pp. 61–62; Revesz 1976, pp. 9–13.
5. Conze 1940, pp. 39–52.
6. Revesz 1976, pp. 3–5, 100–101.
7. Chirot 1976, pp. 43–51.
8. Revesz 1976, pp. 5–9, 101–105.
9. Kaser 1990, pp. 70–71.
10. Ibid., p. 78.
11. Kaser 1992, 1995.
12. Stoianovich 1992, pp. 1–77.
13. Busch-Zantner 1937, pp. 72–81.
14. Kochanowicz 1983, pp. 153–166; Kula 1976, pp. 192–203.
15. Plakans 1975a, pp. 630–651.
16. Revesz 1976, pp. 17–25; Robinson 1932, pp. 11–13; Stahl 1986, pp. 1–50; Stahl 1980.
17. Hajnal 1965.
18. Hajnal 1983, pp. 65–69.
19. Ibid., pp. 97–99.
20. Mitterauer 1990b, pp. 26–28.
21. Mitterauer 1994. Also see Higounet 1986. It is important to point out that the colonization border is the same as the Hajnal line. Hajnal thought that the difference he noted did not evolve until modern times.
22. Mitterauer 1994.
23. Ibid.
24. Ibid.
25. Ibid.
26. Ogris 1971, p. 954.
27. Winner 1977, pp. 125–134.
28. Revesz 1976, pp. 218–220; Andorka 1976, pp. 340–341.
29. Revesz, 1976, pp. 205–207.
30. Ibid., pp. 205–208; Conze 1940, pp. 18–20; Visniauskaite 1971, pp. 369–376.
31. Todorova 1993, pp. 125–128; Stahl 1986, pp. 26–30, 43.
32. Revesz 1976, p. 208; Constantinescu and Stahl 1968, pp. 13–14.
33. Mitterauer and Kagan 1990, pp. 184–185.
34. Shaffer 1982; Kertzer 1989, p. 4.
35. Stahl 1986, p. 169.
36. Kaser, 1996.
37. Ibid.
38. Ibid.
39. Ibid.
40. Kaser 1986.

41. Andorka and Faragó 1983, pp. 281–307.
42. Palli 1983, pp. 207–216.
43. Plakans 1975b, pp. 2–35; Plakans 1983, pp. 167–206.
44. Plakans 1983, pp. 167–206.
45. Visniauskaite 1971, pp. 369–377; Conze 1940, pp. 31–39.
46. Conze 1940, p. 122.
47. Mitterauer and Kagan 1990, pp. 147–190; Czap 1982, pp. 5–26.
48. Czap 1982, pp. 5–26.
49. Wagner 1994, pp. 232–233.
50. Czap 1982, p. 20.
51. Plakans 1975b, p. 27.
52. Mitterauer and Kagan 1990, pp. 178–182.
53. Ibid.
54. Plakans 1983, pp. 200–210.
55. Mitterauer and Kagan 1990, pp. 163–165.
56. Glatzer and Bollig 1983, pp. 307–325; Campbell 1976; Kaser 1995, pp. 63–66.
57. Revesz 1976, pp. 164–166; Andorka and Faragó 1983, p. 282; Palli 1971, pp. 205–219; Czap 1982, p. 7.
58. Kaser 1995, pp. 233–257.
59. Ibid.
60. Ibid., pp. 180–182.
61. Ibid., pp. 176–178.
62. Shinn 1961, pp. 601–621.

CHAPTER 3

1. For overviews, see Kriedte et al. 1981; Mendels 1984; Clarkson 1985; Ogilvie and Cerman 1996.
2. Pfister 1996, pp. 75–81.
3. Mendels 1972; Medick 1976; Levine 1977; Braun 1978, 1990; Kriedte et al. 1981; Levine et al. 1984.
4. Levine 1977, pp. 61–64; Wrigley et al. 1997, pp. 128–139, 183–187.
5. Braun 1990, p. 42.
6. Pfister 1992b, pp. 210–214; Kriedte et al. 1993, pp. 219–226; Ogilvie and Cerman 1996, pp. 9, 228–229.
7. Lehning 1980, pp. 67–70; Gutmann and Leboutte 1984; Ebeling and Klein 1988, pp. 34–38; Schlumbohm 1994, pp. 99–108; Ogilvie 1997, pp. 242–251.
8. Merzario 1989, pp. 160–162.
9. Gullickson 1986, pp. 138–144; Merzario 1989, pp. 167–172.
10. Schlumbohm 1983.
11. Kussmaul 1990, pp. 7–11, 27, ch. 6; Fitz 1985, pp. 102–104; Göbel 1988, pp. 207–219; for the general argument cf. Kriedte et al. 1981, p. 91; for contrary evidence see Ogilvie 1997, pp. 251–254.
12. Pfister 1994a, pp. 77–81.
13. Braun 1990, pp. 139–141.
14. See especially Mendels 1972, pp. 249–253; Gutmann 1987, pp. 168–170; Pfister 1989b, pp. 646–653.
15. For a typology of population growth in proto-industrial regions see Pfister 1992b, pp. 210–214.
16. Mager 1982, pp. 437, 442–446, 462; Schlumbohm 1994, pp. 152–160; Merzario 1989, p. 160.
17. Cf. Pfister 1992b, pp. 202–210 for a theoretical statement of the following relationships; for a survey of the literature, cf. Kriedte et al. 1993, pp. 226–232.
18. Pfister 1992a, pp. 387–388.
19. Lehning 1980, pp. 40–42; Claverie and Lamaison 1981, p. 212; Schlumbohm 1982, pp. 324–329; Medick 1983, pp. 288–290, 1996, pp. 191–205; Terrier 1996, pp. 139–141; Ogilvie 1997, pp. 281–282; for the interpretation of the results of Lehning and Medick, cf. Pfister 1992b, pp. 228, notes 6 and 7.
20. Ogilvie 1990, pp. 86–97, 1997, pp. 64, 303, 353.
21. Schlumbohm 1982, pp. 325–330.
22. Pfister 1992a, pp. 286–289.
23. Schlumbohm 1982, pp. 319–321, 1994, pp. 69–72.
24. Medick 1976, pp. 301–303; Kriedte et al. 1981, ch. 2.
25. Ogilvie 1997, pp. 281–288.
26. Derived from Ogilvie 1997, p. 265.

27. Levine 1977, pp. 48–50; Wall 1986, pp. 275–276; Pfister 1989a, pp. 95–97, 1992a, pp. 324–325, 387–389.
28. See, for instance, Ogilvie 1997, pp. 267–268, 294–296.
29. Pfister 1992a, pp. 310–313.
30. Wall 1987, pp. 84–87.
31. Ogilvie 1990, pp. 86–89.
32. Mitterauer 1986, p. 232.
33. Gaunt 1978, p. 251, Lehning 1980, pp. 105–110; Collins 1982, p. 134; Mitterauer 1986, p. 237.
34. Pfister 1992a, pp. 298–303.
35. Merzario 1989, pp. 163–165, 167, 173–175.
36. Ogilvie 1997, pp. 296–299; for similar results, see Levine 1977, pp. 50–52; Fitz 1985, pp. 142–145; Schlumbohm 1994, pp. 264, 281–285; cf. also Medick 1976, pp. 307–308.
37. Medick 1976, pp. 304–305; Kriedte et al. 1981, ch. 2.
38. Tilly and Scott 1978, chs 4–6.
39. Wall 1986, pp. 263–266.
40. Collins 1982, pp. 133–134.
41. Merzario 1989, pp. 169–170; Pfister 1992a, pp. 374–376.
42. Saito 1981, pp. 642–650; Wall 1986, pp. 275–276; Braun 1990, p. 141; Pfister 1989a, p. 93; for the general argument cf. Medick 1976, pp. 310–312.
43. Hufton 1975, pp. 14–17; Wall 1987, pp. 94–97; Pfister 1989a, pp. 92–96.
44. Wall 1986, p. 278.
45. Thompson 1967, pp. 71–72; Quataert 1985.
46. Gullickson 1986, pp. 101–102; Pfister 1992a, pp. 262–263.
47. Braun 1990, pp. 55–59.
48. Examples include Gaunt 1978, pp. 251–252; Braun 1990, pp. 134–135; Pfister 1992a, pp. 394–395; Medick 1996, pp. 218–224 and *passim*; for a theoretical discussion of the threat of departure, see Hirschman 1970.
49. Gullickson 1991.
50. Pfister 1989a, 1992a, pp. 315–365, 387–389.

51. Medick 1976, pp. 303–305; Kriedte et al. 1981, ch. 3; Braun 1990, pp. 43–47.
52. King 1998, pp. 137–139, 149–150.
53. Medick 1976, p. 305; Kriedte et al. 1981, ch. 3; Levine et al. 1984, pp. 39–41, 97–99. This perspective draws heavily on Chayanov's (1966) analysis of the peasant economy.
54. For the following, see Pfister 1992b, pp. 220–222; cf. also Ghez and Becker 1975; Modigliani 1980.
55. Pfister 1992a, pp. 370–374; Hendrickx 1997, pp. 194–196, 199–204.
56. Medick 1996, p. 222 and *passim*; Terrier 1996, pp. 122–138; Pfister 1994a, pp. 75–77; 1994b, pp. 10–12.
57. Pfister 1992a, pp. 348–349, 374–377.
58. Ibid., pp. 380–386, 1994b, pp. 10–12; cf. Braun 1990, pp. 64–83.
59. Pfister 1992a, p. 369; for the general argument, cf. Medick 1976, p. 306.

CHAPTER 4

1. Kornhauser 1993, pp. 63–111.
2. Murray 1984.
3. An exception is the special issue of the journal *Continuity and Change* (6, part 3) on "Legal Systems and Family Systems: Jack Goody Revisited."
4. Mitterauer and Seider 1982, pp. 2–3.
5. Saller 1986, pp. 7–22.
6. Ibid., pp. 54–59; see also Flandrin 1976.
7. It is prudent not to footnote such a remark.
8. The medieval and early modern equivalent of private international law, the law governing international commerce.
9. See cases in which manorial courts in England determined whether a couple was validly married, in Poos and Bonfield 1998.
10. The vitality of the laws on blasphemy were tested in the late 1980s by opponents of the sale of Salman Rushdie's *Satanic Verses* in the UK.

11. See for example Cailisse 1969, pp. 533–537, and Brissaud 1912, pp. 82–86.

12. We must remember that by our period there was a division in Christendom between the Roman Church and the Eastern Orthodox Church. In a number of respects, both the theological and the institutional structures of the two Churches differed. More attention will be given to the Roman Church in this chapter, because it held sway over a larger segment of Christian Europe, and during our period its theology and structure underwent significant changes affecting family law due to the Reformation. Moreover, in the Eastern Church, the use of vernacular language (rather than the unifying Latin of the Roman Church) in liturgy and in theology led to a variety of differences amongst churches in various nations of Eastern Europe. For a more detailed account of the diversity of the Slavic states, see Levin 1989.

13. Tabuteau 1988, pp. 223–229.

14. Saller 1986, pp. 7–9.

15. Kaser 1984, pp. 354–356; Jolowicz and Nicholas 1972, pp. 242–255.

16. For a summary of a recent case in Lincolnshire, see *The Times*, London, July 20, 1995.

17. Brundage 1995, p. 5.

18. For a detailed exposition of the effect that the Christianization of Europe had upon the law of the family in the West see Goody 1983.

19. The description of canon law set out herein largely refers to the law of the Roman Church. The Eastern Orthodox Church developed its own authorities. Levin 1989, p. 26.

20. For a more detailed exposition, see Brundage 1995.

21. Levin 1989, p. 23.

22. See generally, Donahue 1983, pp. 144–158 and 1992, pp. 338–366.

23. For England, see for example, Ingram 1987; and Brundage 1987, pp. 300–314, 341, 517–536.

24. Outhwaite 1995.

25. The literature analyzing the logic of these principles established by Pope Alexander III is the subject of considerable academic debate. See, amongst others, Donahue 1976, p. 252.

26. Brundage 1987, pp. 331–337.

27. Pollock and Maitland 1968, pp. 368–369.

28. Donahue 1992 and Helmholz 1974.

29. In Eastern Orthodox theology, consummation was not required for a valid marriage to be formed. Nor was non-consummation grounds for annulment.

30. Donahue 1976.

31. The canon law of the Eastern Orthodox Church required parental consent. Marriages in Russia seem, by West European standards, more likely to be arranged. Levin 1989, pp. 90–95.

32. Smith 1986.

33. An encyclical of 1059 forbade marriages within the seventh degree of kinship. Precisely how the degrees were to be calculated was a matter of controversy, until the "germanic" method was adopted in the twelfth century. For an elaborate discussion see Goody 1983, pp. 134–146.

34. Even spiritual kinship created a bar to marriage. An individual was not only forbidden to marry those within the prohibited degrees by virtue of blood or by marriage, but might not marry those within the prohibited degrees of his or her godparents.

35. For a discussion of the effects of the extension of the prohibited degrees, see ibid.

36. Given the dearth of priests in some parts of Eastern Europe, it is likely that other ceremonies were sufficient to create a recognized marriage. But by the sixteenth century, such mar-

riages were less secure. Levin 1989, pp. 84–88.

37. Brundage 1987, pp. 442–444.

38. For a summary of the "Protestant" view, see Ozment 1983, pp. 25–49.

39. Robisheaux 1989, pp. 98–99.

40. Ozment 1983, pp. 39–40.

41. Ibid., p. 40.

42. Ibid., pp. 44–49.

43. Robisheaux 1989, pp. 95–99.

44. Ibid., p. 105.

45. Ozment 1983, pp. 38–41.

46. Robisheaux 1989, pp. 107–110.

47. Ozment 1983, pp. 41–44.

48. Ibid.

49. Ibid.; Stone 1977.

50. Cailisse 1969, pp. 538–555.

51. Ibid., pp. 553–554.

52. Brissaud 1912, p. 107.

53. Ibid., 108.

54. With the exception of a brief period during the Interregnum.

55. For a detailed discussion, see Outhwaite 1995.

56. 26 Geo. II, c. 33.

57. Gerber 1994.

58. Starr 1992, pp. 4–5.

59. MacNeill 1967, pp. 244, 337–338.

60. Transfers from groom to bride upon marriage were not unknown in Christendom; the morning gift in Anglo-Saxon England is an example, as was the later institution of pin money, in which the groom undertook to pay a yearly sum to his wife.

61. Jennings 1975, pp. 75–80.

62. See, for example, the important study by Goody, *Production and Reproduction* (1976).

63. For a discussion of the marriage settlement process in England, see Bonfield 1982.

64. Marsot 1995, pp. 33–34.

65. El-Nahal 1979, pp. 44–45.

66. Rheinstein 1972, pp. 196–197.

67. The much remarked upon text "What therefore God has joined together let no man put asunder" is from Matthew 19: 3–9. Professor Brundage argues that Jesus did not

prohibit divorce entirely; he wished only to limit the circumstances in which divorce might be sanctioned. St. Paul took a less tolerant view. 1987, p. 58.

68. For a discussion of the law with commentary on the sources, see Hunter 1994, pp. 509–514.

69. Brundage 1987, pp. 53–54.

70. Hunter 1994, p. 508.

71. Ibid., pp. 199–205, 243–245.

72. Ibid., pp. 370–376.

73. R. H. Helmholz (1974) has found that less than 20 percent of the instances of marriage litigation he studied were actions to annul marriages. For the continental evidence, see Phillips 1991, pp. 5–7.

74. The odd case in which divorce was permitted is noted ibid., pp. 509–511.

75. Noonan.

76. Brundage 1987, p. 344.

77. Phillips 1991, pp. 14–18.

78. Ozment 1983, p. 93.

79. Phillips 1991, pp. 13–20.

80. Stone 1990, pp. 303–308.

81. For examples see the case studies in Stone 1993.

82. Phillips 1991 discussing Canon VII, p. 12.

83. For a more detailed account of developments in French law after the Council of Trent, see Traer 1980, pp. 31–47.

84. Stoljar 1989, pp. 139–140.

85. Phillips 1991, p. 55.

86. Ibid.

87. Ibid., pp. 53–54.

88. Ibid., pp. 49–50.

89. Levin 1989, pp. 114–121.

90. Brundage 1987, pp. 513–514.

91. Levin 1989, pp. 105–114.

92. El-Nahal 1979, pp. 46–47.

93. Jennings 1975, pp. 82–87.

94. For the argument for England, see Macfarlane 1982.

95. For a summary discussion see Flandrin 1976, pp. 71–78.

96. In England, for example, although the predominant inheritance custom

was that of male primogeniture, there were local variations. The most notable was that of the county of Kent where according to the custom of gavelkind, lands held by a particular form of tenure (socage) descended in equal shares amongst all sons, or if the holder died without male issue, passed in equal shares to all daughters. See generally, Simpson 1986, pp. 57–62.

97. Ladurie 1976, pp. 37–70.

98. For a discussion see Cooper 1976, pp. 196–197.

99. Ibid., pp. 233–305.

100. For early modern England, see Bonfield 1984, pp. 653–658.

101. In contrast with Christianity, the Qur'an set out the right of women, albeit unequal to that of men, to inherit property. Accordingly, a man inherited a whole part of an ancestor's property, a woman a half-share. This inequality in shares was explained by the fact that a woman was free to deal with her own inheritance, while a man was required to support his family with his. Some commentators have regarded the more expansive obligation assumed by men as the source of Qur'an-sanctioned male dominance: men are the guardians of women and of the family. Marsot 1995, p. 9.

102. Ozment 1983, pp. 152–154.

103. By landed families I mean larger landowners who lived primarily off the rent generated by their estates. In different parts of Europe, the income and social stature of the landed class might vary. English historians use the term "gentry" to signify landed families who are not members of the aristocracy; the gentry was not a legally defined class, while the aristocracy was. While such nuances might differ elsewhere in Europe, the term "landed class" is used to signify the greater landholders, and peasantry (and yeomanry for England) is

employed to describe the holder/occupier of land.

104. For a discussion see Bonfield 1982.

105. For a different view of the operation of strict settlement, see Spring 1993.

106. Bonfield 1986b, pp. 155–176.

107. See for example, cases in Poos and Bonfield 1997.

108. For a summary, see my "Introduction" to Bonfield 1992, pp. 7–11.

109. Feenstra, ibid., pp. 37–53.

110. Godding, ibid., pp. 15–36.

111. Bellomo, Romano, and Zorzoli: all ibid.

112. Calvero, ibid., pp. 215–254.

113. Kagan 1981, pp. 25–28.

114. The approach of the nobility in Burgundy, where more equal distributions of property were effected mostly by use of testament, exhibits many of the same tensions between providing for an heir, and distributing property amongst all children that occurred in England. See Petitjean 1992.

115. For an example of marriage contracts in eighteenth-century France, see Forster and Forster, pp. 274–284.

116. Rebel 1983, pp. 175–178.

117. This issue is discussed for France by Ladurie 1974, pp. 95–97. For England, see Spufford 1974.

118. Wrightson and Levine 1979, p. 99.

119. Robisheaux 1989, pp. 123–128.

120. Kagan 1981, pp. 25–28, 80–84, 259.

121. Handley 1994.

122. See generally, Baker 1990, pp. 550–557.

123. McIntosh 1986, pp. 170–176; Bennett 1987, pp. 104–114.

124. See generally, Erickson 1993.

125. Ibid., ch. 7.

126. Kagan 1981, ch. 3.

127. Handley 1994, pp. 121–123.

128. Degler 1978.

129. Ibid., p. 236.

130. Jennings 1975, pp. 63–67.

131. Marsot 1995, pp. 54–65.

132. El-Nahal 1979, pp. 49–50; Jennings 1975, pp. 89–91. By way of contrast, women in Castile (with the exception

of widows) were not permitted to bring suit without a male representative. Kagan 1981, p. 10.

133. Jennings 1975, pp. 58–59, 71. Although women were underrepresented as litigants in Ottoman courts, ranging from about 10 to 25 percent, depending upon the court studied. The women who did appear in court frequently did so because their "male protector" (father or husband) had died. Inheritance claims were those most frequently pursued. Zarinebaf-Shahr 1996.

134. Houlbrooke 1984, pp. 102–110; for a recent study of inter-spousal relationships in individual families see Larminie 1995, pp. 78–92.

135. Earle 1989, pp. 160–174.

136. Ericson 1993, pp. 158–162. Wrightson and Levine 1979, pp. 99–100.

CHAPTER 5

1. Harrington 1995, pp. 25–47.
2. Bels 1968, p. 78.
3. Wiesner 1993, p. 22.
4. Bucer, *De Regno Christi* (n. 61), cap. 18; quoted in Carlson 1994, p. 76.
5. Bels 1968, p. 78; Esmein 1929–1935, vol. 2, pp. 144–145.
6. Köhler 1932–1942; Phillips 1988, pp. 62, 64; Roper 1989, pp. 69–70; Watt 1992, pp. 50–53.
7. Seeger 1989, p. 24; Watt 1994, p. 246.
8. Glendon 1980, pp. 103–104; Harrington 1995, pp. 103–104, 273–278; Watt 1992, pp. 261–278.
9. Brundage 1987, p. 356; Ozment 1983, pp. 44–45; Viollet 1905, pp. 428–430.
10. Goody 1983, pp. 181–182; Ozment 1983, pp. 45–46. Luther was not altogether consistent on the question of impediments. On one occasion, he maintained that first cousins could marry and that a man could marry the sister of his deceased wife or fiancée; elsewhere, he declared these marriages prohibited.

11. Harrington 1995, p. 86; Safley 1984, p. 32; Watt 1992, pp. 43–44.
12. Esmein 1929–1935, vol. 1, pp. 28, 100–101; Helmholz 1974, pp. 26–27; Viollet 1905, p. 445.
13. Brundage 1987, pp. 146, 433; Esmein 1929–1935, vol. 2, pp. 56–57, 106; Helmholz 1974, p. 100; Phillips 1988, pp. 13–14.
14. Phillips 1988, p. 90.
15. Ibid., pp. 93–94.
16. Ibid., p. 86.
17. Brundage 1987, pp. 334, 374; Phillips 1988, p. 91.
18. Phillips 1988, pp. 48, 53–57, 62–63.
19. Ibid., pp. 69–71.
20. Ibid., pp. 50, 62.
21. Harrington 1995, pp. 269–270; Köhler 1932–1942, vol. 1, p. 413; Roper 1989, p. 158; Safley 1984, p. 167; Seeger 1989, p. 417; Staehelin 1957, pp. 181–198; Watt 1992, p. 123.
22. Davis 1983, p. 33.
23. Archives de l'Etat de Neuchâtel (hereafter AEN), Justice Matrimoniale de Neuchâtel 2: 192v–193, 211, 215.
24. Seeger 1989, pp. 423–424; Watt 1992, pp. 128–129.
25. Harrington 1995, pp. 226–227; Kingdon 1995, p. 183; Köhler 1932–1942, vol. 1, p. 109; Monter 1980, p. 195; Pittard 1946, pp. 31–34; Roper 1989, p. 198; Safley 1984, p. 175; Staehelin 1957, pp. 181–198; Watt 1992, pp. 130–131.
26. Harrington 1995, p. 269, n. 217; Safley 1984, p. 142; Staehelin 1957, pp. 181–198; Watt 1992, pp. 121–124.
27. Darmon 1979, p. 91.
28. Ibid., p. 29; Watt 1992, p. 136.
29. AEN, Consistoire de Valangin (hereafter CSV) 1: 46.
30. Lambert and Watt 1996, pp. 104–105.
31. Roper 1989, p. 188. Safley 1984, pp. 137–139, 142, found 19 cases from sixteenth-century Basel in which abuse was cited as a ground for divorce. Among those examples he provides, however, the *Ehegericht*

awarded divorces only when abuse was accompanied by adultery. In such decisions, the infidelity almost certainly played a more important role than abuse.

32. Blaisdell 1982, p. 71; 1988, pp. 242–244.

33. Seeger 1989, pp. 420–421, 441–442.

34. Phillips 1988, pp. 87, 89–90.

35. The Reformation also produced no significant changes concerning the remarriage of widows. In the early Middle Ages, the Roman Catholic Church strongly discouraged second marriages. Eventually, however, the Church at least tolerated such second marriages and, borrowing a practice from Roman law, prescribed a minimum waiting period (usually nine months) following the death of the spouse before one could remarry. Protestants continued this practice, although the courts rarely enforced the waiting period either before or after the Reformation. Evidence indicates that, for social and economic reasons, both Protestants and Catholics often remarried soon after their spouses' deaths without incurring the wrath of judicial authorities. A high percentage of widows and widowers remarried within six months of a spouse's death in sixteenth- and seventeenth-century France, for example; Flandrin 1979, pp. 115–116; Harrington 1995, p. 242; Safley 1984, p. 24; Watt 1992, p. 159, n. 83.

36. Houlbrooke 1985, pp. 83, 348; Ingram 1987, p. 366; Roper 1989, p. 160; Safley 1984, pp. 170–173; Watt 1992, pp. 58, 113–114.

37. Carlson 1994, pp. 130–131.

38. See Gennep 1960, pp. 132–133; Watt 1992, pp. 65–69.

39. AEN, CSV 3: 268, 272, 274.

40. One notable difference was that abandoned fiancés were not required to wait as long as spouses to be released from their engagements.

According to Genevan marriage laws, while abandoned spouses might have to wait ten years to obtain a divorce, women whose fiancés left the country for legitimate reasons had to wait only one year to be freed from their engagements. There was no fixed delay for men whose fiancées had left the country for whatever reason, nor for women whose fiancés had maliciously abandoned them before the wedding; Watt 1992, p. 72, n. 35.

41. Ibid., p. 199. Protestants in some areas did alter their stance on betrothal during the course of the Reformation period. In 1612, six years before the Quarthier/Milliods case in Valangin, the reformed churches in France decided that betrothal was not a binding marriage promise; Mentzer 1991, p. 175.

42. Ingram 1987, p. 197; Mitchison and Leneman 1989, p. 100; Phillips 1988, p. 31; Segalen 1981, p. 11; Watt 1992, pp. 91–92, 97.

43. Brundage 1982, p. 18; Goody 1976a, p. 14; Schama 1988, pp. 405–406.

44. Carlson 1994; Ingram 1987.

45. Harrington 1995, p. 61.

46. Ibid., p. 245.

47. Ibid., pp. 162–166.

48. Stone 1977, pp. 180–193.

49. Watt 1992, p. 63.

50. Houlbrooke 1979, pp. 62–64; Roper 1989, pp. 156–157; Watt 1992, pp. 83–87.

51. AEN, CSV 1: 72r–v.

52. Ingram 1987, pp. 200–201, 203–204, 210; Robisheaux 1989, pp. 105–116; Schama 1988, pp. 441–442; Watt 1992, pp. 62–63.

53. Kingdon 1998.

54. Strauss 1978, p. 4.

55. Cunningham 1995, pp. 49–50; Ozment 1983, pp. 170–172; Sommerville 1990, p. 101; Strauss 1978, p. 163; Watt 1993, p. 432.

56. Ozment 1983, p. 134.

57. Sommerville 1990, pp. 102–103.

58. Ibid., pp. 125–129; quotation from p. 129.
59. Cunningham 1990, p. 48; Schnucker 1990, pp. 108–121; Sommerville 1990, p. 129.
60. Sommerville 1990, pp. 130–133.
61. Cunningham 1995, p. 51.
62. Sommerville 1990, pp. 104–105.
63. Ibid., pp. 104–105.
64. Strauss 1978, pp. 1–28, 123–131, 202; Wiesner 1993, pp. 121–122.
65. Cunningham 1995, pp. 59–61; Sommerville 1990, pp. 108–111. Cf. Ariès 1962, pp. 137–336.
66. Wiesner 1993, pp. 122–123.
67. Safley 1984, pp. 1, 185, 195.
68. Watt 1992, pp. 100, 105. In prosecuting illicit sexuality, most Protestant magistrates did not share the zeal of those in certain Reformed areas. In sixteenth-century Valangin, the Consistory was known to punish couples who were already married but had engaged in sexual relations before the wedding; AEN, CSV 1: 41v–42v.
69. Graham 1996, pp. 286–289; Harrington 1995, pp. 239, 255; Kingdon 1995, p. 179; Watt 1992, pp. 106–107.
70. Otis 1985, pp. 40–45; Roper 1989, pp. 104–108; Wiesner 1986, p. 101.
71. Harrington 1995, p. 251.
72. Kertzer 1993, pp. 18–19.
73. Ibid., pp. 10, 12, 16–17; Watt 1992, pp. 102–104.
74. Ferrante 1990, pp. 46–72.
75. Cavalla and Cerutti 1990, pp. 73–109. By the eighteenth century, in Italy men were actually protected from being identified publicly as the fathers of illegitimate children; Kertzer 1993, pp. 17, 60.
76. Kertzer 1993, p. 19.
77. Ibid., pp. 27–28.
78. Harrington 1995, p. 251; Kertzer 1993, pp. 20, 138–144.
79. Wiesner 1993, p. 21.
80. *Dr. Martin Luthers Sämmtliche Werke*, ed. Ernst Ludwig, Johann Georg Plochmann, and Johann Conrad Irmischer (Erlangen and Frankfurt: Heyder & Zimmer, 1826–1857), vol. 20, p. 84, quoted in Wiesner 1993, p. 9.
81. "Predigt am 2. Sonntag nach Ephiphanias" on 1 Peter 3: 7 (1524), in *D. Martin Luthers Werke: Kritische Gesamtausgabe* (Weimar: Hermann Bohlaus Nachfolger, repr. 1964–1968), vol. 15, pp. 419–420, quoted in Harrington 1995, p. 72.
82. Harrington 1995, p. 72.
83. Ibid., pp. 73–84; Wiesner 1993, p. 24. The religious turmoil associated with the Reformation may well have nurtured growing misogyny, contributing to the unprecedented mass witch trials of the late sixteenth and early seventeenth centuries. Of the tens of thousands of people who were tried for witchcraft, roughly half of whom were executed, probably 80 percent were women. In the Middle Ages, women had been singled out as adherents to heretical groups, some of which allowed them to play more active religious roles than did the Roman Catholic Church hierarchy. And some of the Reformation's radical sects allowed greater female participation, providing ammunition for Catholic, Lutheran, and Reformed authorities who associated women with religious deviance. Both Protestant and Catholic theologians and leaders sought to reform popular religious practices and took special aim at those which they considered forms of witchcraft. Sixteenth-century thinkers continued to embrace the medieval belief that women were more lustful than men. In the Reformation era more than ever before, religious and lay leaders conceived of witchcraft in sexual terms, believing that witches participated in orgies with the devil. Women were believed to be especially prone to make pacts with the devil, and misogynistic elements were

quite prominent in campaigns against popular religion; Klaits 1985, pp. 58–59, 70–72.

84. The office of deaconess did exist in at least one Reformed community, the town of Wesel along the Rhine. Entrusted with care for the sick and poor, deaconesses were elected from 1568 until the early seventeenth century, when the elections apparently died out; Olson 1989, pp. 81–82.

85. Watt 1993, pp. 433–434; Wiesner 1993, pp. 192–195.

86. Cohen 1989, pp. 166–188; Marshall 1989, pp. 120–139; Schama 1988, p. 404; Willen 1989, pp. 140–165.

87. Wiesner 1993, pp. 196–197, 213.

88. Davis 1986, pp. 167–197; Howell 1986.

89. Jacobsen 1989, pp. 54, 57; Karant-Nunn 1989, p. 43.

90. Safley 1984, pp. 173, 180. Roper 1989, p. 203, argues that the Augsburg city council did offer more protection to married women than ever before; in so doing, however, these Protestant magistrates were acting in a paternalistic manner, based on the idea of wifely subordination, which mirrored a real loss of status for women.

91. Carlson 1994, pp. 112–113; Houlbrooke 1985, p. 342; Mitchison and Leneman 1989, p. 89; Watt 1992, p. 98. The majority of plaintiffs to contract disputes were women, however, in Reformation Augsburg, Basel, and Constance; Roper 1989, p. 160; Safley 1984, p. 173.

CHAPTER 6

1. Meuvret 1946, 1965.
2. Meuvret 1965, p. 507.
3. Dupâquier 1997, pp. 241–245.
4. Pfister 1997, pp. 519–520.
5. Galloway 1988.
6. Lunn 1991, p. 137.
7. Livi Bacci 1987; Walter and Schofield 1989, pp. 17–21; Perrenoud 1997, pp. 298–300.

8. Biraben, 1975, p. 197.
9. Hollingsworth and Hollingsworth 1971, p. 144.
10. Biraben 1975, pp. 218–225; Del Panta 1980, pp. 41–48.
11. Hansen 1979.
12. Flinn 1974, p. 317; Sonnino 1996, pp. 84–85.
13. Calvi 1984, p. 21.
14. Chiappa Mauri 1994.
15. Wrigley and Schofield 1981, pp. 234–236.
16. Ibid., pp. 236–248.
17. Andorka 1995, p. 130.
18. Bruneel 1977, pp. 368–371; Pérez Moreda 1980, pp. 146–154; Vandenbroeke et al. 1983; Imhof 1990; Sonnino 1996, pp. 85–88; Reher 1997, pp. 122–123.
19. Houdaille 1984, pp. 87–90.
20. Wrigley et al. 1997, pp. 268–280.
21. For Germany see Knodel 1988, pp. 35–69, and Imhof 1990; for Scandinavia, see Turpeinen 1979, Lithell 1981, Brändström 1993, Moring 1998.
22. Ransel 1991.
23. Turpeinen 1979, p. 14; Lithell 1981, p. 183.
24. Matthews Grieco 1991, pp. 16–19.
25. Lithell 1981, p. 189; Ransel 1991, p. 119.
26. Reher 1988, p. 108.
27. Viazzo 1994a; Kytir et al. 1995.
28. Dobson 1997, pp. 167–174.
29. Landers 1993, 1996.
30. Hollingsworth 1977, pp. 325–328; Woods et al. 1993, pp. 35–39.
31. Galliano 1966, p. 139; Houdaille 1980, p. 94; Sussman 1982, pp. 101–188.
32. Laslett 1971, p. 106.
33. Smith 1977, p. 23
34. Hajnal 1965; Bonnain 1986, p. 119; Viazzo 1989.
35. Wrigley et al. 1997, pp. 477–494.
36. Knodel 1988; Lithell 1981, p. 191.
37. Garden 1975, pp. 46–84.
38. Hunecke 1989, p. 307.

39. Corsini 1974; Bideau et al. 1988, p. 373.
40. Garden 1975, p. 63; Bideau et al. 1994, p. 164.
41. Houdaille 1984, p. 91.
42. Wrigley et al. 1997, p. 355.
43. Netting 1981, pp. 129–168.
44. Lesthaeghe 1992, pp. 277–279.
45. Livi Bacci 1986; Perrenoud 1990.
46. For Glarus, see Head 1988; for the Trans-Danube area see Andorka 1971 and Vasary 1989.
47. Bideau et al. 1988, pp. 373–398 (the passage from Moheau is quoted on p. 397).
48. Henry and Houdaille 1978, 1979.
49. Langer 1972, p. 98.
50. Hoffer and Hull 1981.
51. Wrightson 1982a, pp. 14–15.
52. Hunecke 1991.
53. On England, see Laslett and Oosterveen 1973 and Adair 1996; on the general tendency in Europe, see Flinn 1981, pp. 118–120.
54. The theory of the "first sexual revolution" supported by Shorter 1975, is criticized by Mitterauer 1983, pp. 86–113.
55. Meyer 1980, p. 252.
56. The quotation is taken from Viazzo et al. 1997, p. 182. On the geography of abandonment and on the widely differing attitudes to illegitimacy see Hunecke 1991, pp. 56–61, Kertzer 1993, pp. 71–102, and Valverde 1994.
57. Hunecke 1991, pp. 56–61; Da Molin 1993, pp. 77-78; Pérez-Moreda 1996, pp. 8–9; Sá 1996.
58. Fildes 1988, pp. 159–189; Ransel 1988, pp. 45–50.
59. Pérez Moreda 1996, p. 7.
60. Knodel and De Vos 1980; Wall 1981a; Weir 1983, pp. 143–150; Gavitt 1996.
61. Hunecke 1991, pp. 46–47; Kertzer 1993, pp. 110–112.
62. Wrigley et al. 1997, pp. 299–300.
63. Henry 1987, pp. 97–104.
64. Bardet et al. 1981; Gutierrez and Houdaille 1983; Schofield 1986;

Knodel 1988, pp. 102–115; Vandenbroeke 1991; Wrigley et al. 1997, pp. 307–323.
65. Bruneel 1977; Benigno 1996.
66. Davis 1973, pp. 94–95; Benigno 1996, pp. 295–296.
67. Imhof 1981; Shorter 1982.
68. Bideau 1986; Henry 1987, pp. 106–111.
69. Benigno 1996, p. 280.
70. Perrenoud 1981, pp. 327–328; Brändström 1988.
71. Livi Bacci 1987, pp. 90–93.
72. Dobson 1997, pp. 172–183.
73. Perrenoud 1997, p. 300.
74. Hollingsworth 1977, p. 328; Houdaille 1992, p. 15.
75. Livi Bacci 1987, p. 93.
76. Wrigley 1978; Smith and Oeppen 1993, pp. 296–298.
77. For the "Mediterranean" population an average age of marriage has been suggested of 20 years for the women and 30 for the men and a life expectancy at birth of 25 years (Saller 1994, pp. 132–142); for the two English populations the simulations are based on empirical estimates of an average age for the first marriage of 24 for women and 26 for men, and for both a life expectancy of 36.2 years for the sixteenth century and 38.6 for the eighteenth (Smith and Oeppen 1993, p. 290).
78. Ben-Amos 1994, pp. 48–54.
79. Baulant 1972, pp. 967–968; Laslett 1977, p. 166; Mayhew 1991, pp. 217–219; Ben-Amos 1994, pp. 58–67; Viazzo 1994b, pp. 34–38.
80. Baulant 1972, pp. 961–963; Fontaine 1995, pp. 141–142; Fauve-Chamoux 1996.
81. Pullan 1989, pp. 19–20.
82. Fauve-Chamoux 1996, p. 9.

CHAPTER 7

1. Chavarria 1988; Fletcher 1994; Gouge 1622; Logan 1994; Ozment 1983.

2. De Mause 1974; O'Day 1994; Pollock 1983; Stone 1977.

3. Grubb 1996, ch. 2; Houlbrooke 1984, ch. 6; Hufton 1996, ch. 5; Kuchowicz and Libiszowska 1982; McLaren 1984; Ozment 1983, ch. 3; Pollock 1990; Strauss 1978, p. 91.

4. De Mause 1974, p. 34; Flandrin 1984, pp. 195–198.

5. Farge 1993, p. 52; Fairchilds 1984, p. 194; Fildes 1988, chs 4–6; Lindemann 1981; Romano 1996, p. 241; Schnucker 1974; Senior 1983.

6. Newall 1990; Senior 1983; Wrightson 1982a.

7. Clark 1987; Fairchilds 1984, p. 196; Fildes 1988, ch. 6; Lindemann 1981; Motley 1990, pp. 25–27; Romano 1996, p. 165; Ross 1976, p. 189; Senior 1983.

8. Farge 1993, pp. 52–53; Sussman 1980.

9. Cohen 1986; Cunningham 1995, p. 42; Fairchilds 1984, pp. 198–201; Houlbrooke 1984, p. 146; Motley 1990, ch. 1; Ransel 1991; Raeff 1966, p. 123; Schama 1988, pp. 538, 541–544, citing Pollock 1987, p. 73.

10. Flinn 1981, pp. 16–17; Kuchowicz and Libiszowska 1982; Riley 1989; Ransel 1991; Schama 1988, p. 521. Quote from Motley 1990, p. 28.

11. Martinson 1992, p. 18; Morel 1983; Ozment 1983, pp. 121–126; 1986, pp. 96–101; Pollock 1987, pp. 107–115; Strauss 1978, p. 86.

12. Davis 1995, pp. 32, 57; MacDonald 1981, pp. 82–84; Marshall 1983, pp. 121–122; Martinson 1992, p. 22; Morel 1983; Pollock 1987, pp. 123–127; Ransel 1991; Schama 1988, pp. 517–521. Quote from Ozment 1986, p. 101.

13. Ben-Amos 1994, pp. 8–9; Kuchowicz and Libiszowska 1982; Mitterauer 1992, pp. 32–33; Motley 1990, ch. 1; Pollock 1996a; Strauss 1978, p. 96.

14. Brewer 1980; Ezell 1983; Gottlieb 1993, p. 143; Okenfuss 1980, p. 75; Pollock 1996a; Schnucker 1990.

15. Ben-Amos 1994, ch. 1; Griffiths 1996, ch. 1; Pollock 1996a.

16. Fletcher 1994; Hoch 1986, p. 181; Houlbrooke 1984, p. 141; Kuchowicz and Libiszowska 1982; Motley 1990, pp. 43–44; Ozment 1983, pp. 144–159; Pollock 1983, ch. 5; Roodenburg 1985; Schama 1988, p. 556; Schnucker 1990; Sommerville 1992, pp. 94–95; Tovrov 1978.

17. Houlbrooke 1984, pp. 144–145, 169; Hughes 1984; Mitterauer 1992, p. 32; Motley 1990, pp. 36, 42, 61; Pollock 1996a. Quote from Ozment 1986, p. 94.

18. Ago 1997; Ben-Amos 1994, pp. 232–234; Czap 1978; Logan 1994; Macfarlane 1986, ch. 7; Ozment 1983, pp. 38–40; Pollock 1987, pp. 247–248; Robisheaux 1981; Sabean 1990, p. 329; Tovrov 1978; Wrightson 1982b, pp. 71–79, 115–116.

19. Griffiths 1996, pp. 80–81; Macfarlane 1970, pp. 120–123; Ozment 1990, pp. 8–9, citing Fichtner 1989, p. 83.

20. Brewer 1980; Cohen 1986; Cunningham 1995, pp. 106–110; Hughes 1984; Levine and Wrightson 1991, pp. 321–329; Martinson 1992, pp. 18, 20, 48; Raeff 1966, p. 123; Roche 1983; Strauss 1978, p. 122.

21. Ben-Amos 1994, pp. 158–165; Houlbrooke 1984, p. 143. Quote from Pollock 1987, p. 57.

22. Brown, J. 1986; Charlton 1988; Fletcher 1994; Greaves 1983; Logan 1994; Motley 1990, pp. 53–55; Strauss 1978, pp. 4–8, 116–118, 123.

23. Charlton 1994; Houston 1983; Motley 1994; Wiesner 1993, p. 118. Quote from Spufford 1979, pp. 417–418.

24. Cressy 1977; Houston 1983; Pollock 1996b.

25. Levine and Wrightson 1991, pp. 324–327; Moriceau 1993; O'Day 1982, pp. 61, 125; Raeff 1966, pp. 111–119; Spufford 1974, pp. 193–199; Wallbank 1979, citing Spufford 1979, p. 415.

26. Bowden 1996; McMullen 1977; O'Day 1982, p. 185; Pollock 1989a; Wiesner 1993, pp. 119–123.

27. Kuchowicz and Libiszowska 1982; Motley 1994; Pollock 1989a; 1996a; Schlumbohm 1980.

28. Ago 1989; Cohen 1992; Fairchilds 1984, p. 204; Fletcher 1995, chs 15, 16; Motley, 1990, p. 47; Petschauer 1983; Pollock 1996a; Raeff 1966, pp. 128–147; Tovrov 1978.

29. Fletcher 1995, chs 18, 19; Motley 1990, pp. 50, 61; Pollock 1989a; Schama 1988, p. 511; Tovrov 1978.

30. Ben-Amos 1994, pp. 40–47; Cunningham 1990; 1995, pp. 86–86; Kuchowicz and Libiszowska 1982; Lundh 1995; Martinson 1992, pp. 79–81; Pfister 1989; Romano 1996, p. 152; Vassberg 1983.

31. Ben-Amos 1994, p. 40; Cunningham 1990; Rose 1989; Vassberg 1983.

32. Cunningham 1995, p. 88; Jordanova 1987.

33. Ben-Amos 1994, pp. 55, 158–159; Houlbrooke 1988, pp. 188–189; Lundh 1995; Mitterauer 1990a; Roche 1983; Wall 1987.

34. Kussmaul 1981, pp. 22–24, 26; Laslett 1977, pp. 29–35; Lundh 1995; Mitterauer 1990a; Romano 1996, pp. 153, 155–156; Seleski 1995; Wall 1987; Wiesner 1993, p. 93.

35. Arru 1990; Ben-Amos 1994, pp. 70–71; Guttormsson 1991; Kertzer 1989; Mayhew 1991; Mitterauer 1990a; Da Molin 1990; Romano 1996, pp. 155, 186.

36. Houlbrooke 1984, pp. 174, 177; Mitterauer and Sieder 1982, pp. 105, 107; Mitterauer 1990.

37. Hill 1981, ch. 3; Houlbrooke 1984, pp. 175–176; Maza 1983, ch. 4; Mitterauer and Sieder 1982, p. 105; Romano 1996, ch. 6; Rushton 1991; Seleski 1995; Smith 1977.

38. Brewer 1980; Goody 1976b; Hurwich 1993; Ladurie 1976; Pedlow 1982; Siddle 1986.

39. Bonfield 1986a; Derouet 1993; Garcia 1992; Spring 1993.

40. Farrow 1996; Garcia 1992; Lundh 1995; Wheaton 1980.

41. Farrow 1996; Hurwich 1993; Lundh 1995; Pedlow 1982; Rudolph 1992.

42. Collomp 1984; Cooper 1976; Cooper 1992; Farrow 1996; Garcia 1992; Houlbrooke 1984, ch. 9; Howell 1976; Lundh 1995; Siddle 1986; Spufford 1976; Wheaton 1980. Quote from Burguière and Lebrun 1996a, p. 65.

43. Macfarlane 1970, pp. 120–123; Sabean 1990, pp. 256, 298–300, 305, 322, 416–418; Wheaton 1980.

44. Collomp 1984; Fichtner 1989, pp. 66–67; Goody 1976b; Rudolph 1992; Sabean 1990, pp. 250–251; Segalen 1977; Wheaton 1980.

45. Collomp 1984; Macfarlane 1970, pp. 131–132; Rudolph 1992; Staves 1996; Stone 1977, pp. 115–116; Tadmor 1992, citing Slater 1984, pp. 34–35.

46. Ben-Amos 1994; Fairchilds 1984, pp. 68–69; Pollock 1989b; 1998. Quote from Macfarlane 1970, p. 131.

47. Ben-Amos 1994, pp. 53–54; Brodsky 1986; Charlton 1994; Collins 1991; Roche 1983; Schubnel 1985; Wrigley and Schofield 1981, p. 258.

48. Dos Guimarães Sá 1994; Kertzer 1993; Tilly et al. 1992; Ulbricht 1985.

49. Delasselle 1978; Kertzer 1993, p. 25; Sherwood 1988, p. 111; Viazzo 1991; Wilson 1989.

50. Delasselle 1978; Fildes 1990; Hufton 1974, pp. 321, 332; Kertzer 1993, pp. 172–173; Larquié 1985; Sherwood 1988, p. 115; Tilly et al. 1992; Valverde 1994; Wilson 1989.

51. Delasselle 1978; Fildes 1990; Kertzer 1993, p. 178; Wilson 1989. Quote from Gottlieb 1993, p. 142.

52. Hoffer and Hull 1981; Jackson 1996; Leboutte 1991; Malcolmson 1977; Schama 1988, pp. 459, 521; Wrightson 1982a.

53. De Mause 1974; Martini 1986; Pollock 1983, pp. 91–95; Schama 1988, p. 521.

54. Forbes 1986; Houlbrooke 1984, p. 139.
55. Cohen 1986; Dekker and Groenendijk 1991; Motley 1990, p. 67; Strauss 1978, p. 122; Wrightson 1982b, ch. 4.
56. Cunningham 1995, p. 61; Flandrin 1984, pp. 136, 154–155; Hughes 1984; Burguière and Lebrun 1996b; Plumb 1975; Ransel 1991; Strauss 1978, pp. 8, 88.

CHAPTER 8

1. Fauve-Chamoux 1988, 1995a.
2. Hajnal 1965, 1982, 1983.
3. Dupâquier et al. 1981; Dupâquier 1988.
4. Henry 1968.
5. Garden 1970; Fauve-Chamoux 1983, 1995b.
6. Eiras-Roel 1991.
7. Henry and Houdaille 1978.
8. Dupâquier 1979.
9. Perrenoud 1979.
10. Benedict 1991.
11. Ovidius 1929.
12. Garden 1970.
13. Knodel 1988; Möring 1996; Schlumbohm 1991.
14. Bonnain 1986.
15. Flinn 1981.
16. Head-König 1993.
17. Shorter 1974.
18. Lepecq de la Cloture 1778.
19. Goody 1983.
20. Héritier 1994.
21. Burguière 1996.
22. Gouesse 1986.
23. Murru-Corriga 1996.
24. Goody 1983.
25. Sauvain-Dugerdil 1990.
26. Pelissier 1996.
27. Dulong 1987.
28. Dupâquier 1979.
29. Diefendorf 1982; Goody et al. 1976; Klapisch-Zuber 1981; Lorcin 1981; Vassberg 1994; Wintjes 1982.
30. Kertzer and Laslett 1995.

31. Cabourdin 1981.
32. Boulton 1990.
33. Bideau 1980.
34. Fauve-Chamoux 1994, 1995b.
35. Fauve-Chamoux and Wall 1997.
36. Fauve-Chamoux 1983.
37. Dupâquier et al. 1981.
38. Wall 1991.
39. Session XXIV of the Coucil of Trent, chapter 1, see Lottin et al. 1975.
40. Bels 1968.
41. Dessertine 1981.
42. Lottin et al. 1975.
43. Ibid.
44. Ibid.
45. Ibid.
46. Phillips 1988.
47. Stone 1992.
48. Wrigley and Schofield 1981.
49. Baulant 1976.

CHAPTER 9

1. Goody 1996b.
2. Burckhardt 1951.
3. Anz 1998.
4. Ozment 1983.
5. Anz, p. 9.
6. Huizinga 1953.
7. Rusinek 1973.
8. Barthélemy 1988, p. 90.
9. Herlihy 1995, p. 115.
10. Alberti, 1960 p. 182.
11. Paludan, 1995.
12. Pepys 1985, p. 246.
13. Tadmor 1996, pp. 111–140; Tadmor 1989.
14. Sarrazin 1902, p. 398.
15. Kent 1977, pp. 8–9.
16. Casey 1989, pp. 193–195.
17. Ozment 1997.
18. Goody 1983, p. 268; Jones 1990; Maranda 1974.
19. Bloch 1965, p. 284; Casey 1989, pp. 25–26; Klapisch-Zuber 1990, p. 45.
20. Barthélemy 1988, pp. 88–93.
21. Herlihy 1995, pp. 143–146, 164–167; Schmid 1983; Duby 1973.
22. Elias 1978, pp. 17–36.

23. Heers 1993.
24. Cited in Kent 1977, p. 14.
25. Herlihy 1985, p. 92.
26. Heers 1993, pp. 157–172; Herlihy 1985, p. 90.
27. Goodwin 1999, p. 101.
28. Davies 1990, p. 209.
29. Bieniak 1984, p. 133.
30. Philpotts 1913, pp. 132–133.
31. Malcolm 1998, pp. 164–166.
32. Kaser 1994, pp. 45–68.
33. Patterson 1994, pp. 239–240; Reaney 1991, p. liv.
34. Goody 1983; Gaunt 1996, pp. 211–234.
35. Thirsk 1976, p. 190.
36. Cooper, 1976, pp. 296, 303; Kamen 1984, p. 119.
37. Zanetti 1972, pp. 83–84; Litchfield 1969, p. 197; Davis 1962, p. 72.
38. Thirsk 1976, p. 178; Cooper 1976, p. 236. The creation of new entailments was prohibited in Sweden in 1810 and in Denmark in 1849.
39. Cited in Forster 1971, p. 4.
40. Ibid., pp. 133–134.
41. Hunecke 1995.
42. Elliott 1963, p. 38.
43. McDonogh 1986, pp. 42–44, 153.
44. Beizais 1958, pp. 88–110.
45. Kamen 1984, p. 103; Gager 1996; Sicroff 1960.
46. Bossy 1985, p. 58.
47. Israel 1995, pp. 97–98.
48. Magocsi 1983, pp. 87–88.
49. Pepys 1985, p. 73.
50. Von Haxthausen 1847, p. 109.
51. Bossy 1985, pp. 9, 11.
52. Herlihy 1995, pp. 332–334.
53. Klapisch-Zuber 1990, p. 83.
54. Dauzat 1945, pp. 38–40; Gottschald 1982.
55. Skautrup 1947, p. 261.
56. Zernicki-Szeliga 1900, p. 12.
57. Baroja 1965, p. 91.
58. Cellini 1956, pp. 16–17.
59. Romson 1921, pp. 70–78.
60. Gager 1996, p. 86.
61. Davis 1995.
62. *Namenforschung* 1996.
63. Fauve-Chamoux 1995a; Elliott 1963, p. 31.
64. Cited in Flandrin 1976, p. 11.
65. *Richard III*, III. i, written in the 1590s.
66. Fortes 1969, p. 251; Pitt-Rivers 1973, pp. 89–106.
67. Mousnier 1974.
68. Forster 1971.
69. Tillyard 1994.
70. Flandrin 1979, pp. 23–33.
71. Hunt 1996.
72. Stone 1977, p. 124.
73. Schröcker 1981, pp. 90–93.
74. Kaminski 1993, p. 32.
75. Brunner 1968, pp. 103–127.
76. Sabean 1992, pp. 113–132.
77. Gaunt 1997, pp. 103–128.
78. Demetz 1997, pp. 237–240.
79. Ehmer 1998, p. 52.
80. Davis 1977, p. 92.
81. Wormald 1980, pp. 54–97.
82. Philpotts 1913.
83. Whitaker 1968.
84. Quoted in Wormald 1980, p. 94.
85. Pitt-Rivers 1973, p. 94.
86. Ibid., pp. 94, 326.
87. Hammel 1968, pp. 87–88.
88. Tegnæus 1952, p. 28; Krauss 1885, pp. 19–43; Cisewski 1897.
89. Flandrin 1979, p. 19.
90. Klapisch-Zuber 1990, pp. 9–10, 45.
91. Gatterer 1788.

REFERENCES

Adair, Richard. 1996. *Courtship, Illegitimacy and Marriage in Early Modern England*. Manchester: Manchester University Press.

Ago, Renata. 1989. "Farsi uomini. Giovani nobili nella Roma barocca." *Memoria: Rivista di Storia delle Donne* 27: 7–21.

Ago, Renata. 1997. "Young Nobles in the Age of Absolutism: Paternal Authority and Freedom of Choice in Seventeenth-Century Italy," pp. 283–322 in *A History of Young People in the West. Ancient and Medieval Rites of Passage*, vol. 1. Cambridge, Mass.: Belknap Press.

Alberti, Leon Battista. 1960. *Opera volgari*, vol. 1, edited by C. Grayson. Bari: Laterza.

Andorka, Rudolf. 1971. "La Prévention des naissances en Hongrie dans la région Ormánság depuis la fin du XVIIIe siècle." *Population* 25: 63–78.

Andorka, Rudolf. 1976. "The Peasant Family Structure in the 18th and 19th Centuries," pp. 321–348 in *Acta Ethnographica Academiae Scientarium Hungaricae*. Budapest: Akademiai Kiado.

Andorka, Rudolf. 1995. "Household Systems and the Lives of the Old in Eighteenth- and Nineteenth-Century Hungary," pp. 129–155 in *Aging in the Past*, edited by David I. Kertzer and Peter Laslett. Berkeley: University of California Press.

Andorka Rudolf and Tamás Faragó. 1983. "Pre-industrial Household Structure in Hungary," pp. 281–307 in *Family Forms in Historic Europe*, edited by Richard Wall. Cambridge: Cambridge University Press.

Anon. 1789. *L'Ami des enfants: motion en faveur du divorce*. Paris.

Anon. 1790. *L'Homme mal marié, ou questions à l'auteur de Du divorce*. Paris.

Anz, Christoph. 1998. *Gilden im mittelalterlichen Skandinavien*. Veröffentlichungen des Max-Planck-Instituts für Geschichte 139. Göttingen: Vandenhoeck & Ruprecht.

Ariès, Philippe. 1960. *L'Enfant et la vie familiale sous l'Ancien Régime*. Paris: Librairie Plon.

Ariès, Philippe. 1962. *Centuries of Childhood: A Social History of Family Life*, translated by Robert Baldick. New York: Vintage Books.

Ariès, Philippe, and George Duby (eds.). 1986, tr. It. 1987. *La vita privata dal Rinascimento all'Illuminismo*. Rome and Bari: Laterza. First published Paris: Seuil.

Arru, Angiolina. 1990. "The Distinguishing Features of Domestic Service in Italy." *Journal of Family History* 15: 547–566.

Arru, Angiolina. 1995. *Il servo. Storia di una carriera nel Settecento*. Bologna: Il Mulino.

Aymard, Maurice (ed.). 1995. *Storia d'Europa, 4: L'età moderna, secoli XVI–XVIII*, Turin: Einaudi.

Baker, J. H. 1990. *An Introduction to English Legal History*, third edn. London: Butterworth.

Barbagli, Marzio. 1991. "Three Household Formation Systems in Eighteenth- and Nineteenth-Century Italy," pp. 250–270 in *The Family in Italy*, edited by David I. Kertzer and Richard P. Saller. New Haven: Yale University Press.

Barbagli, Marzio. 1996. *Sotto lo stesso tetto. Mutamenti della famiglia in Italia dal XV al XX secolo*. Bologna: Il Mulino.

Barbieri, Giuseppe and Lucio Gambi (eds.). 1970. *La casa rustica in Italia*. Florence: Olschki.

Bardet, Jean-Pierre. 1983. *Rouen aux XVIIᵉ et XVIIIᵉ siècles, les mutations d'un espace social*. Paris: SEDES.

Bardet, Jean-Pierre and Jacques Dupâquier (eds.). 1997. *Histoire des populations de l'Europe. I Des origines aux prémices de la révolution démographique*. Paris: Fayard.

Bardet, Jean-Pierre et al. 1981. "La Mortalité maternelle autrefois." *Annales de Démographie Historique* 18: 31–48.

Barley, M. W. 1985. "Rural Building in England," pp. 590–682 in *The Agrarian History of England and Wales*, vol. 5, edited by Joan Thirsk. Cambridge: Cambridge University Press.

Baroja, Julio Caro. 1965. "Honour and Shame. A Historical Account of Several Conflicts," in *Honour and Shame*, edited by J. G. Peristany. London: Weidenfeld & Nicolson.

Barthélemy, Dominique. 1988. "Kinship," in *A History of Private Life*, vol. 2: *Revelations of the Medieval World*, edited by Philippe Ariès and Georges Duby. Cambridge, Mass.: Harvard University Press.

Battaglia, Salvatore. 1961. *Grande Dizionario della lingua italiana*. Turin: Utet.

Baulant, Micheline. 1972. "La Famille en miettes: sur un aspect de la démographie du XVIIᵉ siècle." *Annales ESC* 27: 959–968.

Baulant, Micheline. 1976. "The Scattered Family: Another Aspect of Seventeenth-century Demography," pp. 104–116 in *Family and Society*, edited by Robert Forster and Orest Ranum. Baltimore, Maryland: Johns Hopkins University Press.

Baumgarten, Karl. 1965. "Die Tischordnung im alten Mecklenburgischen Bauernhaus." *Deutsches Jahrbuch für Volkskunde* 11: 5–15.

Beizais, Haralds. 1958. "Hedniska seder och bruk bland lettiska bönder." *Kyrkohistorisk årsskrift*: 58: 88–110.

Bellomo, Manlio. 1992. "La struttura patrimoniale della famiglia italiana nel tardo medioevo," pp. 53–70 in *Marriage, Property, and Succession*, edited by Lloyd Bonfield. Berlin: Duncker & Humboldt.

Bels, Pierre. 1968. *Le Mariage des protestants français jusqu'en 1685. Fondements doctrinaux et pratiques juridiques*. Paris: Librairie générale de droit et de jurisprudence.

Ben-Amos, Ilana Krausman. 1994. *Adolescence and Youth in Early Modern England*. New Haven and London: Yale University Press.

Benedict, Philip. 1991. *The Huguenot Population of France, 1600–1685: The Demographic Fate and Customs of a Religious Minority*. Philadelphia: The American Philosophical Society.

Benevolo, Leonardo. 1996. *La città nella storia d'Europa*. Rome and Bari: Laterza. First published 1993.

Benigno, Francesco. 1996. "I dannati del primo sole. Ipotesi sulla mortalità di genere in Italia meridionale tra XVII e XX secolo." *Meridiana* 26–27: 277–310.

Bennett, Judith. 1987. *Women in the Medieval Countryside: Gender and Household in Brigstock before the Plague*. Oxford: Oxford University Press.

Bérélowitch, W. 1997. "La Russie," in *Histoire des populations d'Europe. I Des origines aux prémices de la révolution démographique*, edited by J-P. Bardet and J. Dupâquier. Paris: Fayard.

Berkner, Lutz K. 1972. "The Stem-family and the Developmental Cycle of the Peasant Household: An Eighteenth-century Austrian Example." *American Historical Review* 77: 398–418.

Berkner, Lutz K. and F. F. Mendels. 1978. "Inheritance Systems, Family Structure, and Demographic Patterns in Western Europe, 1700–1900," pp. 209–223 in *Historical Studies of Changing Fertility*, edited by Charles Tilly. Princeton: Princeton University Press.

Bideau, Alain. 1980. "A Demographic and Social Analysis of Widowhood and Remarriage: the Example of the Castellany of Thoissey-en-Dombes, 1670–1840." *Journal of Family History* 1: 28–43.

Bideau, Alain. 1986. "Fécondité et mortalité après 45 ans. L'Apport des recherches en démographie historique." *Population* 41: 59–72.

Bideau, Alain and Alfred Perrenoud. 1981. "Remariage et fécondité. Contribution à l'étude des mécanismes de récupération des populations anciennes," pp. 547–559 in *Marriage and Remarriage in Populations of the Past*, edited by Jacques Dupâquier et al. London: Academic Press.

Bideau, Alain, Jean-Pierre Bardet, and Jacques Houdaille. 1988. "La Fécondité," pp. 349–411 in *Histoire de la population française*, edited by Jacques Dupâquier, vol. 2. Paris: Presses Universitaires de France.

Bideau, Alain, Guy Brunet, and Michel Floquet. 1994. "Mortalité différentielle des enfants indigènes et des enfants en nourrice." *Annales de Dèmographie Historique* 31: 151–168.

Bieniak, Janusz. 1984. "Knight Clans in Medieval Poland," in *The Polish Nobility in the Middle Ages*, edited by Antoni Gasiorowski. Wrocław: Zaklad Narodowy im. Ossolinskich.

Biraben, Jean-Noël. 1975. *Les Hommes et la peste en France et dans les pays européens et méditerranéens*, vol. 1. Paris: Mouton.

Biraben, Jean-Noël. 1979. "Essai sur l'évolution du nombre des hommes." *Population* 1: 13–25.

Blaisdell, Charmarie J. 1982. "Calvin's Letters to Women: the Courting of Ladies in High Places." *Sixteenth Century Journal* 13: 67–84.

Blaisdell, Charmarie J. 1988. "Calvin's and Loyola's Letters to Women: Politics and Spiritual Counsel in the Sixteenth Century," pp. 235–253 in *Calviniana: Ideas and Influence of Jean Calvin*, edited by Robert V. Schnucker. Kirksville, Mo.: Sixteenth Century Journal Publishers.

Blayo, Yves. 1975. "La Mortalité en France de 1740 à 1829." *Population*, numéro spécial 30: 123–142.

Bloch, Marc. 1965. *Feudal Society*, vol. 2, tr. L. A. Manyon. London: Routledge.

Blok, Anton. 1995. "Dietro le quinte: compare la sfera del privato," pp. 597–622 in *Storia d'Europa*, vol. 4, edited by Aymard.

Blom, Ida. 1991. "The History of Widowhood: a Bibliographic Overview." *Journal of Family History* 4: 191–210.

Bonfield, Lloyd. 1982. *Marriage Settlements, 1660–1740: the Adoption of the Strict Settlement*. Cambridge: Cambridge University Press.

Bonfield, Lloyd. 1984. "Contrasting Sources: Court Rolls and Settlements as Evidence of Hereditary Transmission of Land amongst Small Landholders in Early Modern England." *University of Illinois Law Review* 1984: 653–658.

Bonfield, Lloyd. 1986a. "'Affective Families', 'Open Élites' and Strict Family Settlements in Early Modern England." *Economic History Review* 2nd ser. 49: 341–354.

Bonfield, Lloyd. 1986b. "Normative Rules and Property Settlement: Reflections on the Link between Marriage and Inheritance in Early Modern England," pp. 155–176 in *The World We Have Gained: Histories of Population and Social Structure*, edited by Lloyd Bonfield, Richard Smith, and Keith Wrightson. Oxford: Basil Blackwell.

Bonfield, Lloyd (ed.). 1992. *Marriage, Property, and Succession*. Berlin: Duncker & Humboldt.

Bonnain, Rolande. 1981. "Nuptialité, fécondité et pression démographique dans les Pyrénées 1769–1836." pp. 87–121 in *Les Baronnies des Pyrénées*, edited by Isac Chiva and Joseph Goy, vol. 2. Paris: Editions de l'Ecole des Hautes Etudes en Sciences Sociales.

Bossy, John. 1985. *Christianity in the West 1400–1700*. Oxford: Oxford University Press.

Boulton, Jeremy. 1990. "London Widowhood Revisited: the Decline of Female Remarriage in the Seventeenth and Early Eighteenth Centuries." *Continuity and Change* 3: 323–355.

Bowden, Caroline M. K. 1996. "Parental Attitudes towards the Education of Girls in Late Sixteenth- and Early Seventeenth-century England," pp. 105–124 in *Education and Cultural Transmission: Historical Studies of Continuity and Change in Families, Schooling and Youth Cultures*, edited by Johan Strum, Jeroen Dekker, Richard Aldrich, and Frank Simon.

Paedagogica Historica, supplementary series 2: 105–124. Ghent, Belgium: C.S.H.P.

Brändström, Anders. 1988. "The Impact of Female Labour Conditions on Infant Mortality." *Social History of Medicine* 1: 329–358.

Brändström, Anders. 1993. "Infant Mortality in Sweden, 1750–1950," pp. 19–34 in *The Decline of Infant Mortality in Europe, 1800–1950*, edited by Carlo A. Corsini and Pier Paolo Viazzo. Florence: UNICEF and Istituto degli Innocenti.

Braudel, Fernand. 1979. *Civilisation matérielle, économie et capitalisme (XVᵉ –XVIIIᵉ siècle). Les Structures du quotidien: le possible et l'impossible.* Paris: Colin (tr. It. Turin: Einaudi, 1993).

Braun, Rudolf. 1978. "Protoindustrialization and Demographic Changes in the Canton Zürich," pp. 289–334 in *Historical Studies of Changing Fertility*, edited by Charles Tilly. Princeton: Princeton University Press.

Braun, Rudolf. 1990. *Industrialisation and Everyday Life.* Cambridge: Cambridge University Press.

Bremmer, Jan and Lourens van den Bosch (eds.). 1995. *Between Poverty and the Pyre. Moments in the History of Widowhood.* London: Routledge.

Brewer, John. 1980. "Childhood Revisited. The Genesis of the Modern Toy." *History Today* 30 (December): 32–39.

Brewer, John and Roy Porter (eds.). 1993a. *Consumption and the World of Goods.* London and New York: Routledge.

Brewer, John and Roy Porter. 1993b. "Introduction," pp. 1–15 in *Consumption and the World of Goods.* London and New York: Routledge.

Brissaud, Jean. 1912. *A History of French Private Law.* Boston: Little, Brown.

Brodsky, Vivien. 1986. "Widows in Late Elizabethan London: Remarriage, Economic Opportunity and Family Orientations," pp. 122–154 in *The World We Have Gained. Histories of Population and Social Structure*, edited by Lloyd Bonfield, Richard Smith, and Keith Wrightson. Oxford: Basil Blackwell.

Brown, Frank E. 1986. "Continuity and Change in the Urban House: Developments in Domestic Space Organization in Seventeenth-Century London." *Comparative Studies in Society and History* 28: 558–590.

Brown, Judith. 1986. "A Woman's Place Was in the Home: Women's Work in Renaissance Tuscany," pp. 206–226 in *Rewriting the Renaissance. The Discourses of Sexual Difference in Early Modern Europe*, edited by Margaret W. Ferguson, Maureen Quilligan, and Nancy J. Vickers. Chicago: University of Chicago Press.

Brundage, James A. 1982. "Concubinage and Marriage in Medieval Canon Law," pp. 118–128 in *Sexual Practices and the Medieval Church*, edited by Vern L. Bullough and James A. Brundage. Buffalo, New York: Prometheus Books.

Brundage, James. 1987. *Law, Sex and Christian Society in Medieval Europe.* Chicago: University of Chicago Press.

Brundage, James. 1995. *Medieval Canon Law.* London: Longman.

Bruneel, Claude. 1977. *La Mortalité dans les campagnes: le duché de Brabant aux XVIIe et XVIIIe siècles*. Louvain: Editions Neuwelaerts.

Brunner, Otto. 1968. "Das 'Ganze Haus' und die alteuropäische Ökonomik," pp. 103–127 in *Neue Wege der Verfassungs- und Sozialgeschichte*. Göttingen: Vandenhoeck & Ruprecht.

Burckhardt, Jacob. 1951. *The Civilization of the Renaissance in Italy*. London: Phaidon Press.

Burgelin, Olivier. 1977. "Abbigliamento," pp. 79–104 in *Enciclopedia*, vol. 1. Turin: Einaudi.

Burguière, André. 1996. "'Cher cousin': les usages matrimoniaux de la parenté proche dans le France du XVIIIe siècle". Paper presented at the Société de Démographie Historique.

Burguière, André and François Lebrun. 1986. "Les Cent et une familles de l'Europe," pp. 17–92 in *Histoire de la Famille*, vol. 2, edited by Burguière et al. Paris: Armand Colin.

Burguière, André and François Lebrun. 1996a. "The One Hundred and One Families of Europe," pp. 1–94 in *A History of the Family. Volume Two: the Impact of Modernity*, edited by André Burguière, Christiane Klapisch-Zuber, Martine Segalen, and Françoise Zarabend, translated by Sarah Hanbury Tenison. Cambridge, Mass.: Belknap Press.

Burguière, André and François Lebrun. 1996b. "Priest, Prince and Family," pp. 95–158 in *A History of the Family. Volume Two: the Impact of Modernity*, edited by André Burguière, Christiane Klapisch-Zuber, Martine Segalen, and Françoise Zarabend, translated by Sarah Hanbury Tenison. Cambridge, Mass.: Belknap Press.

Busch-Zantner, Richard. 1937. "Tschiftlikwesen und Zadruga in Südosteuropa. Ein Beitrag zur Geschichte der balkanischen Agrarverfassung." *Vierteljahrschrift für Sozial- und Wirtschaftsgeschichte* 30: 72–81.

Cabourdin, Guy. 1981. "Le Remariage en France sous l'Ancien Régime (seizième-dix-huitième siècles)," pp. 273–286 in *Marriage and Remarriage in Populations of the Past*, edited by Jacques Dupâquier et al. London: Academic Press.

Cailisse, Carlo. 1969. *A History of Italian Law*. New York: Rothman Reprint.

Calvi, Giulia. 1984. *Storie di un anno di peste*. Milan: Bompiani.

Campbell, John K. 1976. *Honor, Family and Patronage*. New York: Oxford University Press.

Camporesi, Piero. 1980. *Il pane selvaggio*. Bologna: Il Mulino.

Camporesi, Piero. 1989. *La terra e la luna. Alimentazione folklore società*. Milan: A. Mondadori.

Capatti, Alberto and Massimo Montanari. 1999. *La cucina italiana. Storia di una cultura*. Rome and Bari: Laterza.

Carlson, Eric Josef. 1994. *Marriage and the English Reformation*. Oxford: Basil Blackwell.

Casey, James. 1989. *The History of the Family*. Oxford: Basil Blackwell.

Cavalla, Sandra and Simona Cerutti. 1990. "Female Honor and the Social

Control of Reproduction in Piedmont between 1600 and 1800," translated by Mary M. Gallucci, pp. 73–109 in *Sex and Gender in Historical Perspective*, edited by Edward Muir and Guido Ruggiero. Baltimore, Maryland and London: Johns Hopkins University Press.

Cellini, Benvenuto. 1956. *Autobiography*. Harmondsworth: Penguin.

Cerfvol de [pseud.]. 1770. *Cri d'une honnête femme qui réclame le divorce conformément aux loix de la primitive Eglise, à l'usage actuel du Royaume catholique de Pologne, et à celui de tous les peuples de la terre qui existent ou qui ont existé, excepté nous*. London.

Charlton, Kenneth. 1988. "'Not Publike Onely but Also Private and Domesticall': Mothers and Familial Education in Pre-industrial England." *History of Education* 17: 1–20.

Charlton, Kenneth. 1994. "Mothers as Educative Agents in Pre-industrial England." *History of Education* 23: 129–156.

Chavarria, Elisa N. 1988. "Ideologia e comportamenti familiari nei predicatori italiani tra cinque e settecento. Tematiche e modelli." *Rivista Storica Italiana* 100: 679–723.

Chayanov, Alexander V. 1966. *The Theory of Peasant Economy*. Homewood, Ill.: Free Press.

Chiappa Mauri, Luisa. 1994. "Testamenti lombardi in tempo di peste," pp. 215–252 in Michel Mollat et al., *La Peste Nera*. Spoleto: Centro Italiano di Studi sull'Alto Medioevo.

Chirot, Daniel. 1976. *Social Change in a Peripheral Society. The Creation of a Balkan Colony*. New York: Pine Forge Press.

Cisewski, S. 1897. *Kunstliche Verwandtschaft bei den Südslawen*. Leipzig.

Clark, Gillian. 1987. "A Study of Nurse Children 1550–1750." *Local Population Studies* 39: 8–23.

Clarkson, Leslie A. 1985. *Proto-industrialization: The First Phase of Industrialization?* Basingstoke: Macmillan.

Claverie, Elisabeth and Pierre Lamaison. 1981. "Der Ousta als Produktions- und Wohneinheit im Haut-Gévaudan im 17., 18. und 19. Jahrhundert," pp. 202–213 in *Familie zwischen Tradition und Moderne: Studien zur Geschichte der Familie in Deutschland und Frankreich vom 16. bis zum 18. Jahrhundert*, edited by Neithard Bulst and Jochen Hoock. Göttingen: Vandenhoeck & Ruprecht.

Clavero, Bartolomé. 1992. "Favor maioratus, usus Hispaniae: moralidad de linaje entre Castilla y Europa," pp. 215–254 in *Marriage, Property, and Succession*, edited by Lloyd Bonfield. Berlin: Duncker & Humboldt.

Clunas, Craig. 1999. "Modernity Global and Local: Consumption and the Rise of the West," in *American Historical Review* 104: 1497–1511.

Cohen, Elizabeth. 1986. "Fond Fathers, Devoted Daughters? Family Sentiment in Seventeenth-century France." *Histoire Sociale—Social History* 19: 343–363.

Cohen, Michèlle. 1992. "The Grand Tour: Constructing the English Gentleman in Eighteenth-century France." *History of Education* 21: 241–257.

Cohen, Sherrill. 1989. "Asylums for Women in Counter-Reformation Italy," pp. 166–188 in *Women in Reformation and Counter-Reformation Europe*, edited by Sherrin Marshall. Bloomington: Indiana University Press.

Collins, Brenda. 1982. "Proto-industrialization and Pre-famine Emigration." *Social History* 7: 127–146.

Collins, S. 1991. "British Stepfamily Relationships, 1500–1800." *Journal of Family History* 16: 331–344.

Collomp, Alain. 1983. *La Maison du père, famille et village en Haute Provence aux XVIIᵉ et XVIIIᵉ siècles*. Paris: Presses Universitaires de France.

Collomp, Alain. 1984. "Tensions, Dissensions, and Ruptures inside the Family in Seventeenth- and Eighteenth-century Haute Provence," pp. 145–170 in *Interest and Emotion: Essays on the Study of Family and Kinship*, edited by Hans Medick and David Warren Sabean. Cambridge: Cambridge University Press.

Collomp, Alain. 1987 (tr. It.). "Famiglie. Abitazioni e coabitazioni," pp. 393–425 in *La vita privata*, vol. 3, edited by Philippe Ariès and Georges Duby. (First published Paris: Seuil, 1985).

Condorcet, Jean Antoine Nicolas Caritat, Marquis de. 1794. *Esquisse d'un tableau historique des progrès de l'esprit humain*. Paris: Agasse.

Constantinescu, N. N. and Henri H. Stahl. 1968. "Der Wandel der gesellschaftlichen Struktur in Rumänien seit 1945," pp. xiii, 1–19 in *Von der Agrar- zur Industriegesellschaft. Sozialer Wandel auf dem Lande in Südosteuropa*, edited by Franz Ronneberger and Gerhard Teich. Darmstadt: Hoppenstedt.

Conze, Werner. 1940. *Agrarverfassung und Bevölkerung in Litauen und Weißrußland*. Leipzig: S. Hirzel.

Cooper, J. P. 1976. "Patterns of Inheritance and Settlement by Great Landowners from the Fifteenth to the Eighteenth Centuries," pp. 192–327 in *Family and Inheritance. Rural Society in Western Europe 1200–1800*, edited by Jack Goody, Joan Thirsk, and E. P. Thompson. Cambridge: Cambridge University Press.

Cooper, Sheila M. 1992. "Intergenerational Social Mobility in Late-Seventeenth- and Early-Eighteenth-Century England." *Continuity and Change* 7: 283–301.

Corsini, Carlo A. 1974. "La Fécondité naturelle de la femme mariée. Le cas des nourrices." *Genus* 30: 243–259.

Corso, Raffaele. 1948. *Popoli dell'Europa. Usi e costumi*. Naples: Pironti.

Cosenza, Luigi. 1974. *Storia dell'abitazione*. Milan: Vangelista.

Cressy, David. 1977. "Levels of Illiteracy in England, 1530–1730." *The Historical Journal* 20: 1–23.

Cuisenier, Jean. 1991. *La Maison rustique: logique sociale et composition architecturale*. Paris: Presses Universitaires de France.

Cunningham, Hugh. 1990. "The Employment and Unemployment of Children in England *c.*1680–1851." *Past and Present* 126: 115–150.

Cunningham, Hugh. 1995. *Children and Childhood in Western Society since 1500*. London and New York: Longman.

Czap, Peter Jr. 1978. "Marriage and the Peasant Joint Family in the Era of

Serfdom," pp. 103–123 in *The Family in Imperial Russia. New Lines of Historical Research*, edited by David L. Ransel. Urbana: University of Illinois Press.

Czap, Peter Jr. 1982. "The Perennial Multiple Family Household, Mishino, Russia, 1782–1858." *Journal of Family History* 7: 5–26.

Da Molin, Giovanna. 1990. "Family Forms and Domestic Service in Southern Italy from the Seventeenth to the Nineteenth Centuries." *Journal of Family History* 15: 503–528.

Da Molin, Giovanna. 1993. *Nati e abbandonati*. Bari: Cacucci.

Darmon, Pierre. 1979. *Le Tribunal de l'impuissance. Virilité et defaillance conjugales dans l'Ancienne France*. Paris: Editions du Seuil.

Dauzat, Albert. 1945. *Les Noms de famille de France*. Paris: Payot.

Davidson, Caroline. 1982. *A Woman's Work Is Never Done. A History of Housework in the British Isles 1650–1950*. London: Chatto & Windus.

Davies, Norman. 1990. *God's Playground. A History of Poland*, vol. 1: *The Origins to 1795*. Oxford: Clarendon Press.

Davis, J. C. 1962. *The Decline of the Venetian Nobility as a Ruling Class*. Baltimore, Maryland: Johns Hopkins University Press.

Davis, John. 1973. *Land and Family in Pisticci*. London: Athlone Press.

Davis, Natalie Zemon. 1977. "Ghosts, Kin, and Progeny: Some Features of Family Life in Early Modern France." *Daedalus* 106(2): 87–114.

Davis, Natalie Zemon. 1983. *The Return of Martin Guerre*. Cambridge, Mass.: Harvard University Press.

Davis, Natalie Zemon. 1986. "Women in the Crafts in Sixteenth-Century Lyon," pp. 167–197 in *Women and Work in Preindustrial Europe*, edited by Barbara A. Hanawalt. Bloomington: Indiana University Press.

Davis, Natalie Zemon. 1995. *Women on the Margins. Three Seventeenth-Century Lives*. Cambridge, Mass.: Harvard University Press.

De Maddalena, Aldo. 1974. "L'Europa rurale 1500–1750," pp. 209–285 in *Storia economica d'Europa*, vol. 2, edited by Carlo Cipolla. Turin: UTET.

De Mause, Lloyd. 1974. "The Evolution of Childhood," pp. 1–74 in *The History of Childhood*, edited by Lloyd de Mause. London: Souvenir Press.

De Vries, Jan. 1984. *European Urbanization 1500–1800*. London: Methuen; Cambridge, Mass.: Harvard University Press.

De Vries, Jan. 1993. "Between Purchasing Power and the World of Goods: Understanding the Household Economy in Early Modern Europe," pp. 85–132 in *Consumption and the World of Goods*, edited by John Brewer and Roy Porter. London and New York: Routledge.

Deffontaines, Pierre. 1972. *L'Homme et sa maison*. Paris: Gallimard.

Degler, Ian. 1978. "Turkish Woman in the Ottoman Age," pp. 229–244 in *Women in the Muslim World*, edited by L. Beck and N. Kiddie. Cambridge, Mass.: Harvard University Press.

Dekker, J. J. H. and Groenendijk, L. F. 1991. "The Republic of God or the Republic of Children? Childhood and Child-rearing after the Reformation." *Oxford Review of Education* 17: 317–335.

Del Panta, Lorenzo. 1980. *Le epidemie nella storia demografica italiana (secoli XIV–XIX)*. Turin: Loescher.

Delasselle, Claude. 1978. "Abandoned Children in Eighteenth-Century Paris," pp. 47–82 in *Deviants and the Abandoned in French Society. Selections from the Annales Economies, Sociétés, Civilisations*, vol. 4, edited by Robert Forster and Orest Ranum. Baltimore, Maryland: Johns Hopkins University Press.

Demetz, Peter. 1997. *Prague in Black and Gold. The History of a City*. London: Penguin.

Derouet, Bernard. 1993. "Le Partage des frères: héritage masculin et reproduction sociale en Franche-Comté aux XVIIIe et XIXe siècles." *Annales ESC* 48: 453–474.

Derouet, Bernard. 1996. "Nuptiality and Family Reproduction in Male-Inheritance Systems: Reflections on the Examples of the France-Comté, Seventeenth-Eighteenth Centuries." *The History of the Family* 2: 139–158.

Dessertine, Dominique. 1981. *Divorcer à Lyon sous la révolution et l'empire*. Lyon: Presses Universitaires de Lyon.

Dessureault, Christian, John A. Dickinson, and Thomas Wien. 1994. "Living Standards of Norman and Canadian Peasants, 1690–1835."

Di Simplicio, Oscar. 1994. "Il divorzio in Italia in antico regime. Problemi di ricerca." Paper presented at the Convegno internazionale Mutamenti della famiglia nei paesi occidentali, Bologna, October 6–8.

Diderot, Denis. 1786. *Supplément au voyage de Bougainville*. Paris.

Diefendorf, Barbara B. 1982. "Widowhood and Remarriage in Sixteenth-century Paris." *Journal of Family History* 4: 379–395.

Dobson, Mary J. 1997. *Contours of Death and Disease in Early Modern England*. Cambridge: Cambridge University Press.

Donahue, Charles, Jr. 1976. "The Policy of Alexander the Third's Consent Theory of Marriage," pp. 252–283 in *Proceedings of the Fourth International Congress of Medieval Canon Law*, edited by S. Kuttner. Vatican: Biblioteca Apostolica Vaticana.

Donahue, Charles, Jr. 1983. "The Canon Law on the Formation of Marriage and Social Practice in the Later Middle Ages." *Journal of Family History* 8: 144–158.

Donahue, Charles, Jr. 1992. "English and French Marriage Cases in the Later Middle Ages: Might the Difference be Explained by Differences in Property Law?" pp. 338–366 in *Marriage, Property, and Succession*, edited by Lloyd Bonfield. Berlin: Duncker & Humboldt.

Dos Guimarães Sá, Isabel. 1994. "Child Abandonment in Portugal: Legislation and Institutional Care." *Continuity and Change* 9: 69–89.

Dos Guimarães Sá, Isabel. 1996. "Abandono de crianças, ilegitimate e concepções pré-nupciais em Portugal," pp. 37–58 in *Expostos e ilegítimos na realidade ibérica do século XVI ao presente*, edited by Vicente Pérez Moreda. Porto, Portugal: Edições Afrontamento.

Douglas, Mary and Baron Isherwood. 1979. *The World of Goods: Toward an Anthropology of Consumption.* New York: Basic Books. (Italian trans. Bologna: Il Mulino, 1984).

Drummond, Jack Cecil and Anne Wilbraham. 1958. *The Englishman's Food. A History of Five Centuries of English Diet.* London: Cape. (First published 1939).

Duby, Georges. 1973. *Hommes et structures du Moyen Age.* Paris: Mouton.

Dülmen, Richard van (ed.). 1990. *Kultur und Alltag in der frühen Neuzeit. 1 Das Haus und seine Menschen 16.–18. Jahrhundert.* Munich: Beck.

Dulong, Claude. 1987. "Madame de La Fayette et ses placements immobiliers." *XVIIe Siècle* 3: 241–265.

Dunn, Patrick P. 1974. "'That Enemy is the Baby.' Childhood in Imperial Russia," pp. 383–406 in *The History of Childhood*, edited by Lloyd de Mause. London: Souvenir Press.

Dupâquier, Jacques. 1979. *La Population rurale du Bassin Parisien à l'époque de Louis XIV.* Paris: Presses de l'Université de Lille.

Dupâquier, Jacques (ed.). 1988. *Histoire de la population française*, vol. 2. Paris: Presses Universitaires de France.

Dupâquier, Jacques. 1997. "Les Vicissitudes du peuplement (XVe–XVIIIe siècles)," pp. 239–261 in *Histoire des populations de l'Europe*, vol. 1, edited by Jean-Pierre Bardet and Jacques Dupâquier. Paris: Fayard.

Dupâquier, Jacques, Etienne Hélin, Peter Laslett, Massimo Livi-Bacci, and Solvi Sogner (eds.). 1981. *Marriage and Remarriage in Populations of the Past.* London: Academic Press.

Earle, Peter. 1989. *The Making of the English Middle Classes: Business, Society and Family Life in London, 1660–1730.* London: Methuen.

Ebeling, Dietrich and Peter Klein. 1988. "Das soziale und demographische System der Ravensberger Protoindustrialisierung," pp. 27–48 in *Bevölkerungsgeschichte im Vergleich: Studien zu den Niederlanden und Nordwestdeutschland*, edited by Ernst Hinrichs and Henk van Zon. Zurich: Ostfriesische Landschaft.

Ehmer, Josef. 1998. "Traditionelles Denken und neue Fragestellungen zur Geschichte von Hantwerk und Zunft," in *Handwerk, Hausindustrie und die historische Schule der Nationalökonomie*, edited by Friedrich Lenger. Bielefeld: Verlag für Regionalgeschichte.

Eiras-Roel, Antonio. 1991. "A propos de la démographie urbaine d'Ancien Régime: l'exemple des petites villes de la Galice traditionnelle," pp. 399–410 in *Historiens et populations. Liber Amicorum Etienne Hélin.* Academia: Louvain-la-Neuve.

Elias, Norbert. 1969. *Über den Prozess der Zivilisation. I. Wandlungen des Verhaltens in den weltlichen Oberschichten des Abendlandes.* Frankfurt: Suhrkampf. (First published 1939; Italian trans. Bologna: Il Mulino, 1982.)

Elias, Norbert. 1975. *Die höfische Gesellschaft.* Darmstadt-Neuwied: Luchterhand Verlag. (Italian trans. Bologna: Il Mulino, 1980.)

Elias, Norbert. 1978. *Über den Prozeß der Zivilisation*, vol. 1: *Wandlungen des*

Verhaltens in den weltlichen Oberschichten des Abendlandes. Frankfurt: Suhrkamp.

Elliott, J. H. 1963. *The Revolt of the Catalans. A Study in the Decline of Spain 1598–1640.* Cambridge: Cambridge University Press.

El-Nahal, Galal. 1979. *The Judicial Administration of Ottoman Egypt in the Seventeenth Century.* Minneapolis: Bibliotheca Islamica.

Erickson, Amy Louise. 1993. *Women and Property in Early Modern England.* London: Routledge.

Esmein, Adhémar. 1929–1935. *Le Mariage en droit canonique.* 2 vols, second edn. Paris: Librairie du Recueil Sirey.

Evans, Robin. Ger trans. 1996. "Menschen, Türen, Korridore" [German trans.] *Arch+*, December: 85–97. (First published in *Architectural Design* 4 (1978): 267–277.)

Ezell, Margaret J. 1983. "John Locke's Images of Childhood. Early Eighteenth Century Response to *Some Thoughts Concerning Education.*" *Eighteenth-Century Studies* 17: 139–155.

Faccioli, Emilio. 1973. "La cucina," pp. 981–1030 in *Storia d'Italia, V: I documenti,* I. Turin: Einaudi.

Fairchilds, Cissie. 1984. *Domestic Enemies. Servants and their Masters in Old Regime France.* Baltimore, Maryland: Johns Hopkins University Press.

Farago, Tamas. 1994. "Seasonality of Marriages in Hungary from the Eighteenth to the Twentieth Century." *Journal of Family History* 4: 333–350.

Farge, Arletter. 1993. *Fragile Lives. Violence, Power and Solidarity in Eighteenth-century Paris,* translated by C. Shelton. Cambridge, Mass.: Harvard University Press.

Farrow, Lee. 1996. "Peter the Great's Law of Single Inheritance: State Imperatives and Noble Resistance." *Russian Review* 55: 429–447.

Fauve-Chamoux, Antoinette. 1983. "The Importance of Women in an Urban Environment: the Example of the Rheims Household at the Beginning of the Industrial Revolution," pp. 475–492 in *Family Forms in Historic Europe,* edited by Richard Wall, Jean Robin, and Peter Laslett. Cambridge: Cambridge University Press.

Fauve-Chamoux, Antoinette. 1988. "Les Structures familiales en France aux XVIIᵉ et XVIIIᵉ siècles," pp. 317–347 in *Histoire de la population française,* vol. 2, edited by Jacques Dupâquier. Paris: Presses Universitaires de France.

Fauve-Chamoux, Antoinette. 1994. "Female Surplus and Preindustrial Work: the French Urban Experience," pp. 31–50 in *Socio-economic Consequences of Sex-Ratios in Historical Perspective, 1500–1980,* edited by Solvi Sogner and Antoinette Fauve-Chamoux. Milan: Università Bocconi.

Fauve-Chamoux, Antoinette. 1995a. "The Stem Family, Demography and Inheritance: The Social Frontiers of Auto-regulation," pp. 88–113 in *The European Peasant Family and Society,* edited by Richard L. Rudolph. Liverpool: Liverpool University Press.

Fauve-Chamoux, Antoinette. 1995b. "Female Mobility and Urban Population in

Preindustrial France (1500–1900)," pp. 43–71 in *Internal Migrations and Medium Distance Migrations in Historical Europe*, edited by A. Eiras-Roel and O. Rey Castelao. Santiago de Compostela: CIDH.

Fauve-Chamoux, Antoinette. 1996. "Beyond Adoption: Orphans and Family Strategies in Pre-Industrial France." *The History of the Family* 1: 1–13.

Fauve-Chamoux, Antoinette and Richard Wall. 1997. "Nuptialité et famille," in *Histoire de la population européenne*, edited by Jean-Pierre Bardet and Jacques Dupâquier. Paris: Fayard.

Feenstra, Robert. 1992. "Family, Property and Succession in the Province of Holland during the Sixteenth, Seventeenth and Eighteenth Centuries," pp. 37–53 in *Marriage, Property and Succession*, edited by Lloyd Bonfield. Berlin: Duncker & Humboldt.

Ferrante, Lucia. 1990. "Honor Regained: Women in the Casa del Soccorso di San Paolo in Sixteenth-Century Bologna," translated by Margaret M. Gallucci, pp. 46–72 in *Sex and Gender in Historical Perspective*, edited by Edward Muir and Guido Ruggiero. Baltimore, Maryland and London: Johns Hopkins University Press.

Fichtner, Paula Sutter. 1989. *Protestantism and Primogeniture in Early Modern Germany*. New Haven: Yale University Press.

Fildes, Valerie A. 1986. *Breasts, Bottles and Babies. A History of Infant Feeding*. Edinburgh: Edinburgh University Press.

Fildes, Valerie. 1988. *Wet Nursing: A History from Antiquity to the Present*. Oxford: Basil Blackwell.

Fildes, Valerie. 1990. "Maternal Feelings Re-assessed: Child Abandonment and Neglect in London and Westminster, 1550–1800," pp. 139–178 in *Women as Mothers in Pre-Industrial England*, edited by Valerie Fildes. London: Routledge.

Finlay, Roger. 1981a. "Differential Child Mortality in Pre-industrial England: the Example of Cartmel, Cumbria, 1600–1750." *Annales de Démographie Historique* 67–80.

Finlay, Roger. 1981b. *Population and Metropolis. The Demography of London 1580–1650*. Cambridge: Cambridge University Press.

Finzi, Roberto. 1990. "Differenze: la pellagra nella donna fertile." *Annali dell'Istituto 'Alcide Cervi'* 12: 201–210.

Fitz, Arno J. 1985. *Die Frühindustrialisierung Vorarlbergs und ihre Auswirkungen auf die Familienstruktur*. Dornbirn: Vorarlberger Verlagsanstalt.

Flandrin, Jean-Louis. 1976. *Familles, parenté, maison, sexualité dans l'ancienne société*. Paris: Hachette.

Flandrin, Jean-Louis. 1979. *Families in Former Times. Kinship, Household and Sexuality*. Cambridge: Cambridge University Press.

Flandrin, Jean-Louis. 1996a. "Les Temps modernes," pp. 549–575 in *Histoire de l'alimentation*, edited by Jean-Louis Flandrin and Massimo Montanari. Paris: Fayard.

Flandrin, Jean-Louis. 1996b. "L'Alimentation paysanne en économie de subsistence," pp. 597–627 in *Histoire de l'alimentation*, edited by Jean-Louis Flandrin and Massimo Montanari. Paris: Fayard.

Flandrin, Jean Louis. 1996c. "Choix alimentaires et art culinaire (XVIe–XVIIIe siècle)," pp. 657–681 in *Histoire de l'alimentation*, edited by Jean-Louis Flandrin and Massimo Montanari. Paris: Fayard.

Flandrin, Jean-Louis and Massimo Montanari (eds.). 1996. *Histoire de l'alimentation*. Paris: Fayard.

Fletcher, Anthony. 1994. "Prescription and Practice: Protestantism and the Upbringing of Children, 1560–1700," pp. 325–346 in *The Church and Childhood*, edited by Diana Wood. Oxford: Basil Blackwell.

Fletcher, Anthony. 1995. *Gender, Sex and Subordination in England 1500–1800*. New Haven: Yale University Press.

Flinn, Michael. 1974. "The Stabilisation of Mortality in Pre-Industrial Western Europe." *Journal of European Economic History* 3: 285–318.

Flinn. Michael W. 1981. *The European Demographic System, 1500–1820*. Baltimore, Maryland: Johns Hopkins University Press; Brighton: Harvester Press.

Fontaine, Laurence. 1995. "Devoluzione dei beni nelle valli alpine del Delfinato (XVII–XVIII secolo)." *Quaderni Storici* 30: 135–154.

Forbes, Thomas R. 1986. "Deadly Parents: Child Homicide in Eighteenth- and Nineteenth-century England." *Journal of the History of Medicine* 41: 175–199.

Forster, Robert. 1971. *The House of Saulx-Tavanes. Versailles and Burgundy 1700–1830*. Baltimore, Maryland: Johns Hopkins University Press.

Forster, Robert and Elborg Forster (eds.). 1969. *European Society in the Eighteenth Century*. New York: Harper & Row.

Fortes, Meyer. 1969. *Kinship and the Social Order*. Chicago: Aldine.

Fragnito, Gigliola. 1988. "'Parenti' e 'familiari' nelle corti cardinalizie del Rinascimento," pp. 565–587 in *"Familia" del Principe e Famiglia aristocratica* edited by Cesare Mozzarelli. Rome: Bulzoni.

Fragnito, Gigliola. 1991. "La trattatistica cinque e seicentesca sulla corte cardinalizia. 'Il vero ritratto di una bellissima e ben governata corte'." *Annali dell'Istituto storico italo-germanico in Trento* 17: 135–185.

Frati, Luigi. 1923. *Il settecento a Bologna*. Palermo: Sandron.

Gager, Kristin Elizabeth. 1996. *Blood Ties and Fictive Ties. Adoption and Family Life in Early Modern France*. Princeton: Princeton University Press.

Gagliani, Dianella and Mariuccia Salvati (eds.). 1995. *Donne e spazio nel processo di modernizzazione*. Bologna: Clueb.

Galliano, Paul. 1966. "La Mortalité infantile (indigènes et nourrissons) dans la banlieu sud de Paris à la fin du XVIIIe siècle." *Annales de Démographie Historique* 3: 139–177.

Galloway, Patrick R. 1988. "Basic Patterns in Annual Variations in Fertility, Nuptiality, Mortality, and Prices in Pre-Industrial Europe." *Population Studies* 42: 275–309.

Gambi, Lucio. 1976. "La casa contadina," pp. 479–504 in *Storia d'Italia*, vol. 6: *Atlante*. Turin: Einaudi.

Garcia, J. M. P. 1992. "Rural Family Life in La Huerta de Valencia during the Eighteenth Century." *Continuity and Change* 4: 71–101.

Garden, Maurice. 1970. *Lyon et les Lyonnais au XVIIIe siècle*. Paris: Les Belles Lettres/Flammarion, 1975.

Garnot, Benoît. 1994. "La Culture matérielle dans les villes françaises au XVIIIe siècle," pp. 21–29 in *"Material Culture: Consumption, Life-style, Standard of Living, 1500–1900," Proceedings of the Eleventh International Economic History Congress, Milan, September 1994*, edited by Anton J. Shuurman and Lorena Walsch. Milan: Università Bocconi.

Gatterer, Johann Christoph. 1788. *Abriß der Genealogie*. Göttingen: Vandehoek & Ruprecht.

Gaudemet, Jean. 1987. *Le Mariage en Occident*. Paris: Editions du Cerf.

Gaunt, David. 1978. "Familie, Haushalt und Arbeitsintensität: eine Interpretation demographischer Variationen in Schweden im 17. und 18. Jahrhundert," pp. 219–260 in *Biologie des Menschen in der Geschichte*, edited by Arthur Imhof. Stuttgart: Frommann-Holzboog.

Gaunt, David. 1996. *Familjeliv i Norden*. Stockholm: Gidlund.

Gaunt, David. 1997. "Urban Clannishness and the Nuclear Kin: Trends in Swedish Family Life," pp. 103–128 in *Family and Kinship in Europe*, edited by Marianne Gullestad and Martine Segalen. London: Pinter.

Gavitt, Philip. 1996. "Infant Death in Late Medieval Florence," pp. 137–153 in *Medieval Family Roles*, edited by Cathy Jorgensen Intyre. New York and London: Garland.

Gennep, Arnold van. 1960. *The Rites of Passage*, trans. Monika B. Vizedom and Gabrielle L. Caffee. Chicago: University of Chicago Press.

Gerber, Haim. 1994. *State, Society, and Law in Islam: Ottoman Law in Comparative Perspective*. Albany: State University of New York Press.

Ghez, Gilbert R. and Gary S. Becker. 1975. *The Allocation of Time and Goods over the Life Cycle*. New York: Columbia University Press.

Gillis, John. 1985. *For Better for Worse*. Oxford: Oxford University Press.

Giorgetti, Cristina. 1992. *Manuale di storia del costume e della moda*. Florence: Cantini.

Glatzer, B. and M. Bollig. 1983. "Herds and Households among Pashtun Pastoral Nomads: Limits of Growth." *Ethnology* 22: 307–325.

Glendon, Mary Ann. 1980. "Legal Concepts of Marriage and the Family," pp. 95–109 in *Loving, Parenting and Dying: the Family Cycle in England and America, Past and Present*, edited by Vivian C. Fox and Martin H. Quitt. New York: Psychohistory Press.

Glennie, Paul. 1995. "Consumption within Historical Studies," pp. 164–203 in *Acknowledging Consumption. A Review of New Studies*, edited by Daniel Miller. London and New York: Routledge.

Göbel, Gerhard W. 1988. *Bevölkerung und Ökonomie: historisch-demographische Untersuchung des Kirchspiels Siegen in der Nassau-Oranischen Zeit 1742–1806*. St. Katharinen, Germany: Scripta Mercaturae.

Godding, Philippe. 1992. "Le Droit au service du patrimoine familial: les Pays-Bas Méridionaus", pp. 15–36 in *Marriage, Property and Succession*, edited by Lloyd Bonfield. Berlin: Duncker & Humboldt.

Goldthwaite, Richard A. 1993. *Wealth and the Demand for Art in Italy 1300–1600*. Baltimore and London: Johns Hopkins University Press.

Goodwin, Jason. 1999. *Lords of the Horizons. A History of the Ottoman Empire*. London: Vintage.

Goody, Jack. 1976a. *Production and Reproduction: A Comparative Study of the Domestic Domain*. Cambridge: Cambridge University Press.

Goody, Jack. 1976b. "Introduction," pp. 1–9 in *Family and Inheritance. Rural Society in Western Europe*, edited by Jack Goody, Joan Thirsk, and E. P. Thompson. Cambridge: Cambridge University Press.

Goody, Jack. 1983. *The Development of the Family and Marriage in Europe*. Cambridge: Cambridge University Press.

Goody, Jack. 1996a. "Comparing Family Systems in Europe and Asia: Are There Different Sets of Rules?" *Population and Development Review* 22: 1–20.

Goody, Jack. 1996b. *The East in the West*. Cambridge: Cambridge University Press.

Goody, Jack. 2000. *The European Family*. Oxford: Basil Blackwell.

Goody, Jack, Joan Thirsk, and E. P. Thompson (eds.). 1976. *Family and Inheritance: Rural Society in Western Europe 1200–1800*. Cambridge: Cambridge University Press.

Gottlieb, Beatrice. 1993. *The Family in the Western World. From the Black Death to the Industrial Age*. New York: Oxford University Press.

Gottschald, Max. 1982. *Deutsche Namenkunde*. Berlin: Walter de Gruyter.

Goubert, Pierre. 1960. *Beauvais et le Beauvaisis de 1600 à 1730*. Paris: S.E.V.P.E.N.

Goubert, Pierre. 1982. *La Vie quotidienne des paysans français au XVIIe siècle*. Paris: Hachette.

Gouesse, Jean-Marie. 1986. "Mariages de proches parents (XVIe–XXe siècles)," pp. 31–62 in *Le Modèle familial européen. Normes, déviances, contrôle du pouvoir*. Rome: Ecole française de Rome.

Gouge, William. 1622. *Of Domestical Duties*. London.

Graham, Michael F. 1996. *The Uses of Reform: "Godly Discipline" and Popular Behavior in Scotland and Beyond, 1560–1610*. Leiden: E. J. Brill.

Grassi, Luigi, Mario Pepe, and Giancarlo Sestieri. 1992. *Dizionario di antiquariato. Dizionario storico-critico di Arte e Antiquariato dall'antichità all'inizio del Novecento*. Milan: Vallardi-Garzanti. (First published 1989.)

Greaves, Richard L. 1983. "The Role of Women in Early English Nonconformity." *Church History* 52: 299–311.

Green Carr, Louis. 1994. "Emigration and the Standard of Living: the Eighteenth-century Chesapeake," pp. 83–94 in *"Material Culture: Consumption, Life-style, Standard of Living, 1500–1900," Proceedings of the Eleventh International Economic History Congress, Milan, September, 1994*, edited by Anton J. Schuurman and Lorena Walsh. Milan: Università Bocconi.

Grieco, Allen J. 1996. "Alimentation et classes sociales à la fin du Moyen Âge et à la Renaissance," pp. 479–490 in *Histoire de l'alimentation*, edited by Jean-Louis Flandrin and Massimo Montanari. Paris: Fayard.

Griffiths, Paul. 1996. *Youth and Authority. Formative Experiences in England 1560–1640*. Oxford: Clarendon Press.

Groppi, Angela (ed.). 1996. *Il lavoro delle donne*. Rome and Bari: Laterza.

Grubb, James S. 1996. *Provincial Families of the Renaissance. Private and Public Life in the Veneto*. Baltimore, Maryland: Johns Hopkins University Press.

Guenzi, Alberto. 1982. *Pane e fornai a Bologna*. Venice: Marsilio.

Guenzi, Alberto. 1983. "L'area protoindustriale del canale Reno in città nel secolo XVIII," pp. 173–210 in *Problemi d'acque a Bologna. Atti del II colloquio, 10–11 ottobre 1981*. Bologna: Istituto per la Storia di Bologna.

Guenzi, Alberto. 1990. "La tessitura femminile tra città e campagna. Bologna, secoli XVII–XVIII", in Istituto Internazionale di Storia Economica "F. Datini", Prato, *La donna nell'economia, secc. XIII–XVIII*, edited by Simonetta Cavaciocchi. Florence: Le Monnier.

Gullickson, Gay L. 1986. *Spinners and Weavers of Auffay: Rural Industry and the Sexual Division of Labor in a French Village, 1750–1850*. Cambridge: Cambridge University Press.

Gullickson, Gay L. 1991. "Love and Power in the Proto-industrial Family," pp. 205–226 in *Markets and Manufacture in Early Industrial Europe*, edited by Maxine Berg. London: Routledge.

Gutierrez, Hector and Jacques Houdaille. 1983. "La Mortalité maternelle en France au XVIIIᵉ siècle." *Population* 38: 975–994.

Gutmann, Myron P. 1987. "Protoindustrialization and Marriage Ages in Eastern Belgium," *Annales de démographie historique 1987*: 143–173.

Gutmann, Myron P. and René Leboutte. 1984. "Rethinking Proto-industrialization and the Family." *Journal of Interdisciplinary History* 14: 587–607.

Guttormsson, Loftur. 1991. "Pietism and the Definition of Childhood: Evidence from Eighteenth-century Iceland." *History of Education* 20: 27–35.

Hajnal, John. 1965. "European Marriage Pattern in Perspective," pp. 101–135 in *Population in History*, edited by David V. Glass and David E. C. Eversley. London: Edward Arnold.

Hajnal, John. 1982. 'Household Formation Patterns in Historical Perspective." *Population and Development Review* 3: 449–494.

Hajnal, John. 1983. "Two Kinds of Pre-Industrial Household Formation Systems," pp. 65–104 in *Family Forms in Historic Europe*, edited by Richard Wall. Cambridge: Cambridge University Press.

Hammel. E. A. 1968. *Alternative Social Structures and Ritual Relations in the Balkans*. Englewood Cliffs, N.J.: Prentice-Hall.

Hammel, E. A. and P. Laslett. 1974. "Comparing household structure over time and between cultures." *Comparative Studies in Society and History* 16: 73–109.

Handley, Sarah. 1994. "The Monarchic State in Early Modern France: Marital Regime Government and Male Right," pp. 107–126 in *Politics, Ideology, and the Law in Early Modern Europe: Essays in Honor of J. H. M. Salmon*, edited by Adrianna Bakos. Rochester, N.Y.: University of Rochester Press.

Hansen, Hans-Oluf. 1979. "Some Age Structural Consequences of Mortality Variations in Pre-Transitional Iceland and Sweden," pp. 113–133 in *The Great Mortalities*, edited by Hubert Charbonneau and André Larose. Liège: Ordina Editions.

Harrington Joel. F. 1995. *Reordering Marriage and Society in Reformation Germany*. Cambridge: Cambridge University Press.

Hasluck, M. 1954. *The Unwritten Law in Albania*. Cambridge: Cambridge University Press.

Hauser, Andrea. 1994. *Dinge des Alltags. Studien zur historischen Sachkultur eines schwäbischen Dorfes*. Tübingen: Tübinger Vereinigung für Volkskunde e. V.

Hayward, Helena. 1965, Italian trans. 1992. *Storia del mobile di tutti i paesi dall'antichità ai nostri giorni*. Reggio Emilia: Magis Book. (First published London: Hamlyn, 1965.)

Head, Anne-Lise. 1988. "Le Contrôle de la fécondité en milieu préalpin: l'exemple de paroisses protestantes dans le pays glaronais (XVIIIᵉ–XIXᵉ siècles)." *Annales de Démographie Historique* 25: 99–109.

Head-König, Anne-Lise. 1993. "Forced Marriage and Forbidden Marriages in Switzerland: State Control of the Formation of Marriage in Catholic and Protestant Cantons in the Eighteenth and Nineteenth Centuries." *Continuity and Change* 3: 441–466.

Heers, Jacques. 1993. *Le Clan familial au Moyen Age. Étude sur les structures politiques et sociales des milieux urbains*. Paris: Presses Universitaires de France.

Helmholz, R. H. 1974. *Marriage Litigation in Medieval England*. Cambridge: Cambridge University Press.

Helvétius, Claude Adrien. 1795. *Réflexions morales*. Paris.

Hendrickx, Franciscus M. 1997. *In Order Not to Fall into Poverty: Production and Reproduction in the Transition from Proto-industry to Factory Industry in Borne and Wierden. The Netherlands, 1800–1900*. Amsterdam: International Institute of Social History.

Hennet, Albert Joseph Ulpien. 1789. *Du divorce*. Paris.

Henry, Louis. 1968. "Problèmes de la nuptialité. Considérations de méthodes." *Population* 5: 835–844.

Henry, Louis. 1987. "Mortalité des hommes et des femmes dans le passé." *Annales de Démographie Historique* 24: 87–118.

Henry, Louis and Jacques Houdaille. 1978. "Célibat et âge au mariage aux XVIIIᵉ et XIXᵉ siècles en France, I: célibat définitif." *Population* 33: 43–84.

Henry, Louis and Jacques Houdaille. 1979. "Célibat et âge au mariage aux XVIIIᵉ et XIXᵉ siècles en France, II: âge au premier mariage." *Population* 34: 403–442.

Héritier, Françoise. 1994. *Les Deux soeurs et leur mère*. Paris: Odile Jacob.

Herlihy, David. 1985. *Medieval Households*. Cambridge, Mass.: Harvard University Press.

Herlihy, David. 1995. *Women, Family and Society in Medieval Europe. Historical Essays 1978–1991*. Providence, RI: Berghahn.

Higounet, Charles. 1986. *Die deutsche Ostsiedlung im Mittelalter*. Berlin: Siedler Verlag.

Hill, Christopher. 1981. "In Death They Were Still Divided." *New Society* July 30.

Hirschman, Albert O. 1970. *Exit, Voice, and Loyalty: Responses to Decline in Firms, Organizations, and States*. Cambridge, Mass.: Harvard University Press.

Hoch, Steven L. 1986. *Serfdom and Social Control in Russia. Petrovskoe, a Village in Tambov*. Chicago: University of Chicago Press.

Hochstrasser, Olivia. 1993. *Ein Haus und seine Menschen 1549–1989*. Tübingen: Tübinger Vereinigung für Volkskunde e. V.

Hoffer, Peter C. and N. E. H. Hull. 1981. *Murdering Mothers: Infanticide in England and New England 1558–1803*. New York: New York University Press.

Hollingsworth, Mary F. and Thomas H. Hollingsworth. 1971. "Plague Mortality Rates by Age and Sex in the Parish of St Botolph's without Bishopsgate, London, 1603." *Population Studies* 25: 131–146.

Hollingsworth, Thomas H. 1977. "Mortality in the British Peerage Families since 1600." *Population* 32: 323–352.

Horn, James. 1994. "Domestic Standards of Living in England and the Chesapeake, 1650–1700," pp. 71–81 in *"Material Culture: Consumption, Life-style, Standard of Living, 1500–1900," Proceedings of the Eleventh International Economic History Congress, Milan, September 1994*, edited by Anton J. Schuurman and Lorena Walsh. Milan: Università Bocconi.

Horn, Pamela. 1975. *The Rise and Fall of the Victorian Servant*. Dublin: Gill & Macmillan / New York: St. Martin's Press.

Houdaille, Jacques. 1980. "La Mortalité des enfants en Europe avant le XIXe siécle," pp. 85–118 in *La Mortalité des enfants dans le monde et dans l'histoire*, edited by Paul-Marie Boulanger and Dominique Tabutin. Liège: Ordina Editions.

Houdaille, Jacques. 1984. "La Mortalité des enfants dans la France rurale de 1690 à 1779." *Population* 39: 77–106.

Houdaille, Jacques. 1992. "L'Inégalité devant la mort au XVIIIe et XIXe siècle," pp. 13–23 in *Démographie et différences* edited by Jacques Houdaille et al. Paris: Presses Universitaires de France.

Houlbrooke, Ralph. 1979. *Church Courts and the People during the English Reformation 1520–1570*. Oxford: Oxford University Press.

Houlbrooke, Ralph A. 1984. *The English Family 1450–1700*. London: Longman.

Houlbrooke, Ralph. 1985. "The Making of Marriage in Mid-Tudor England: Evidence from the Records of Matrimonial Contract Litigation." *Journal of Family History* 10: 339–352.

Houlbrooke, Ralph A. (ed.). 1988. *English Family Life 1576–1716. An Anthology from Diaries*. Oxford: Oxford University Press.

Houston, R. A. 1983. "Literacy and Society in the West 1500–1850". *Social History* 8: 269–293.

Howell, Cicely. 1976. "Peasant Inheritance Customs in the Midlands, 1280–1700," pp. 112–155 in *Family and Inheritance. Rural Society in Western Europe 1200–1800*, edited by Jack Goody, Joan Thirsk, and E. P. Thompson. Cambridge: Cambridge University Press.

Howell, Martha C. 1986. *Women, Production, and Patriarchy in Late Medieval Cities*. Chicago: University of Chicago Press.

Huetz de Lemps, Alain. 1996. "Boissons coloniales et essor du sucre," pp. 629–641 in *Histoire de l'alimentation*, edited by Jean-Louis Flandrin and Massimo Montanari. Paris: Fayard.

Hufton, Olwen H. 1974. *The Poor of Eighteenth-Century France 1750–1789*. Oxford: Clarendon Press.

Hufton, Olwen H. 1975. "Women and the Family Economy in Eighteenth-century France." *French Historical Studies* 9: 1–22.

Hufton, Olwen H. 1984. "Women without Men. Widows and Spinsters in Britain and France in the Eighteenth Century." *Journal of Family History* 4: 355–376.

Hufton, Olwen H. 1995. "Women without Men. Widows and Spinsters in Britain and France in the Eighteenth Century," pp. 122–155 in *Between Poverty and the Pyre. Moments in the History of Widowhood*, edited by Jan Bremmer and Lourens van den Bosch. London: Routledge.

Hufton, Olwen H. 1996. *The Prospect before Her. A History of Women in Western Europe 1500–1800*. New York: Knopf/Milan: Mondadori, 1996. (First published London: Harper Collins, 1995).

Hughes, Diane Owen. 1983. "Sumptuary Law and Social Relations in Renaissance Italy," pp. 69–99 in *Disputes and Settlements: Law and Human Relations in the West*, edited by John Bossy. Cambridge: Cambridge University Press.

Hughes, Mary J. 1984. "Child-rearing and Social Expectations in Eighteenth-century England: the Case of the Colliers of Hastings." *Studies in Eighteenth Century Culture* 13: 79–100.

Huizinga, Johan. 1953. *Erasmus*. Stockholm: Natur och kultur.

Hunecke, Volker. 1989. *I trovatelli di Milano. Bambini esposti e famiglie espositrici dal XVII al XIX secolo*. Bologna: Il Mulino.

Hunecke, Volker. 1991. "Intensità e fluttuazioni degli abbandoni dal XV al XIX secolo," pp. 27–72 in *Enfance abandonnée et société en Europe, XIVe–XXe siècle*, edited by Philippe Boutry. Rome: Ecole Française de Rome.

Hunecke, Volker. 1995. *Der venezianische Adel am Ende der Republik 1646–1797. Demographie, Familie, Haushalt*. Tübingen: Bibliotek des Deutschen Historischen Instituts im Rom.

Hunt, Margaret R. 1996. *The Middling Sort. Commerce, Gender and the Family in England 1680–1780*. Berkeley: University of California Press.

Hunter, William. 1994. *A Systematic and Historical Exposition of Roman Law*. London: Gaunt Reprint. (First published 1876.)

Hurwich, J. 1993. "Inheritance Practices in Early Modern Germany." *Journal of Interdisciplinary History* 23: 699–718.

Hyman, Philip and Mary Hyman. 1996. "Imprimer la cuisine: les livres de cuisine en France entre le XVe et le XIXe siècle," pp. 643–655 in *Histoire de l'alimentation*, edited by Jean-Louis Flandrin and Massimo Montanari. Paris: Fayard.

Imhof, Arthur E. 1981. "La Surmortalité des femmes mariées en âge de pro-création." *Annales de Démographie Historique* 18: 81–87.

Imhof, Arthur E. 1990. *Lebenserwartungen in Deutschland vom 17. bis 19. Jahrhundert*. Weinheim: VCH Acta Humaniora.

Ingram, Martin. 1987. *Church Courts, Sex and Marriage in England, 1570–1640*. Cambridge: Cambridge University Press.

Israel, Jonathan. 1995. *The Dutch Republic. Its Rise, Greatness and Fall 1477–1806*. Oxford: Oxford University Press.

Istituto Internazionale di Storia Economica "F. Datini", Prato. 1997. *Alimentazione e nutrizione, secc. XIII–XVIII*, edited by Simonetta Cavaciocchi. Florence: Le Monnier.

Jackson, Mark. 1996. *New-Born Child Murder. Women, Illegitimacy and the Courts in Eighteenth-Century England*. Manchester: Manchester University Press.

Jacobsen, Grethe. 1989. "Nordic Women and the Reformation," pp. 47–67 in *Women in Reformation and Counter-Reformation Europe*, edited by Sherrin Marshall. Bloomington: Indiana University Press.

Jennings, Ronald. 1975. "Woman in Early Seventeenth Century Ottoman Judicial Records." *Journal of the Economic and Social History of the Orient* 18: 75–80.

Jolowicz, H. F. and Barry Nicholas. 1972. *Historical Introduction to the Study of Roman Law*, third edn. Cambridge: Cambridge University Press.

Jones, William Jervis. 1990. *German Kinship Terms 750–1500*. Studia linguistica germanica 27. Berlin: Walter de Gruyter.

Jordanova, Ludmilla L. 1987. "Conceptualising Childhood in the Eighteenth Century: the Problem of Child Labor." *British Journal for Eighteenth-Century Studies* 10: 189–200.

Kagan, Richard. 1981. *Lawsuits and Litigants in Castile: 1500–1700*. Chapel Hill: University of North Carolina Press.

Kamen, Henry. 1984. *European Society 1500–1700*. London: Routledge.

Kaminski, Andrzej Sulima. 1993. *Republic vs. Autocracy. Poland-Lithuania and Russia 1686–1697*. Cambridge, Mass.: Harvard University Press.

Kaplan, Steven. 1996. *The Bakers of Paris and the Bread Question, 1700–1775*. Durham, NC: Duke University Press. (French trans. Paris: Fayard, 1996.)

Karant-Nunn, Susan C. 1989. "The Women of the Saxon Silver Mines," pp. 29–46 in *Women in Reformation and Counter-Reformation Europe*, edited by Sherrin Marshall. Bloomington: Indiana University Press.

Kaser, Karl. 1986. *Freier Bauer und Soldat. Die Militarisierung der agrarischen Gesellschaft in der kroatisch-slawonischen Militärgrenze (1535–1881)*. Graz: Abteilung für Südosteuropäische Geschichte.

Kaser, Karl. 1990. "Im Schatten der europäischen Weltwirtschaft. Die Verfestigung der Agrarstrukturen und die Peripherisierung Südosteuropas im 16. Jahrhundert," pp. 49–81 in *Südosteuropa-Fallstudien. 20 Jahre "Südosteuropäische Geschichte" in Graz*, edited by Horst Haselsteiner. Graz: Abteilung für Südosteuropäische Geschichte.

Kaser, Karl. 1992. *Hirten, Kämpfer, Stammeshelden. Ursprünge und Gegenwart des Balkanischen Patriarchats*. Vienna, Cologne, and Weimar: Böhlau Verlag.

Kaser, Karl. 1994. "The Balkan Joint Family Household: Seeking its Origins." *Continuity and Change* 9: 45–68.

Kaser, Karl. 1995. *Familie und Verwandschaft auf dem Balkan. Analyse einer untergehenden Kultur*. Vienna, Cologne, and Weimar: Böhlau Verlag.

Kaser, Karl. 1996. "Household and Family Contexts in the Balkans: Introduction." *The History of the Family* 1: 375–386.

Kaser, Max. 1984. *Roman Private Law*. Fourth edn, trans. Rolf Dannenberg. Pretoria: University of South Africa Press.

Kent, Francis W. 1977. *Household and Lineage in Renaissance Florence*. Princeton: Princeton University Press.

Kertzer, David I. 1989. "The Joint Family Household Revisited: Demographic Constraints and Household Complexity in the European Past." *Journal of Family History* 14: 1–16.

Kertzer, David I. 1993. *Sacrificed for Honor. Italian Infant Abandonment and the Politics of Reproductive Control*. Boston: Beacon Press.

Kertzer, David I. and Peter Laslett (eds.). 1995. *Aging in the Past*. Berkeley: University of California Press.

King, Steven A. 1998. "English Historical Demography and the Nuptiality Conundrum: New Perspectives." *Historical Social Research* 23: 130–156.

Kingdon, Robert M. 1990. "The Geneva Consistory as Established by John Calvin." *On the Way: Occasional Papers of the Wisconsin Conference of the United Church of Christ* 7: 30–44.

Kingdon, Robert M. 1995. *Adultery and Divorce in Calvin's Geneva*. Cambridge, Mass.: Harvard University Press.

Klaits, Joseph. 1985. *Servants of Satan: the Age of the Witch Hunts*. Bloomington: Indiana University Press.

Klapisch-Zuber, Christiane. 1981. "La 'Mère cruelle': maternité, veuvage et dot dans la Florence des XIV–XVᵉ siècles." *Annales ESC*. 5: 1097–1109.

Klapisch-Zuber, Christiane. 1982. "Le Complexe de Griselda. Dot et dons de mariage au Quattrocento." *Mélanges de l'École Française de Rome. Moyen Age-Temps Modernes*, 94(1): 7–43. (Italian trans. in Klapisch-Zuber 1988, pp. 153–191.)

Klapisch-Zuber, Christiane. 1988. *La famiglia e le donne nel Rinascimento a Firenze*. Rome and Bari: Laterza.

Klapisch-Zuber, Christiane. 1990. *La Maison et le nom. Stratégies et rituels dans l'Italie de la Renaissance*. Paris: Editions de l'Ecole des Hautes Etudes en Sciences Sociales.

Klapisch-Zuber, Christiane and Michel Demonet. 1972. " 'A uno pane e uno vino': La famille rurale toscane au début du XV siècle." *Annales ÉSC* 27: 873–901.

Knodel, John E. 1988. *Demographic Behavior in the Past. A Study of Fourteen German Village Populations in the Eighteenth and Nineteenth Centuries.* Cambridge: Cambridge University Press.

Knodel, John and Susan DeVos. 1980. "Preferences for the Sex of Offspring and Demographic Behavior in Eighteenth- and Nineteenth-Century Germany." *Journal of Family History* 5: 145–166.

Kochanowicz, Jacek. 1983. "The Peasant Family as an Economic Unit in the Polish Feudal Economy of the Eighteenth Century," pp. 153–166 in *Family Forms in Historic Europe*, edited by Richard Wall. Cambridge: Cambridge University Press.

Köhler, Walther. 1932–1942. *Züricher Ehegericht und Genfer Konsistorium*, 2 vols. Leipzig: M. Heinsius Nachfolger.

Komlos, John. 1998. "Shrinking in a Growing Economy? The Mystery of Physical Stature during the Industrial Revolution." *Journal of European Economic History* 58: 779–802.

Kornhauser, Marjorie E. 1993. "Love, Money and the IRS: Family, Income Sharing, and the Joint Income Tax Return," *Hastings Law Journal* 45: 63–111.

Krauss, E. S. 1885. *Sitte und Brauch der Südslawen*. Vienna.

Kriedte, Peter, Hans Medick, and Jürgen Schlumbohm. 1981. *Industrialization before Industrialization: Rural Industry and the Genesis of Capitalism.* Cambridge: Cambridge University Press.

Kriedte, Peter, Hans Medick, and Jürgen Schlumbohm. 1993. "Proto-industrialization Revisited: Demography, Social Structure, and Modern Domestic Industry." *Continuity and Change* 8: 217–252.

Kuchowicz, Zbigniew and Zofia Libiszowska. 1982. "The Child in the Polish Family in the Eighteenth Century." *Polish Review* 27: 70–83.

Kuklo, Cezary. 1990. "Marriage in Pre-industrial Warsaw in the Light of Demographic Studies." *Journal of Family History* 3: 239–260.

Kula, Witold. 1976. "The Seigneury and the Peasant Family in Eighteenth-Century Poland," pp. 192–203 in *Family and Society. Selections from the Annales. Economies, Sociétés, Civilisations*, edited by R. Forster and O. Ranum. Baltimore, Maryland: Johns Hopkins University Press.

Kussmaul, Ann. 1981. *Servants in Early Modern England*. Cambridge: Cambridge University Press.

Kussmaul, Ann. 1990. *A General View of the Rural Economy of England 1538–1840*. Cambridge: Cambridge University Press.

Kytir, Josef, Christian Köck, and Rainer Münz. 1995. "Historical Regional Patterns of Infant Mortality in Austria." *European Journal of Population* 11: 243–259.

Ladurie, Emmanuel Le Roy. 1974. *The Peasants of Languedoc*. Urbana: Illinois University Press.

Ladurie, Emmanuel Le Roy. 1976a. "Family Structures and Inheritance Customs in the Sixteenth Century," pp. 37–70 in *Family and Inheritance: Rural Society in Western Europe 1200–1800*, edited by Jack Goody, Joan Thirsk, and E. P. Thompson. Cambridge: Cambridge University Press.

Ladurie, Emmanuel 1976b. "A System of Customary Law: Family Structures and Inheritance Customs in Sixteenth-century France," pp. 75–103 in *Family and Society. Selection from the Annales Economies, Sociétiés, Civilisations*, edited by R. Forster and O. Ranum. Baltimore, Maryland: Johns Hopkins University Press.

Lambert, Thomas and Isabella M. Watt (eds.). 1996. *Registres du Consistoire de Genève au temps de Calvin, 1542–1544*. With the assistance of Jeffrey R. Watt; under the Supervision of Robert M. Kingdon. Geneva: Droz.

Landers, John. 1993. *Death and the Metropolis. Studies in the Demographic History of London 1670–1830*. Cambridge: Cambridge University Press.

Landers, John. 1996. "Mortality in Eighteenth-Century London: A Note." *Continuity and Change* 11: 303–310.

Langer, William L. 1972. "Checks on Population Growth: 1750–1850." *Scientific American* 226 (2): 92–99.

Larminie, Vivienne. 1995. *Wealth, Kinship and Culture: the Seventeenth Century Newdigates of Arbury and Their World*. London: Boydell.

Larquié, Claude. 1985. "La Mise en nourrice des enfants madrilènes au XVIIe siècle." *Revue d'Histoire Moderne et Contemporaine* 32: 125–144.

Laslett, Peter. 1971. *The World We Have Lost*, second edn. London: Methuen.

Laslett, Peter. 1977. *Family Life and Illicit Love in Earlier Generations*. Cambridge: Cambridge University Press.

Laslett, Peter. 1989. *A Fresh Map of Life: The Emergence of the Third Age*. London: Weidenfeld & Nicolson.

Laslett, Peter and Karla Oosterveen. 1973. "Long-Term Trends in Bastardy in England." *Population Studies* 27: 255–286.

Laslett, Peter, Jim Oeppen, and James E. Smith. 1993. "La parentela estesa verticalmente nell'Italia del XXI secolo." *Polis* 7: 121–139.

Laudani, Simona. 1996. "Mestieri di donne, mestieri di uomini: le corporazioni in età moderna," pp. 183–204 in *Il lavoro delle donne* edited by Angela Groppi (1996).

Leboutte, René. 1991. "Offense against Family Order: Infanticide in Belgium from the Fifteenth through the Early Twentieth Centuries." *Journal of the History of Sexuality* 2: 159–185.

Lehning, James R. 1980. *The Peasants of Marlhes: Economic Development and Family Organization in Nineteenth-Century France*. Chapel Hill: University of North Carolina Press.

Lepecq de la Cloture, Louis. 1778. *Collections d'observations sur les maladies et constitutions épidémiques . . . ainsi qu'avec l'histoire naturelle et médicale de Normandie*. Rouen.

Lesthaeghe, Ron. 1992. "Motivation et légitimation: conditions de vie et régimes de fécondité en Belgique et en France du XVIe au XVIIIe siècle," pp. 275–316 in *Modèles de la démographie historique*, edited by Alain Blum et al. Paris: INED and Presses Universitaires de France.

Levi, Giovanni. 1979. "Innovazione tecnica e resistenza contadina: il mais nel Piemonte del '600." *Quaderni storici* 42: 1092–1100.

Levi, Giovanni. 1991. "L'energia disponibile," pp. 141–168 in *Storia dell'economia Italiana*, edited by Ruggiero Romano. Turin: Einaudi.

Levi, Giovanni. 1996. "Comportements, ressources, procès: avant la 'révolution' de la consommation," pp. 186–207 in *Jeux d'échelles. La micro-analyse à l'esperience*, edited by Jacques Revel. Paris: Seuil/Gallimard.

Levi Pisetsky, Rosita. 1995. *Il costume e la moda nella societá italiana*. Turin: Einaudi. (First published 1978.)

Levin, Eve. 1989. *Sex and Society in the World of the Orthodox Slavs, 900–1700*. Ithaca, N.Y.: Cornell University Press.

Levine, David. 1977. *Family Formation in an Age of Nascent Capitalism*. New York: Academic.

Levine, David and Keith Wrightson. 1991. *The Making of an Industrial Society: Whickham 1560–1765*. Oxford: Clarendon Press.

Levine, David et al. 1984. *Proletarianization and Family History*. Orlando: Academic.

Lindemann, Mary. 1981. "Love for Hire: the Regulation of the Wet-nursing Business in Eighteenth-century Hamburg." *Journal of Family History* 6: 379–395.

Litchfield, R. B. 1969. "Demographic Characteristics of Florentine Patrician Families." *Journal of Economic History* 19: 191–205.

Lithell, Ulla-Britt. 1981. "Breast-Feeding Habits and their Relations to Infant Mortality and Marital Fertility." *Journal of Family History* 6: 182–194.

Livi Bacci, Massimo. 1983. "Ebrei, aristocratici e cittadini: pecursori del declino della fecondità." *Quaderni storici* 54: 913–939.

Livi Bacci, Massimo. 1986. "Social-Group Forerunners of Fertility Control in Europe," pp. 182–200 in *The Decline of Fertility in Europe*, edited by Ansley J. Coale and Susan Cotts Watkins. Princeton: Princeton University Press.

Livi Bacci, Massimo. 1987. *Popolazione e alimentazione. Saggio sulla storia della demografia europea*. Bologna: Il Mulino.

Livi Bacci, Massimo. 1997. *La popolazione nella storia d'Europa*. Bari: Laterza.

Livi Bacci, Massimo and Marco Breschi. 1990. "Italian Fertility: An Historical Account." *Journal of Family History* 15: 385–408.

Logan, Oliver. 1994. "Counter-Reformatory Theories of Upbringing in Italy," pp. 275–284 in *The Church and Childhood*, edited by Diana Wood. Oxford: Basil Blackwell.

Lorcin, Marie Thérèse. 1981. "Veuve noble et veuve paysanne en Lyonnais d'après les testaments des XIVe et XVe siècles," *Annales de Démographie Historique*: 273–288.

Lorence-Kot, Bogna. 1985. *Child-Rearing and Reform. A Study of the Nobility in Eighteenth-century Poland*. Westport, Conn.: Greenwood Press.

Lottin, Alain et al. 1975. *La Désunion du couple sous l'Ancien Régime, l'exemple du Nord*. Paris: Presses Universitaires de Lille.

Lundh, C. 1995. "Households and Families in Pre-industrial Sweden." *Continuity and Change* 10: 33–68.

Lunn, Peter G. 1991. "Nutrition, Immunity, and Infection," pp. 131–145 in *The Decline of Mortality in Europe*, edited by Roger Schofield et al. Oxford: Oxford University Press.

McDonogh, Gary W. 1986. *Good Families of Barcelona*. Princeton: Princeton University Press.

MacEverdy Colin and Richard Jones. 1978. *Atlas of World Population History*. London. Allen Lane.

Macfarlane, Alan. 1970. *The Family Life of Ralph Josselin, a Sevententh-Century Clergyman*. Cambridge: Cambridge University Press.

Macfarlane, Alan. 1979. "The Family, Sex and Marriage in England 1500–1800." *History and Theory* 18: 103–123.

Macfarlane, Alan. 1982. *The Origins of English Individualism*. Oxford: Basil Blackwell.

Macfarlane, Alan. 1986. *Marriage and Love in England. Modes of Reproduction 1300–1840*. Oxford: Basil Blackwell.

McIntosh, Marjorie K. 1986. *Autonomy and Community: The Royal Manor of Havering, 1200–1500*. Cambridge: Cambridge University Press.

McKendrick, Neil. 1982. "Introduction. The Birth of a Consumer Society: The Commercialization of Eighteenth-century England," pp. 1–6 in *The Birth of a Consumer Society* by Neil McKendrick, John Brewer, and J. H. Plumb. Bloomington: Indiana University Press.

McKendrick, Neil, John Brewer, and J. H. Plumb. 1982. *The Birth of a Consumer Society: The Commercialization of Eighteenth-century England*. Bloomington: Indiana University Press.

McLaren, Angus. 1984. *Reproductive Rituals: the Perception of Fertility in England from the Sixteenth to the Nineteenth Century*. London: Methuen.

McMullen, Norma. 1977. "The Education of English Gentlewomen 1540–1640." *History of Education* 6: 87–101.

MacNeill, William. 1967. *A World History*. New York: Oxford University Press.

Mager, Wolfgang. 1982. "Protoindustrialisierung und agrarisch-heimgewerbliche Verflechtung in Ravensberg während der frühen Neuzeit." *Geschichte und Gesellschaft* 8: 435–474.

Magocsi, Paul R. 1983. *Galicia. A Historical Survey and Bibliographic Guide*. Toronto: University of Toronto Press.

Malanima, Paolo. 1990. *Il lusso dei contadini. Consumi e industrie nelle campagne toscane del sei e settecento*. Bologna: Il Mulino.

Malanima, Paolo. 1994. "Changing Patterns in Rural Living Conditions: Tuscany in the Eighteenth Century," pp. 115–124 in *"Material Culture: Consumption, Life-style, Standard of Living, 1500–1900,"* Proceedings of the Eleventh International Economic History Congress, Milan, September 1994, edited by Anton J. Schuurman and Lorena Walsh. Milan: Università Bocconi.

Malanima, Paolo. 1995. *Economia preindustriale. Mille anni. Dal IX al XVIII secolo*. Milan: Bruno Mondadori.

Malcolm, Noel. 1998. *Kosovo. A Short History*. London: Macmillan.

Malcolmson, R. W. 1977. "Infanticide in the Eighteenth Century," pp. 187–209 in *Crime in England 1550–1800*, edited by J. S. Cockburn. Princeton: Princeton University Press.

Manciulli, Andrea. 1996. "Le arti della tavola," pp. 325–345 in *Et coquatur ponendo. Cultura della cucina e della tavola in europa tra medioevo ed età moderna*. Istituto Internazionale "F. Datini", Prato.

Maranda, Pierre. 1974. *French Kinship: Structure and History*. The Hague: Mouton.

Marshall, Rosalind K. 1983. *Virgins and Viragos. A History of Women in Scotland from 1080–1980*. London: Collins.

Marshall, Sherrin. 1989. "Protestant, Catholic, and Jewish Women in the Early Modern Netherlands," pp. 120–139 in *Women in Reformation and Counter-Reformation Europe*, edited by Sherrin Marshall. Bloomington: Indiana University Press.

Marsot, Afaf Lutfi al-Sayyd. 1995. *Women and Men in Late Eighteenth Century Egypt*. Austin: University of Texas Press.

Martigny, Hilaire Joseph Hubert de. 1789. *Traité philosophique, théologique et politique de la loi du divorce, demandée aux Etats généraux par S. A. S. Mgr. Louis Philippe Joseph d'Orléans, premier Prince du Sang, où l'on traite la question du célibat des deux sexes, et des causes morales de l'adultère*. Paris.

Martini, Gabriele. 1986. "Rispetto dell'infanzia e violenza sui minori nella Venezia del seicento." *Società e Storia* 9: 793–817.

Martinson, Floyd M. 1992. *Growing Up in Norway*. Carbondale: Southern Illinois University Press.

Matthaiou, Anna. 1997. "La Longue durée de l'alimentation: permanences rurales et différences urbaines en Grèce sous la domination ottomane," pp. 313–323 in Istituto Internazionale di Storia Economica "F. Datini", Prato, *Alimentazione e nutrizione, secc. XIII–XVIII*, edited by Simonetta Cavaciocchi. Florence: Le Monnier.

Matthews Grieco, Sara F. 1991. "Breastfeeding, Wet Nursing and Infant Mortality in Europe (1400–1800)," pp. 15–62 in *Historical Perspectives on Breastfeeding* edited by Sara F. Matthews Grieco and Carlo A. Corsini. Florence: UNICEF and Istituto degli Innocenti.

Mayhew, Graham. 1991. "Life-Cycle Service and the Family Unit in Early Modern Rye." *Continuity and Change* 6: 201–226.

Maza, Sarah. 1983. *Servants and Masters in Eighteenth Century France. The Uses of Loyalty*. Princeton: Princeton Univesity Press.

Medick, Hans. 1976. "The Proto-Industrial Family Economy: the Structural Function of Household and Family during the Transition from Peasant Society to Industrial Capitalism." *Social History* 3: 291–315.

Medick, Hans. 1983. "Privilegiertes Handelskapital und 'kleine Industrie': Produktion und Produktionsverhältnisse im Leinengewerbe des altwürttembergischen Oberamts Urach im 18. Jahrhundert." *Archiv für Sozialgeschichte* 23: 267–310.

Medick, Hans. 1995. "Une Culture de la considération. Les vêtements et leur couleur à Laichingen entre 1750 et 1820." *Annales Histoire, Sciences Sociales* 50: 753–774. (Also in *Quaderni storici* 89: 1087–1115.)

Medick, Hans. 1996. *Leben und Überleben in Laichingen 1650–1900: Lokalgeschichte als allgemeine Geschichte.* Veröffentlichungen des Max-Planck-Instituts für Geschichte 126. Göttingen: Vandenhoeck & Ruprecht.

Meldrum, Tim. 1999. "Domestic Service, Privacy and the Eighteenth-century Metropolitan Household." *Urban History* 26: 27–39.

Mendels, Franklin F. 1972. "Proto-Industrialization: the First Phase of the Industrialization Process." *Journal of Economic History* 32: 241–261.

Mendels, Franklin F. 1984. "Des Industries rurales à la proto-industrialisation: historique d'un changement de perspective." *Annales, ESC* 39: 977–1008.

Mennell, Stephen. 1985. *All Manners of Food (Eating and Taste in England and France from the Middle Ages to the Present).* Oxford: Basil Blackwell.

Mentzer, Raymond A., Jr. 1991. "Ecclesiastical Discipline and Communal Reorganization among Protestants of Southern France." *European History Quarterly* 21: 165–185.

Merzario, Raul. 1989. *Il capitalismo nelle montagne: strategie famigliari nella prima fase di industrializzazione nel Comasco.* Bologna: Il Mulino.

Merzario, Raul. 1996. "Donne sole nelle valli e nelle montagne," pp. 229–246 in *Il lavoro delle donne*, edited by Angela Groppi. Rome and Bari: Laterza.

Metken, Sigrid. 1996. *Der Kampf um die Hose. Geschlechterstreit und die Macht im Haus. Die Geschichte eines Symbols.* Frankfurt and New York: Campus; Paris: Éditions de la Fondation Maison des Sciences de l'Homme.

Meuvret, Jean. 1946. "Les Crises de subsistances et la démographie de la France d'Ancien Régime." *Population* 1: 643–650.

Meuvret, Jean. 1965. "Demographic Crisis in France from the Sixteenth to the Eighteenth Century," pp. 507–522 in *Population in History*, edited by David V. Glass and D. E. C. Eversley. London: Edward Arnold.

Meyer, Jean. 1980. "Illegitimates and Foundlings in Pre-Industrial France," pp. 249–263 in *Bastardy and its Comparative History*, edited by Peter Laslett Karla Oosterveen and Richard Smith. London: Edward Arnold.

Mintz, Sidney. 1985. *Sweetness and Power. The Place of Sugar in Modern History.* New York and London: Penguin Books. (Italian trans. Turin: Einaudi, 1990.)

Mitchison, Rosalind and Leah Leneman. 1989. *Sexuality and Social Control: Scotland 1660–1780.* Oxford: Basil Blackwell.

Mitterauer, Michael. 1983. *Ledige Mütter.* Munich: Beck.

Mitterauer, Michael. 1986. "Formen ländlicher Wirtschaft: Historische Ökotypen und familiale Arbeitsorganisation im österreichischen Raum," pp. 187–323 in *Familienstruktur und Arbeitsorganisation in ländlichen Gesellschaften*, edited by Michael Mitterauer und Joseph Ehmer. Vienna: Böhlau.

Mitterauer, Michael. 1990a. "Servants and Youth." *Continuity and Change* 5: 11–38.

Mitterauer, Michael (ed.). 1990b. *Historisch-anthropologische Familien-forschung. Fragestellungen und Zugangsweisen.* Vienna: Böhlau.

Mitterauer, Michael. 1990c. "Komplexe Familienformen in sozialhistorischer Sicht," pp. 109–122 in *Historisch-anthropologische Familienforschung. Fragestellungen und Zugangsweisen,* edited by Michael Mitterauer. Vienna and Cologne: Böhlau.

Mitterauer, Michael. 1992. *A History of Youth,* trans. G. Dunphy. Oxford: Basil Blackwell.

Mitterauer, Michael. 1994. "Medieval Roots of European Family Developments," manuscript.

Mitterauer, Michael and Alexander Kagan. 1982. "Russian Family Structures from a Central European Point of View." *Journal of Family History* 7: 103–131.

Mitterauer, Michael and Alexander Kagan. 1990. "Russische und mittel-europäische Familienstrukturen im Vergleich," pp. 147–190 in *Historisch-anthropologische Familienforschung,* edited by Michael Mitterauer. Vienna: Böhlau.

Mitterauer, Michael and Reinhard Seider. 1982. *The European Family: Patriarchy to Partnership from the Middle Ages to the Present,* trans. Karla Oosterveen and Manfred Horzinger. Oxford: Basil Blackwell.

Modigliani, Franco. 1980. "The Life Cycle Hypothesis of Saving Twenty Years Later," pp. 41–75 in *The Collected Papers of Franco Modigliani,* vol. 2, edited by Andrew Abel. Cambridge, Mass.: MIT Press.

Montanari, Massimo. 1991. *Nuovo Convivio. Storia e cultura dei piaceri della tavola nell'età moderna.* Rome and Bari: Laterza.

Montanari, Massimo. 1994. *La fame e l'abbondanza. Storia dell'alimentazione in Europa.* Rome and Bari: Laterza. (First published 1993).

Montenegro, Riccardo. 1996. *Abitare nei secoli. Storia dell'arredamento dal Rinascimento ad oggi.* Milan: Leonardo Arte.

Monter, E. William. 1980. "Women in Calvinist Geneva (1550–1800)." *Signs* 6: 189–209.

Montesquieu, Charles de Secondat. 1721. *Les Lettres persanes.* Paris. Lettre 116.

Montesquieu, Charles de Secondat. 1748. *De l'Esprit des lois.* Paris. Book XVI, ch. 15.

Morel, Marie-France. 1983. "Les Parents devant la maladie de leurs enfants dans la France moderne (XVIe–XVIIIe siècles)." *Asclepio* 35: 359–374.

Morelly, M. 1755. *Code de la nature.* Paris.

Moriceau, Jean-Marc. 1993. "Le Laboureur et ses enfants: formation profes-sionnelle et mobilité sociale en Île-de-France." *Revue d'Histoire Moderne et Contemporaine* 40: 387–414.

Morineau, Michel. 1996. "Croître sans savoir pourquoi: structures de produc-tion, démographie et rations alimentaires," pp. 577–595 in *Histoire de l'alimentation,* edited by Jean-Louis Flandrin and Massimo Montanari. Paris: Fayard.

Möring, Béatrice. 1996. "Marriage and Social Change in South-western Finland, 1700–1870." *Continuity and Change* 1: 91–114.

Möring, Béatrice. 1998. "Motherhood, Milk, and Money. Infant Mortality in Pre-Industrial Finland." *Social History of Medicine* 11: 177–196.

Motley, Mark. 1990. *Becoming a French Aristocrat. The Education of the Court Nobility 1580–1715*. Princeton: Princeton University Press.

Motley, Mark. 1994. "Educating the English Gentleman Abroad: the Verney Family in Seventeenth-century France and Holland." *History of Education* 23: 243–256.

Mousnier, Roland. 1974. *Les Institutions de la France sous la monarchie absolue 1598–1789*, vol. 1: *Société et état*. Paris: Presses Universitaires de France.

Murray, Charles. 1984. *Losing Ground: American Social Policy*. New York: Basic Books.

Murru, Corriga Giannetta. 1996. *La discendenza in Sardegna (XVI–XVIII sec.)*. Caglairi: Annali della Facoltà di Magistero.

Namenforschung. Ein internationales Handbuch zur Onomastik, vol 2. 1996. Berlin: de Gruyter.

Nazarov, Vladislav. 1997. "L'Alimentation d'élite de l'Etat Russe (XVe–XVIIe siècles)," pp. 841–849 in Istituto Internazionale di Storia Economica "F. Datini", Prato, *Alimentazione e nutrizione, secc. XIII–XVIII*, edited by Simonetta Cavaciocchi. Florence: Le Monnier.

Nenadic, Stana. 1994. "Household Possessions and the Modernising City: Scotland, c.1720 to 1840," pp. 147–159 in *"Material Culture: Consumption, Life-style, Standard of Living, 1500–1900," Proceedings of the Eleventh International Economic History Congress, Milan, September, 1994*, edited by Anton J. Schuurman and Lorena Walsh. Milan: Università Bocconi.

Netting, Robert M. 1981. *Balancing on an Alp*. Cambridge: Cambridge University Press.

Newall, Fiona. 1990. "Wet Nursing and Child Care in Aldenham, Hertfordshire, 1595–1726: Some Evidence on the Circumstances and Effects of Seventeenth-century Child Rearing Practices," pp. 122–138 in *Women as Mothers in Pre-Industrial England. Essays in Memory of Dorothy McLaren*, edited by Valerie Fildes. London: Routledge.

Nigro, Giampiero. 1997. "Mangiare di grasso, mangiare di magro. Il consumo di carni e pesci tra Medioevo ed Età moderna," pp. 113–146 in Istituto Internazionale di Storia Economica "F. Datini", Prato, *Alimentazione e nutrizione, secc. XIII–XVIII*, edited by Simonetta Cavaciocchi. Florence: Le Monnier.

Nimkoff, M. F. and R. Middleton. 1960. "Types of Family and Types of Economy." *American Journal of Sociology* 66: 215–225.

O'Day, Rosemary. 1982. *Education and Society 1500–1800. The Social Foundations of Education in Early Modern Britain*. London: Longman.

O'Day, Rosemary. 1994. *The Family and Family Relationships, 1500–1900, England, France and the United States of America*. New York: St. Martin's Press.

Ogilvie, Sheilagh C. 1990. "Women and Proto-industrialisation in a Corporate Society: Württemberg Woolen Weaving, 1590–1760," pp. 76–103 in

Women's Work and the Family Economy in Historical Perspective, edited by Pat Hudson and William R. Lee. Manchester: Manchester University Press.

Ogilvie, Sheilagh C. 1997. *State Corporatism and Proto-industry: the Württemberg Black Forest, 1580–1797*. Cambridge: Cambridge University Press.

Ogilvie, Sheilagh C. and Markus Cerman. 1996. *European Proto-industrialization*. Cambridge: Cambridge University Press.

Ogris, W. 1971. "Erbengemeinschaft," p. 954 in *Handwörterbuch zur deutschen Rechtsgeschichte*, vol. 1, edited by Adalbert Erler. Berlin: Erich Schmidt Verlag.

Okenfuss, Max J. 1980. *The Discovery of Childhood in Russia. The Evidence of the Slavic Primer*. Newtonville, Mass.: Oriental Research Partners.

Olson, Jeannine E. 1989. *Calvin and Social Welfare: Deacons and the "Bourse française."* Selinsgrove, Pa.: Susquehanna University Press.

Ortmayer, Norbert. 1995. "Late Marriage: Causes and Consequences of the Austrian Alpine Marriage Pattern," pp. 88–113 in *The European Peasant Family and Society*, edited by Richard R. Rudolph. Liverpool: Liverpool University Press.

Otis, Leah L. 1985. *Prostitution in Medieval Society: the History of an Urban Institution in Languedoc*. Chicago: University of Chicago Press.

Outhwaite, R. B. 1995. *Clandestine Marriage in England 1500–1850*. London: Hambleton Press.

Ovidius Naso, Publius. 1929. *Fasti*, London: Macmillan.

Ozment, Steven. 1983. *When Fathers Ruled. Family Life in Reformation Europe*. Cambridge, Mass.: Harvard University Press.

Ozment, Steven. 1986. *Magdalena & Balthasar. An Intimate Portrait of Life in 16th-Century Europe Revealed in the Letters of a Nuremberg Husband and Wife*. New Haven, Conn.: Yale University Press.

Ozment, Steven. 1990. *Three Behaim Boys Growing Up in Early Germany. A Chronicle of Their Lives*. New Haven, Conn.: Yale University Press.

Ozment, Steven. 1997. *The Bürgermeister's Daughter. Scandal in a Sixteenth Century German Town*. New York: Harper.

Palazzi, Maura 1985. "Pigioni e inquilini nella Bologna del '700: le locazioni delle 'case e botteghe di città,'" pp. 337–434 in *Popolazione ed economia dei territori bolognesi durante il Settecento. Atti del 3° colloquio, Bologna, 15 gennaio 1983*. Bologna: Istituto per la Storia di Bologna.

Palli, H. 1971. "Historical Demography of Estonia in the 17th–18th Centuries and Computers," pp. 205–219 in *Studia historica in honorem Hans Kruus*, Tallinn. Eest: NSV Teadusle Alxadeemia.

Palli, H. 1983. "Estonian Households in the Seventeenth and Eighteenth Centuries," pp. 207–216 in *Family Forms in Historic Europe*, edited by Richard Wall. Cambridge: Cambridge University Press.

Paludan, Helge. 1995. *Familia og familie. To europæiske kulturelementers møde i højmiddelalderens Danmark*. Aarhus: Aarhus universitetsforlag.

Pardailhé-Galabrun, Annik. 1988. *La Naissance de l'intime. 3000 foyers parisiens XVIIᵉ–XVIIIᵉ siècles.* Paris: Presses Universitaires de France.

Patterson, Nerys Thomas. 1994. *Cattle-Lords and Clansmen. The Social Structure of Early Ireland.* South Bend, Ind.: University of Notre Dame Press.

Pedlow, Gregory W. 1982. "Marriage, Family Size, and Inheritance among Hessian Nobles 1650–1900." *Journal of Family History* 7: 333–352.

Pelissier, Jean-Pierre. 1996. "Mobilités et aires matrimoniales." Paper presented at the Société de Démographie Historique.

Pepys, Samuel. 1985. *The Shorter Pepys*, edited by Robert Latham. London: Bell & Hyman.

Pérez Moreda, Vicente. 1980. *Las crisis de mortalidad en la España interior (siglos XVI–XIX).* Madrid: Siglo Veintiuno Editores.

Pérez Moreda, Vicente. 1996. "Infancia abandonada e ilegitimidad en la historia de las poblaciones hibéricas," pp. 7–35 in *Expostos e ilegítimos na realidade ibérica do século XVI ao presente*, edited by Vicente Pérez Moreda. Porto, Portugal: Edições Afrontamento.

Perrenoud, Alfred. 1979. *La Population de Genève XVIᵉ–XIXᵉ siècles.* Geneva: A. J. Champion.

Perrenoud, Alfred. 1981. "Les Aspects socio-économiques de la mortalité différentielle des enfants dans le passé," pp. 323–340 in *Proceedings of the International Population Conference, Manila 1981*, vol. 2. Liège: International Union for the Scientific Study of Population.

Perrenoud, Alfred. 1990. "Aspects of Fertility Decline in an Urban Setting: Rouen and Geneva," pp. 243–263 in *Urbanization in History*, edited by Ad van der Woude et al. Oxford: Oxford University Press.

Perrenoud, Alfred. 1997. "La Mortalité," pp. 287–315 in *Histoire des populations de l'Europe*, vol. 1, edited by Jean-Pierre Bardet and Jacques Dupâquier. Paris: Fayard.

Petitjean, Michel. 1992. "Eléments d'une politique patrimoniale de l'aristocratie à travers l'example bourguignon," pp. 225–286 in *Marriage, Property, and Succession*, edited by Lloyd Bonfield. Berlin: Duncker & Humboldt.

Petschauer, Peter. 1983. "Growing Up Female in Eighteenth-Century Germany." *Journal of Psychohistory* 11: 167–207.

Pfister, Christian. 1997. "L'Allemagne: du XVIᵉ au XVIIIᵉ siècle," pp. 515–526 in *Histoire des populations de l'Europe*, edited by Jean-Pierre Bardet and Jacques Dupâquier, vol 1. Paris: Fayard.

Pfister, Ulrich. 1989a. "Work Roles and Family Structure in Proto-industrial Zurich." *Journal of Interdisciplinary History* 20: 83–105.

Pfister, Ulrich. 1989b. "Proto-industrialization and Demographic Change: the Canton of Zürich Revisited." *Journal of European Economic History* 18: 629–662.

Pfister, Ulrich. 1992a. *Die Züricher Fabriques: protoindustrielles Wachstum vom 16. zum 18. Jahrhundert.* Zurich: Chronos.

Pfister, Ulrich. 1992b. "The Proto-industrial Household Economy: toward a Formal Analysis." *Journal of Family History* 17: 201–232.

Pfister, Ulrich. 1994a. "Volumes et prix sur le marché immobilier de trois communes zurichoises au XVIIIe siècle," pp. 71–94 in *Les Mouvements longs des marchés immobiliers ruraux et urbains en Europe. XVIe–XIXe siècles*, edited by Michel Dorban and Paul Servais. Louvain-la-Neuve: Académia.

Pfister, Ulrich. 1994b. "Proto-industry and the Life Course: Evidence from Early Modern Zurich." Paper presented at the 6th Annual International Conference on Socio-Economics. The Society for the Advancement of Socio-Economics, July 15–17. Jouy en Josas, France.

Pfister, Ulrich. 1996. "A General Model of Proto-industrial Growth," pp. 73–92 in *Proto-industrialisation: recherches récentes et nouvelles perspectives, Mélanges en souvenir de Franklin Mendels*, edited by René Leboutte. Geneva: Droz.

Phillips, Roderick. 1988. *Putting Asunder. A History of Divorce in Western Society*. Cambridge: Cambridge University Press.

Phillips, Roderick. 1991. *Untying the Knot: A Short History of Divorce*. Cambridge: Cambridge University Press.

Philpotts, Bertha Surtees. 1913. *Kindred and Clan in the Middle Ages and After*. Cambridge: Cambridge University Press.

Pittard, Thérèse. 1946. *Femmes de Genève aux jours d'autrefois*. Geneva: Labor et Fides.

Pitt-Rivers, Julian. 1973. "The Kith and the Kin," pp. 89–106 in *The Character of Kinship*, edited by Jack Goody. Cambridge: Cambridge University Press.

Plakans, Andrejs. 1975a. "Seigneurial Authority and Peasant Family Life: the Baltic Area in the Eighteenth Century." *Journal of Interdisciplinary History* 5: 630–651.

Plakans, Andrejs. 1975b. "Peasant Farmsteads and Households in the Baltic Littoral, 1797." *Comparative Studies in Society and History* 17: 2–35.

Plakans, Andrejs. 1983. "The Familial Contexts of Early Childhood in Baltic Serf Society," pp. 167–206 in *Family Forms in Historic Europe*, edited by Richard Wall. Cambridge: Cambridge University Press.

Plumb, J. H. P. 1975. "The New World of Children in Eighteenth-century England." *Past and Present* 67: 64–93.

Pollock, Sir Frederick and Frederic William Maitland. 1968. *The History of English Law before the Time of Edward I*, second edn., vol. 2 Cambridge: Cambridge University Press.

Pollock, Linda A. 1983. *Forgotten Children: Parent–Child Relations from 1500 to 1900*. Cambridge: Cambridge University Press.

Pollock, Linda A. 1987. *A Lasting Relationship. Parents and Children over Three Centuries*. London: Fourth Estate.

Pollock, Linda A. 1989a. " 'Teach Her to Live Under Obedience': the Making of Women in the Upper Ranks of Early Modern England." *Continuity and Change* 4: 231–258.

Pollock, Linda A. 1989b. "Younger Sons in Tudor and Stuart England." *History Today* 39 (June): 23–29.

Pollock, Linda A. 1990. "Embarking on a Rough Passage: the Experience of

Pregnancy in Early-modern Society," pp. 39–67 in *Women as Mothers in Pre-Industrial England. Essays in Memory of Dorothy McLaren*, edited by Valerie Fildes. London: Routledge.

Pollock, Linda A. 1996a. "'Training a Child in the Way He/She Should Go.' Cultural Transmission and Child-rearing within the Home in England, *circa* 1550–1800," pp. 79–104 in *Education and Cultural Transmission: Historical Studies of Continuity and Change in Families, Schooling and Youth Cultures* edited by Johan Strum, Jeroen Dekker, Richard Aldrich, and Frank Simon. *Paedagogica Historica* Supplementary Series 2.

Pollock, Linda A. 1996b. "Teacher–Pupil Relations in Eighteenth- and Nineteenth-Century Britain," pp. 15–29 in *Listening to Children in Education*, edited by Ron Davie and David Galloway. London: David Fulton.

Pollock, Linda A. 1998. "Rethinking Patriarchy and the Family in Seventeenth-century England." *Journal of Family History* 23: 3–27.

Pomata, Gianna. 1983. "La storia delle donne: una questione di confine," pp. 1434–1469 in *Il mondo contemporaneo*, edited by Giovanni De Luna, Peppino Ortoleva, Marco Revelli, and Nicola Tranfaglia, *Gli strumenti della ricerca—2, Questioni di metodo*. Florence: La Nuova Italia.

Poni, Carlo. 1993. "Moda e innovazione: le strategie dei mercanti di seta di Lione nel secolo XVIII," pp. 17–55 in Istituto Internazionale di Storia Economica "F. Datini", Prato. 1993. *La seta in Europa, sec. XIII–XX*, edited by Simonetta Cavaciocchi. Florence: Le Monnier.

Poni, Carlo. 1994. "Tecnologie, organizzazione produttiva e divisione sessuale del lavoro: il caso dei mulini da seta," pp. 269–296 in *Il lavoro delle donne* edited by Angela Groppi. Rome and Bari: Laterza.

Poos, L. R. and Lloyd Bonfield. 1997. *Select Cases in Manorial Courts, 1250–1550*, vol. 113. London: Selden Society.

Poos, L. R. and Lloyd Bonfield. 1998. *Select Pleas in Manorial Courts: Family and Property Law*, vol. 114. London: Selden Society.

Pounds, Norman J. G. 1989. *Hearth & Home. A History of Material Culture*. Bloomington: Indiana University Press.

Pullan, Brian. 1989. *Orphans and Foundlings in Early Modern Europe*. Reading: University of Reading Press.

Quataert, Jean H. 1985. "Combining Agrarian and Industrial Livelihood: Rural Households in the Saxon Oberlausitz in the Nineteenth Century." *Journal of Family History* 10: 145–162.

Raeff, Marc. 1966. *Origins of the Russian Intelligentsia. The Eighteenth-century Nobility*. New York: Harcourt, Brace & World.

Ransel, David L. 1988. *Mothers of Misery: Child Abandonment in Russia*. Princeton: Princeton University Press.

Ransel, David L. 1991. "Infant-Care Cultures in the Russian Empire," pp. 113–134 in *Russia's Women. Accommodation, Resistance, Transformation*, edited by Barbara Evans Clements, Barbara Alpern Engel and Christine D. Worobec. Berkeley: University of California Press.

Ranum, Orest. 1986, Italian trans. 1987. "I rifugi dell'intimità," pp. 161–204 in *La vita privata dal Rinascimento all' Illuminismo*, edited by Philippe Ariès and George Duby. Rome and Bari: Laterza. (First published Paris: Seuil, 1986.)

Reaney, P. H. 1991. *A Dictionary of English Surnames*. London: Routledge.

Rebel, Hermann. 1983. *Peasant Classes: the Bureaucratization of Property and Family Relations under Early Hapsburg Absolutism, 1511–1636*. Princeton: Princeton University Press.

Reher, David S. 1988. *Familia, población y sociedad en la provincia de Cuenca, 1700–1970*. Madrid: Siglo Veintiuno Editores.

Reher, David S. 1997. *Perspectives on the Family in Spain, Past and Present*. Oxford: Oxford University Press.

Reher, David. 1998. "Families' Ties in Western Europe: Persistent Contrasts." *Population and Development Review* 24: 203–234.

Revesz, L. 1976. *Der osteuropäische Bauer: seine Rechtslage im 17. und 18. Jahrhundert*. Bern: Schweizerisches Ost-Institut.

Rheinstein, Max. 1972. *Marriage Stability, Divorce, and the Law*. Chicago: University of Chicago Press.

Ribeiro, Aileen. 1984. *Dress in Eighteenth Century Europe 1715–1789*. London: Batsford.

Riley, James C. 1989. "The Sickness Experience of the Josselins' Children." *Journal of Family History* 14: 347–363.

Robinson, Gerald T. 1932. *Rural Russia under the Old Regime*. London: Longmans.

Robisheaux, Thomas. 1981. "Peasants and Pastors: Rural Youth Control and the Reformation in Hohenlohe, 1540–1680." *Social History* 6: 281–300.

Robisheaux, Thomas. 1989. *Rural Society and the Search for Order in Early Modern Germany*. Cambridge: Cambridge University Press.

Roche, Daniel. 1981. *Le Peuple de Paris. Essai sur la culture populaire au XVIIIᵉ siècle*. Paris: Aubier Montaigne. (Italian trans. Bologna: Il Mulino, 1986.)

Roche, Daniel. 1983. "L'Amour paternel à Paris au XVIII siecle." *Annales de Démographie Historique 1983*: 73–80.

Roche, Daniel. 1989. *La culture des apparences. Une histoire du vêtement (XVIIᵉ–XVIIIᵉ siècle)*. Paris: Fayard.

Roche, Daniel. 1997. *Histoire des choses banales. Naissance de la consommation XVIIᵉ–XIXᵉ siècle*. Paris: Fayard.

Romani, Marzio Achille. 1997. "Regalis coena: aspetti economici e sociali del pasto principesco (Italia settentrionale, secoli XVI–XIX)," pp. 719–740 in Istituto Internazionale di Storia Economica "F. Datini", Prato, *Alimentazione e nutrizione, secc. XIII–XVIII*, edited by Simonetta Cavaciocchi. Florence: Le Monnier.

Romano, Andrea. 1992. "Successioni e difesa del patrimonio famigliare nel Regno di Sicilia," pp. 155–214 in *Marriage, Property and Succession*, edited by Lloyd Bonfield. Berlin: Duncker & Humboldt.

Romano, Dennis. 1996. *Housecraft and Statecraft. Domestic Service in Renais-*

sance Venice 1400–1600. Baltimore, Maryland: Johns Hopkins University Press.

Romano, Ruggiero. (ed.). 1991. *Storia dell'economia italiana* II: *L'età moderna: verso la crisi*. Turin: Einaudi.

Romson, Märta Björnbom. 1921. "Gift kvinnas släktnamn." *Svenska jurist tidning* 2: 70–78.

Roodenburg, Herman W. 1985. "The Autobiography of Isabella de Moerloose: Sex, Childrearing and Popular Belief in Seventeenth-century Holland." *Journal of Social History* 18: 517–540.

Roper, Lyndal. 1989. *The Holy Household: Women and Morals in Reformation Augsburg*. Oxford: Clarendon Press.

Rosanvallon, Pierre. 1992. *Le Sacre du citoyen. Du suffrage universel en France*. Paris: Gallimard. (Italian trans. Milan: Anabasi, 1994.)

Rose, Mary B. 1989. "Social Policy and Business: Parish Apprenticeship and the Early Factory System." *Business History* 31: 5–32.

Rösener, Werner. 1995. *I contadini nella storia d'Europa*. Rome and Bari: Laterza.

Ross, James Bruce. 1976. "The Middle-class Child in Urban Italy, Fourteenth to Early Sixteenth Century," pp. 183–228 in *The History of Childhood*, edited by Lloyd de Mause. London: Souvenir Press.

Roux, Simone. 1976. *La Maison dans l'histoire*. Paris: Albin Michel. (Italian trans. Rome: Editori Riuniti, 1982.)

Rudolph, R. L. 1992. "The European Family and Economy: Central Themes and Issues." *Journal of Family History* 17: 119–138.

Rusinek, Michal. 1973. *Ziemia Kopenika*. Warsaw: Turystyka.

Sabean, David Warren. 1990. *Property, Production and Family in Neckarhausen, 1700–1870*. Cambridge: Cambridge University Press.

Sabean, David Warren. 1992. "Social Background to Vetterleswirtschaft: Kinship in Neckarhausen," pp. 113–132 in *Frühe Neuzeit—Frühe Moderne? Forschungen zur Vielgeschichtigkeit von Übergangsprozessen*, edited by Rudolf Vierhaus. Göttingen: Veröffentlichung des Max-Planck-Instituts für Geschichte.

Safley, Thomas Max. 1984. *Let No Man Put Asunder. The Control of Marriage in the German Southwest: A Comparative Study, 1550–1600*. Kirksville, Mo.: Sixteenth Century Journal Publishers.

Saito, Osamu. 1981. "Labour Supply Behavior of the Poor in the English Industrial Revolution." *Journal of European Economic History* 10: 633–652.

Salaman, Roger. N. 1985 (1948[1]). *The History and Social Influence of the Potato*. Cambridge: Cambridge University Press. (Italian trans. Milan: Garzanti, 1989.)

Saller, Richard P. 1986. "*Patria Potestas* and the Stereotype of the Roman Family." *Continuity and Change* 1: 7–22.

Saller, Richard P. 1994. *Patriarchy, Property and Death in the Roman Family*. Cambridge: Cambridge University Press.

Sarrazin, Gregor, 1902. *Shakespeare-Lexicon*. Berlin: Reimer.

Sarti, Raffaella. 1994a. "Per una storia del personale domestico in Italia. Il caso di Bologna (secc. XVIII–XIX)." Doctoral thesis, Università degli Studi di Torino.

Sarti, Raffaella. 1994b. "Donne e famiglia. A margine di un volume sul caso friulano". *Rassegna degli Archivi di Stato* 3: 675–688.

Sarti, Raffaella. 1995. "Spazi domestici e identità di genere tra etá moderna e contemporanea," pp. 13–41 in *Donne e spazio nel processo di modernizzazione*, edited by Dianella Gagliani and Mariuccia Salvati. Bologna: Clueb.

Sarti, Raffaella. 1999a. *Vita di casa. Abitare, mangiare, vestire nell'Europa moderna*. Rome and Bari: Laterza.

Sarti, Raffaella. 1999b. "'Comparir con equiggio in scena'. Servizio domestico e prestigio nobiliare (Bologna, fine XVII–inizio XX secolo)," *Cheiron*.

Sarti, Raffaella. Forthcoming. "The True Servant. Self-definition of Male Domestics in an Italian city (Bologna, 17th–18th centuries)", *The History of the Family*.

Sauvain-Dugerdil, Claudine. 1990. "Les Isolats alpins ont-ils existé? Réflexion à partir de 250 ans d'histoire généalogique d'une valée valaisanne," pp. 297–322 in *Approche pluridisciplinaire des isolats humains*, edited by A. Chaventré and D. F. Roberts. Paris: INED.

Schama, Simon. 1988. *The Embarrassment of Riches: an Interpretation of Dutch Culture in the Golden Age*. Berkeley: University of California Press.

Schlumbohm, Jürgen. 1980. "'Traditional' Collectivity and 'Modern Individuality': Some Questions and Suggestions for the Historical Study of Socialization. The Examples of the German Lower and Upper Bourgeoisies around 1800." *Social History* 5: 71–103.

Schlumbohm, Jürgen. 1982. "Agrarische Besitzklassen und gewerbliche Produktionsverhältnisse: Grossbauern, Kleinbesitzer und Landlose als Leinenproduzenten im Umland von Osnabrück und Bielefeld während des frühen 19. Jahrhunderts," pp. 315–334 in *Mentalitäten und Lebensverhältnisse: Beispiele aus der Sozialgeschichte der Neuzeit. Festschrift Rudolf Vierhaus.* Göttingen: Vandenhoeck & Ruprecht.

Schlumbohm, Jürgen. 1983. "Seasonal Fluctuations and Social Division of Labour: Rural Linen Production in the Osnabrück and Bielefeld Regions and the Urban Woollen Industry in the Niederlausitz. c.1770–c.1850," pp. 92–123 in *Manufacture in Town and Country before the Factory*, edited by Maxine Berg, Pat Hudson, and Michael Sonenscher. Cambridge: Cambridge University Press.

Schlumbohm, Jürgen. 1991. "Social Differences in Age at Marriage: Examples from Rural Germany during the Eighteenth and Nineteenth Centuries," pp. 593–608 in *Historiens et populations. Liber Amicorum Etienne Hélin.* Louvain-la-Neuve: Academia.

Schlumbohm, Jürgen. 1994. *Lebensläufe, Familien, Höfe: Die Bauern und Heuerleute des osnabrückischen Kirchspiels Belm in proto-industrieller Zeit, 1650–1860.* Veröffentlichungen des Max-Planck-Instituts für Geschichte 110. Göttingen: Vandenhoeck & Ruprecht.

Schmid, Karl. 1983. *Gebetsdenken und adliges Selbstverständnis im Mittelalter.* Sigmaringen: Thorbecke.

Schnucker, Robert V. 1974. "The English Puritans and Pregnancy, Delivery and Breast Feeding." *History of Childhood Quarterly* 1: 637–658.

Schnucker, Robert V. 1990. "Puritan Attitudes towards Childhood Discipline, 1560–1634," pp. 108–121 in *Women as Mothers in Pre-Industrial England,* edited by Dorothy McLaren and Valerie Fildes. London: Routledge.

Schofield, Roger. 1986. "Did the Mothers Really Die? Three Centuries of Maternal Mortality in 'The World We Have Lost,'" pp. 231–260 in *The World We Have Gained,* edited by Lloyd Bonfield et al. Oxford: Basil Blackwell.

Schröcker, Alfred. 1981. *Die Patronage des Lothar Franz von Schönborn 1655–1729.* Wiesbaden: Franz Steiner Verlag.

Schubnel, A. 1985. "Education et apprentissage d'un métier en 1518." *Revue d'Alsace* 111: 47–55.

Schuurman, Anton J. and Lorena Walsh S. 1994. "*Material Culture: Consumption, Life-style, Standard of Living, 1500–1900," Proceedings of the Eleventh International Economic History Congress, Milan, September 1994.* Milan: Università Bocconi.

Schwarz, Gabriele. 1989. *Allgemeine Siedlungsgeographie,* 4th edn. Berlin and New York: Walter de Gruyter.

Seeger, Cornelia. 1989. *Nullité de mariage, divorce et séparation de corps à Genève au temps de Calvin.* Lausanne: Société d'Histoire de la Suisse Romande.

Segalen, Martine. 1977. "'Avoir sa part': Sibling Relations in Partible Inheritance Brittany," pp. 129–144 in *Interest and Emotion: Essays on the Study of Family and Kinship,* edited by Hans Medick and David Warren Sabean. Cambridge: Cambridge University Press.

Segalen, Martine. 1981 (with Josselyne Charmat). *Amours et mariages de l'ancienne France.* Paris: Berger-Levrault.

Seleski, Patty. 1995. "Women, Work and Cultural Change in Eighteenth- and Early Nineteenth-century London," pp. 143–167 in *Popular Culture in England c.1500–1850,* edited by Tim Harris. New York: St. Martin's Press.

Senior, Nancy. 1983. "Aspects of Infant Feeding in Eighteenth-century France." *Eighteenth Century Studies* 16: 367–388.

Sereni, Emilio. 1981. "Note di storia dell'alimentazione nel Mezzogiorno: i Napoletani da 'mangiafoglia' a 'mangiamaccheroni'," pp. 292–371 in *Terra nuova e buoi rossi e altri saggi per una storia dell'agricoltura,* edited by Emilio Sereni. Turin: Einaudi. (First published 1958.)

Serventi, Silvano and Françoise Sabban. 2000. *La pasta: storia e cultura di un cibo universale.* Rome and Bari: Laterza.

Shaffer, John W. 1982. *Family and Farm. Agrarian Change and Household Organization in the Loire Valley, 1500–1900.* Albany: State University of New York Press.

Shammas, Carole. 1994. "The Decline of Textile Prices in England and British America prior to Industrialization." *Economic History Review* 48: 483–507.

Sherwood, Joan. 1988. *Poverty in Eighteenth-century Spain. The Women and Children of the Inclusa*. Toronto: University of Toronto Press.

Shinn, William T. 1961. "The Law of the Russian Peasant Household." *Slavic Review* 20: 601–621.

Shorter, Edward. 1974. "Différences de classe et sentiment depuis 1750." *Annales ESC* 4: 1034–1057.

Shorter, Edward. 1975. *The Making of the Modern Family*. New York: Basic Books.

Shorter, Edward. 1982. *A History of Women's Bodies*. New York: Basic Books.

Sicroff, Albert. 1960. *Les Controverses des statuts de "pureté de sang" en Espagne du XVᵉ au XVIIᵉ siècle*. Paris: Didier.

Siddle, David. 1986. "Inheritance Strategies and Lineage Development in Peasant Society." *Continuity and Change* 1: 333–362.

Simoncini, Giorgio (ed.). 1995a. *L'uso dello spazio privato nell'età dell'Illuminismo*. Florence: Olschki.

Simoncini, Giorgio. 1995b. "Residenze signorili, borghesi e popolari fra tardo Seicento e fine Settecento," pp. 1–24 in *L'uso dello spazio privato nell'età dell'Illuminismo*, edited by Giorgio Simoncini. Florence: Olschki.

Simpson, A. W. B. 1986. *An Historical Introduction to the Land Law*, 2nd edn. Oxford: Clarendon Press.

Skautrup, Peder. 1947. *Det danske sprogs historie*, vol. 2. Copenhagen: Gyldendal.

Slater, Miriam. 1984. *Family Life in the Seventeenth Century. The Verneys of Claydon House*. London: Routledge & Kegan Paul.

Smith, Daniel Scott. 1977. "A Homeostatic Demographic Regime: Patterns in West European Family Reconstitution Studies," pp. 19–51 in *Population Patterns in the Past*, edited by Ronald D. Lee. London: Academic Press.

Smith, James E. and Jim Oeppen. 1993. "Estimating Numbers of Kin in Historical England Using Demographic Microsimulation," pp. 280–317 in *Old and New Methods in Historical Demography*, edited by David S. Reher and Roger Schofield. Oxford: Oxford University Press.

Smith, Richard M. 1984. "The Structural Dependence of the Elderly: a Recent Development. Some Sceptical Thoughts." *Ageing and Society* 4: 409–428.

Smith, Richard M. 1986. "Marriage Processes in the English Past: Some Continuities," pp. 42–99 in *The World We Have Gained: Histories of Population and Social Structure*, edited by Lloyd Bonfield, Richard Smith, and Keith Wrightson. Oxford: Basil Blackwell.

Soler, Jean. 1996. "Les raisons de la Bible: règles alimentaires hébraïques," pp. 73–84 in *Histoire de l'alimentation* edited by Jean-Louis Flandrin and Massimo Montanari. Paris: Fayard.

Sommerville, C. John. 1990. *The Rise and Fall of Childhood*. Revised edn. New York: Vintage Books.

Sommerville, C. John. 1992. *The Discovery of Childhood in Puritan England*. Athens: University of Georgia Press.

Sonnino, Eugenio. 1996. "L'età moderna (secoli XVI–XVIII)," pp. 73–130 in *La popolazione italiana dal medioevo a oggi*, edited by Lorenzo Del Panta et al. Rome and Bari: Laterza.

Spring, Eileen. 1993. *Law, Land and Family, Aristocratic Inheritance in England, 1300–1800*. Chapel Hill: University of North Carolina Press.

Spufford, Margaret. 1974. *Contrasting Communities: English Villagers in the Sixteenth and Seventeenth Centuries*. Cambridge: Cambridge University Press.

Spufford, Margaret. 1976. "Peasant Inheritance Customs and Land Distribution in Cambridgeshire from the Sixteenth to the Eighteenth Centuries," pp. 156–176 in *Family and Inheritance. Rural Society in Western Europe 1200–1800*, edited by Jack Goody, Joan Thirsk, and E. P. Thompson. Cambridge: Cambridge University Press.

Spufford, Margaret. 1979. "First Steps in Literacy: the Reading and Writing Experiences of the Humblest Seventeenth-century Spiritual Autobiographers." *Social History* 4: 407–437.

Staehelin, Adrian. 1957. *Die Einführung der Ehescheidung in Basel zur Zeit der Reformation*. Basel: Helbing & Lichtenhahn.

Stahl, Henri H. 1980. *Traditional Romanian Village Communities*. Cambridge: Cambridge University Press.

Stahl, Paul H. 1986. *Household, Village and Village Confederation in Southeastern Europe*. New York: Columbia University Press.

Starr, June. 1992. *Law as Metaphor: from Islamic Courts to the Palace of Justice*. Albany: State University of New York Press.

Staves, Susan. 1996. "Resentment or Resignation? Dividing the Spoils among Daughters and Younger Sons," pp. 194–220 in *Early Modern Conceptions of Property*, edited by John Brewer and Susan Staves. London: Routledge.

Stoianovich, Traian. 1992. "The Conquering Balkan Orthodox Merchant," pp. 1–77 in *Between East and West. The Balkan and Mediterranean Worlds*, vol. 2, edited by Traian Stoianovich. New Rochelle: Aristide Caratzas.

Stoljar, Samuel. 1989. "A History of the French Law of Divorce—I." *International Journal of Law and the Family* 3: 139–140.

Stone, Lawrence. 1977. *The Family, Sex and Marriage in England 1500–1800*. London: Weidenfeld & Nicolson.

Stone, Lawrence. 1990. *The Road to Divorce: England 1530–1987*. Oxford: Oxford University Press.

Stone, Lawrence. 1993. *Broken Lives: Separation and Divorce in England 1660–1857*. Oxford: Oxford University Press.

Stone, Lawrence and Jeanne C. Fawtier Stone. 1984 and 1986. *An Open Elite? England 1540–1880*. Oxford: Oxford University Press. (Italian trans. Bologna: Il Mulino, 1989.)

Strauss, Gerald. 1978. *Luther's House of Learning. Indoctrination of the Young in the German Reformation*. Baltimore, Maryland: Johns Hopkins University Press.

Sussman, George D. 1980. "The End of the Wet-nursing Business in France," pp. 224–252 in *Family and Sexuality in French History*, edited by Robert Wheaton and Tamara K. Hareven. Philadelphia: University of Pennsylvania Press.

Sussman, George D. 1982. *Selling Mother's Milk: the Wet-Nursing Business in France, 1715–1914*. Urbana: University of Illinois Press.

Tabuteau, Emily Zack. 1988. *Transfers of Property in Eleventh-Century Norman Law*. Chapel Hill: University of North Carolina Press.

Tadmor, Naomi. 1989. "Family and Friend in *Pamela*." *Social History* 14: 289–306.

Tadmor, Naomi. 1992. "Dimensions of Inequality among Siblings in Eighteenth-Century English Novels: the Cases of *Clarissa* and *The History of Miss Betsy Thoughtless*." *Continuity and Change* 7: 303–333.

Tadmor, Naomi. 1996. "The Concept of the Household-Family in Eighteenth Century England." *Past and Present* 151: 111–140.

Tegnæus, Harry. 1952. *Blood-Brothers: an Ethno-Sociological Study of the Institution of Blood-Brotherhood with Special Reference to Africa*. Stockholm: Ethnographic Museum.

Terrier, Didier. 1996. *Les Deux âges de la protoindustrialisation: les tisserands du Cambrésis et du Saint-Quentinois 1730–1880*. Paris: EHESS.

Teti, Vito. 1978. *Il pane, la beffa e la festa. Cultura alimentare e ideologia dell'alimentazione nelle classi subalterne*. Rimini and Florence: Guaraldi. (First published 1976.)

Thirsk, Joan. 1976. "The European Debate on Customs of Inheritance 1500–1700," in *Family and Inheritance. Rural Society in Western Europe 1200–1800*, edited by Jack Goody. Cambridge: Cambridge University Press.

Thirsk, Joan. 1997. "The Preparation of Food in the Kitchen, in Europe North of the Alps, 1500–1700," pp. 423–439 in Istituto Internazionale di Storia Economica "F. Datini", Prato, *Alimentazione e nutrizione, secc. XIII–XVIII*, edited by Simonetta Cavaciocchi. Florence: Le Monnier.

Thompson, Edward P. 1967. "Time, Work Discipline and Industrial Capitalism." *Past and Present* 38: 56–97.

Thornton, Peter. 1991. *The Italian Renaissance Interiors*. New York: Harry N. Abrams. (Italian trans. Milan: Leonardo, 1992.)

Tian-Shanskaia, Olga Semyonova. 1993. *Village Life in Late Tsarist Russia*, edited by David L. Ransel. Bloomington: Indiana University Press.

Tilly, Louise A. and Joan W. Scott. 1978. *Women, Work and the Family*. New York: Holt.

Tilly, Louise A., Rachel G. Fuchs, David I. Kertzer, and David L. Ransel. 1992. "Child Abandonment in European History: A Symposium." *Journal of Family History* 17: 1–23.

Tillyard, Stella. 1994. *Aristocrats*. London: Chatto & Windus.

Toaff, Ariel. 2000. *Mangiare alla giudia. La cucina ebraica in Italia dal Rinascimento all'età moderna*. Bologna: Il Mulino.

Tocci, Giovanni. 1988. "'Forma urbis' e modi di vita nelle città," pp. 118–139 in *Vita civile degli italiani. Società, economia e cultura materiale. Men-*

talità, comportamenti e istituzioni tra Rinascimento e decadenza 1550–1700, edited by Giuseppe Galasso. Milan: Electa.

Todorova, Maria. 1993. *Balkan Family Structure and the European Pattern. Demographic Developments in Ottoman Bulgaria*. Washington, D. C.: American University Press.

Tolstoy, Leo. 1942. *War and Peace*, trans. Louise and Aylmer Maude. New York: Simon & Schuster.

Tovrov, Jessica. 1978. "Mother–Child Relationships among the Russian Nobility," pp. 15–43 in *The Family in Imperial Russia*, edited by David L. Ransel. Urbana: University of Illinois Press.

Traer, James. 1980. *Marriage and the Family in Eighteenth Century France*. Ithaca, N.Y.: Cornell University Press.

Turpeinen, Oiva. 1979. "Infant Mortality in Finland 1749–1865." *Scandinavian Economic History Review* 27: 1–21.

Ulbricht, Otto. 1985. "The Debate about Foundling Hospitals in Enlightenment Germany: Infanticide, Illegitimacy, and Infant Mortality Rates." *Central European History* 18: 211–256.

Valeri, Renée. 1977. "Alimentazione," pp. 344–361 in *Enciclopedia*, vol. 1. Turin: Einaudi.

Valverde, Lola. 1994. "Illegitimacy and the Abandonment of Children in the Basque Country, 1550–1800," pp. 51–65 in *Poor Women and Children in the European Past*, edited by John Henderson and Richard Wall. London: Routledge.

Vandenbroeke, Christiaan. 1991. "Quelques précisions au sujet de la mortalité maternelle en Flandre (XVIIᵉ–XIXᵉ siècles)," pp. 195–202 in *Historiens et populations*, edited by Michel Poulain et al. Louvain-la-Neuve: Académia.

Vandenbroeke, Christiaan, Frans van Poppel, and Ad van der Woude. 1983. Le Développement séculaire de la mortalité aux jeunes âges dans le territoire du Bénélux." *Annales de Démographie Historique* 20: 257–289.

Van der Woude, Ad. 1983. "La Ville néerlandaise," pp. 309–388 in *Etudes sur les villes en Europe occidentale*, vol. 2, edited by Alain Lottin et al. Paris: Sedes.

Van der Woude, Ad and Frans van Poppel. 1996. "The Role of Migration in the Demographic System of the Dutch Republic," pp. 181–201 in *Les Systémes démographiques du passé*, edited by Alain Bideau. Lyon: Centre Jacques Cartier.

Vasary, Ildiko. 1989. " 'The Sin of Transdanubia': the One-Child System in Rural Hungary." *Continuity and Change* 4: 429–468.

Vassberg, David E. 1983. "Juveniles in the Rural Work Force of Sixteenth-Century Castile." *Journal of Peasant Studies* 11: 62–75.

Vassberg, David E. 1994. "The Status of Widows in Sixteenth-century Rural Castille," pp. 180–195 in *Poor Women and Children in the European Past*, edited by John Henderson and Richard Wall. London: Routledge.

Veinstein, Gilles. 1995. "L'Islam ottomano nei Balcani e nel Mediterraneo," pp. 57–82 in *Storia d'Europa*, vol. 4: *L'età moderna. Secoli XVI–XVIII*, edited by Maurice Aymard. Turin: Einaudi.

Viazzo, Pier Paolo. 1989. *Upland Communities*. Cambridge: Cambridge University Press.

Viazzo, Pier Paolo. 1991. "Family Structures and the Early Phase in the Individual Life Cycle. A Southern European Perspective," pp. 31–50 in *Poor Women and Children in the European Past*, edited by John Henderson and Richard Wall. London: Routledge.

Viazzo, Pier Paolo. 1994a. "Les Modèles alpins de mortalité infantile." *Annales de Démographie Historique* 31: 97–117.

Viazzo, Pier Paolo. 1994b. "Family Structures and the Early Phase in the Individual Life Cycle," pp. 31–50 in *Poor Women and Children in the European Past*, edited by John Henderson and Richard Wall. London: Routledge.

Viazzo, Pier Paolo, Maria Bortolotto, and Andrea Zanotto. 1997. "Riforme dei regolamenti e oscllazioni della mortalità infantile allo Spedale degli Innocenti di Firenze nella seconda metà del Settecento," pp. 177–217 in *Senza famiglia*, edited by Giovanna Da Molin. Bari: Cacucci.

Vickery, Amanda. 1993. "Women and the World of Good: a Lancashire Consumer and her Possessions," pp. 274–301 in *Consumption and the World of Goods*, edited by John Brewer and Roy Porter. London and New York: Routledge.

Vigarello, Georges. 1985. *Le Propre et le sale. L'hygiène du corps depuis le Moyen Age*. Paris: Seuil. (Italian trans. Venice: Marsilio, 1988).

Viollet, Paul. 1905. *Histoire du droit civil français*. Paris: Librairie de la Société du Recueil Général des Lois et des Arrêts.

Visceglia, Maria Antonietta. 1991. "I consumi in Italia in età moderna," pp. 211–241 in *Storia dell'economia italiana* edited by Ruggiero Romano. Turin: Einaudi.

Visniauskaite, A. J. 1971. "The Development of the Lithuanian Peasant Family," pp. 369–376 in *VII Congres International des Sciences Anthropologiques et Ethnologiques*, Moscow (1964), vol. 11. Moscow.

Von Haxthausen, August. 1847. *Studien zur Zustände das Volksleben und insbesonderen die ländlichen Einrichtungen Russlands*. Hannover.

Wagner, William G. 1994. *Marriage, Property, and Law in Late Imperial Russia*. Oxford: Clarendon Press.

Wall, Richard. 1981a. "Inferring Differential Neglect of Females from Mortality Data." *Annales de Démographie Historique 1981* 18: 119–140.

Wall, Richard. 1981b. "Woman Alone in English Society." *Annales de Démographie Historique 1981*: 303–317.

Wall, Richard. 1983. "The Household: Demographic and Economic Change in England 1650–1970," pp. 493–512 in *Family Forms in Historic Europe*, edited by Richard Wall et al. Cambridge: Cambridge University Press.

Wall, Richard. 1986. "Work, Welfare and the Family: an Illustration of the Adaptive Family," pp. 261–294 in *The World We Have Gained: Histories of Population and Social Structure*, edited by Lloyd Bonfield, Richard M. Smith, and Keith Wrightson. Oxford: Basil Blackwell.

Wall, Richard. 1987. "Leaving Home and the Process of Household Formation in Pre-industrial England." *Continuity and Change* 2: 77–102.

Wall, Richard. 1991. "European Family and Household Systems," pp. 617–636 in *Historiens et populations. Liber Amicorum Etienne Hélin.* Louvain-la-Neuve: Académia.

Wallbank, M. V. 1979. "Eighteenth-Century Public Schools and the Education of the Governing Elite." *History of Education* 8: 1–19.

Walter, John and Roger Schofield. 1989. "Famine, Disease and Crisis Mortality in Early Modern Society," pp. 1–73 in *Famine, Disease and the Social Order in Early Modern Europe*, edited by John Walter and Roger Schofield. Cambridge: Cambridge University Press.

Watt, Jeffrey R. 1992. *The Making of Modern Marriage: Matrimonial Control and the Rise of Sentiment in Neuchâtel, 1550–1800.* Ithaca, N.Y. and London: Cornell University Press.

Watt, Jeffrey R. 1993. "Women and the Consistory in Calvin's Geneva." *Sixteenth Century Journal* 14: 431–441.

Watt, Jeffrey R. 1994. "The Marriage Laws Calvin Drafted for Geneva," pp. 245–255 in *Calvinus Sacrae Scripturae Professor*, edited by W. H. Neuser. Grand Rapids, Mich.: Eerdman's.

Weatherill, Lorna. 1988. *Consumer Behaviour & Material Culture in Britain 1660–1760.* London and New York: Routledge.

Weir, David R. 1983. *Fertility Transition in Rural Europe, 1740–1829.* Ann Arbor, Mich.: University Microfilms.

Wheaton, R. 1980. "Affinity and Descent in Seventeenth-Century Bordeaux," pp. 111–134 in *Family and Sexuality in French History*, edited by Robert Wheaton and Tamera K. Hareven. Philadelphia: University of Pennsylvania Press.

Whitaker, Ian. 1968. "Tribal Structure and National Politics in Albania 1910–1950," pp. 253–293 in *History and Anthropology*, edited by I. M. Lewis. London: Tavistock.

Wiesner, Merry E. 1986. *Working Women in Renaissance Germany.* New Brunswick, N.J.: Rutgers University Press.

Wiesner, Merry E. 1993. *Women and Gender in Early Modern Europe.* Cambridge: Cambridge University Press.

Wijsenbeek-Olthuis, Thera. 1994. "A Matter of Taste. Lifestyle in Holland in the Seventeenth and Eighteenth Centuries," pp. 43–54 in *"Material Culture: Consumption, Life-style, Standard of Living, 1500–1900," Proceedings of the Eleventh International Economic History Congress, Milan, September 1994*, edited by Anton Schuurman and Lorena Walsh. Milan: Università Bocconi.

Willen, Diane. 1989. "Women and Religion in Early Modern England," pp. 140–165 in *Women in Reformation and Counter-Reformation Europe*, edited by Sherrin Marshall. Bloomington: Indiana University Press.

Wilson, Adrian. 1989. "Illegitimacy and its Implications in Mid-eighteenth-century London: the Evidence of the Foundling Hospital." *Continuity and Change* 4: 103–164.

Wilson, Chris. 1984. "Natural Fertility in Pre-industrial England, 1600–1799." *Population Studies* 38: 225–240.

Winner, Irene Portis. 1977. "The Question of the Zadruga in Slovenia: Myth and Reality in Zerovnica." *Anthropological Quarterly* 50: 125–134.

Wintjes, Sherrin Marshall. 1982. "Survivors and Status: Widowhood and Family in the Early Modern Netherlands." *Journal of Family History* 4: 396–405.

Woods, Robert, Naomi Williams, and Chris Galley. 1993. "Infant Mortality in England, 1550–1950," pp. 35–50 in *The Decline of Infant Mortality in Europe, 1800–1950*, edited by Carlo A. Corsini and Pier Paolo Viazzo. Florence: UNICEF and Istituto degli Innocenti.

Wormald, Jenny. 1980. "Blood Feud, Kindred and Government in Early Modern Scotland." *Past and Present* 87: 54–97.

Wrightson, Keith. 1982a. "Infanticide in European History." *Criminal Justice History* 3: 1–20.

Wrightson, Keith. 1982b. *English Society 1580–1680*. London: Hutchinson.

Wrightson, Keith and David Levine. 1979. *Poverty and Piety in an English Village: Terling 1525–1700*. Oxford and New York: Clarendon Press.

Wrigley, Edward A. and Roger S. Schofield. 1981. *The Population History of England 1541–1871. A Reconstruction*. Cambridge: Cambridge University Press.

Wrigley, Edward A., R. S. Davies, J. E. Oeppen, and Roger S. Schofield. 1997. *English Population History from Family Reconstitution 1580–1837*. Cambridge: Cambridge University Press.

Wrigley, Tony. 1978. "Fertility Strategy for the Individual and the Group," pp. 135–154 in *Historical Studies of Changing Fertility*, edited by Charles Tilly. Princeton: Princeton University Press.

Yun, Bartolomé. 1994. "Peasant Material Culture in Castile (1750–1900)," pp. 125–136 in *"Material Culture: Consumption, Life-style, Standard of Living, 1500–1900," Proceedings of the Eleventh International Economic History Congress, Milan, September 1994*, edited by Anton J. Schuurman and Lorena Walsh. Milan: Università Bocconi.

Zanetti, D. E. 1972. *La demografia del patriziato milanese*. Pavia: Università di Pavia.

Zarinebaf-Shahr, Faribra. 1996. "Women, Law, and Imperial Justice in Ottoman Istanbul in the Late Seventeenth Century," pp. 81–95 in *Women, the Family, and Divorce Laws in Islamic History*, edited by Amira El Azhary Sonbol. Syracuse, N.Y.: Syracuse University Press.

Zernicki-Szeliga, Emilian. 1900. *Der polnische Adel und die demselben hinzugetretenen andersländischen Adelsfamilien*. Hamburg: Grand.

Zorzoli, Maria Carla. 1992. "Della famiglia e suo patrimonio: Riflessioni sull'uso del fedecommesso in Lombardia tra cinque e seicento," pp. 71–154 in *Marriage, Property, and Succession*, edited by Lloyd Bonfield. Berlin: Duncker & Humboldt.

AUTHORS

Marzio Barbagli is Professor of Sociology in the Faculty of Statistics at the University of Bologna. He is the author of many sociological and historical books dealing with family, education, politics, social stratification, criminality, and immigration. Among these are *Education for Unemployment* (Columbia University Press, 1982), *Sotto lo stesso tetto. Mutamenti della famiglia in Italia dal XV al XIX secolo* (Il Mulino, 1984), *Provando e riprovando. Matrimonio, famiglia e divorzio in Italia e in altri paesi occidentali* (Il Mulino, 1990), and *Immigrazione e criminalità in Italia* (Il Mulino, 1998).

Lloyd Bonfield is Professor of Law at Tulane University. His publications include *Marriage Settlements, 1660–1700* (Cambridge University Press, 1983) and *Select Cases in Manorial Courts: Family and Property Law* (with L. R. Poos, Selden Society, 1997), and he is completing a monograph on probate litigation. In addition to editing the journal *Continuity and Change*, Bonfield has edited three collections of essays on social and legal history.

Antoinette Fauve-Chamoux is Maître de conferences at the École des Hautes Études en Sciences Sociales, Paris, General Secretary of the International Commission of Historical Demography, and Co-Chair of the Family/Demography network of the European Social Science History Association. She has edited several books and published articles on historical demography, family formation, parental attitudes, and female migration. She is currently working both on demographic transition and comparative family transmission systems in Eurasia.

David Gaunt is Professor of History at University College of South Stockholm and Director of the Baltic and East European Graduate School. His work on family history includes *Familjeliv i Norden* (second edn., Gidlund, 1996) and he has also written on the history of the Swedish bureaucracy, old age, the labor movement, and questions of historical anthropology. His present research concerns the praxis of tolerance of ethnic and religious minorities in the Polish-Lithuanian commonwealth.

Karl Kaser received his doctorate in Southeast European History in 1980 from the Karl-Franzens Universität Graz. Since October 1980, he has been affiliated with the Department for Southeast European Studies of the Institute for History of the University of Graz, where he was appointed Professor in 1996. Since 1998, he has been the Director of the Center for the Study of Balkan Societies and Cultures. His recent publications include: *Macht und Erbe. Männerherrschaft, Besitz und Familie im östlichen Europa*

(1500–1900), (Böhlau, 2000) and *Freundschaft und Feindschaft auf dem Balkan. Euro-balkanische Herausforderungen* (Wieser, 2001).

David I. Kertzer is the Paul Dupee University Professor of Social Science at Brown University, where he is also Professor of Anthropology and Italian Studies. He is the author of many books, including, most recently, *Sacrificed for Honor: Italian Infant Abandonment and the Politics of Reproductive Control* (Beacon, 1993); *Politics and Symbols: The Italian Communist Party and the Fall of Communism* (Yale University Press, 1996); *The Kidnapping of Edgardo Mortara* (Knopf, 1997), and *The Popes against the Jews* (Knopf, 2001).

Ulrich Pfister holds the Chair of Social and Economic History at the University of Munster, Germany. He has published two books (in German, 1982 and 1992) on the demography of contraception in seventeenth-century Zurich and on the proto-industrial development of early modern Zurich. Apart from proto-industrialization and family history, his articles relate to the history of religion and agrarian history during the early modern period as well as the financial history of Third World countries during the twentieth century.

Linda A. Pollock is Professor of History at Tulane University. She is author of *Forgotten Children: Parent–Child Relations from 1500 to 1900* (Cambridge University Press, 1983) and *With Faith and Physic: The Life of a Tudor Gentlewoman: Lady Grace Mildmay 1552–1620* (St. Martin's, 1993). She is currently completing a study of conflict amongst the landed elite, entitled "Turbulent Waters: Family Conflict and the Politics of Accommodation in Early Modern England."

Raffaella Sarti was Marie Curie Fellow at the Centre de Recherches Historiques of the École des Hautes Études en Sciences Sociales in Paris from 1998 to 2000, of which she is now an associated member. Currently Researcher in Early Modern History at the University of Urbino (Italy), she is the author of *Vita di casa. Abitare, mangiare, vestire nell'Europa moderna* (Laterza, 2000; English translation, Yale University Press, forthcoming) and of articles on the history of material culture, women's and gender history, family history, the history of domestic service, and of slavery.

Pier Paolo Viazzo is Associate Professor of Social Anthropology at the University of Turin. He is the author of several books including *Upland Communities: Environment, Population and Social Structure in the Alps since the Sixteenth Century* (Cambridge University Press, 1989) and *Introduzione all'antropologia storica* (Laterza, 2000) and co-editor, with C. A. Corsini, of *The Decline of Infant and Child Mortality: The European Experience, 1750–1990* (Martinus Nijhoff, 1997).

Jeffrey R. Watt is Professor of History at the University of Mississippi where he has taught since 1988. His publications include *Choosing Death: Suicide and Calvinism in Early Modern Geneva* (Truman State University Press, 2001) and *The Making of Modern Marriage: Matrimonial Control and the Rise of Sentiment in Neuchâtel, 1550–1800* (Cornell University Press, 1992). Watt is currently involved in research on the Consistory in Calvin's Geneva and on the Inquisition in Modena, Italy.

INDEX

Page references to maps and tables are in italics